The Innovative Campus
Nurturing the Distinctive Learning Environment

by
Joy Rosenzweig Kliewer

AMERICAN COUNCIL ON EDUCATION ★
ORYX PRESS ★
Series on Higher Education
1999

The rare Arabian Oryx is believed to have inspired the myth of the unicorn. This desert antelope became virtually extinct in the early 1960s. At that time, several groups of international conservationists arranged to have nine animals sent to the Phoenix Zoo to be the nucleus of a captive breeding herd. Today, the Oryx population is over 1,000, and over 500 have been returned to the Middle East.

© 1999 The Oryx Press
4041 North Central at Indian School Road
Phoenix, Arizona 85012-3397

Published simultaneously in Canada
Printed and bound in the United States of America

∞ The paper used in this publication meets the minimum requirements of American National Standard for Information Science—Permanence of Paper for Printed Library Materials, ANSI Z39.48, 1984.

Library of Congress Cataloging-in-Publication Data
Kliewer, Joy Rosenzweig.
    The innovative campus: nurturing the distinctive learning environment / by Joy Rosenzweig Kliewer.
        p. cm. — (American Council on Education/Oryx Press series on higher education)
    Includes bibliographical references and index.
    ISBN 1-57356-236-X (alk. paper)
    1. Education, Higher—United States—Case studies. 2. Educational change—United States—Case studies. 3. Universities and colleges—United States—Sociological aspects—Case studies. 4. Subculture—United States—Case studies. I. Title. II. Series.
LA227.4.K55 1999
378.73—dc21   98-27878
                                                  CIP

CONTENTS

TABLES
AND FIGURES

TABLES

FIGURES

ACKNOWLEDGMENTS

In every intellectual undertaking, every creative project or endeavor, there are individuals who serve as our guides or resource persons, nurturing and supporting us along the way. In these pages, I wish to acknowledge the individuals who served as my guides and support persons, those who believed in telling the stories of the innovative campuses and who helped to ensure that this project was a success.

First, I am grateful to the faculty of Claremont Graduate University for their generous award of a research grant to fund this investigation. The grant enabled me to travel across the United States to visit distinctive colleges and universities and to capture the history and culture of these unique institutions. I wish to express my heartfelt appreciation to three professors in the Center for Educational Studies at Claremont Graduate University who helped to nourish this project and who generously gave of their time and talents to consult with me and review drafts of the manuscript. Thanks to Daryl G. Smith, David E. Drew, and especially Jack H. Schuster, my dear teacher, mentor, and guide, whose continuous support and scholarly insights have been such a gift to me.

I wish to express my gratitude to L. Jackson Newell, president of Deep Springs College and professor of higher education at the University of Utah, for his spirited guidance and valuable comments on the manuscript. Dr. Newell's works on maverick colleges have been an inspiration to me. Thanks also to Professor Laurin Raiken of the Gallatin School of Individualized Study at New York University for all of his passion about the topic and for his important feedback on the manuscript.

There are a number of individuals who assisted in various phases of the project research. I am particularly grateful to the 19 scholars and practitioners who offered consultation in the institutional selection process (see appendix A). A special note of thanks to Robert E. Engel of the University of Iowa for bestowing upon me his "treasure chest" of writings, notes, and articles that he gathered during his own journeys to innovative campuses in 1970 and 1971.

I would especially like to acknowledge the presidents, chancellors, and executive officers of the six campuses that I visited for welcoming me into their communities. Thanks to Marilyn Chapin Massey, president of Pitzer College; Gordon E. Michalson, Jr., former dean and warden of New College of the University of South Florida; Gregory S. Prince, Jr., president of Hampshire College; Karl S. Pister, former chancellor of the University of California (UC), Santa Cruz; Jane L. Jervis, president of The Evergreen State College; and Mark L. Perkins, chancellor of the University of Wisconsin (UW)-Green Bay.

Thanks to the outstanding efforts of James Feeney at New College; Tom Levitan, former dean of students at Hampshire College; Daniel Spielmann at UW-Green Bay; and Jeannie Chandler at Evergreen for their assistance in the scheduling of interviews and coordinating the site visits.

The following individuals went out of their way to provide access to historical documents and institutional data: Werner Warmbrunn, Lois Dumont, and Anna Ganahl at Pitzer College; James Feeney at New College; Lynda Block Hill at University of South Florida at Sarasota/New College; Larry Beede and Susan Dayall at Hampshire College; Debbie Furlong at UW-Green Bay; Robert James, Randy Nelson, and Ophelia Zalamea at UC Santa Cruz; and Barbara Leigh Smith at Evergreen. Edward W. Weidner, founding chancellor of UW-Green Bay, provided me with a variety of archival materials from his personal files. The late Dean McHenry, founding chancellor of UC Santa Cruz, and his wife Jane graciously welcomed me to Santa Cruz and shared their memories about the campus' life and history. Dean McHenry was a visionary and a legend at UC Santa Cruz and I was honored to have the privilege of meeting him.

I am extremely grateful to all of the spirited and pioneering faculty members, administrators, and alumnae/i who shared their voices and rich stories and experiences in this study. More than 150 hours of interviews were conducted in places as diverse as board rooms, Chinese restaurants, campus cafeterias, faculty offices, and deli counters. Thank you to all of the interviewees for the most enriching dialogs and discussions of my life. In some ways, this is as much your story as it is the story of these six institutions.

I owe a special debt of gratitude to those individuals at each campus who took the time to review drafts of the case study chapters: Thanks to Werner Warmbrunn and Stephen L. Glass, founding professors at Pitzer College, and to Anna Ganahl, former director of communications at Pitzer, for reviewing chapter 2. I am grateful to Gordon E. Michalson, Jr.; James Feeney, director of special project development; Kathleen Killion, director of admissions; Steve Miles, chair of humanities; and Tom Levitan, former director of student affairs at New College, for their important feedback on chapter 3. Thanks to Larry Beede, associate dean of faculty at Hampshire College, and Tom Levitan, again, for reviewing chapter 4. I am so appreciative of Chancellor Mark L. Perkins and the following individuals at the University of Wisconsin-Green Bay who read chapter 5: Myron Van de Ven, assistant vice chancellor for enrollment services; Carol Pollis, dean of liberal arts and sciences; Tim Sewall, alumnus and director of assessment and testing services; Mike Murphy, professor of humanistic studies and associate dean of liberal arts and sciences; and Dean Rodeheaver, assistant chancellor for planning and budget. R. Michael Tanner, former executive vice chancellor of UC Santa Cruz, offered important feedback on chapter 6. President Jane L. Jervis; founding president, Charles McCann; and particularly Academic Vice President and Provost Barbara Leigh Smith at Evergreen, provided valuable insights in their reviews of chapter 7.

My colleagues at Western University of Health Sciences have been especially supportive and encouraging throughout the publication process. A big thank you to Vivian Curato in the Office of Strategic Planning for her cheerful assistance with the mailing of the manuscripts. My warmest thanks to Carl E. Trinca, vice provost/vice president for strategic planning, for his kind support in enabling me to follow my dream of publishing a book on innovative colleges and universities.

This publication would also not have been possible without the commitment of the staff of The Oryx Press and the American Council on Education. A special thank you to Susan Slesinger, senior vice president at Oryx, for her dedication to this project and to Christine Davis for her excellent editorial skill. Thanks also to James J. Murray III, vice president and director of the Division of External Affairs at the American Council on Education, and to James W. Hall, chancellor of Antioch University, for recommending this book for publication.

Finally, I wish to express my appreciation to my family—to my wonderful parents, Sylvia and Herbert Rosenzweig, and to my sister, Marcy, for their unending support, and to the love of my life, my husband Todd Kliewer, whose creative and rebellious spirit has brought poetry and philosophy into my life. Thanks to each and every one of my support persons, colleagues, and guides. You have been by my side throughout this process. Your guidance has enriched this journey inside the worlds of innovative campuses.

INTRODUCTION

There are places I'll remember
All my life, though some have changed
Some forever, not for better,
Some have gone and some remain
All these places had their moments
With lovers and friends I still can recall . . .
In my life, I've loved them all . . .[1]

John Lennon and Paul McCartney, 1965

BACKGROUND AND OVERVIEW

In the 1960s and early 1970s, academic planners, reformers, countercultural gurus, faculty members, and students converged upon mountaintops, held retreats in the woods, and occupied classrooms and board rooms for days at a time, to give life to new and radically different institutions of higher education. Scores of innovative or experimental colleges and subcolleges burst onto the scene against a backdrop of social and political turbulence, heated and passionate student demonstration, rapid enrollment growth, economic upswings, and countercultural lifestyle exploration.[2]

Witness the birth of the Alternative One College at Keene State in New Hampshire; the Aquarian University, built on a "spiritual commune" in Baltimore; the Student Center College in Mendocino, California; the College Within at Tufts; and the College of the Person in Washington, D.C. There was the College of the Atlantic in Bar Harbor, Maine, founded "in part to help the island's economy and in part to make a difference in the world" (Hall 1994,

52); the Campus-Free College in Arlington, Massachusetts; the Colleges-Within-The-College at the University of Kansas; the cluster colleges of the University of the Pacific (at Elbert Covell College, every course was taught in Spanish); free-spirited Franconia College in the "round green mountains of New Hampshire"; Prescott College in Arizona; and the Experimental College at Fresno State—here students enrolled in courses on Love and Violence, Basic Mountaineering, and the Practice of Yoga. There was the student-run Experimental College at San Francisco State; the neoclassical experiments at University of California (UC), Berkeley, and San Jose State; the alternative New Jersey campuses of Ramapo and Stockton State; the encounter group college (Johnston) of the University of Redlands (now the Johnston Center for Integrative Studies); New College in Florida; Hampshire College in Massachusetts; The Evergreen State College, a public experimental college on the outskirts of Olympia, Washington; and UC Santa Cruz, an innovative university built in the middle of a redwood forest (Coyne and Hebert 1972; Gaff 1970a, b; Grant and Riesman 1978; Hall 1991; Kuh et al. 1991; McDonald and O'Neill 1988; Tussman 1969).

Although most of these dazzling departures thrived in the 1960s and early 1970s, many of them attracting international "celebrity" faculty, top-notch applicants, and antiestablishment attendees, by the mid-1970s, the years of prosperity and high hopes gave way to stagnation and decline. Friends and founders began to flee. Faculty and students ran for cover. Severe economic hardships, declines in the rate of enrollment growth, and shifting student values (materialistic or careerist student goals and aspirations) brought an end to the age of experimentation. The University of California, Santa Cruz, began the "long, mutinous march back to the familiar lines of academic responsibility" (Adams 1984, 24); Johnston College was absorbed into the University of Redlands (Blume 1981); the phone lines were cut, the learning "huts" taken away, the office doors padlocked at the Experimental College at San Francisco State (Grand and Bebout 1981). One by one, the bold new campuses began to close their doors or abandon their visions of educational innovation. One by one, the institutional families gathered up their belongings and bid a fond farewell to the dreams.

When the storm cleared and the enrollments stabilized, only a few beautiful little experiments were left intact or operational (e.g., College of the Atlantic, Hampshire College, The Evergreen State College). What kept these imaginative ventures healthy and strong? What are some of the keys to the survival or longevity of academic innovations?

This study examines how and why innovative colleges and universities have preserved and/or transformed their original pioneering visions or early imaginative ideals. To gain insight into the history and endurance of institutional innovations in higher education, site visits were conducted to a group of distinctive colleges and universities across the United States: Pitzer College in

Claremont, California; New College of the University of South Florida in Sarasota; Hampshire College in Amherst, Massachusetts; the University of Wisconsin-Green Bay; the University of California, Santa Cruz; and The Evergreen State College in Olympia, Washington.

The goal of the research was to capture the stories of the institutional lives and histories of the innovative colleges and universities to understand how and why distinctive institutions of higher education keep alive and/or transform their original pioneering visions or dreams. The ultimate purpose of the study (and the significance of the investigation) was the hope of inspiring future efforts at institutional renewal and reform in American higher education.

This introduction provides an overview, a guide to the investigation. It begins with a definition of innovation and innovative institutions of higher education. From there, it presents the research questions that guided this investigation. The next section reviews the literature on experimental colleges and universities and institutional change, and discusses how the current study expands the literature base. The next section presents an overview of the methodological design, institutional selection procedures, and data gathering techniques. The following section discusses the significance of the research for educational policy makers, researchers, students, and their communities. The chapter concludes with a discussion and a preview of the chapters of the volume.

DEFINITION:
WHAT IS AN INNOVATIVE COLLEGE OR UNIVERSITY?

It is a challenge to grasp, put your fingers around, touch and feel the idea of innovation in higher education (Townsend, Newell, and Wiese 1992). Different authors conceptualize reform in different ways, and there are "a cornucopia of typologies to choose from" (Levine 1980, 4). There are those who single out alternative campuses for their out-of-the-ordinary programs, their "wacky," "handmade," "one-of-a-kind" designs—e.g., the mountain hiking classes, the Zen and You workshops (Gehret 1972; Levine 1980; Townsend et al. 1992). Friends and foes conjure up images of caterpillars about to become butterflies; educational paradises or Gardens of Eden; classical Greek societies; and "hairy," "messy" homes for the radically inclined (Childs 1981; Coyne and Hebert 1972; Greening 1981b; Martin 1982; Von der Muhll 1984).

In one of the more well-known conceptions, Gerald Grant and David Riesman (1978) divide experimental institutions into the "telic" (the counter-revolutionary, that is, reforms in the underlying purpose or philosophy of undergraduate education) and the "popular" (reforms in the processes, the means or delivery of higher education). James W. Hall (1991), chancellor of Antioch University, categorizes innovative colleges along curricular lines (i.e., integrated or interdisciplinary, human development, and cluster models).

Arthur Levine (1980) offers a typology based on structural reform: new experimenting organizations; innovative enclaves within existing organizations; holistic and piecemeal changes; and peripheral, environmental reforms. And L. Jackson Newell and Katherine C. Reynolds (1993a) place experimental or "maverick colleges" into a four-quadrant schema based on student selection (who should attend, arrayed on a continuum ranging from open to elite institutions) and educational methods (how best to integrate theoretical and practical knowledge, on a continuum ranging from campuses that connect theory to practice at "immediate times and locations" [inside the classroom] to those that prefer to keep experiential practice distant from the classroom setting or entirely separate from the college or university program).

For the purposes of this study, "innovation" has been operationally defined as any significant departure from traditional practices in American higher education (Levine 1980). In this study, "innovative," "experimental," or "distinctive" colleges and universities refers to those campuses that were founded amidst the social, political, economic, and demographic transformations of the 1960s and early 1970s as alternatives to the mainstream American college or university. How do these campuses "depart" from the mainstream? Drawing on the literature, there appear to be five dimensions that "mark out the territory" of innovative institutions of higher education (each of these characteristics is described in greater detail in chapter 1):

1. Interdisciplinary teaching and learning: cross-disciplinary study and collaboration in curricular and cocurricular activity (Grant and Riesman 1978; Newell 1984)
2. Student-centered education: students engineer or "take charge of" their academic programs (e.g., students invent their own academic majors, design courses, and assist in curricular planning and development) (Adams 1993; Frazier 1977; Grand and Bebout 1981; Newell 1984)
3. Egalitarianism: participatory governance structures—town meetings, general assemblies, and/or community forums where administrators, faculty, and students share equal voice in decision making; an absence of status symbols, such as titles and ranks; close-knit relations between faculty and students; narrative evaluations as opposed to letter grades; and cooperation and collaboration, rather than competition in teaching and learning (Grant and Riesman 1978; Hall 1994; Kuh et al. 1991; Townsend et al. 1992)
4. Experiential learning: out-of-classroom projects, theses, and/or internships are integral to the academic program (Adams 1993; Newell 1984)
5. An institutional focus on teaching rather than research and/or publication: there is an intensity, a spirit of vocation about teaching that "permeates these communities" (Grant and Riesman 1978, 33)

While some colleges and universities today may refer to themselves as "distinctive" or "innovative," this study focuses specifically on those campuses that were founded as part of the educational reform movement of the 1960s and early 1970s and that typically embodied these distinctive characteristics at the time of their inception.

RESEARCH QUESTIONS

This study asks how and why do innovative colleges and universities maintain their founding principles, their distinctive, offbeat original designs? What keeps the dream, the spirit of reform, alive (or leads to its compromise or demise)? What does it take to preserve the visions, the start-up hopes and plans of distinctive learning institutions? Most importantly, what do these colleges and universities, their life cycles, stories, and experiences, have to teach us about the processes of innovation and the preservation of reform efforts in higher education? What are the lessons to be learned from the lives of the distinctive campuses that made their initial mark on the 1960s and 1970s higher education scene and have managed for over two decades or so to survive the pressures—sometimes even to thrive—or to conform, to compromise the dream? These questions formed the heart of this investigation. They served as the guides, the research road maps, to a qualitative, multi-campus journey inside the worlds of six innovative colleges and universities in the mid-1990s (both those that appeared to have remained, for the most part, distinctive, and those that seemed to have compromised or transformed their original missions of innovation).

THE LITERATURE ON INNOVATIVE COLLEGES AND UNIVERSITIES: THE PHOTO ALBUM

Researchers have tried their hands at explaining or accounting for why the innovative higher education movement of the 1960s and 1970s lost its magical, mystical momentum, and why some innovative campuses abandoned their early visions or simply collapsed, while others endured or succeeded in preserving their missions. Yet there have been no empirical, up-to-date investigations that examine these phenomena across institutions. With few exceptions (e.g., Grant and Riesman 1978; Levine and Weingart 1973), the bulk of the writings in this creative corner of the higher education literature are nonempirical pieces (memoirs, personal thoughts, treasured moments, and reflections), usually based on a single-campus experience. Systematic investigations that contemplate the question of how and why innovative colleges and universities sustain or transform their distinctive founding missions and practices are few and far between. This section explores the writings, the texts of the researchers, visitors, and guests to the innovative campuses of the 1960s and 1970s, identifying key works, comparing and contrasting formats and findings, and charting out the openings for an original study of alternative institutions in the 1990s.

Exploring the literature on innovative colleges and universities of the 1960s and 1970s is like opening up a photo album or scrapbook filled with memories, stories, and snapshots of bold, creative ventures. The literature abounds with beautiful and telling portraits (usually nonempirical slices or tales) of single-campus experiences—for example: Anzulovic's (1976) account of the "rise and fall of Prescott College"; Coyne's (1972) portrait of the death of a dream at Bensalem College; Grand and Bebout's (1981) "passionate discourse" on the Experimental College at San Francisco State; Kahn's (1981) remembrance of Kresge College (a humanistic, encounter group or "T-grouping" cluster college at UC Santa Cruz); Ruopp and Jerome's (1973) story of "love and death" at Franconia College; Von der Muhll's (1984) report on the rise and fall of "Educational Eden" at UC Santa Cruz; founder Joseph Tussman's (1969) history of the Experimental College at UC Berkeley.

These memoirs and portraits, tucked away in journals and books from the 1960s and beyond, recall tales of institutional vision, struggle, and dampened dreams. Story after story (and storyteller after storyteller) reveals the years of hope and desperation—from the bountiful founding days of the 1960s when the economy was booming, college and university enrollments were skyrocketing, the applicant pool was overflowing, and anything seemed possible. Anything could be done until the economic downturns of the 1970s, when the flower children were no more, when a depressed economy and faculty marketplace turned the tide against the dreamers. Now "the brightest blooms in the garden of the University of California's newest, most daringly-conceived campus [had] faded," Von der Muhll (1984, 86) laments, and "with an inevitability suggesting the operation of gravitational law, the enterprise [at Santa Cruz, as elsewhere] beg[an] to sink" (51).

Reading these pieces is like taking a walk through history. They pull at you, touch you, in their emotional accounts of the stories and the shattered visions. Take the bittersweet tale of Franconia College, told by Ruopp and Jerome in 1973: "What happened at Franconia had to do with love and death. In the spring of 1968 many cried at Franconia. They cried because it is hard, very hard to find a place to be human in, to find people to be human with. Humanness in all its weakness and strength, humanness with its kaleidoscopic mixture of openness and selfishness, warmth and fear" (114–15).

These single-campus accounts and sentimental journeys are accompanied by a smaller group of empirical research studies and institutional histories (e.g., Arthur's [1995] history of New College in Florida; McDonald and O'Neill's [1988] account of the first 10 years of Johnston College). Perhaps the most influential of these writings is a landmark work by Gerald Grant and David Riesman (1978). In their classic study, *The Perpetual Dream*, the authors invite us inside the worlds of seven experimental colleges and universities, recounting the founding years and planning rituals, introducing us to an assortment of serious and eccentric characters such as Alan Chadwick of UC Santa Cruz, a self-described "philosophical gardener" who was brought in to "nurture growth at Santa Cruz" (260) and fellow Englishman Jasper Rose "who wears his King's College gown while lecturing [and who] organized Shakespearean readings." (The authors describe their first meeting: "Rose greeted us effervescently, clapping our hands between his and leading us into his office with its red walls, an Oriental rug, roll-top desk, and quaint hanging lamp.") (261) Grant and Riesman tell of the communal bonding and kin group experiences at UC Santa Cruz's Kresge College and the early days of Stockton State College in New Jersey when students lived in the "rather seedy" Mayflower Hotel on the Atlantic City boardwalk while their dormitories were being completed. They also study Ramapo College in New Jersey and devote a chapter to the College for Human Services (now Audrey Cohen College), a social change–oriented campus whose early students were drawn from those living on welfare in New York City. In their chapter on St. John's College, an institution that "sought to restore the classical curriculum with new intensity and purity," Grant and Riesman describe the Great Books seminars "that often continue[d] past midnight in the coffee shop" and the Irregular Ellipsoid Hurling Contests (egg throws) and Epicycle races that offered a release from the strict, relentless "St. Johnny" schedule.

Through these stories and scenes, through these amazing and intersecting casts of characters and flashbacks (captured through seven years in the field), Grant and Riesman create a kind of portrait or dreamscape of experimentation in American higher education. Their "modest proposal" calls for the creation of a group of UC Santa Cruz–style cluster colleges (with "gray-headed" academics, common core programs, peer learning, preprofessional courses, and rigorous standards of evaluation, including at least "one tough requirement" for students—e.g., a thesis, a publication). This recipe for reform is flavored with some clues about why experimental campuses succumb. These range from clashes in personality—"like marriages they [the experiments] involve very subtle matchings"—to the "pervasive" cost to the careers of faculty "who join such efforts within research-oriented universities" (i.e., "bucking" the dominant reward system by joining a teaching subcollege) (370). What might be some other reasons? After reading Grant and Riesman, one longs for a more complete explanation of what happens to the dreams.

Flash forward to 1980. Along comes Arthur Levine (1980) who tackles the issue head-on. In his widely hailed study of the foundings and fates of 14 innovative subcolleges that came to life at the State University of New York

(SUNY), Buffalo, in the 1960s (the subcolleges dissolved their distinctive missions in the 1970s), the author is charged with the task of discovering "why innovation fails": Why do innovations "prosper, persist, decline, and fail after they have been adopted"? (10). Drawing on interviews, observations, historical fact finding, and institutional document analyses, Levine carefully reconstructs the founding years, reassembles the planning teams, and captures the distinctive curricular accents of the fallen colleges (e.g., College A with its "radically progressive philosophy" and its storefront home on Buffalo's Main Street; College H, the health college; and Rachel Carson, the environmental campus cluster).

Through his studies and searchings, Levine uncovers two critical ingredients to successful innovation: "compatibility" and "profitability." Compatibility is the degree of congruence—the fit—between the norms, values, and goals of the host institution (SUNY, Buffalo) and the innovation (College A, H, etc.). Profitability refers to the extent to which the innovation satisfies the needs of the campus and its constituencies. When there is compatibility and profitability between parent institution and experimental offspring, there is "successful" innovation. When there is incompatibility and unprofitability, there is "failure" or termination ("Camelot dies").[3]

Levine's classic work, however, speaks only to the worlds of the inner colleges or subcolleges. It does not encompass the patterns of success or failure (how "Camelot lives and dies") at the free-standing or holistic innovative ventures that grew out of the countercultural decade (the Hampshires, the Prescotts, the Evergreens). Nor does this work offer a glimpse into the cultures and fates of the subcolleges that sprang up beyond the walls of SUNY, Buffalo, a distinctive university that had been extensively reorganized in the late 1960s by a president who took the pieces of the campus apart—and soon thereafter left. (The research is centered on the life and times of the Buffalo 14.) Still, Levine's book is the only innovative college or university study to date that focuses exclusively on the issue of why and how distinctive campuses prosper or persist and why and how distinctive campuses abandon or transform their opening visions or dreams. Since the writing of Levine (1980), there have been no empirical investigations (and there have been no cross-campus research studies) that single-mindedly explore the life cycles (the birthings, changes, evolutions) of alternative colleges and universities of the countercultural era.

Innovation or reform in higher education is also examined in studies of institutional change in colleges and universities (e.g., Bensimon 1993; Blackwell 1996; Corak and Wharton 1992; Curry 1992; Hefferlin 1969; Kemp and McBeath 1994; Louis 1989; Steeples 1990; Teitelbaum 1994). These investigations describe the processes and strategies by which existing campuses have adopted and/or sustained "innovations" such as curricular reforms, new programs, policies, and initiatives.

Perhaps the earliest and most highly regarded work on institutional change in higher education is *Dynamics of Academic Reform* by J.B. Lon Hefferlin (1969). In this classic study, Hefferlin examined a randomly selected sample of 110 colleges and universities across the United States between 1962 and 1967 to "uncover the forces within institutions which tend to preserve and nourish a readiness to change" (xi). The purpose of the research was to "learn how changes come about in the educational program: how colleges and universities alter their services, revamp their requirements, and reorganize their courses" to effect change (188). Hefferlin discovered that the sources or origins of institutional reform were not internally driven (from *within* the college or university), but were shaped by forces outside of the institution. Hefferlin concluded that external factors—the market for higher education, the competition among institutions, the pressure for innovation—were fundamental to institutional reform. He explained that "while the responsiveness of an institution to change can be significantly affected by internal factors, the institution will seldom alter its functions without external influence. Outsiders initiate; insiders react" (146).

Hefferlin also found that while no one factor distinguished the "dynamic" from the less dynamic (or "static") institutions, there were a series of interrelated factors that seemed to permit and to encourage change in colleges and universities. Dynamic institutions tended to be religious colleges, campuses that were located in metropolitan areas, institutions whose faculties were changing by a combination of expansion and turnover, and campuses that were more financially dependent on attracting students. Static institutions, on the other hand, were more likely to be independent universities, campuses where students had relatively little influence in curricular decisions, institutions where the presidents were viewed as conservative or change-resistant, and campuses with a higher proportion of tenured faculty.

While Hefferlin's classic work and other institutional change studies offer insights into the initiation and endurance of reforms that are embraced within existing institutions, they do not address the question of how innovative *institutions* (reform-based campuses) endure or successfully sustain their innovations over time. In general, what is known about the endurance and transformation of distinctive institutions of higher education of the 1960s and 1970s grows out of collections of reflections and personal accounts (memoirs and moments, portrait pieces out of a research "photo album")—with perhaps a paragraph or brief section devoted to the struggle to keep hold of original innovative plans and dreams.

Why did Johnston College, early Kresge, or the Experimental College at San Francisco State go under? The gurus and founders (and interested third-party observers) point to the following reasons for the termination of experimentation: utopian visions and planning, economic hardships, enrollment declines, faculty recruitment struggles, philosophical differences among early academic cohorts and new recruits, faculty overwork, student attrition, and institutional stereotypes or public image problems (Bloch and Nylen 1974; Blume 1981; Coyne and Hebert 1972; Greening 1981a; Kahn 1981; Weidner 1977; Wofford 1973).

At the same time, these memoirs and tales told by participant-observers single out the following reasons for long-lasting innovation or the survival (or longevity) of distinctive institutions: administrative commitment and leadership, the continuing presence of a core group of founding faculty, free-standing organizations (as opposed to subcolleges of larger institutions), private or independent institutional control, partnerships or collaborative teaching and learning networks with nearby "traditional" campuses, and later start-up dates (Elmendorf 1975; Frazier 1977; Hall 1991; Hahn 1984; Meister 1982; Youtz 1984).

In short, while other authors—besides Grant and Riesman (1978) and Levine (1980)—have ventured into this research territory, offering ideas and explanations about the endurance and transformation, and the life or death of innovative institutions, these offerings are usually based on personal reflections, individual moments, and encounters at a single unorthodox institution. Many of the stories of institutional growth and transformation have yet to be told. Many of the stories are incomplete.

Not only are the studies of innovative campuses usually based on memoirs and reflective musings, but the edges of the campus portraits are curling, the images are fading. Those authors who put pen to paper and recorded the tales of turbulence of the experimental college or university did so long ago (usually in the 1970s) when the ashes were still smoldering and the surviving innovative campuses were just beginning to get back on their feet; that is to say, much of the literature is dated. In Gaff and Associates' (1970) singular study of cluster colleges, for example, the authors acknowledge, "In a fundamental sense the [experimental college] movement probably is too young for a full assessment" (Gaff 1970c, 68). While Gaff and cohorts do review some of the major problems of the cluster (or sub-) colleges (e.g., utopian visions, faculty immobility, the loss of a charismatic leader), in 1970 it was too early to gauge the full scope of the movement or the factors affecting the rise and fall, and the endurance and transformation of innovative institutions. At many campuses, the experiment was still in its infancy.

Cardozier (1993b) and his cast of presidential characters and commentators of innovative colleges and universities set out to resolve this dilemma, to update the stories in a recent work (*Important Lessons from Innovative Colleges and Universities*). In the opening pages, Cardozier explains: "Some of the previous reports appeared before the institutions [in this study] opened and focus only on institutional plans. Others appeared shortly after the institutions opened, when the innovations had not yet been tested adequately" (2). The overarching goal of the book is to "describe the innovations, to assess how well each worked, and in the cases of those that did not succeed or that did not live up to the planners' expectations, to discuss reasons" (1). The "case studies,"the descriptions and explanations, here are based principally on the authors' (founding presidents' or leaders') opinions and recollections, along with some institutional data. Once more, these are rich and vital stories and voices, but there is often little original research and/or empirical foundation. There is only a brief section of the editor's notes connecting the various contributors' stories and campus experiences.

Townsend, Newell, and Wiese's (1992) recent addition to this spirited innovative colleges literature is a summary report and a review of the histories and features of "uncommon" colleges and universities (both those that grew out of the 1960s and 1970s and those that came to life at the turn of the century or around the time of the progressive era: 1900–1920). The book stands out as a valuable resource on alternative colleges and universities and a future-directed handbook for institutions that seek to "become distinct and maintain a sense of distinctiveness over time" (xvi), but this writing is primarily based on a "synthesis and evaluation of various literature bases" (69). Like Cardozier's (1993b) piece and others, it is an important work, but not an original investigation.

Perhaps the only contemporary empirical study of distinctive institutions that highlights some "survival" and "failure" themes is a monograph edited by Newell and Reynolds (1993b). This report, which emerges from a graduate seminar in higher education, tells the stories of 10 "maverick" colleges (seven of which were founded in the late nineteenth or early twentieth century). Each piece opens with a college portrait, sometimes striking in its picturesque feeling and imagery: "Towering pine trees march in measured cadence down rocky slopes to the sea, interspersed with staccato notes of giant granite boulders. The tangy salty sea air is underscored by the wheeling cries of sea birds on the brisk New England wind. This is the setting for the College of the Atlantic...." (Wardle 1993, 118). The authors move on to describe the origins and evolutions of the colleges, the demographics, and current campus teaching and learning climates and scenes. While this vivid collection of maverick college portraits offers insight into the life courses and cycles of experiments in higher education, the treatment of this issue is fairly brief and the campus studies are based primarily on literature reviews, catalog accounts, and a few interviews with founders and leaders. (There is no detailed methodological protocol or design described.) At the same time, the authors point out, the report does not include the stories of "middle ground" institutions—"colleges that gradually forfeit their distinctive characteristics" (Newell 1993, 136). There appears to be an opening for a study that steps inside the worlds of the innovative and formerly innovative institutions, one that incorporates the voices of multiple campus characters, founders, and leaders, and pursues an in-depth methodological strategy (campus site visits, interviews, observation techniques).

In sum, empirical, up-to-date cross-campus investigations of innovative colleges and universities of the 1960s and 1970s are a rare find in the literature. Nearly all of the existing research studies reflect here and there upon, but do not thoroughly respond to, the question of why and how innovative campuses keep hold of their founding plans and principles. Most studies were either written at a time when the campuses were too young for a full assessment (e.g., Gaff and Associates 1970; Grant and Riesman 1978) or are recent accounts and summary reports that incorporate single (and often beautifully captured) institutional histories and present concerns, but without a broader multi-institutional framework or analysis of how and why these spirited colleges and universities transformed or preserved their founding visions. This study strives to add a new portrait, a new series of research snapshots of the existing landscape of collegiate impressions, one that weaves together multiple campus experiences and voices to capture for today the stories of innovative college and university lives, lessons, and dreams.

METHODOLOGY

To examine the history and durability of innovation at alternative institutions, four- to five-day site visits were conducted at six distinctive colleges and universities across the United States. Institutional selection was based on a comprehensive review of previously published guides on alternative campuses and interdisciplinary programs in higher education (e.g., Bear 1980; Coyne and Hebert 1972; Heiss 1973; Lichtman 1972; Newell 1986), and the readings and research on innovative colleges and universities. Campus "nominations" were also sought through consultation with a panel of nationally recognized experts on reform in higher education—faculty, administrators, and researchers who had extensive contact or association with alternative colleges or universities (see appendix A).

Drawing on the literature review and the information provided by the expert panel, a "master list" of 314 innovative colleges and universities was generated (appendix B). From this master list, I compiled a "candidate" list of 22 free-standing institutions that remained open in the 1990s, from which the sample of six case study sites was drawn (appendix C).

Four decision rules guided the final selection of institutions from the candidate list. First, every effort was made to select campuses from different regions of the country. Second, I attempted to include at least some institutions that had not been thoroughly investigated in the research literature.

Third, I tried to achieve a balance between public and private ventures. Fourth, I tried to select both those institutions that seemed to have maintained their founding principles and those that appeared to have transformed themselves or moved away from their opening missions.

The final sample of institutions included two small private liberal arts colleges (Pitzer College and Hampshire College), two small public colleges (The Evergreen State College and New College), and two distinctive public universities (University of California, Santa Cruz, and University of Wisconsin-Green Bay). Three alternate sites were also selected in the event that the proposal to participate in the research project was declined by one or more of the campuses. (Table 1 provides an overview of the final sample of institutions and alternate campus sites.)

The Six Innovative Institutions

The Evergreen State College was selected as a research site because of the institution's remarkable perseverance as a distinctive college in the public sector of higher education. Although there had been a number of studies written about Evergreen and its distinctive learning communities (e.g., Jones 1981; Lyons 1991; McCann 1977; Nkabinde 1993; Schuster 1989; Tommerup 1993; Youtz 1984), there had been no contemporary research investigations that focused exclusively on the topic of the evolution and the preservation of the campus' pioneering start-up visions. Based on a review of the literature and consultation with the expert panel, the Evergreen campus seemed to stand out as a "pure type" example of an institution that had maintained its distinctive founding heritage. Evergreen was, thus, a natural choice for inclusion in this research project.

Hampshire College, too, was singled out by the consultants and in the research literature as a campus with an exceptional ability to keep hold of its pioneering original visions. Like Evergreen, there had been a number of studies published about the college (e.g., Alpert 1980; Astin, Milem, Astin, Ries, and Heath 1991; Birney 1993; Holmquist, Nisonoff, and Rakoff 1984), but none that addressed the topic of the endurance and/or transformation of the early distinctive ideals of the institution from an empirical research perspective. What especially qualified Hampshire College as a case study site was its status as a private distinctive college in western Massachusetts. There was no other campus like Hampshire in that region of the country.

New College of the University of South Florida was identified as another excellent case study site because of its remarkable longevity as a distinctive public college. Based on preliminary reviews of institutional catalogs and consultation with the expert panel, New College appeared to have carried on over the decades with its rebellious founding philosophies intact (e.g., an absence of grades, contract-based learning)—despite a merger with a public

TABLE 1

FINAL LIST OF INNOVATIVE INSTITUTIONS AND ALTERNATE SITES

Institution	Founding Year	Carnegie Classification[a]	Control	Location (State)	Enroll- ment	Writings/ Reports[b]	Presumed Status[c]
Selected Sites							
1. The Evergreen State College	1967	BA II	Public	WA	3,477	X	M
2. Hampshire College	1965	BA I	Private	MA	1,050	X	M
3. New College of the University of South Florida	1960	not listed*	Public	FL	526	X	M
4. Pitzer College	1963	BA I	Private	CA	890		NM
5. University of California, Santa Cruz	1962	Res II	Public	CA	10,173	X	NM
6. University of Wisconsin-Green Bay	1965	MA II	Public	WI	5,205		NM
Alternate Sites							
1. College of the Atlantic	1969	BA I	Private	ME	217		M
2. Ramapo College of New Jersey	1969	BA II	Public	NJ	4,683		NM
3. The Richard Stockton College of New Jersey (formerly Stockton State College)	1969	BA I	Public	NJ	5,619		NM

Note. The data in column 3 (Carnegie Classification) are from *A Classification of Institutions of Higher Education 1994 Edition*, 1994, Princeton, NJ: The Carnegie Foundation for the Advancement of Teaching. The data in columns 2, 4, 5, and 6 are from the *1995 Higher Education Directory* by M.P. Rodenhouse (Ed.), 1995, Falls Church, VA: Higher Education Publications.

[a] BA I = Baccalaureate I institutions, BA II = Baccalaureate II institutions, MA II = Master's II institutions, Res II = Research II institutions (*A Classification of Institutions of Higher Education*, 1994).

[b] X = The institution has been the subject of six or more journal articles, books, chapters in edited volumes, and/or scholarly reports.

[c] M = Presumption that the institution *maintained* its founding principles, NM = Presumption that the institution *did not maintain* its founding principles. (Based on a review of the literature and current campus catalogs, and consultation with a panel of experts on innovation in American higher education.)
*The Carnegie classification for the University of South Florida is Res II.

university system (the University of South Florida). The campus was one of a selected group of innovative institutions visited by researchers Gerald Grant and David Riesman in the 1970s, and since that time, there had been no comprehensive original research studies that examined New College's innovative heritage. The New College story was a story worth telling.

University of California, Santa Cruz, was chosen as a case study site because it was singled out in the literature and in communications with the consultants as a campus that had been transformed over the years into a more mainstream university. Although there had been a number of writings about the Santa Cruz campus (e.g., UC Santa Cruz and one of its residential colleges—Kresge College—were featured as case studies in Grant and Riesman's 1978 work; other writings about Santa Cruz include McHenry 1977, 1993; and Von der Muhll 1984), there had been no recent accounts that examined the evolution of this unusual public university from an empirical or qualitative research perspective. The Santa Cruz site was, thus, another "natural" choice for this investigation.

University of Wisconsin-Green Bay was selected because of the campus' innovative heritage as an interdisciplinary, environmentally oriented institution in Green Bay, Wisconsin. The campus had been mentioned in the literature and in the guidebooks on innovative higher education of the 1960s and 1970s (e.g., Coyne and Hebert 1972; Grant and Riesman 1978; Heiss 1973), but there were few studies of the history and evolution of the innovative founding ideals of the university. Like UC Santa Cruz, UW-Green Bay was a fascinating subject for a case study because of its status as a historically distinctive public university in a mainstream higher education system. Green Bay was also selected because of its geographic location in the Midwest.

Pitzer College was identified as a research site because of the college's distinctive founding heritage as an institution devoted to interdisciplinary education and participatory governance frameworks. Pitzer's status as a private innovative college affiliated with a consortium of institutions—The Claremont Colleges—in the western United States also distinguished this campus from other potential candidates for investigation. In addition, there were few published works about the college, although the campus had a rich history of innovation.

Data-Gathering Techniques

At each campus, approximately 25 semi-structured interviews were conducted with faculty members, administrators, trustees, and selected students and active alumnae/i. Key informants were drawn from the ranks of the veteran and charter faculty and administrators, the forward-thinking planners and leaders who gave "life" to these campuses (and who remained on campus or in the vicinity). Altogether, 151 interviews were held with 164 faculty, administrators, students, trustees, and alumnae/i during the six field visits. All interviews were tape recorded and nearly all 151 interviews were transcribed verbatim.

The interviews were supplemented with extensive archival research and institutional document analysis, along with observations of key campus activities, programs, and meetings. Data were analyzed inductively both within and across campus sites, generating rich insights about the endurance and transformation of innovative campus missions. (A more detailed description of the methodological procedures is presented in appendix D.)

SIGNIFICANCE OF THE STUDY

This investigation is important to higher education for several reasons. First, there is the social climate and the timing. Disruptions in the social fabric (turbulence and uprisings), Newell (1993) reminds us, brought the experimental colleges and universities of the 1960s and 1970s to life. In this era (the 1990s) when campuses are witnessing continued and heated protests over threats to student aid, budget cuts, affirmative action, and ethnic studies; when urban malaise and environmental crises and accelerated student and public concerns and criticisms about higher education (student neglect, research specialization, etc.) are colliding (Townsend et al. 1992), the ground may be fertile, the times ripe, for the founding of a new movement of radical departures in higher education. The lessons learned from the colleges and universities that grew out of the most recent reform period in American higher education will serve as teachers and guides for those departures that may be on the educational horizon.

At the same time, telling the tales of these campuses will inform innovations on the inside (those creative approaches, programs, and practices that are taken up within existing or mainstream colleges and universities) (Cardozier 1993a). Newell (1993) argues that financial crises often provide fertile ground for innovative proposals and strategies. (Campuses "become willing to entertain radical ideas and consider sweeping changes that wouldn't warrant their glance in good times.") (133) In the current fiscal climate, when college and university budgets continue to tighten, when higher education policy makers and players may be searching for new models for reinvigorating traditional and fledging practices, departments, and programs, innovative college and university strategies and designs (their lessons and distinctive approaches) will become vital. In the words of Townsend, Newell, and Wiese (1992),

> Higher education is in need of visions. We urge educators—faculty, staff, administration, and system leaders—to commit to a cherished value or a compelling vision and then to articulate a purpose that challenges the commitment of others. The callings, causes, and cries that make up the innermost commitments of people can become

educational missions that chart new paths for higher education (69–70).

It was with spirit and hope for preserving and revitalizing student-centered venues for knowledge and consciousness raising in higher education, that this study of innovative campuses was undertaken.

ORGANIZATION OF THE CHAPTERS

The remainder of this volume is organized into eight chapters. The historical chapter, chapter 1, establishes the context for the founding of the innovative colleges and universities. It describes the conditions that gave rise to the alternative higher education movement of the period and examines how the distinctive campuses of the 1960s and 1970s departed from the mainstream of American higher education. This chapter also discusses the older and progressive roots of campus innovation, and describes the general shifts in the economy and the social and cultural environment in the mid- to late 1970s that brought the innovative higher education movement to a close.

Chapters 2 through 7 present the results of the six campus case studies. Each chapter paints a portrait of a unique college or university world, capturing the spirit of the early or founding days of the campus, describing the evolution and endurance of the pioneering principles that shaped the guiding visions of the founders and planners of the institution. Each account draws on the data gathered in the interviews, document analyses, and observations at the campuses, and includes a demographic profile of the interview participants, a discussion of the key issues or challenges to innovation at the institutions, an examination of the campus' survival or longevity, and a reflection on the implications of the findings for innovation and reform in American higher education.

Chapter 8, the conclusion, summarizes and synthesizes the key findings of the case studies, comparing and contrasting the six campus studies of educational innovation and transformation. The chapter discusses the implications of the results for the wider higher education community and distinctive institutions, and offers suggestions for future research on campus reform.

NOTES

1. I owe the musical reference to Jim Bebout and Tom Greening, editors of the *Journal of Humanistic Psychology* (vol. 21, spring 1981), who wove John Lennon lyrics throughout the writings of this special issue on "humanistic" colleges. This particular excerpt appears in Greening (1981a), page 3. Lyrics used by permission from Sony/ATV Songs LLC (Renewed).
2. The terms "innovative," "experimental," "distinctive," "radical," and "alternative" are used interchangeably in this study (as they are in the research literature) to refer to the

institutional departures in higher education that grew out of the social, political, and demographic transformations of the 1960s and early 1970s.

3. This study is one of three key works by Arthur Levine on reform and innovation in higher education. Two other important writings by Levine are *Reform of Undergraduate Education* (with John Weingart in 1973) and the comprehensive *Handbook on Undergraduate Curriculum* (Levine 1978), which includes concise case studies of selected innovative institutions of the 1960s and 1970s.

REFERENCES

Adams, E.A. 1993. Prescott: From parson to parsimony. In *Maverick colleges: Ten notable experiments in American undergraduate education*, edited by L.J. Newell and K.C. Reynolds, 89–103. Salt Lake City: Utah Education Policy Center, Graduate School of Education, The University of Utah.

Adams, W. 1984. Getting real: Santa Cruz and the crisis of liberal education. *Change* (May-June): 19–27.

Alpert, R.M. 1980. Professionalism and educational reform: The case of Hampshire College. *Journal of Higher Education* 51 (5): 497–518.

Anzulovic, B. 1976. The rise and fall of Prescott College. *The University Bookman*, XVI (3): 51–57.

Arthur, F.C. 1995. *New College: The first three decades*. Sarasota, Fla.: The New College Foundation.

Astin, H.S., J.F. Milem, A.W. Astin, P. Ries, and T. Heath. 1991. *The courage and vision to experiment: Hampshire College, 1970–1990*. Los Angeles: Higher Education Research Institute, Graduate School of Education, University of California, Los Angeles.

Bear, J. 1980. *The alternative guide to college degrees & non-traditional higher education*. New York: Stonesong.

Bensimon, E.M. 1993. *Creating an institutional identity out of "differences": A case study of multicultural organizational change*. Paper presented at the Annual Meeting of the College Reading and Learning Association, Kansas City, Mo., April. (ERIC Document Reproduction Service No. ED 358 777)

Birney, R.C. 1993. Hampshire College. In *Important lessons from innovative colleges and universities*, edited by V.R. Cardozier, 9–22. *New Directions for Higher Education* no. 82 (summer).

Blackwell, P. 1996. Reform under adversity. *Teacher Education Quarterly* 21 (1): 19–26.

Bloch, P., and N. Nylen. 1974. Hampshire College: New intents and old realities. *Change* (October): 38–42.

Blume, F. 1981. The role of personal growth groups at Johnston College. *Journal of Humanistic Psychology* 21 (2): 47–61.

Cardozier, V.R. 1993a. Editor's notes. In *Important lessons from innovative colleges and universities*, edited by V.R. Cardozier, 1–7. *New Directions for Higher Education* no. 82 (summer).

————, ed. 1993b. Important lessons from innovative colleges and universities. *New Directions for Higher Education* no. 82 (summer).

Childs, B. 1981. The obligatory inspirational commencement address (Johnston College graduation, May 1980). *Journal of Humanistic Psychology* 21 (2): 143–46.

Corak, K.A., and D.P. Wharton. 1992. *Strategic planning and organizational change: Implications for institutional researchers.* Paper presented at the Annual Forum of the Association for Institutional Research, Atlanta, May. (ERIC Document Reproduction Service No. ED 349 889)

Coyne, J. 1972. Bensalem: When the dream died. *Change* (October): 39–44.

Coyne, J., and T. Hebert. 1972. *This way out: A guide to alternatives to traditional college education in the United States, Europe and the Third World.* New York: E.P. Dutton.

Curry, B.K. 1992. *Instituting enduring innovations: Achieving continuity of change in higher education.* ASHE-ERIC Higher Education Report No. 7. Washington, D.C.: The George Washington University, School of Education and Human Development.

Elmendorf, J. 1975. *Transmitting information about experiments in higher education: New College as a case study.* New York: Academy for Educational Development.

Frazier, N. 1977. Freedom and identity at Hampshire College. *Change* (November): 14–17.

Gaff, J.G. 1970a. The cluster college concept. In *The cluster college*, J.G. Gaff and Associates, 3–32. San Francisco: Jossey-Bass.

————. 1970b. Organizing learning experiences. In *The cluster college*, J.G. Gaff and Associates, 33–62. San Francisco: Jossey-Bass.

————. 1970c. Promises and products. In *The cluster college*, J.G. Gaff and Associates, 65–70. San Francisco: Jossey-Bass.

Gaff, J.G., and Associates. 1970. *The cluster college.* San Francisco: Jossey-Bass.

Gehret, K.G. 1972. Reports: Washington's Evergreen College. *Change* (May): 17–19.

Grand, I.J., and J. Bebout. 1981. Passionate discourse: The experimental college at San Francisco State. *Journal of Humanistic Psychology* 21 (2): 79–95.

Grant, G., and D. Riesman. 1978. *The perpetual dream: Reform and experiment in the American college.* Chicago: The University of Chicago Press.

Greening, T. 1981a. The first days of Johnston College. *Journal of Humanistic Psychology* 21 (2): 3–15.

————. 1981b. Power, decision making, and coercion in experimental colleges. *Journal of Humanistic Psychology* 21 (2): 97–109.

Hahn, J. 1984. Disciplinary professionalism: Second view. In *Against the current: Reform and experiment in higher education*, edited by R.M. Jones and B.L. Smith, 19–33. Cambridge, Mass.: Schenkman.

Hall, J.W. 1991. *Access through innovation: New colleges for new students.* New York: The National University Continuing Education Association, American Council on Education, and Macmillan.

Hall, M. 1994. A distaste for walls. *Harvard Magazine* (November-December): 52–57.

Hefferlin, JB L. 1969. *Dynamics of academic reform.* San Francisco: Jossey-Bass.

Heiss, A. 1973. *An inventory of academic innovation and reform.* Berkeley: The Carnegie Commission on Higher Education.

Holmquist, F.W., L. Nisonoff, and R.M. Rakoff. 1984. The labor process at Hampshire College. In *Against the current: Reform and experiment in higher education*, edited by R.M. Jones and B.L. Smith, 183–214. Cambridge, Mass.: Schenkman.

Jones, R.M. 1981. *Experiment at Evergreen.* Rochester, Vt.: Schenkman.

Kahn, M. 1981. The Kresge experiment. *Journal of Humanistic Psychology* 21 (2): 63–69.

Kemp, J., and R.J. McBeath. 1994. Higher education: The time for systemic and systematic change. *Educational Technology* 34, no. 5 (May-June): 14–19.

Kuh, G.D., J.H. Schuh, E.J. Whitt, R.E. Andreas, J.W. Lyons, C.C. Strange, L.E. Krehbiel, and K.A. MacKay. 1991. *Involving colleges: Successful approaches to fostering student learning and development outside the classroom.* San Francisco: Jossey-Bass.

Levine, A. 1978. *Handbook on undergraduate curriculum.* San Francisco: Jossey-Bass.

————. 1980. *Why innovation fails.* Albany: State University of New York Press.

Levine, A., and J. Weingart. 1973. *Reform of undergraduate education.* San Francisco: Jossey-Bass.

Lichtman, J. 1972. *Free university directory.* Washington, D.C.: American Association for Higher Education.

Louis, K.S. 1989. Surviving institutional change: Reflections on curriculum reform in universities. In *Improving undergraduate education in large universities*, edited by C.H. Pazandak, no. 66 (summer): 9–25.

Lyons, J.W. 1991. An eclipse of the usual: The Evergreen State College. In *The role and contribution of student affairs in involving colleges*, edited by G.D. Kuh and J.H. Schuh, 173–98. Washington, D.C.: The National Association of Student Personnel Administrators.

Martin, W.B. 1982. The legacy of the sixties: Innovation—bloodied but unbowed. *Change* (March): 35–38.

McCann, C.J. 1977. Academic administration without departments at The Evergreen State College. In *Academic departments: Problems, variations, and alternatives*, D.E. McHenry and Associates, 147–69. San Francisco: Jossey-Bass.

McDonald, W., and K. O'Neill. 1988. *"As long as you're havin' a good time." A history of Johnston College 1969–1979.* San Francisco and Redlands, Calif.: Forum Books.

McHenry, D.E. 1977. Academic organizational matrix at the University of California, Santa Cruz. In *Academic departments: Problems, variations, and alternatives*, D.E. McHenry and Associates, 86–116. San Francisco: Jossey-Bass.

————. 1993. University of California, Santa Cruz. In *Important lessons from innovative colleges and universities*, edited by V.R. Cardozier, 37–53. *New Directions for Higher Education* no. 82 (summer).

Meister, J.S. 1982. A sociologist looks at two schools—the Amherst and Hampshire experiences. *Change* (March): 26–34.

Newell, L.J. 1993. Conclusion: Making sense of irrepressible dreams. In *Maverick colleges: Ten notable experiments in American undergraduate education*, edited by L.J. Newell and K.C. Reynolds, 129–39. Salt Lake City: Utah Education Policy Center, Graduate School of Education, The University of Utah.

Newell, L.J., and K.C. Reynolds. 1993a. Introduction. In *Maverick colleges: Ten notable experiments in American undergraduate education*, edited by L.J. Newell and K.C. Reynolds, ii–vii. Salt Lake City: Utah Education Policy Center, Graduate School of Education, The University of Utah.

Newell, L.J., and K.C. Reynolds, eds. 1993b. *Maverick colleges: Ten notable experiments in American undergraduate education*. Salt Lake City: Utah Education Policy Center, Graduate School of Education, The University of Utah.

Newell, W.H. 1984. Interdisciplinary curriculum development in the 1970's: The Paracollege at St. Olaf and the Western College Program at Miami University. In *Against the current: Reform and experiment in higher education*, edited by R.M. Jones and B.L. Smith, 127–47. Cambridge, Mass.: Schenkman.

————. 1986. *Interdisciplinary undergraduate programs: A directory*. Oxford, Ohio: Association for Integrative Studies.

Nkabinde, Z. 1993. Evergreen: Ever green? In *Maverick colleges: Ten notable experiments in American undergraduate education*, edited by L.J. Newell and K.C. Reynolds, 104–17. Salt Lake City: Utah Education Policy Center, Graduate School of Education, The University of Utah.

Ruopp, R.R., and J. Jerome. 1973. Realities: Death in a small college. In *Five experimental colleges: Bensalem, Antioch-Putney, Franconia, Old Westbury, Fairhaven*, edited by G.B. MacDonald, 114–56. New York: Harper and Row.

Schuster, J.H. 1989. The Evergreen State College. Site visit report for the Carnegie Foundation for the Advancement of Teaching's Campus Community Project, Claremont, Calif., 27 June. Draft.

Steeples, D.W., ed. 1990. Managing change in higher education. *New Directions for Higher Education* no. 71 (fall).

Teitelbaum, H. 1994. Changing the campus environment. *NACADA Journal* [*The Journal of the National Academic Advising Association*] 14 (1): 32–37.

Tommerup, P.D. 1993. Adhocratic traditions, experience narratives and personal transformation: An ethnographic study of the organizational culture and folklore of The Evergreen State College, an innovative liberal arts college. *Dissertation Abstracts International* 54 (03): 1051. (University Microfilms No. AAC93-20067)

Townsend, B.K., L.J. Newell, and M.D. Wiese. 1992. *Creating distinctiveness: Lessons from uncommon colleges and universities*. ASHE-ERIC Higher Education Report No. 6. Washington, D.C.: The George Washington University, School of Education and Human Development.

Tussman, J. 1969. *Experiment at Berkeley*. New York: Oxford University Press.

Von der Muhll, G. 1984. The University of California at Santa Cruz: Institutional-izing Eden in a changing world. In *Against the current: Reform and experiment in higher education*, edited by R.M. Jones and B.L. Smith, 51–92. Cambridge, Mass.: Schenkman.

Wardle, B. 1993. College of the Atlantic: Spirit of time and place. In *Maverick colleges: Ten notable experiments in American undergraduate education*, edited by L.J. Newell and K.C. Reynolds, 118–28. Salt Lake City: Utah Education Policy Center, Graduate School of Education, The University of Utah.

Weidner, E.W. 1977. Problem-based departments at the University of Wisconsin-Green Bay. In *Academic departments: Problems, variations, and alternatives*, D.E. McHenry and Associates, 63–85. San Francisco: Jossey-Bass.

Wofford, H. 1973. Dreams and realities: How big the wave? In *Five experimental colleges: Bensalem, Antioch-Putney, Franconia, Old Westbury, Fairhaven*, edited by G.B. MacDonald, 158–91. New York: Harper and Row.

Youtz, B.L. 1984. The Evergreen State College: An experiment maturing. In *Against the current: Reform and experiment in higher education*, edited by R.M. Jones and B.L. Smith, 93–118. Cambridge, Mass.: Schenkman.

CHAPTER 1

Historical Background

The Rise and Fall of the Innovative Higher Education Movement

INTRODUCTION

The 1960s ushered in a decade of reform and experimentation in American higher education. America witnessed the birth of hundreds of experimental colleges and universities and subcolleges as the economy thrived, enrollments soared, and students across the nation sought alternatives to the mainstream college or university.

This chapter sets the stage for the present investigation by describing the historical and social context for the establishment of the innovative colleges and universities of the 1960s and 1970s. The discussion begins in the 1960s with an overview of the rise of innovative institutions. It moves on to profile the dynamics and dimensions, the early or founding characteristics of the higher education reforms of this era. The next section briefly traces the progressive and early educational roots of the alternative campuses of the 1960s and 1970s. The chapter concludes with an examination of the dramatic shifts in the economic, social, and political climate that brought the era of campus reform to a close.[1]

ORIGINS AND SOCIAL CONTEXT OF THE INNOVATIVE COLLEGE AND UNIVERSITY MOVEMENT

In his retrospective on Johnston College, former faculty fellow John Watt (1981) explains that "this was no ordinary college" (41). These were also no

1

"ordinary" times. The mood was antiwar and earthy, individuals were getting in touch with nature and were commune bound, campuses cast off their shrouds of silence—student voices were heard! In these heated, exciting days, the conditions were ripe for radical experimentation. Looking back, it seems that there were five dominant sociocultural conditions that gave rise to the innovative college and university movement of the 1960s and 1970s: (1) the skyrocketing economy; (2) the swelling in the ranks of undergraduate enrollments; (3) turbulence and dissent on campus; (4) the black student movement and the women's liberation movement; and (5) the dawning of a counterculture.

The Skyrocketing Economy

In the 1960s, the nation was riding the tide of an economic boom. The stock market was up, inflation was down, and unemployment had reached a new low. In the years following the 1957 Russian launching of Sputnik, the world's first artificial satellite, America turned its attention to higher education (and education in general) as an arena for promoting national growth and scientific development (Kerr 1971). Colleges and universities received "massive infusions" of state and federal support (Grant and Riesman 1978; Kerr 1971). Institutions were "blessed with heretofore unprecedented levels of . . . private sources of money" (Hahn 1984, 21). According to Earl F. Cheit (1971), foundation support for education (at the elementary, secondary, and college/university levels) grew from $70 million in 1954-55 to $350 million in 1964-65—a 500 percent increase in just 10 years. Alumnae/i, non-alumnae/i, and "business" support for colleges and universities rose by more than 50 percent during the decade.

These were, then, lively, optimistic days in higher education, in James W. Lyons' recollection, "a time when educational ideals and aspirations knew no boundaries; anything could be done" (Lyons 1991, 177). George Von der Muhll (1984) reflects on the hope and fortune that sustained the chartering of UC Santa Cruz: "California in those affluent years was rapidly becoming the wealthiest, most populous state in the Union. In that fabulous kingdom by the sea, the most dazzling anticipations soon merged with reality" (52).

The Swelling in the Ranks of Undergraduate Enrollments

As the economy soared, so did the demand for higher education (Von der Muhll 1984). According to U.S. Department of Education figures, total enrollments in American colleges and universities rapidly grew from 3,610,007 in 1960-61 to 7,571,636 in 1968-69, "more than doubling" during an eight-year period (Gaff 1970a). The arrival of the post-World War II baby boomers to the campuses, "added to the growth in the number of high school graduates," caused an "unprecedented demographic bulge" (Grant and Riesman 1978,

191). Many new and experimenting institutions were founded to meet the demands of rapidly increasing enrollments (Hahn 1984). Sub- or cluster colleges were added to the research "multiversities" to foster a sense of the small, personalized learning community. With the thriving economy of the 1960s, and the extraordinary rate of growth in the college and university applicant pool, there was room for innovation—for campus visionaries to follow their hearts, jump on the bandwagon, and found new and unconventional institutions of higher education.

Turbulence and Dissent on Campus

The charismatic leaders of alternative ventures in higher education were not only following their own hearts. They were guided by the actions and voices of students, voices like that of Berkeley's Mario Savio, a leader of the 1964 Free Speech Movement at Berkeley. Savio called upon the student masses assembled on Sproul Plaza to rise up against the "mechanized" multiversity:

> There is a time when the operation of the machine [the university] becomes so odious, makes you so sick at heart, that you can't take part; you can't even passively take part, and you've got to put your bodies upon the gears and upon the wheels, upon the levers, upon all the apparatus and you've got to make it stop. And you've got to indicate to the people who run it, to the people who own it, that unless you're free, the machine will be prevented from working at all. (cited in Gitlin 1987, 291)

Students of the 1960s were putting their bodies up against more than the gears of the university machine. They were challenging the system of government, the capitalistic order that ran the machine, that sponsored weapons and war industry research and sent American troops to fight the battles in Vietnam. Across the nation, campuses were rocked by heated and passionate demonstrations against the war in Southeast Asia. Students of the "New Left" organized massive strikes, marches, sit-ins, and rallies. According to Helen Lefkowitz Horowitz (1987), the early civil rights sit-ins and Freedom Rides in the South, the battles over segregation and discrimination against African Americans, "moved rebellious college students off the campus and into politics, taught them techniques of non-violent protest, and gave them a complicated, but exhilarating education about American society" (226).

What were the students' demands? Undergraduates (and graduate students) demanded an end to the draft, to the ROTC, and university-run military and weapons research. They demanded revised and "relevant" curricular options (including ethnic and women's studies and individualized course plans), open dorms, representation on college and university governance committees, and alternatives to the traditional grading system (Hall and

Kevles 1982; Horowitz 1987). They demanded an end to the "dehumanizing" structures of the multiversity, carrying signs bearing the slogan, "I Am A Human Being; do not fold, spindle or mutilate" (Boyer 1984, xv). Most of all, they demanded to be heard: In the spring of 1968, in the wake of intense student uprisings at Columbia University, there were more than 200 "major demonstrations" at more than 100 campuses (Rothman and Lichter 1982). Between October 1967 and May 1969, the U.S. Senate (1969) reports 211 colleges and universities witnessed 471 "disturbances."

Out of the heated student unrest of the 1960s, grew alternatives and additives to higher education (e.g., open admissions, pass/fail grading options, independent studies, African American studies, women's studies, coeducational dorms) and a new family of "counter-institutions" that embodied the participatory, person-centered philosophies of a generation.

The Black Student Movement and the Women's Liberation Movement

The call for civil rights and equality among persons of color and women was also a rallying point of the 1960s. As more and more colleges and universities opened their doors to growing numbers of African American students, there were new demands for African American studies programs and increased representation of African American students, faculty, and administrators in higher education. Calls within the African American community turned from integration to Black Power. Horowitz (1987) reports: "Campuses erupting in protests over the [Vietnam] war had secondary conflicts—sometimes connected, sometimes separate—as black students forced colleges to confront their agenda" (241).

A new wave of feminism also swept the nation as women across the United States began to form consciousness-raising groups and to unite against traditional patriarchal systems and institutions. In her book on the history of women in higher education, Barbara Miller Solomon (1985) writes: "The outpouring of protest, anger, and questions about the place of women came from all directions—colleges, work force, professions, and voluntary organizations—and brought women of different ages and groups into the women's movement" (203). "Thousands of women all over the country," she says, "discovered in consciousness raising that they need not be alone in resolving conflicts of work, study, creativity, and personal relationships" (203). The movement for Black Power and women's liberation collided with the antiwar protests and the New Left movement of the 1960s to create a national climate that was open to radical social, political, and educational reform.

The Dawning of a Counterculture

At the same time, the sociocultural atmosphere was undergoing a kind of physical and mystical, or spiritual, transformation. In the 1960s, "the search for alternative life-styles was on" (Watt 1981, 42). Disillusioned by "a society that could produce the Vietnam crisis . . . and the type of racial and social injustices uncovered by the civil rights movement," Watt (1981, 42) explains, new groups of wanderers, seekers of personal enlightenment, and back-to-nature poets and philosophers—the hippies, diggers, and yippies—kicked off a countercultural movement, "turning on" and "dropping out," exploring alternatives to mainstream, middle-class America. Countercultural beings grew their hair long, donned tie-dye and love beads, experimented with consciousness-changing drugs, psychedelic art, and sitar music; they held love-ins and be-ins and embraced naturalism and sensual experience; they left their homes in the cities to live and play on rural communes and in "revolutionary enclaves" (Grand and Bebout 1981; Martin 1982; Ravitch 1983).

Many of the humanistic or encountering colleges that were founded in the 1960s and early 1970s grew out of this loose, antiestablishment spirit. These new educational habitats answered a longing for schools and communities that were free from rigid rules and bureaucratic structures, creative places and intellectual spaces where the young would feel "whole and human and happy" (David Smillie, New College, Florida faculty member, cited in Riesman 1975, 41).

DEFINITION AND PROFILE OF INNOVATIVE COLLEGES AND UNIVERSITIES

All in all, innovative colleges and universities, born in the context of the radical 1960s, were "most creative and far-out adventure[s]" (Rogers 1983, 243). They came into being as "part of this larger picture of an ongoing process of fermentation in the culture in which things just started bubbling" (Grand and Bebout 1981, 80).

How did the alternative colleges and universities of the 1960s and 1970s depart from the mainstream of American higher education? As indicated in the introduction, there are five distinguishing characteristics of the innovative campuses of the 1960s and 1970s: (1) interdisciplinary teaching and learning approaches; (2) student-centered education programs; (3) egalitarian governance and community life; (4) experiential learning; and (5) an educational mission devoted to undergraduate teaching. Each of these characteristics is described in the following sections.

Interdisciplinary Teaching and Learning

First, the innovative colleges and universities of this era embraced interdisciplinary approaches to teaching and learning. Faculty were often encouraged to team up, to form collaborative partnerships with colleagues outside their specialty areas. It was not uncommon, for example, to find an artist and a philosopher teaching a course on "the problems of perception," or a psychologist and a biologist leading a seminar on the "concepts of human nature" (Alpert 1980, 508). Natural and social scientists offered courses on the "energy crisis" and scientists and humanists coordinated programs on "historical American attitudes toward the environment" (Newell 1984, 142). At UC Santa Cruz, a physicist turned his analytic skills to the study of Meso-American civilizations, an astronomer with "a lifelong engagement with music [offered] a successful course on Beethoven," an historian taught a class on the "19th century Russian novel," and a psychologist analyzed the paintings of Cezanne (Von der Muhll 1984, 65). "Underlying these disparate endeavors," Von der Muhll (1984) relates, "was a common approach: a disengagement from the constricting pressures of the monographic tradition, a joyous affirmation of the capacity of the amateur to bring new life—and sometimes new insight—to old subjects" (65).

Student-Centered Education

Second, students at innovative colleges and universities were encouraged to take ownership of their education. Whether it was a Hampshire College senior "contracting" with faculty to perform a study of tumor immunology, or a San Francisco State Experimental College student organizing a course on the Ecstatic Style of Cosmic Consciousness, the majors and the curricula at these alternative colleges and universities were heavily unprescribed, decidedly individualized, and overwhelmingly student-centered [2] (Adams 1993; Frazier 1977; Grand and Bebout 1981; Newell 1984).

Undergraduates were often freed from conventional requirements or credit structures, and "given . . . more authority over their academic lives" (Alpert 1980, 508). Students could invent their own academic "majors," design independent study programs, and even participate in curricular planning. This was the case at New College in Florida, The Evergreen State College, and a host of other free-spirited alternative campuses of the 1960s and 1970s, including the Experimental College at San Francisco State. Here students exchanged curricular ideas at a registration "marketplace" in the Gallery Lounge:

> All the [student] course organizers would set up at various tables and they would have signs and costumes and music playing. The idea was that people should be able to talk to their course planners about what they were trying to cover in the course and how they were going to

teach it. . . . What resulted was an incredible marketplace of ideas and forms of learning all dealing with innovative educational content and process, swirls of activity. (Grand and Bebout 1981, 82)

Egalitarianism

A third characteristic was a spirit of egalitarian community at the innovative colleges and universities. Status symbols, such as titles and ranks, were surprisingly absent from the faculty and administrative rosters (Blume 1981; Grant and Riesman 1978; Owada 1981; Sullivan 1973; Watt 1981). At Evergreen, students, teachers, administrators, and the president all called each other by their first names (Schuster 1989). Likewise, at Johnston College, "faculty let go of traditional titles and called themselves merely faculty fellows. . . . Faculty and students met on a first-name basis and evaluated each other" (Watt 1981, 44). At the College of the Atlantic, Hampshire College, and many other distinctive campuses, titles were also "taboo." The blurring of the bureaucratic lines was one of the hallmarks of the innovative institutions of the 1960s and 1970s.

Campus decision making and policy drafting was often a dynamic, participatory, open-to-all arena. Town meetings, general assemblies, and community forums replaced closed-door committee meetings. Administrators, faculty, and students were expected to have equal voice in the formulating of campus guidelines and in the setting of institutional policies (Kuh et al. 1991; Lyons 1991; Rogers 1983; Schuster 1989; Williams 1981; Youtz 1984). As Jerry G. Gaff wrote in 1970, the cluster (and other distinctive) colleges strive to "substitute equality for hierarchy, participant democracy for bureaucracy" (Gaff 1970b, 60).

Inside the classroom, seminar scenes were often hailed as "co-learning" opportunities (Grant and Riesman 1978; Owada 1981; Weidner 1977), where student and faculty roles would overlap and where "everyone [was] everyone else's student and everyone else's teacher" (Kahn 1981, 126). Kresge College founder and encounter group enthusiast Michael Kahn described the teacher-learner relationship in the "humanistic" college setting as "a delicate and joyful ballet, in which each partner is continually given the opportunity to reveal unsuspected depths of wisdom in the other" (126).

Experiential Learning

Another characteristic was out-of-classroom projects, theses, and internships. Experiential education was often integral to the academic programs of the innovative colleges and universities (Adams 1993; Newell 1984). At many of these uncommon institutions, education was not limited to the classroom setting. Students were expected to venture out into the world, to take part in

local work, social causes, or community-building experiences that would enhance and expand their readings and seminar discussions.

At Prescott College, for example, where founder Dr. Charles Franklin
Parker dreamed of creating an educational institution that would allow students to actively explore their environment, there is a rich history of outdoor
education—students use "the natural setting of the Southwestern wilderness
as their classroom" (Adams 1993, 89). At early University of Wisconsin-Green
Bay, the community was viewed as a natural "laboratory" for the students, a
"communiversity."

Undergraduate Teaching Missions

Fifth, creativity in undergraduate teaching was a hallmark of the distinctive
colleges and universities of this era. Many faculty came to these new experimental colleges and universities to escape the pressures of "publish or perish,"
to teach "interesting and groovy courses" like Classical Guitar, Meditation
Workshop, Sioux Tipi, and Natural Healing (Grant and Riesman 1978, 106).
In these "topsy-turvy" non-tenure worlds (faculty were often employed under
renewable non-tenure contracts), academics were free to test the limits of
curricular possibility (Frazier 1977; Ingersoll 1984; Perkins 1984). There were
no hangups over traditional "departmental politics and appointment rituals"
because (at many of the innovative institutions) there were no departments
(Lyons 1991, 185). Here, faculty were given the freedom to reshape and
broaden their teaching repertoires, to practice and perfect their craft.

OLDER DISTINCTIVE AND PROGRESSIVE COLLEGES: THE ROOTS OF INNOVATIVE HIGHER EDUCATION IN THE 1960S AND 1970S

Such ideas, of course, were neither new nor unusual in the history of American
higher education. Two of the oldest distinctive campuses in the country,
Antioch College and Berea College, came to life in the mid-nineteenth century
(Townsend, Newell, and Wiese 1992). Other campuses, such as Reed College
and Deep Springs College, were founded in the first three decades of the
twentieth century when the progressive movement in American politics and
John Dewey's educational ideals (emphasizing democratic, person-centered
classroom communities, the performing arts, interdisciplinary study, and the
richness of out-of-class experience) took hold in a generation of new experimental colleges (Alpert 1980; Elmendorf 1975; Newell 1993; Townsend et al.
1992).

There was Black Mountain College, a performing artists' campus-colony,
where scholars and students studied and lived and played in a creative,

bohemian cultural community (Duberman [1972] 1993). "The end of the community" at Black Mountain, Grant and Riesman (1978) explain, "was to foster creativity and to experience beauty . . . and the process of education resembled a studio with its apprenticeship style of mutual creation and criticism" (23). There were new experimental women's colleges such as Bennington and Sarah Lawrence College—centers of artistic energy that fostered student initiative, self expression, and creativity: "The professors [at Bennington] were charged with the responsibility of closing the gap [between life and learning], of making work and play, classroom and theater, classroom and poetry journal, one undifferentiated experience" (Rudolph [1962] 1990, 476–77). Older, established experimental institutions such as Goddard and St. Stephens (Bard) completely overhauled their academic programs at this time, to make way for individualized learning options, interdisciplinary study, and aesthetic ideas and forms.

"The stress that these [older distinctive] colleges put on freedom of choice and students taking charge of their own education," Richard M. Alpert (1980) writes, "including attention and concern for teaching over research, found fresh meaning and vitality" in the 1960s (502). The 1960s and early 1970s experiments in American higher education represented a revival of the progressive "assault" on the authoritarianism, bureaucracy, specialization, and departmentalization of the research university (Alpert 1980). A new generation of experimental thinkers, visionaries, and vanguards set out to transform the college and university world, to liberate the teacher and the student from the mighty hand of the large, bureaucratic university.[3]

THE END OF THE INNOVATIVE COLLEGE AND UNIVERSITY MOVEMENT: SHIFTS IN THE ECONOMIC, POLITICAL, AND SOCIAL CLIMATE

The times they are a-changin'

Bob Dylan, 1963

In the late 1960s and early 1970s, alternative institutions were popular and thriving. Booming experiments at Santa Cruz attracted internationally renowned faculty (an "imposing collection" of Guggenheim and Fulbright scholars) (Adams 1984; Von der Muhll 1984). San Francisco State and its McLuhan, Meditation, and Zen workshops caught the attention of *Time, Newsweek*, and *Esquire* (Grand and Bebout 1981). ("The national news media began to take notice of [the] 'quiet revolution' just across the bay from Berkeley") (Keyes 1967, 296). John Coyne's and Tom Hebert's (1972) words of advice to prospective students of the Hutchins experiment at Sonoma State were: "A nice place for a college, but apply early. This is another one of those colleges a new generation of students has discovered" (252). On the other coast, alternative-minded youth flocked to Hampshire College (Meister 1982), turning down "Radcliffe, Yale, or even Wesleyan to attend" (Grant and Riesman 1978, 380). Gerald Grant (1984) remembers when the campus "opened its doors . . . and there were so many prospective students crowding into its admissions office that they spilled over into the apple orchard" (315).

Then, slowly and surely, "at some unperceived hour in the early seventies" (several cite 1973 as the turning point year) (e.g., Adams 1984; Grubb 1984), the innovative colleges and universities began to lose their momentum. The interest waned. The reporters stopped calling. The charismatic, guru founders abandoned ship. The bold little innovative subcolleges at San Francisco, Berkeley, and San Jose went under. This section examines the dramatic transformations in the economic, social, and political climate in the 1970s that brought the free-wheeling era of experimental college and university founding to a close.

Economic Downturns

First, there were drastic shifts in the national economy. In the 1970s, the days of affluence and opulence in education were over. Money was scarce and the economy was in serious trouble (Hahn 1984; Hall 1991; Mayhew 1977; Meister 1982). According to Cheit (1971), federal funding for higher education, which had increased by 41.9 percent between 1964 and 1965, grew by 30.6 percent in 1966, increased by only 10 percent in 1967, and just 2 percent in 1968. "The increases in federal support in every year since 1967," he warned, "are less than the increases in the price level." In "real terms, federal support is declining" (10). At the same time, private donations to colleges and universities fell short of proposed expenditures. In Cheit's investigation of the financial status of 41 American colleges and universities in 1971, he discovered that 29 of the 41 institutions (71 percent) were either "headed for financial trouble or were in financial difficulty" (139). The new concern for campuses of the 1970s, Cheit writes, is "who will pay the bills" (18).

Higher education in the 1970s was, thus, no longer the dazzling, strike-it-rich landscape for academic innovation. Many colleges and universities were overextended and undercapitalized (Cheit 1971). They had invested huge sums in new programs and buildings in the "golden age" of the 1960s and were not prepared for the economic turnaround of the years ahead. Many new and experimental colleges (that were opened or planned in the 1960s) were caught in a state of partial development (Hall 1991). Subcolleges or colleges within colleges were often lopped off, abandoned when the funds dried up. Whole new experimental enterprises were threatened with closure, extinction (Frazier 1977; Hall 1991; Kuh et al. 1991; Longsworth 1976; Lyons 1991; Youtz 1984).

In the scarcity-conscious days of the 1970s, utopian, experimental campus communities struggled to keep their original dreams and visions intact. Many were victims of the academic depression.

Decline in the Rate of Enrollment Growth

- People only care about me, me, me!
- We're part of the me generation.
- People are looking out for number one.

Voices of college students discussing the mood on American campuses, 1979 (Levine 1980a, 21–22).

Interviewer: Will the United States be a better or worse place to live in the next 10 years?

Student: The U.S. will definitely be a worse place to live.

Interviewer: Then you must be pessimistic about the future.

Student: No, I'm optimistic.

Interviewer (with surprise): Why?

Student: Because I have a high grade point average and I'm going to get a good job, make a lot of money, and live in a nice house.

A conversation "repeated on campuses all across the country" 1979 (Levine 1980a, 103).

Along with the dramatic shifts in the nation's economy, a crisis of a different nature was taking form. Colleges and universities were "running out of students" (Von der Muhll 1984). In the 1970s, the college-going baby boom had ended (Hahn 1984; Levine 1980b; Potter 1980). Nationwide, higher education enrollments failed to keep pace with projections of bountiful recruitment pools. College and university attendance, which had jumped by nearly 50 percent between 1961 and 1969, grew by only about 23 percent between 1971 and 1979. (The total fall enrollment figures are 4,145,065 for 1961 and 8,004,660 for 1969; 8,948,644 for 1971 and 11,569,899 for 1979) (NCES 1993).

This was also the close of the counterculture and the end of the activist season (Adams 1984; Meister 1982). According to a Gallup International poll of 1969 and Carnegie surveys of 1976, the proportion of students participating in demonstrations dropped from 28 percent in 1969 to 19 percent in 1976 (Levine 1980a). The students of the 1970s, Arthur Levine writes, came of age in a decade of unchecked inflation, three recessions, and an "intermittent crisis of unemployment" (Levine 1980a, 65–66). In the wake of the assassinations of Dr. Martin Luther King, Jr., and Robert F. Kennedy, the rioting at the Democratic National Convention, the shootings at Kent and Jackson State, the Watergate scandal, and the war in Southeast Asia, there was a sense of collapse, a feeling of hopelessness, of things falling apart. The youth of America had lost touch with their dreamy, flower-child hopes of communing with others, overthrowing the system, and changing the world. Their heroes gone, and their visions faded, the college generation turned inward.

When probed in 1969 about what was "most essential for them to get out of college," undergraduates ranked "learning to get along with people" and "formulating the values and goals for my life" in the number one and two positions. In 1976, the top objectives were a "detailed grasp of a special field" and "training and skills for an occupation" (Carnegie Commission on Higher Education 1969 Survey, Carnegie Council on Policy Studies in Higher Education 1976 Survey, cited in Levine 1980a).

In the Higher Education Research Institute's annual survey of entering U.S. college and university students, in 1966, 43.8 percent of the participants reported that it was "essential" or "very important" to "be very well off financially"; in 1976, the figure had jumped to 53.1 percent; in 1979, 62.7 percent (Astin, Parrott, Korn, and Sax 1997). At the same time, the proportion of students who indicated that it was essential or very important to "develop a meaningful philosophy of life" steadily declined from a high of 82.9 percent in 1967, to 60.8 percent in 1976, and 50.4 percent in 1980. (See figure 1 for a display of the dramatically shifting student responses to these two survey items in the 1960s and 1970s, and the stability of these trends since the late 1980s.) When asked to indicate "very important reason[s] in deciding to go to college" in 1971, roughly 50 percent of the survey participants checked the category "being able to make more money." In 1979, 63.9 percent made the same choice. "If there are still students who come to school to find themselves, rather than jobs," Levine (1980a) concludes, "they are keeping a low profile" (61).

So suffered the experimental colleges and universities. In the constricted job market of the late 1970s and with the new "vocomania" mood of the student generation (Levine 1980a), an alternative, interdisciplinary, "touchy-feely" campus was not the preferred setting of the college-goer with careerist intentions. Edward W. Weidner (1977), founding chancellor of the University of Wisconsin-Green Bay, commented: Students "today, in the latter part of the 1970s, . . . tend to shy away from . . . any . . . kind of innovation in higher education. They want to play it safe" (79). Gaff (1970c) likewise observed: "Students wonder[ed] whether they will be as well prepared [for the workplace] as they would have been if they had gone to a more traditional school or whether their degrees will mean as much" (231–3). In times of economic downturn, students are less willing to take "educational risks," to join an experimental college or university.

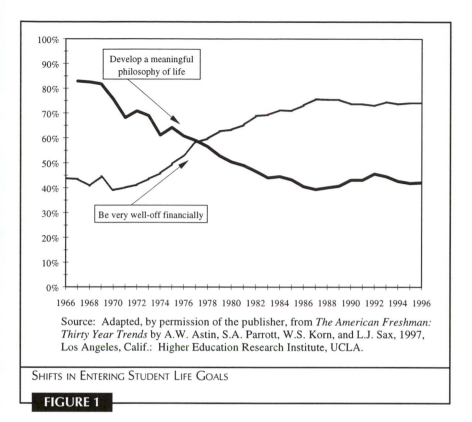

Source: Adapted, by permission of the publisher, from *The American Freshman: Thirty Year Trends* by A.W. Astin, S.A. Parrott, W.S. Korn, and L.J. Sax, 1997, Los Angeles, Calif.: Higher Education Research Institute, UCLA.

SHIFTS IN ENTERING STUDENT LIFE GOALS

FIGURE 1

Shifts in the Academic Labor Market and Faculty Recruitment Struggles

Faculty, too, were impacted by the downturn in the national economy. In the glutted 1970s academic labor market, scholars sought the stability and security of a mainstream, tenure-granting institution or department. As Von der Muhll (1984) reports, "gifted extradisciplinary teaching and imaginative contributions to institution-building" would have little weight "in a dossier otherwise bereft of publications" (73). The twists and turns of the new marketplace ruled the day, drove the academic "masses" away from the innovative colleges and universities (and away from innovative approaches in teaching and learning) that would not guarantee them mobility in the current job market.

DIRECTION OF THIS STUDY

Given the momentous shifts in the social and political attitudes, the economy, and the society in the 1970s, it is remarkable that alternative colleges and universities from the countercultural era survive in the 1990s, and even more striking that some of them carry on with their distinctive philosophies more or less intact. This study enters the worlds of six innovative colleges and universities today to investigate how and why these extraordinary campuses have managed to survive and even to keep their dreams of innovation alive amidst a changing social, economic, and political climate.

NOTES

1. When I speak of the innovative colleges or the innovative college and university movement of the 1960s, "1960s era," or the "countercultural decade," I am actually referring to those campuses that came into being or that were planned in the 1960s. This family of institutions includes those innovative campuses that were opened in the 1970s (but that were established during—and grew out of—the waves of social, economic, and political protest and reform of the previous decade) (e.g., The Evergreen State College, Hampshire College, Ramapo College) (Coyne and Hebert 1972).
2. Two exceptions are worth mention: Joseph Tussman's Experimental College at Berkeley and the Experimental College at San Jose State (in its "first phase"). Both colleges opened in 1965 and offered a fully prescribed "Great Books" curriculum modeled after Alexander Meiklejohn's Experiment at the University of Wisconsin (1927–1932) (Cadwallader 1984; Tussman 1969). "We are not impressed," wrote Tussman in 1969, "with current tendencies to allow or encourage each student to pursue his own 'interests' or to encourage students collectively to participate in curriculum determination. Students will have the rest of their lives to plan their own learning programs; in college, such planning is still the responsibility of the faculty" (112).
3. In the 1920s and 1930s, the nation also witnessed the founding of a number of neoclassical and experimental colleges within larger universities, including Alexander Meiklejohn's Experimental College at the University of Wisconsin in 1927, which offered a single integrated course of study for the entire freshman and sophomore year. The first year, according to Townsend et al. (1992), was dedicated to the study of fifth-century Athens; the second year was devoted to understanding contemporary American life. This era also marked the founding of Robert Maynard Hutchins' College of the University of Chicago, emphasizing the "great books of the Western World" and its direct descendent—a reborn St. John's College—that drew on the ideas of Hutchins' College and Meiklejohn's Experiment at Wisconsin. The St. John's curriculum was organized around some 100 great books in Western civilization.

REFERENCES

Adams, E.A. 1993. Prescott: From parson to parsimony. In *Maverick colleges: Ten notable experiments in American undergraduate education*, edited by L.J. Newell and K.C. Reynolds, 89–103. Salt Lake City: Utah Education Policy Center, Graduate School of Education, The University of Utah.

Adams, W. 1984. Getting real: Santa Cruz and the crisis of liberal education. *Change* (May-June): 19–27.

Alpert, R.M. 1980. Professionalism and educational reform: The case of Hampshire College. *Journal of Higher Education* 51 (5): 497–518.

Astin, A.W., S.A. Parrott, W.S. Korn, and L.J. Sax. 1997. *The American Freshman: Thirty Year Trends*. Los Angeles: Higher Education Research Institute, UCLA.

Blume, F. 1981. The role of personal growth groups at Johnston College. *Journal of Humanistic Psychology* 21 (2): 47–61.

Boyer, E. 1984. Introduction. In *Against the current: Reform and experimentation in higher education*, edited by R.M. Jones and B.L. Smith, xiii–xxi. Cambridge, Mass.: Schenkman.

Cadwallader, M.L. 1984. Experiment at San Jose. In *Against the current: Reform and experiment in higher education*, edited by R.M. Jones and B.L. Smith, 343–66. Cambridge, Mass.: Schenkman.

Cheit, E.F. 1971. *The new depression in higher education: A study of financial conditions at 41 colleges and universities.* New York: McGraw-Hill.

Coyne, J., and T. Hebert. 1972. *This way out: A guide to alternatives to traditional college education in the United States, Europe and the Third World.* New York: E.P. Dutton.

Duberman, M. [1972] 1993. *Black Mountain: An exploration in community.* New York: W.W. Norton.

Elmendorf, J. 1975. *Transmitting information about experiments in higher education: New College as a case study.* New York: Academy for Educational Development.

Frazier, N. 1977. Freedom and identity at Hampshire College. *Change* (November): 14–17.

Gaff, J.G. 1970a. The cluster college concept. In *The cluster college*, J.G. Gaff and Associates, 3–32. San Francisco: Jossey-Bass.

———. 1970b. Organizing learning experiences. In *The cluster college*, J.G. Gaff and Associates, 33–62. San Francisco: Jossey-Bass.

———. 1970c. Problems created and resolved. In *The cluster college*, J.G. Gaff and Associates, 216–38. San Francisco: Jossey-Bass.

Gitlin, T. 1987. *The sixties: Years of hope, days of rage.* New York: Bantam Books.

Grand, I.J., and J. Bebout. 1981. Passionate discourse: The experimental college at San Francisco State. *Journal of Humanistic Psychology* 21 (2): 79–95.

Grant, G. 1984. Whither the progressive college? *Liberal Education* 70 (4): 315–21.

Grant, G., and D. Riesman. 1978. *The perpetual dream: Reform and experiment in the American college.* Chicago: The University of Chicago Press.

Grubb, C. 1984. Innovative politics in defense of innovative education: A case study of a faculty's struggle for survival. In *Against the current: Reform and experiment in higher education*, edited by R.M. Jones and B.L. Smith, 153–81. Cambridge, Mass.: Schenkman.

Hahn, J. 1984. Disciplinary professionalism: Second view. In *Against the current: Reform and experiment in higher education*, edited by R.M. Jones and B.L. Smith, 19–33. Cambridge, Mass.: Schenkman.

Hall, J.W. 1991. *Access through innovation: New colleges for new students.* New York: The National University Continuing Education Association, American Council on Education, and Macmillan.

Hall, J.W., and B.L. Kevles. 1982. The social imperatives for curricular change in higher education. In *In opposition to core curriculum: Alternative models for undergraduate education*, edited by J.W. Hall and B.L. Kevles, 13–38. Westport, Conn.: Greenwood.

Horowitz, H.L. 1987. *Campus life: Undergraduate cultures from the end of the eighteenth century to the present.* Chicago: University of Chicago Press.

Ingersoll, V. 1984. What defines "alternative education" and what are its prospects for the future? In *Against the current: Reform and experiment in higher education,* edited by R.M. Jones and B.L. Smith, 47–49. Cambridge, Mass.: Schenkman.

Kahn, M. 1981. The seminar: An experiment in humanistic education. *Journal of Humanistic Psychology* 21 (2): 119–27.

Kerr, C. 1971. Foreword. In *The new depression in higher education: A study of financial conditions at 41 colleges and universities,* E.F. Cheit, vii–xv. New York: McGraw-Hill.

Keyes, R. 1967. The free universities. *The Nation* (2 October): 294–99.

Kuh, G.D., J.H. Schuh, E.J. Whitt, R.E. Andreas, J.W. Lyons, C.C. Strange, L.E. Krehbiel, and K.A. MacKay. 1991. *Involving colleges: Successful approaches to fostering student learning and development outside the classroom.* San Francisco: Jossey-Bass.

Levine, A. 1980a. *When dreams and heroes died: A portrait of today's college student.* San Francisco: Jossey-Bass.

————. 1980b. *Why innovation fails.* Albany: State University of New York Press.

Longsworth, C.R. 1976. Experimental colleges: Agents of change. *Today's Education. NEA Journal* (January-February): 73–76.

Lyons, J.W. 1991. An eclipse of the usual: The Evergreen State College. In *The role and contribution of student affairs in involving colleges,* edited by G.D. Kuh and J.H. Schuh, 173–98. Washington, D.C.: The National Association of Student Personnel Administrators.

Martin, W.B. 1982. The legacy of the sixties: Innovation—bloodied but unbowed. *Change* (March): 35–38.

Mayhew, L.B. 1977. *Legacy of the seventies: Experiment, economy, equality, and expediency in American higher education.* San Francisco: Jossey-Bass.

Meister, J.S. 1982. A sociologist looks at two schools—the Amherst and Hampshire experiences. *Change* (March): 26–34.

National Center for Education Statistics (NCES). 1993. *Digest of education statistics.* Washington, D.C.: U.S. Department of Education.

Newell, L.J. 1993. Conclusion: Making sense of irrepressible dreams. In *Maverick colleges: Ten notable experiments in American undergraduate education,* edited by L.J. Newell and K.C. Reynolds, 129–39. Salt Lake City: Utah Education Policy Center, Graduate School of Education, The University of Utah.

Newell, W.H. 1984. Interdisciplinary curriculum development in the 1970's: The Paracollege at St. Olaf and the Western College Program at Miami University. In *Against the current: Reform and experiment in higher education,* edited by R.M. Jones and B.L. Smith, 127–47. Cambridge, Mass.: Schenkman.

Owada, Y. 1981. Prefigurative education: A discovery at Johnston College. *Journal of Humanistic Psychology* 21 (2): 129–40.

Perkins, J.H. 1984. Comments on Newell. In *Against the current: Reform and experiment in higher education*, edited by R.M. Jones and B.L. Smith, 149–51. Cambridge, Mass.: Schenkman.

Potter, G.T. 1980. Innovation, experimentation, and higher education: Is the perpetual dream a nightmare? *Liberal Education* 66 (3): 307–14.

Ravitch, D. 1983. *The troubled crusade: American education, 1945–1980*. New York: Basic Books.

Riesman, D. 1975. The noble experiment that . . . ? New College. *Change* (May): 34–43.

Rogers, C.R. 1983. *Freedom to learn for the 80's*. Columbus, Ohio: Charles E. Merrill.

Rothman, S., and S.R. Lichter. 1982. *Roots of radicalism: Jews, Christians, and the New Left*. New York: Oxford University Press.

Rudolph, F. [1962] 1990. *The American college and university: A history*. Athens, Ga.: The University of Georgia Press.

Schuster, J.H. 1989. *The Evergreen State College*. Site visit report for the Carnegie Foundation for the Advancement of Teaching's Campus Community Project, Claremont, Calif., 27 June. Draft.

Solomon, B.M. 1985. *In the company of educated women: A history of women and higher education in America*. New Haven: Yale University Press.

Sullivan, H. 1973. The experimental college: A cool medium. *Improving College and University Teaching and Learning* 21 (August): 265–68.

Townsend, B.K., L.J. Newell, and M.D. Wiese. 1992. *Creating distinctiveness: Lessons from uncommon colleges and universities*. ASHE-ERIC Higher Education Report No. 6. Washington, D.C.: The George Washington University, School of Education and Human Development.

Tussman, J. 1969. *Experiment at Berkeley*. New York: Oxford University Press.

United States Congress, Senate. 1969. Permanent Subcommittee on Investigations of the Committee on Government Operations. *Staff study of campus riots and disorders—October 1967–May 1969*. Washington, D.C.: U.S. Government Printing Office.

Von der Muhll, G. 1984. The University of California at Santa Cruz: Institutionalizing Eden in a changing world. In *Against the current: Reform and experiment in higher education*, edited by R.M. Jones and B.L. Smith, 51–92. Cambridge, Mass.: Schenkman.

Watt, J. 1981. Johnston College: A retrospective view. *Journal of Humanistic Psychology* 21 (2): 41–45.

Weidner, E.W. 1977. Problem-based departments at the University of Wisconsin-Green Bay. In *Academic departments: Problems, variations, and alternatives*, D.E. McHenry and Associates, 63–85. San Francisco: Jossey-Bass.

Williams, E. 1981. A confirmation and critique. *Journal of Humanistic Psychology* 21 (2): 17–21.

Youtz, B.L. 1984. The Evergreen State College: An experiment maturing. In *Against the current: Reform and experiment in higher education*, edited by R.M. Jones and B.L. Smith, 93–118. Cambridge, Mass.: Schenkman.

CHAPTER 2

Pitzer College

Innovation in the Social and Behavioral Sciences

BACKGROUND: SETTING THE SCENE

S hady, tree-lined streets, quaint cottages, and Victorian-style homes charm you as you enter the "downtown" area. Striking, ivy-covered buildings with classical Greek columns and grand stone gateways serenade you along College Avenue. In the backdrop, sunny lawns and sheltered courtyards invite you into their retreats. Accents of the new gracefully mix with the old, New England, Ivy League architectural tradition offering a visual feast here in Claremont, California, the home of a unique consortium of private undergraduate liberal arts colleges and a graduate school, collectively known as The Claremont Colleges (or "the Colleges," for short).

The Claremont Colleges

The Claremont Colleges are nestled at the southern base of the San Gabriel Mountains, about 35 miles east of downtown Los Angeles. On a clear fall or winter day, you can see the snow-peaked ranges of Mount Baldy rising above the rooftops of this six-college town of some 35,000 residents and 6,000 students. Modeled after the Oxford University plan of clusters of small residential colleges, each of the colleges in the Claremont group has a life and a character of its own—a distinct curricular mission; a president, faculty, and board of trustees; independent legal status; and institutional guidelines—while sharing in the resources of the other colleges (e.g., joint academic programs, research opportunities, cross registration) and the central programs and ser-

18

vices of the Claremont consortium (the library, health services, counseling center, bookstore, etc.). According to group plan pioneer Robert J. Bernard (1982), it was early Pomona College president James A. Blaisdell's dream to create "centers of learning" that would "combine the special virtues of the small college and the advantages of the large university" (7). In a now-famous letter to Ellen Browning Scripps, dated October 1923, Blaisdell expressed his vision for an Oxford-style campus in Claremont:

> My own very deep hope is that instead of one great, undifferentiated university, we might have a group of institutions divided into small colleges—somewhat in the Oxford type—around a library and other utilities which they would use in common. In this way I should hope to preserve the inestimable *personal* values of the small college while securing the facilities of the great university. Such a development would be a new and wonderful contribution to American higher education. (Clary 1970, 2)

On October 14, 1925, the Articles of Incorporation were filed with the State of California and "The Claremont Colleges" officially came into being. Pomona College, the founding institution (established in 1887), offers the baccalaureate in all major fields of the arts, humanities, natural sciences, and social sciences. The current enrollment at Pomona College is 1,521. Claremont Graduate University, chartered in 1925, is the graduate degree-granting institution of The Claremont Colleges, awarding master's and doctoral degrees in fields spanning education, humanities, social sciences, fine arts, botany, mathematics, management, and information science. The graduate university enrolls some 928 students. Scripps College was founded in 1926 as a liberal arts college for women with an interdisciplinary emphasis and a special focus on the fine arts and humanities. Scripps has an enrollment of 687 undergraduates. Claremont McKenna College (CMC)—formerly Claremont Men's College—was established in 1947 with a curricular concentration in economics and public affairs. Claremont McKenna has an enrollment of 957 students and became coeducational in 1976. In 1955, Harvey Mudd College was founded as the science, engineering, and mathematics member of the consortium. Today, the campus enrolls 686 students. In the early 1960s, one more undergraduate institution was to come to life in Claremont, California, as Blaisdell's dream flourished and the saga of pioneering new Oxford-style colleges on the West Coast continued.

Pitzer College: The "New College on the Block"

Modern white buildings that face inward; hexagonal faculty offices; a tall white clock tower; an organic garden; a 1904 California bungalow that doubles as a coffee house/art gallery/poetry spot—scenes and images from Pitzer College, the newest "kid" on The Claremont Colleges' block. Pitzer College was founded in 1963 as an undergraduate residential liberal arts college for women with a curricular emphasis on the social and behavioral sciences (e.g., the study of anthropology, psychology, sociology, economics, political studies, etc.). The campus encompasses 20 acres of land on the eastern edge of The Claremont Colleges, just north of the Claremont McKenna College athletic field.

The Founding of Pitzer College

The Pitzer College story begins in 1959 when the Future Colleges Committee (a standing committee of the board of fellows of The Claremont Colleges—composed of the chairs of the boards of trustees of each of The Claremont Colleges, the managing director and three other members of the board of fellows, and the college presidents) gathered to recommend to the Intercollegiate Council of the board of fellows that "it draw up plans for one or more new colleges" (Clary 1970, 179). Following the successful establishment of Harvey Mudd College, Bernard (1982) explains, and the continuing growth in higher education enrollments, the time was ripe for the consideration of a sixth college in Claremont.

Two subcommittees were appointed by the Intercollegiate Council—a joint trustee-faculty subcommittee and an all-faculty subcommittee—to explore the possibilities for curricular design and to determine whether the new campus should be for men, for women, or coeducational. On December 5, 1960, the faculty subcommittee recommended to the Intercollegiate Council, with the second subcommittee's blessing, that a "liberal arts college for women, with emphasis on the social and behavioral sciences" be founded and that "the new college should be residential, like the other colleges in Claremont" (Clary 1970, 180).

According to Bernard (1982), the decision to found a women's college was sparked by the realization that ever-growing numbers of women were applying for admission to The Claremont Colleges and "being turned away here every year" (588). "It was remembered," offers an early high-ranking Pitzer administrator, "that the last college that was founded was Harvey Mudd—that was primarily men. . . . So, Claremont Men's, Harvey Mudd, two men's colleges, time for a woman's college." And time it was. Scripps College was not seeking to increase its enrollment and then-president Frederick Hard "endorsed the establishment of another women's college. [Hard] pointed out that the major field of emphasis would be quite different from Scripps . . . and that The Claremont Colleges would increase both in stature and strength with the establishment of each new institution" (Bernard 1982, 589).[1]

As for the social sciences emphasis, the planners recognized the "growing interest women are demonstrating in [the social sciences] and . . . the great need for women well prepared for careers in such fields as teaching, medicine, business, government, and social work" (*Pitzer College Bulletin* 1963, 9). At the same time, "Exciting new developments in the behavioral sciences made that new field seem promising, and from this starting point the ideas of the founders evolved into a genuine rededication to 'the study of man'" (9).

In 1961 and 1962, actions and resolutions were brought before the board of fellows of The Claremont Colleges and, after a series of meetings and discussion sessions, and after a "generous donor" had been identified,[2] the planning and development of the new institution was underway. Dr. John W. Atherton (a poet, scholar, and former dean of the faculty at Claremont Men's College) was appointed president of Pitzer College, and in 1963 the ground was broken on an expanse of sagebrush and chaparral with the San Gabriel Mountains in the backdrop.

The campus opened in the fall of 1964 with two buildings completed (a residence hall and a combination administration-classroom building) and an entering class of 153 students. In 1970, the college began admitting men as enrollment grew and planners "came to envisage Pitzer as an institution with a broader impact and appeal" (Bernard 1982, 622).

Pitzer College Today

Today this newest sibling of the Claremont consortium enrolls 869 students, 508 (58 percent) of whom are female and 361 (42 percent) of whom are male. Seven percent of Pitzer students are African American, 11 percent are Asian American, 14 percent are Latino, 1 percent are Native American, 56 percent are European American, and 11 percent are international students or members of other (or unknown) ethnic groups. Sixty-six percent of the students live on campus and 60 percent hail from the state of California (Office of Communications 1997).

There are 122 administrators and staff members at Pitzer College. The faculty is comprised of 63 full-time and eight part-time academics. Thirty-four percent of the faculty are female, 66 percent are male, and 25 percent are persons of color. The student-to-faculty ratio at Pitzer is nine to one (Office of Communications 1997).

Today, the college continues to dedicate itself to the study of the social and behavioral sciences, along with the arts, humanities, and natural sciences. The recently formalized Educational Objectives of Pitzer College, as put forth in the 1996-97 catalog, articulate the educational mission of the institution. The goals of a Pitzer education are as follows: (1) breadth of knowledge; (2) understanding in depth; (3) critical thinking, formal analysis, and effective expression; (4) interdisciplinary perspective; (5) intercultural understanding; and (6) concern with social responsibility and the ethical implications of knowledge and action. These six educational objectives are intended to serve as "guides" for undergraduates and their faculty advisors. According to the current catalog, "the College believes that students should take an active part in formulating their individualized plans of study, bringing a spirit of inquiry and adventure to the process of planning" (9).

In addition to a broad range of course offerings in the social and behavioral sciences, the campus has developed a variety of special academic programs, including interdisciplinary classes, independent study, internships, a New Resources program for adult and reentry students, and freshman seminars—titles range from Religion, Politics, and Cyberspace and Environmental Awareness and Responsible Action to Freedom and Responsibility and The Lotus and the Robot ("an overview of how Eastern and Western civilizations have dealt with such issues as the individual's relationship to society, nature, success, and religion") (*Pitzer College Catalogue* 1996, 18). The college also sponsors an External Studies program (off-campus study in the United States and abroad) that is, in many ways, quite nontraditional. Pitzer undergraduates can be found living with families in Zimbabwe; exploring acupuncture, herbology, and acupressure in China; or trekking across the Himalayas in Nepal. More than half of Pitzer graduates participate in some type of External Studies program.

ORGANIZATION OF THIS CHAPTER

This chapter presents an account of the creation, the early missionary ideals, the endurance, and the transformation of innovation at Pitzer College. The case study begins with a demographic profile of the interview participants, the current and past generations of the Pitzer College "family" who shared their voices and memories of the campus in this investigation. The next section examines the original distinctive educational missions of the college. The discussion then focuses on the evolution of the early ideals (i.e., where and how the campus has kept alive its innovative philosophies and where and how the institution has changed or transformed itself). The next section examines key issues or challenges to innovation at Pitzer College. The case study concludes with a summary and a reflection on the Pitzer College story and its implications for reform and innovation in higher education.

INTERVIEW PARTICIPANT PROFILE

To explore the history and current status of innovation at Pitzer College, 27 semi-structured interviews were conducted with 25 founding and/or current faculty members, administrators, students, and trustees in September and October of 1995.[3] Each interview lasted about 50 minutes. The participants included 14 faculty members (eight of whom had been at the college for 25 years or more), nine administrators (including the current president, the founding president, and two former presidents), five alumnae (three of whom were students in the charter class), and two members of the board of trustees. (Some individuals occupied more than one role at the institution.) The interviewees included 13 men and 12 women spanning several different "generations" of the Pitzer College community: Seven of the participants joined Pitzer in either its founding year or opening year (1963, 1964), six started in years two to four (1965–1967), three arrived at Pitzer in the college's sixth or seventh year (1969, 1970), another three came to the institution in its 10th or 11th year (1973, 1974), and five joined the college in its 16th year or later (1979–1992). Excluding the alumnae, the "tenure" for the interviewees at Pitzer College ranged from three to 31 years, with an average length of stay of 19.2 years at the institution.

DISTINCTIVE EARLY IDEALS AT PITZER COLLEGE

The early dynamics of Pitzer consisted of a poet-president, an assortment of young, free-spirited founding faculty, and an adventurous group of charter class students, all with a desire and a charge to build a college from the ground up. The founders' stories of the early years of Pitzer College often begin with a series of comments or remembrances about the feeling or spirit of the place in 1964. "You have to realize this moment," relates one of the original Pitzer faculty, "in which there's nothing but some buildings coming out of the ground and you know you have to open school in September." Imagine it, others offered: No fixed structures, no rules in place. It was an open academic landscape, a clean slate: "We [the charter faculty] were all young and the most aged among us I don't think exceeded the mid-40s. So while we were still young and idealistic, we sought one of the most singular chances we could possibly imagine. We get to start our own college. . . . Everything that you take for granted in a college, you're responsible for evolving."

For the early students, too, there was a sense of pioneering spirit, as a charter class graduate reveals:

> We had this sort of feeling of adventure and of anticipation [in the beginning]. Every time [we'd] come back from summer vacation, there'd be a new building. [When] we started off, there was Sanborn and Scott [Hall] and then Holden and then . . . Bernard and Avery and then Mead Hall was up . . . and then McConnell Center. So, it was kind of exciting. And [the campus back then] was *never* landscaped beautifully because there was always this "back 40," so to speak, that was going to be developed. . . . [Y]ou'd walk across [boulders] to get to your classes.

"I remember [when I was] growing up, my family building a home," a classmate reveals, "and it was that kind of thing [at early Pitzer]. You'd go out

and walk around on the foundation and the next week they'd be setting up...
the drywall or whatever and it was just kind of like, 'Oh, look at this room!' 'Oh
maybe I can live in this dorm. . . .' It was just kind of fun."

Indeed, a glance through the early Pitzer catalogs and yearbooks shows
photographs of students walking on long planks across the dirt and rocks near
the main buildings. One photograph is particularly striking: a young President
Atherton gazing out toward the rocky landscape. In essence, Pitzer College in
its opening years, conveyed a sense and wonder and unlimited possibility, the
spirit of creation, of giving birth to an entirely new type of enterprise. It was also
the 1960s, Atherton explains in a recent campus publication:

> It was an exciting, challenging, and ominous era in which we began.
> An assassin in Dallas had destroyed the American symbol of youth and
> hope. Powerful stirrings in the South and many northern cities fore-
> told the coming violence in Newark, Selma, and Watts. Just as our first
> class was coming to Pitzer, Katherine Towles, dean of students at the
> University of California, Berkeley, closed the campus "to all student
> political action." President Johnson and British Prime Minister Alec
> Douglas-Home had recently endorsed each other's policies in Malay-
> sia and South Vietnam. And on Sunday, September 20, 1964, in
> Claremont, California, the first students were to arrive at Pitzer Col-
> lege. (Looking Back 1995, 12)

This, then, was the feeling and spirit of place that captured the imaginations
of the earliest faculty members, administrators, and students of Pitzer College.
And this was the feeling that guided and shaped the early ideals of the campus.

What were some of the founding missions of Pitzer College? Long-time
faculty members, alumnae, administrators, and trustees were asked to talk
about the distinctive ideals of the campus at its inception.[4] Woven together,
their stories and comments (along with campus archival research and historical document analyses), point to four key themes of educational innovation at
early Pitzer College. The first was a strong sense of community, an egalitarian
ethos fostered through participatory governance and close ties among the
students, faculty, and staff. The second distinctive philosophy was the notion
of individualism or students taking charge of or shaping their own educational
programs. The third common theme was a spirit of freedom, of adventure and
creativity in faculty teaching and scholarship. The fourth ideal was
interdisciplinarity in learning and scholarly activities. Each of these themes is
discussed in greater detail in the following sections.

Community

Ask a charter class alumna, an administrator, faculty member, or trustee, to tell
you about the distinctive ideals of Pitzer College at its birth and they will,
without a doubt, mention "community." "We really started as a community,"

an alumna reveals, "and the myth that continues to revolve or evolve at Pitzer is the myth of community." "Community, of course, was the closest that we came to distinctiveness," an emeritus professor recalls. And an academic of 30 years relates: "The notion of community was very strong, ideologically, and I think it was a word that was bandied about a lot, talking about the college" in its "golden age."

Community Governance

Just what did the founders mean by "community"? And how was this philosophy expressed or lived out at early Pitzer College? First, according to interviewees, there was a concerted effort to begin the college with as few rules as possible. The idea was that every student, every faculty member, every staff person would have a voice in campus decision making. "We wanted not to create the institution for the students coming in," a charter academic recalls, "but just to create the necessary skeletal structure of an operating college, so that the classes coming in the next two years would have as much say as possible in what the college ought to look like." He adds:

> The faculty simply said, "[Governance is] something we're going to work out over the first couple of years. We're all going to sit together in a big room, the whole student body, all the faculty, and all the administrators, and the janitors if they want to come, and we're going to talk about what we want the place to look like governmentally because governmentally it's going to sort of reflect popular attitudes and so on."

And, sure enough, when "we arrived," a charter class alumna reveals, "there were no rules—well there were curfews; we got rid of them as soon as we could—but it was up to us to develop . . . what the place should look like." "The students, the faculty, the administration, trustees, were all involved together," a student from the class of 1970 agrees. There was a feeling of "being involved in it [the college] and I think the feeling that it was so small that you owned it, that you, particularly in the early years, were creating it."

In addition to having students, professors, and administrators serving together on key committees, the fundamental vehicle for what became known as "community governance" at Pitzer College was the town meeting. Based on the model of a roots-based, participatory democracy, the town meeting (usually held weekly) was an open, free-for-all gathering where, in the words of one long-time professor, "the whole college would get into one room essentially and discuss things." "It was obsessive in those days," a professor of history recalls, "you know, . . . even the janitors vote[d]." There would be heated debates and position papers, and discussions would go round and round (a phrase known to insiders as "Pitzering") until a consensus had been reached.

The faculty itself had "tremendous" power, according to several founding fathers. "When you look at the governance structure of those early years," a charter professor explains, "or if you look at the bylaws, ... all matters of education policies are in the hands of the faculty and come to the president as recommendations." "It's ... a governance tradition ... where faculty have been very much in charge," a political studies professor agrees. "Not a top-down run place." A long-time academic explains: "In the early years, ... faculty *assumed* that everything in the college was within their purview ... probably because ... they'd been involved in the hard work of setting the place up, and they expected that what they got out of that was some reciprocal power." Thus, "we thought that it was all right to [just] walk into the president's office and [make demands of] the president of the college. ... When the college center was built, the first president moved his office over there, but the faculty rebelled and wouldn't let him stay there. That's right!"

Even though early academics were granted a high degree of freedom in directing their own affairs and the affairs of the institution, this was not to the exclusion of students. At the new and daring Pitzer College, students participated on many campus committees, including the admissions and financial aid committees, and, after several years, the committee that granted promotions and tenure to faculty. "The remarkable thing about Pitzer," a founding academic marvels, "was Pitzer's incredible openness. ... Whatever went on here was very public knowledge. Students attended faculty meetings, wrote articles about it in the college newspaper ... . *Everybody* kn[ew] what [went] on in the faculty meetings here!" "The governance, alone, was so unusual," an early alumna agrees, "because usually students [in colleges and universities] weren't fully involved in everything and we were pretty much on every committee." "The idea that students and faculty would meet together to plan a college," a charter professor adds, "was considered very odd by colleges ... . [T]he idea that students could come to our faculty meetings and listen in and even *speak* if they felt so moved, that was really what [shocked] even my most liberal colleagues at other institutions!"

Why the desire for a participatory community? Why did the campus wish to give students voice in the goals and directions of the institution? It was the 1960s, a founding high-ranking official explains, a time when large bureaucratic institutions were under criticism for their impersonality and disconnection to students:

> [This was] the time of *all* the unrest ... at Berkeley ..., and *all* the screams about big institutions and impersonality, all this talk about the faculty and administration that doesn't care ... about the students, that the students have nothing to say about their education. So, we thought, [it's a] wonderful time, ... we're a brand new school. We will emphasize student participation, ... students decid[ing] what they

want to do. . . . This [was] one of our fundamental things, [that] every part of the new college, from the trustees to the administration, student body, security, janitorial force, everybody's going to be involved. Everybody's going to have a voice in what goes on at the school.

Close-Knit Community

"Community" at early Pitzer College meant more than participatory governance opportunities. There was a deep communal spirit, a feeling of closeness and bonding among the early participants of the college. The distance between faculty and students was considerably narrowed in the opening years. In planning the institution, a charter professor recalls, "[We] wanted . . . as honest and friendly relationship[s] between faculty and students as possible. . . . [The faculty] wanted students to be friends." There was "that notion that somehow we were in a cooperative enterprise," another charter professor recollects, "in which students and faculty and administration were not as distinct as they were in other places."

Students and faculty members were often on a first-name basis. "That shocked our parents very much," one alumna confesses. "'Why do you call him Steve?,'" Mom or Dad would ask. The classes, too, were scaled down to allow for small and intimate learning groups, interaction, and exchange. The size of the classes "encouraged . . . participation from everyone," an early alumna stresses. "They weren't large lecture halls. . . . Pitzer was very personal." Take the early freshman seminars (required of all entering students),[5] where coffee breaks, creative group excursions, and small classes held in professors' homes became occasions for community bonding and togetherness: "What I remember most," an alumna from the class of 1970 recalls, "is that . . . the [freshman seminars] were *very* small. They were like 10 [people], so it [gave] you an opportunity to get close to a professor, . . . to get close to a group of students, and [the seminars were] held in the evenings [in my professors' homes] and generally in more . . . informal circumstances."

Outside the classroom, too, collegial relationships flourished between early Pitzer professors and students. "You would never be afraid to go and see a faculty member or go and spend time with them in their office or babysit for their kids," a graduate of 1968 reflects. "It was just very much all one big family kind of thing." The entire college, she says, would take hikes or go on retreats and there would be picnics where faculty and staff would bring their children. "You could know your professors, you could hang out with them," another early graduate discloses. "I was on committees with [my professors] and they were around, so there was more of a feeling of family to that." Also, the faculty were young and so there was not so much of an age or generational barrier between teachers and students.

The faculty, themselves, "were very close indeed." "They practically lived in each other's pockets," a professor of English Literature remembers. "Oh yes and . . . socially, they were constantly doing dinners and they were Pitzering . . ., *constantly* discussing this college."

"Essentially, we were all in this together, in this fascinating and semi-dangerous enterprise," a professor who has been at the institution for 31 years recollects. "You know, starting a college which continually might not make it. And the relationship between the students in that class and the early faculty in those days still remains exceedingly strong." In the words of one spirited graduate of 1970, "I think that what ties you to a place is that intimacy. I wasn't a number [at Pitzer]. . . . People knew me. I knew them. And *that's* what takes you back. . . . [Pitzer] was a personal place for me and it was there for me."

Individualism: "Following Your Own Path"

Along with the communitarianism, the hikes and the picnics, the Pitzering, and the all-college retreats, there was a spirit of "do your own thing," "follow your own path." On the one hand, we were very much a community-centered place, an emeritus scholar explains. "We'd all work together. We did have lots of . . . town hall meetings. But at the same time, it was also the spirit of the sixties, let it all hang out, let the individual be the individual and that was contradictory to community." "I think the whole idea that Pitzer was founded on is that you're an individual and that you can create and do whatever you want to do," a graduate of 1968 relates. A classmate agrees: This "is a place that started off really honoring the individual and the . . . individual differences of people. . . . It was a place where they wanted each individual to find their own path."

Students were given "a great deal of freedom" in putting together their own academic programs, an early official relates. "The founding concept was that students ought to participate directly in designing their educations," Atherton recalls (Looking Back 1995, 2). While there was a rather strict set of general education requirements in the beginning,[6] students, from the very start, were encouraged to formulate their own classes, create curricula, and design independent study options to meet their academic interests or needs.

According to one founding faculty member in an interview in 1983, "'We were all very much sixties-type thinkers. We were going to give students tremendous latitude, the tremendous kind of responsibility for their own lives in so far as we could do that. We were all very committed to that'" (Dillon 1983). If you wanted to create your own class, you could do it. If you wanted to major in an interdisciplinary field, the college was open to this independent creativity. "Strange and unusual" student-designed majors with words such as "consciousness" in the titles were pursued at early Pitzer College. There was a sense of adventure and risk taking.

An early graduate shares a story of how she and her classmates were encouraged to individualize their course work and express themselves creatively:

> [In Professor Carl Hertel's] class . . ., we went to the L.A. County Art Museum and there was a selection of maybe six paintings and he said, "Compare and contrast this one and any one of these three." We . . . took notes and we were going to write a paper and then we thought, Let's do it on tape! It was Christmastime [and] we did do our discussion about these pictures on tape, but we also wove in readings from the Bible and singing of Christmas carols with lutes and just dropped the tape off at his office door. And that kind of thing was not only acceptable, but encouraged. So, [the idea] was . . . to be different and to be who you were or try to find out who that was.

Faculty Freedom, Creative Classrooms, and Spellbinding Teaching

The sense of creativity and adventure at early Pitzer College was not limited to students. Faculty, too, had a tremendous amount of freedom in teaching and scholarship. In the early years, a lively professor declares, the college set out to recruit "kooky and excellent" people and we were always encouraged to pursue individual interests, to invent new courses, and to undertake unique approaches to classroom teaching. A former president recalls that there was "a genuine belief that teaching [was] the main responsibility, and mostly, a great deal of respect for teaching styles."

Differences were prized back then, even nourished, he reveals. That was the beauty of the place—the great varieties of teachers and teaching. On the one hand, he says, you would have "a Harvey Botwin," an economist, who "could, in front of a hundred students be spellbinding, just a master and you'd walk away thinking, This lecture, this is extraordinary, which it was." Or, you would come across a

> Lucian Marquis . . . who could take 150 students and . . . [they would] be eating up every word, and he could get participation from them and just stroke them like a huge orchestra. You would then find an Al Schwartz who . . . really didn't believe in teaching as such: "Let's just get together and talk about baseball. Let's just talk about life. . . ." Or Lew Ellenhorn, a social psychologist, who would *organize* his students to have confrontations with [the president] and other people because that's how they would learn what social psychology was all about. . . . Or someone like Ruth Munroe—and I put Lucian Marquis in this category—where if you would look at an introductory course in political studies or psychology, they were as rigorous and as traditional as

you'd find at Harvard. And these courses . . . would co-exist, then,
with these nontraditional courses and teaching styles.

A Pitzer graduate, now a trustee, recalls a spirited seminar with Lew
Ellenhorn:

> [Lew Ellenhorn is a] jazz musician and . . . psychiatrist and he did "The
> Psychology of Jazz" [class] which became "Psychology of the Creative
> Experience." It was a *dynamite* place. You *never* knew what was going
> to go on. . . . [T]hat was the first time I even knew about drug
> addiction because we went and saw Alanon and tr[ied] to figure out
> why people were turning to that and what recovery was all about, and
> [we] went to art galleries and talked to artists and saw them paint and
> we had to do some performing or painting ourselves, getting in touch
> with that. Oh, it was wonderful.

Interdisciplinarity: Sharing the Same Hallways

Next, the charter faculty and administrators of Pitzer College set out to create
an institution that would resist traditional disciplinary organization and the
tensions and turf wars associated with budgeted academic departments. "It is
hoped that the faculty will operate as a committee-of-the-whole and through
functional committees," the founding faculty and staff announced at preliminary (pre-college opening) meetings, "and that departmental stratification and
organization will be avoided as long as possible" (Pitzer College Summary 1964,
1).

In the early years of the college, the Pitzer faculty formed "field groups"
(groupings of faculty with similar disciplinary interests) rather than traditional
academic departments. The field groups would have "conveners" as opposed to
department chairs, and the academic budget would be centrally coordinated,
rather than being administered through individual field groups or disciplines.[7]
According to a recent account on interdisciplinary study at Pitzer College,
"The system was intended to deflect political clashes over budget allocations
and other territorial issues, and to encourage interaction among disciplines,
whether through collaborative teaching or excursions into fields related to or
beyond an initial area of training" (Ganahl 1995, 19).

Out of this cooperative, cross-disciplinary framework came a certain degree
of flexibility for academics, a liberation from the bounds of conventional
disciplinary structures. Sociologists teamed up with psychologists to teach
courses; art historians and anthropologists co-taught seminars. "I had many,
many courses at Pitzer that were team taught through different disciplines," a
graduate of 1968 recalls. Faculty members at Pitzer did not have to conform to
prescribed departmental processes or politics. They had the freedom to step
out on the edge, to teach in new and unexplored fields. Students, too, were

given the opportunity to test out individualized, interdisciplinary studies and majors.

Even the physical organization of the campus reflected the early interdisciplinary spirit of Pitzer College. "All of our offices," a long-time professor explains, "were set up [in] an effort to put people from different disciplines next to one another if it was possible . . . in hopes that out of that would come a diverse and interdisciplinary curriculum."

ENDURANCE AND TRANSFORMATION OF THE DISTINCTIVE EARLY IDEALS AT PITZER COLLEGE

But dreams change as people change and as the campus ages, the early visions of the institution, so near and dear to the hearts and souls of the founders, the creators, are transformed into new passions and new dreams. This section examines the endurance and transformation of Pitzer's innovative founding ideals (community, individualism, faculty freedom and creativity, and interdisciplinarity). It then explores the "survival" or longevity of the institution and offers a summary of the key reasons for the endurance and/or transformation of the distinctive founding themes.

Community

Many interviewees, as noted, echo a certain sentimentality about the early days of the town meetings, the Pitzering, and the togetherness that characterized the college's pioneering era. When asked to describe the campus today and to reflect upon the preservation of the original community ideals, founding and current faculty, administrators, and alumnae indicated that the initial, all-consuming commitment to community governance had faded, but that the participatory structures or style of governance—the opportunities for involvement and the expectation that all voices would be heard—had remained.

Community Governance

Structurally, much of the community governance "stuff of the early years" is still there, a long-time professor of anthropology relates. What Pitzer has maintained, an emeritus professor agrees, is a kind of "ambiance . . . [of] community governance. On many, many committees, students and faculty serv[e] together." A long-time professor of sociology confirms: "We continue to incorporate students in the governance. . . . They sit on . . . virtually every committee." "We have an Academic Planning Committee with equal numbers of faculty and students," a professor of 30 years explains. "We have a Curriculum Committee with equal numbers of faculty and students. Things like that."

What especially continues to single out Pitzer from traditional colleges and universities is the "serious" involvement of undergraduates (as elected or designated representatives) on the institution's appointments, promotion, and tenure committee (Faculty Executive Committee). "I don't know of any other college," a professor of political studies declares, "where students are voting members of a committee that determines tenure for faculty." "I find that this [participation of students on the personnel committee] is the one thing that surprises people when I go to conferences and talk to people about the college," a long-time academic reveals.

What still amazes many interviewees, too, is the level of faculty power. In the words of a long-time professor, "I think [Pitzer] faculty [still] make decisions that in other schools in Claremont [are] certainly beyond [the decision-making powers of the faculties] or [are] made more by administrators. We expect to share much more in budgeting, setting of priorities, all sorts of policy decisions." How many faculties do you know of, a charter academic declares, where the faculty vote on the budgets outside of their departments? "Most faculty in other colleges never even see the budget outside of their own departmental budget."

The 1989 Pitzer reaccreditation self-report makes reference to "the total commitment of the Pitzer community to participatory governance" (22). "The committee system," the authors state, "remains fully participatory and sensitive at each step to community opinion and response" (Pitzer College Application for Re-Accreditation 1989, 23).

What has kept the innovative structure of community governance alive at Pitzer College? According to several interviewees, Pitzer's unusual "institutional arrangements," its comparatively "light" hierarchical organization and administrative operation, have allowed for a more open and inclusive governance design. "People aren't stuck in academic departments," a political studies professor reports. "Presidents and deans," he says, "don't make all of the decisions around here. They're expected to consult widely within the community as a whole and that kind of openness encourages new ideas."

Some interviewees report that it is the continuing presence of the faculty founders, the pioneers, that sustains the participatory governance ethos. Others point to the arrival of the newer faculty cohorts who have been hired by the founders and who "reinvigorate the place." It is the process of "like hiring like," one lively interviewee observes. Pitzer professors, she says, whether they be "old guard" or "new," have a kind of kindred connection and a flair for innovative processes and governance organization. An alumna and current trustee puts it this way: "That initial faculty who . . . became the leaders . . . hired the next generation and the next and the next."[8]

While the participatory structures and styles of governance remain a hall-mark of the Pitzer College campus today, interviewees report that the sponta-neity and energy, the deep involvement that characterized the community governance arena in the charter years, has faded. "We're much more orga-nized, we're much more institutionalized," states a founding father. "We have more forms to fill out. There are more committees than ever before," a fellow charter academic agrees. "The administrations have grown and become more powerful."

A professor of political studies relates: "I'm a little concerned that we're more administratively run than we have been in the past." An English litera-ture professor, likewise, asserts, "Probably the major shift I see is one that has occurred as a result of there being a lot more students and therefore more faculty. So what used to be a school that could have town meetings and get together in fairly intimate ways . . ., has now become a far more bureaucratic and more organized and committee-run sort of place."

These days, the faculty "can't all fit into each other's pockets." "We can't all get together comfortably [as a college] anymore," a long-time faculty member explains. "You see, we went from roughly 120 students in the first year up to, well, 700 students in a few years," another early professor reports, "and it was just impossible to get everyone into one room" for, say, a town meeting. So, what you have today, he argues, is a college that meets primarily in committees. The once-weekly town hall spectacles of free-for-all debate occur only now and then when the college community gathers to focus on a particular issue.

There was a passion and a spirit of involvement among the charter faculty and students that "can never be recaptured," an alumna relates. "I remember shutting the school down for two days to discuss what was wrong with community," a long-time professor declares. "We cancelled classes. My God, how sixties can you get?! . . . But it did represent something that we took seriously enough that we wanted to do something about it. . . . There's no such animal anymore."

"There isn't the same sense of excitement [among the faculty] about being in the middle of doing something consequential on [college] committees," a professor of anthropology explains. These days, he says, most committee work involves "keeping house." It is a different stage in the institution's develop-ment. Professors are no longer "shaping the campus," he adds, and "so the investment of the faculty is considerably less than it had been." He argues that Pitzer professors tend to gravitate toward what truly "makes a difference" at the college today and "for me," for many, that is teaching: "If you ask folks about where they find their pleasures at Pitzer, it's in what they can teach and in what intellectual conversation they're in with their colleagues. It's very rarely any more government pride. There has been a real shift."

In the early years, a professor of 30 years relates,

> Faculty members . . . were tremendously well informed about what was
> going on in the college because they were intimately involved in a
> number of committees . . . and this helped to develop a stronger sense
> of belonging to the institution than is sometimes the case [today]. . . .
> In latter years, . . . some of the junior faculty have been less involved . . .
> and therefore felt less part in the institution than we [early faculty]
> did. Now, it's not a fair comparison because we were creating a new
> institution. . . . [T]here *was* a great sense of involvement, . . . a very
> high level of commitment.

The faculty meetings "tend to be reports" now, a long-time professor
observes:

> We used to *laugh* at Pomona [College] because . . . their faculty
> meetings were [reports]. Our faculty meetings were fights! . . . Ours are
> reports now. . . . We had fights over things like whether we'd have a
> major in religion—a faculty member saying that he would resign from
> the college if we did. But, we worked that [out]. Once we actually had
> a fist fight. . . . [E]verything seemed to be absolutely *critical* in those
> days. . . . This [college] was a *closed* little world. . . . It's not so closed
> anymore with e-mail, faxes, voice mail. . . . So, yeah, I think the place
> has changed.

Students, too, don't rise up and demand change as they used to, the early
faculty and alumnae/i believe, and it is harder and harder to find students these
days who want to be involved on college committees. An alumna from Pitzer's
charter class remarks:

> I've enjoyed the [current Pitzer] students I've met. . . . They live on the
> fringe, yes, but there's not this sense of community the way I experi-
> enced it. Perhaps part of that is [the] generation. . . . I remember
> signing *lots* of petitions and carrying them around. . . . [Students] wrote
> petitions and said, "We don't want this. . . . We *do* want this. . . . We
> don't want to have so many two o'clocks [classes], so many one
> o'clocks, and then locked in [the dorms] at ten o'clock." I think we
> were *much* more proactive then. I think students now react . . ., but I
> don't see that there have been groundswells.

And so, among the founders there is a sense of loss of the early participatory
governance spirit as the college has grown and become more institutionalized,
and the faculty and student generations have changed. While the community
no longer gathers for regular town meetings, and while the early zeitgeist of
building an institutional home, walking around the foundations and stepping
across the rocks and dirt to get to classes, is but a fond memory, the basic
participatory structure of Pitzer College governance has lived on.

Close-Knit Community

Although the early intensity and intimacy of the founding era has passed, there is still some sense of a close-knit community at Pitzer College today. "There is a greater measure of friendliness" at this college than at many other campuses, a founding professor explains. Students and faculty members still call each other by their first names. Small and creative freshman seminars and interactive classrooms remain a distinctive feature of the institution (although "the way we constructed [the freshman seminars] in the first years, mostly . . . lost now, is that they met for three hours in the evening and were intended deliberately for purposes of socialization," a founding father relates).

"There's another contact" beyond the classroom at this institution, an early alumna and current trustee remarks. Pitzer professors, she says, "know the students . . ., they keep in touch with many of them after graduation. There is a *personal* involvement, not just a teaching involvement with students and that's very unique in . . . undergraduate education today." A long-time professor of sociology agrees:

> [Faculty] do have unusually close relationships with students. . . . [T]hey [students] talk to us. They reach out to us. Yesterday, a student was in crying because of what had happened on her statistics exam and I think [students] really feel comfortable in coming [in], talking about problems, and in getting involved in research programs that we may have going and so forth. . . . I think that . . . many small colleges *say* they do this. I think that we . . . do this mentoring really to an *unusual* degree.

For this kindred professor, her teaching and her whole way of being and growing as an academic has been about guiding and caring for her students:

> I think about modeling my whole life for students and sharing with them what I do when I'm not here. [Pitzer faculty] *are* hoping . . . that we not only intellectually give our students something special, but that they come away with a piece of . . . us as people who care about the world, whether it's in ecology or environmental studies . . . or social issues or justice issues or whatever.

While a closeness and connection among students, faculty, and staff is still a hallmark of the Pitzer education, the early spirit of togetherness, the emotional, familial-like bonding that characterized the founding era of the institution has, again, faded to some degree. There is not that level of intensity, in the words of one of Pitzer's first students:

> My [graduating] class was a very close and strong class. I think some of the [more recent] classes [are not as close]. I work with seniors on the class gift and a lot of students [tell me], "I don't even know who's in my class. . . ." When I came here, we [students] were always in one place.

> It was a very strong, kind of everybody-knew-everybody. It was kind of like a sorority or a camp. We were all together, always feeling part of the fun. I think *that* kind of closeness will never happen again.

We were pioneering an institution, a fellow graduate from the charter class echoes:

> There will never be again in Pitzer's history *that* spirit. . . . [T]here's an excitement about something new . . . and then there's a special bonding . . . of those who pioneered something together and that will never be again. . . . I was interested to look at something that came out of Pitzer not very long ago. . . . These were pictures of the reunions. . . . I was *stunned* that there were so few people who "showed" at some of the later . . . reunions. [At] our class reunion . . ., we were too many for the steps of the Grove House [a bungalow that houses the campus's coffee house]— and that's a class of 75 or so. Maybe the Pitzer commitment and experience was different in the beginning.

"In the first year," a founding father relates, "we assigned two faculty couples to each of the corridors [in the dormitories] so that there would be that [close] level of faculty-student interaction and . . . faculty members quite frequently invited students ... or their advisees ... to their homes and some classes were being held at home. Lucian [Marquis] is about the only one I think that still does that." No more evening, home-y freshman seminars. No more nonstop intensive interactions that are born out of a constant Pitzering, regular lively back-and-forth meetings, and the "shutting down of the college" that captured the spirit of pioneers. The educational blueprint had already been mapped out, the campus' foundations conceived, when the newer generations arrived to this institution. And growth, of course, made it more and more difficult for the campus to gather as a tight-knit community.

One long-time professor, a self-declared cynic, mourns the loss of the "human side of education" at Pitzer College. "Walk out into the hallway," he suggests, "and see if anything's going on. The answer is nothing's going on. There's no one here. . . . [T]here's . . . no contact between students and faculty. Now that may sound like a fairly ordinary thing . . ., but there was a time when you would have expected to see lots more interaction. . . . There . . . really was community."

Individualism: "Doing Your Own Thing" in the 1990s

And what of the early ideal of individualism, the free-spirited 1960s notion of the learner taking charge, following his or her own academic path, doing his or her own thing? Is this still a place for the "strange and unusual" major, the self-designed project, the museum-inspired "homework" recordings of Christmastime singing, lutes, and group dialog-analyses of paintings?

In many ways it is, the interviewees report. While the college has recently adopted a "modest number" of general education requirements (or "educational objectives") as part of the reaccreditation process,[9] there remains a creative edge to the college and its curricular paths. Students can still come here and customize their learning experiences. They can create original independent study projects and design their own majors (or "concentrations," in Pitzer-speak), as an administrator relates:

> There's a process by which to create your own concentration. . . . [S]tudents have to work very closely . . . with their advisors to try to come up with a program that has breadth, that also has depth, that is very much fashioned to *them* as individuals, even with the educational guidelines [that the college] put in place. [The guidelines] are . . . very open ended and the intent is that you work on them by talking with your advisor and figuring out what works for you. The intent is still very much for students to play a strong role in shaping their own course of studies here.

A professor who has been at the institution for 28 years explains:

> Students generally don't feel the crush of bureaucracy at this college and I think that was certainly part of the ideal at the beginning, that the students feel a sense of freedom within the school and a feeling that . . . they can shape their own curriculum to a degree. [Some students] will in fact go to a lot of trouble in order to devise a concentration for themselves and the system is very open to that and willing to consider it. It isn't extraordinarily difficult to do.

In fact, more Pitzer students today are creating their own majors than in the early days. Although the figures remain fairly low,[10] there has been an increase in the proportion of undergraduates who are completing their bachelor's degrees in self-designed or "special" concentrations. From 1972 to 1975, for example, the percentage of all Pitzer College graduates who received a baccalaureate degree in a special concentration was 4.0 percent. Between 1992 and 1995, the figure was nearly twice as high (7.8 percent) (Registrar's Office 1996).[11, 12]

It is a long-standing tradition of fostering student responsibility and freedom for directing one's own education, a founding faculty father observes:

> If you have to pick out one or two attitudes which make the college distinctive [today], one would be that Pitzer sort of likes and trusts its students. Now, that may seem like not much, but actually it's a lot. I went to Pomona [College] and Pomona essentially says, "You people are students and do what you're told." And Pitzer says, "We're going to teach you to make decisions; we're going to give you decisions to make which carry with them genuine consequences. . . . So, we're going to

let you be in charge, to a certain extent, of your own academic
existence here. We'll sit by, we'll give you advisers, but essentially
you've got the opportunity here to do yourself real damage." Now,
that's a very hard way to put it, but what it simply means is that you
give students a considerable amount of latitude to make decisions that
are important . . . both for themselves and for the college. . . . And
that's what grew up with the college.

An early Pitzer graduate and current trustee agrees:

I think what you get at Pitzer is a group of students who aren't docile
from the beginning and who are encouraged to shape that spirit of . . .
questioning and concern. . . . There's a floor underneath, there's a net
underneath these kids where they *can* take risks, they *can* challenge,
they *can* explore their own thoughts and yet not be . . . out so far that
they get completely in trouble for it. And that's part of growing up. I
mean, we thought we were adults at 18 and I'm sure my son believes
the same, but we were kids still shaping our thought process[es] and I
think that's part of the Pitzer spirit, being allowed to do that in a very
open sense, in a trusting sense with faculty.

One charter professor refers to what he calls "the college's essential malleability":

The other [distinctive] aspect [of Pitzer] is what I've always referred to
as the college's essential malleability. [The college] does not really
hold the view that a particular kind of education is the very best. So,
there are students who come here who want to take Old World
disciplines and study them in Old World fashions and earn kind of Old
World degrees, developing Old World talents. And there are students
who come here and want to do things that are really innovative. And
the college's position is that neither one of those things is inherently
superior to the other.

A student can come to Pitzer and "carry on a *very* traditional program," he
marvels, "or you can come to Pitzer and create your own concentration. . . . [A]
student may elect, for example, to do work in urban renewal and combine that
maybe with a certain background in sociology, psychology. We don't *have* a
major in urban renewal," he explains, "but a student may, by virtue of his or her
instinctive interests, develop a particular [major] in that. . . . Students who
have a particular focus that they want to pursue that the existing concentration requirements don't necessarily allow for . . ., will try to design one."

What kinds of majors are students designing? A sampling of the creative,
personalized concentrations for the graduating classes of 1993, 1994, and 1995
is as follows: Studies in Conceptual Frameworks and Systems; Urban Ethnic
Studies; The Study of Education; Political Science and Literature from Africa

and the Diaspora; Bioethics; and Feminine Culture: The Mind, Body and Spirit of Women (Registrar's Office 1996). "Essential malleability"—Pitzer's own spirit and tradition of individualism—is at its finest.

Faculty Freedom and Creativity: "Encouraging the Expression of Our Beings"

When it comes to the faculty, academics on campus today still enjoy a tremendous amount of freedom in inventing new courses, undertaking creative or unusual projects, and following their passions or interests in teaching and scholarly activities. According to the faculty interviewees, the college's decentralized, nondepartmental structure enables and empowers them to continue to experiment, to test and try out new ideas and course themes.

"Most of us at Pitzer have a freedom that faculty at most other institutions don't have," proclaims a lively, long-time academic. "We have a freedom to [radically] change what we teach. We can invent new courses all the time. . . . [There are] core courses that are always offered, but there's an awful lot of freedom to invent new courses." An emeritus professor agrees: "We've never had a departmental structure; we've never had a departmental [chair]. We have a dean of faculty who sort of carries the burden of the department. . . . So, what Pitzer gave to me . . . was the freedom to experiment, to try new things."

Consider the experience of this professor of sociology:

> I came [to Pitzer] primarily as an organizational sociologist. [But I've] done lots of other things [here]. I've written a whole mess about China, I've written a lot about technology and society, I've done a lot professionally for the Society for the History of Technology. . . . Well, you can see some other place where the dean might call you in and say, "Now look here! . . ., where's the sociology in all of this?" And maybe that would happen elsewhere, but [it] certainly doesn't happen here.

A faculty member who has been at the college for 10 years agrees: "If there are projects that you're interested in working on, it's not like you go to your department chair and he can shoot it down. . . . You can do pretty much anything you can dream up and convince yourself that's a good idea. There aren't those levels of bureaucracy that hinder creative kinds of things." In the words of a long-time professor,

> There are not a lot of impediments to doing things [here]. . . . There's not an elaborate hierarchy. At [other institutions], you've got colleges and deans and departmental chairs and so forth and . . . layers of hierarchy. Here, things are . . . almost anarchic at times and if you want to do something different, if you want to teach a new course, if you want to build in a fieldwork component . . ., nobody is going to bug you about it.

"For the most part, we've had very strong administrative support for innovation, for creativity," a professor who has been at Pitzer for 26 years, adds. "We've been blessed with wonderful presidents," an early alumna and trustee agrees, "who have *understood* what Pitzer was supposed to be and what the faculty were committed to have Pitzer be."

A top-level administrator says that it is critical that they are "not forcing faculty" into narrowly defined areas of "intellectual thought" at this college. They try "to respect and let people go where their energies [lie]." It is all about appreciating differences, a former faculty member explains, a certain openness to creative expression:

> I think that Pitzer is a tremendously *tolerant* institution at a time of increased intolerance. Its tolerance extends in various directions, both in terms of its tolerance of people from different backgrounds, ethnicities, classes, sexual orientations, and so forth. . . . It is tolerant both in terms of the kinds of people that it will not only *tolerate*, but encourage[s] the expression of their beings. . . . [I]t is . . . tolerant of people who want to challenge disciplinary boundaries, start new courses, projects, and so forth.

Interdisciplinarity

"In the deep, dark depths of the soul, it is always three o'clock in the morning," states sociology professor Glenn Goodwin, quoting F. Scott Fitzgerald (in an interview with Ganahl 1995, 20). "Existential literature," he says, "calls sociologists' attention to things we do not normally pay much attention to: the suffering, anguish and angst viewed by much of sociology as deviant rather than normative. Literature gives us insight into the human beings who comprise 'groups' . . . [and] sociology must be willing to incorporate insights from the humanities into its inquiry. Philosophy and history . . . are perceived wrongly as being too 'soft' to contribute to the sciences. Even fiction, which is by definition 'non-truth,' is nevertheless often 'very truthful.'"

Goodwin is one of the many creative and collaborative scholars at Pitzer today who carry forward the tradition, the early spark and passion for interdisciplinary teaching. There are others: a sociologist who brings psychological, sociological, and historical literature into her course on violence in intimate relationships; a historian and a political scientist who team teach Introduction to Thought: East and West; an artist and political scientist who teach Crossroads of Art and Politics (Ganahl 1995; Pitzer College Application for Re-Accreditation 1989). Interdisciplinarity—teaching and learning at the intersections of traditional fields of inquiry—has persevered at Pitzer College.

"There's [still] a greater willingness to cross disciplinary boundaries here than in most institutions," states a long-time professor, "and in fact we . . . have quite a lot of team teaching here and it's very often faculty members from different fields [who] get together. . . . I've taught with people in English, psychology, anthropology, sociology, political studies, and they've generally been very good experiences." "I always have a sequence of academic interests," a spirited anthropologist points out. "So, if people look at what I've taught over the years, they might say, 'Look at this bizarre assortment of things.' But it's all linked. . . . Pitzer lets me teach these things. I am not novel at Pitzer in this regard. . . . This is what we *all* can do!" Interdisciplinarity, she exclaims, "enables me to always be fired up about something!"

Indeed, all you have to do is open up the current Pitzer catalog, flip through the pages of the viewbook, review the listings of concentrations, or read the articles in the alumnae/i magazine, to get a sense of the continuing tradition of interdisciplinary education at this institution—e.g., the creative team-taught courses, cross-disciplinary majors, and now clusters and programs that link together the college's diverse academic fields.

In 1993, 1994, and 1995, Pitzer undergraduates were completing degrees in such cross-disciplinary concentrations as Art and Psychology, Economics and Environmental Studies, Psychology and Spanish, English and Psychology, Continental Philosophy and Art, and Psychology and Theater (Registrar's Office 1996).

Interdisciplinarity, is, in fact, one of the "credos" of Pitzer College today, one alumna explains. "It's sort of a *required* thing that you think along more than one line at a time." In 1989, the college adopted "Interdisciplinary Perspective" as one of its six educational objectives (or general education requirements). All students are now expected to integrate an interdisciplinary component into their learning plans.

If you want to get a real flavor for the continuing interdisciplinary tradition, walk through the corridors of Pitzer's academic buildings, where you will still find a lively mixing of scholars housed together from different disciplines—e.g., a sociologist's office situated between that of a political scientist and an English professor; a professor in film whose next door neighbor is a professor in math. One long-time professor observes: "You break out of that traditional [disciplinary] cluster [when your offices are situated like ours], and you find, for example, much higher rates of collaboration when people are on the same floor as opposed to being [separated]." "We're not housed by discipline," another academic proclaims, and that has, in part, kept alive the spirit of team teaching and cross-disciplinary collaboration.

What else has kept alive the interdisciplinary, collaborative approaches at this campus? Long-time Pitzer faculty and administrators insist that it is, again, the flexible, nondepartmentalized structure of the institution as well as an academic reward system that supports cross-disciplinary perspectives. "There was just never a power center established," one professor explains: "From the beginning, you don't have that kind of organizational infrastructure to promote and preserve and protect and defend departmental interests. . . . So that just creates a looser kind of a structure and a greater willingness and a greater tolerance to do [creative, interdisciplinary] things." An administrator puts it this way: "We don't have departments. We don't have [department] chairs. We don't have departmental budgets . . . and that's made it very easy for people to cross disciplinary bounds. I think Pitzer was founded with the intent that [interdisciplinarity] would happen and it *has* happened."

At the same time, the faculty reward structure supports and sustains interdisciplinary teaching. At most other institutions, one scholar remarks, "there is very little incentive to make connections with other fields. Often [academic] promotion is judged by what contribution [faculty] made to their own field, not to some . . . theory between politics and economics." "Very often," he says, "some of the most interesting issues tend to happen on the borders of disciplines . . ., and the opportunity to explore those kinds of intersections is often *very* attractive to other academics but they, in their own institutions, see no rewards [for this]."

According to the 1989 reaccreditation self-report, Pitzer "encourages joint teaching by hiring faculty who are so inclined, by rewarding successful joint teaching in contract renewal, promotion and tenure decisions, by counting a jointly taught course as a full teaching credit for each faculty member participating and, when possible, by making funds available to supplement jointly-taught courses with invited speakers and special events" (53).

Interdisciplinary perspectives are also kept alive, again, by the process of "like hiring like"—the faculty who came to Pitzer in the beginning brought in individuals who shared a kind of spark for crossing traditional disciplinary boundaries and this has kept the interdisciplinary framework intact. In the words of a long-time sociology professor, "We've hired people who are pretty much in our own image and likeness as far as their interests and concerns. I think that's kept things going." An academic who has been at the institution for 26 years exclaims that the younger faculty with their new ideas "rejuvenate us!" She says that they enliven and enrich the cross-disciplinary curriculum: "When we hire someone new, it's like recruiting someone into your family. You take great care and you want to bring someone in who will share your basic values and will bring something new. . . . That's where the continuing life is in the college. . . . [The new faculty] fire us up to go charging off all rejuvenated on something else." In the words of one long-time professor of sociology,

> We tend to hire [faculty] who are like minded. . . . I think we are
> always interested in somebody who can bring a cross-cultural perspec-

tive and an interdisciplinary perspective. We just hired a new sociologist out of . . . 400, 500 applicants, and she doesn't want to teach in sociology. She has a degree in business. *But*, her primary research has been very sociological within a business context. So it never really came up as a big issue. Nobody said, "Well, wait a minute, she's not a 'real' sociologist." Well, she is a real sociologist in terms of what she does. So we're a little less concerned about these [traditional disciplinary] titles.

The Survival of Pitzer College as an Innovative Institution

Thirty-one years later and Pitzer College carries on with much of its original distinctive educational design intact. Given the shifts in the economy since the 1960s, the changes in contemporary attitudes toward education (what some characterize as a conservative shift in public attitudes about reform in education), and the short lives of many of Pitzer's kindred counterparts in the 1960s and 1970s, what has kept this innovative institution healthy and alive? Taking a different turn on the topic, interviewees were asked to comment on Pitzer's longevity—i.e., to share, if they could, some of the reasons why this distinctive college has survived.

The answer was almost always the same: Pitzer College is part of The Claremont Colleges. In the words of a past president of Pitzer,

> I think the presence of the other colleges [was critical]. [S]imply being there, side by side, cheek-by-jowl with those other places, [and] things like a joint science program, a library that would far exceed anything that Pitzer could have afforded [on its own], the opportunities for cross registration . . ., those are powerful, powerful things, and I think that in a cornfield in the middle of Iowa started in 1963, I'm not sure we could've made it as undercapitalized as Pitzer's always been.[13]

"Thank God for the other schools," an early alumna and current trustee declares. "I think [Pitzer is] very lucky because they have the support of the other schools nearby. [Otherwise,] I don't know if they would have been able to keep open. It's a pretty expensive venture. . . . I think it's a good mix, that Claremont mix." A psychology faculty member, likewise, asserts: "I think we benefit from being in Claremont a lot because a lot of those [innovative] schools hit some really hard financial [times]—and we did, too, but we benefit from the fact that we are one part of a larger Claremont institution and we have access to resources that we would not have had."

One emeritus faculty member says it straight out: "In fact, [Pitzer] only survived because it was a part of The Claremont Colleges." A long-time administrator, too, declares, "I don't think [Pitzer] would have survived at all had it not been part of the Colleges":

> I certainly think that that was a distinct advantage—being part of the Colleges, because number one, it was a new College and [people said,] "Who?" "Pitzer what?" You know, "Who's that?" Even in recruiting board members and [faculty and students], being part of The Claremont Colleges was probably very important and if we'd been stuck out somewhere by ourselves, it probably wouldn't have worked as well.

In the words of a long-time professor of sociology,

> For whatever problems it also causes, if we *hadn't* been part of The Claremont Colleges, I think we would have disappeared a long time ago. [The Claremont Colleges name] just confers kind of instant recognition.... I always see people at professional meetings for the first time and [they ask], "Where are you from?" "Pitzer College." "Oh, well, what's that?" "It's one of The Claremont Colleges." "Oh yeah. I know, yeah. *Claremont* Colleges."[14]

According to a number of individuals, Pitzer's affiliation with The Claremont Colleges has not only enabled the college to survive, but to survive as a creative alternative in American higher education. In the words of a top-level administrator,

> I think one of the reasons [that Pitzer remains innovative] is the fact that [we're] a part of a consortium in which there's the opposite or the complement.... [W]e sit next to *much* more traditional institutions, share their resources, are in the dialog with them all the time so that we're not out there all by ourselves. If you're out there all by *yourself*, I think it's much harder to sustain the [innovative dimensions]. Being a part of the Claremont system allows [us to] maintain a difference and last through changes and the mood of the country. . . . A lot of [alternative] colleges [had to give in to] pressures as the national mood changed . . . in the eighties and into the early nineties.

The "genius" of the Claremont system, a former Pitzer president relates, "is that each [Claremont] college is *indeed responsible for everything*. We [at Pitzer] have our own board, our own president, our own faculty." Although other innovative colleges have succumbed to external pressures or the pressures of a larger system, he says, here in Claremont, "We do as we damn well please." "We've been given the security to do things differently," a professor of 28 years agrees:

> [Pitzer has] always been regarded by the other [Claremont] Colleges as the "experimental" school and . . . we've been protected in some way by the fact that there are more traditional schools around us and therefore we have the freedom to do experimental things that maybe the other schools don't do. . . . [T]hat's part of why Pitzer has ... maintained a certain innovative quality: We've been given the secu-

rity to do so. . . . I think that there are certain *kinds* of students that are more drawn to Pitzer as opposed to students that are more drawn to CMC [Claremont McKenna College], for example, and I think that has to do with the sense [that] CMC is more traditional and Pitzer more innovative, and CMC *allows* us, in effect, to maintain that role.

Summing Up the Key Reasons for the Endurance and Transformation of the Distinctive Early Ideals at Pitzer College

Looking across the four innovative themes of the life of Pitzer College (community, individualism, faculty freedom, and interdisciplinarity), what, in summary, are the factors that have kept these distinctive original visions alive? What are the factors that have been linked to the changes or transformations in the early innovative designs of Pitzer College?

When it comes to the endurance of Pitzer's distinctive founding ideals, interviewees single out the college's unusual "institutional arrangements," its "light" hierarchical organization. They emphasize, over and over again, the importance of the nondepartmentalized structure: the free-flowing, interdisciplinary field group system. People are a "thread" at this institution, interviewees observe, and it is the founding faculty members (and incoming cohorts who share the visions of the pioneers) who are the keepers of the dreams, the creators and innovators who fuel the visions and keep the spirit alive. Even the physical organization of the campus, with its English professors housed next to sociologists, perpetuates the distinctive, interdisciplinary campus heritage. Above all, it may be Pitzer's connection with the Claremont consortium, the cross-college collaboration and coordination, that has enabled this extraordinary campus to carry on for more than three decades as an innovative institution.

Where there have been changes in the founding distinctive philosophies, the interviewees point to the natural processes of institutional aging—growth, increasing bureaucratization. The radicalism out of which this campus was born in the 1960s, they say, is no longer, and so the kindred spirit and intensity of pioneering a brand-new venture has faded.

In the end, Pitzer College has moved from the 1960s to the 1990s with a few compromises, but with a sense of style and grace. The heritage of the pioneers, the spirit of small, participatory, student-centered community; of interdisciplinary education; and of creative, nourishing academic pursuits lives on in many ways at Pitzer today.

ISSUES AND CHALLENGES TO INNOVATION

However, some issues and pressures exist. Inherent in any new or creative venture is a sense of excitement—along with some tension. This section explores some of the timeless issues and pressures to innovation that have impacted the lives of the students, faculty, and administrators at this institution. These are participatory governance processes, student involvement in community governance, unfulfilled student expectations and student attrition, campus stereotypes and image problems, faculty retirements and generational differences, and the split between innovative traditions and innovating directions.

Participatory Governance Processes: "Alternately Marvelous and Frustrating"

First, there are the tensions associated with the college's participatory governance system. Faculty report that they are often overwhelmed and overburdened by committee work. It is a balancing act, they point out, to juggle the competing demands of heavy governance assignments, teaching loads, and research responsibilities. "Participation and everybody having a voice and a part in designing curriculum and everything else is time consuming and it's hard work," a founding official reveals. In the early years, he relates, "there were some members of the faculty . . . who would . . . say, 'You just tell me what the curriculum's going to be. I want to work on my own subject. I want to teach what I'm teaching. . . . This is taking too much of my time.'"

One Pitzer professor in 1970 described the process as "alternately marvelous and frustrating, depending upon what you want. If you want swift, decisive, authoritative action, it's frustrating. If you want careful consideration from all possible angles before taking any precipitous steps, it's marvelous. From a professor's point of view, it's absolutely marvelous" (Genesis 1970). You hear the same type of thing today. A long-time academic remarks:

> Our governance system does result in tension and hot discussions and emotional energy that is expended that leaves [faculty] less time for other things. . . . [But] that's what being a little different and having an open format [is all about]. It creates those tensions. And we have to resolve among ourselves some things that might be resolved by deans of faculty [at other places]. . . . [It] is very costly in time, depending on which committee you're on.

"I'm a workaholic," one former faculty member confesses, "and I've never worked more than at Pitzer." Over there, she says, "both faculty and staff [are] extraordinarily overworked—I mean, beyond belief. . . . I would arrive at Pitzer at eight o'clock [in the morning] and have my last meeting at nine o'clock at night."

"Faculty at major universities would *never, ever, ever* do what the Pitzer faculty do in regards to the amount of time on committees," an alumna who works in higher education declares. "Never. Trust me. They just wouldn't make that commitment. . . . It's incredible. . . . [The faculty at my university are] all very involved in hiring faculty and tenure reviews. . . . Faculty in general across the United States spend a lot of time on tenure, promotion, and hiring. The involvement at Pitzer is far beyond that."

And time spent in governance means time spent away from teaching and research. A professor of sociology describes the trade-off: "Well, how much of your energies are you going to put into the college—committee work or just doing things like starting up a recycling center . . . like one faculty member did—and how much are you going to [put into] writing . . . books and doing larger professional things. That's always a dilemma."

In the end, most faculty are not willing to give up this routine. A sociology professor explains:

> Last year, [we] had a fairly substantial reexamination of our gover-nance structure and one of the alternative models was a more conven-tional system where you have *more* administrators doing *more* adminis-trative work, freeing up faculty to do other things. And a lot of people thought, I bet you that's really going to sail through because [faculty] are *so* tired sometimes of the demands of community, but it didn't.

Another faculty member remarks: "We're always looking to figure out how we might cut down the amount of time we do spend in governance, but when push comes to shove, nobody wants to give up the power that the faculty have." Participatory decision making may take an awfully long time, a professor of 30 years agrees, but ultimately, it leads in the right direction:

> There was a lot of grumbling and disillusionment in the early years about how [faculty] would talk [in our meetings] and never get anything done. But I was one of those who did not see that as necessarily a weakness. . . . [Y]ou can have quick, simple solutions that [turn out, in the end, to be] wrong. That's one of the problems with authoritarian regimes. . . . In a more participatory organization, you get more varied points of view and more objections raised, more subtleties brought up. . . . Again and again, I can remember . . . *wonderful* discussions with all kinds of information flowing in. . . . [Even if there was] no resolution . . . , I felt educated. . . . It was a learning experience.

Student Involvement in Community Governance

Second, there is the dilemma of student involvement in participatory gover-nance. According to interviewees, Pitzer has had some difficulty over the years in recruiting students to serve on college committees. Participatory gover-nance is not as glamorous as it is "cracked up" to be, a long-time professor explains: "Serving on a committee *seems* like something that would be very exciting [for undergraduates], until you're actually on the committee and it turns out to be very boring. So, one of the things that we've found over the years, is that student participation in committees tends to be variable, that some students who thought they might like to do this soon find that it's a lot of hard work and it's basically rather boring."

"[Students] get on a college committee and all of a sudden discover that's a lot of agonizingly difficult work," a charter professor relates. "And a lot of them just elect not to do it." They don't want to "put up with that," he says: "The first thing that strikes students when you admit them to a faculty meeting is this is just unbelievably dull. . . . All of a sudden, [students] realize that the routine work of running a college day in and day out is exhausting and they don't want part of it. But we make the opportunity available for those who do."

Another founding faculty member puts it this way: "The whole problem with [participatory] government is . . . there isn't enough exciting stuff to do to keep students involved." A professor of sociology agrees: "It's sometimes hard to get students to serve on [committees]. . . . Often issues just seem kind of remote from their concerns."

Some students are intimidated by the level of knowledge or expertise of their faculty counterparts on campus committees. It takes a tough, strong-minded kind of individual to serve with often tenured scholars who have years of experience with the issues and with the college's governing committees, a charter professor observes: "Some students will come to a committee meeting and they will be cowed by the nature of their colleagues. One of the reasons is, obviously, there is a lot of give and take that goes on at the meetings, and those who control the tools of communication most adroitly are likely to make their points more strongly." A faculty member who has taught at Pitzer for 30 years agrees:

> [One] thing [about participatory governance] which is [hard] to deal with . . . is simply that the faculty know a lot more than the students. . . . [W]hen [a] committee starts to meet . . ., there may be new faculty members on it who know nothing about the institution or who have not been on this particular committee before. It is also possible [that] you'll have a set of faculty . . . who've all been on this committee two or three times before who know a lot about the institution and you've got students who are relatively ignorant. And it's not a question of pulling rank; it's simply that it's very hard to talk as equals.

In the end, the choice often comes down to whether the student is going to spend his or her time on a college committee or be devoted to other tasks or college experiences—course work, campus activities, employment, etc. As this alumna and trustee sees it, the "draw" is often in the non-governance arena:

> My observation of Pitzer over some 28, 30 years is that the students have come and gone and [so has] that understanding of the impor-

tance of their true involvement. In some years, you get a lot of [student] involvement [in governance] and some years you don't. . . . [L]ooking back over the years, there have been some times when [students] weren't as concerned. . . . I mean, it's not because the administration says, "You can't be involved in these decisions." It's rather that [students] had other things to do.

Unfulfilled Student Expectations and Student Attrition

Third, there is the issue of student attrition. There are some students who have come to Pitzer seeking an academically free and easy environment, interviewees report. Applicants read the college's literature, they hear about its founding in the 1960s, and they assume that at this campus they can do whatever they please. Even though Pitzer offers a very flexible program, faculty and administrators explain, undergraduates are not completely on their own, or set free.

It is an age-old issue around here. In the early years, one founder begins, "we said that our campus was going to dare to be different and [that] we're going to attract students who dare to be different. . . . It also meant that we had one of the highest attrition rates in the country. . . . [S]tudents would come, expecting a nontraditional, whatever that meant, experience. They were looking for adventure and we couldn't provide the adventure." There have been some disappointed hopes, he says, for students who were seeking a radically unstructured educational experience:

> If you flash back to the sixties and seventies, and you think of Vietnam and all of the turmoil, I think a lot of students came [to Pitzer] expecting to be able to do whatever they wanted to do. . . . [A] lot of students came [to Pitzer] not wanting to have strong academic experiences. And there has *always* been a group [of faculty] at Pitzer [that] might be nontraditional in spirit . . . , but when you were in class, this was serious business. . . and I think a lot of students were disappointed.

For another group of students, the campus has not been structured enough. There are some students who have come to Pitzer and have had "difficulty dealing with the nontradition" of the place, a founding official asserts. He remembers students in the early years coming up to him and saying, "You tell us what we're supposed to take." "The business of designing your own curriculum," he offers, "is a wonderful experience, but a lot of students don't want it."

Pitzer "was a place where people who were inner directed did very well," an early alumna recalls, "but it wasn't a place for a follower. . . . I think you had to be very flexible and you also had to pretty much know where you wanted to go or at least were willing to try different things and it was a very creative place that way."

Campus Stereotypes and Image Problems

Fourth, Pitzer's countercultural image has often cast a shadow over the innovative educational processes and directions of the institution. Since its inception, Pitzer College, like many alternative campuses of the 1960s and 1970s, has come up against negative stereotyping—e.g., distorted perceptions of the college as a "dope-using," indulgent, nonacademic place. Outsiders have looked upon Pitzer with a bizarre curiosity, a long-time academic reveals in an interview in 1983: "A lot of the early year or two at Pitzer was spent not only trying to build a college . . . but sort of build[ing] in the face of all this condescension, contempt, weird looks when you experiment with something" (Dillon 1983).

Take, for example, the "amount of choice that [we] offered students in developing their own curriculum," a long-time academic and former dean of faculty relates:

> This is a thing that I think Pitzer got bad press on in many ways: the idea that students just could come in and create their own program. And I know it upset a whole lot of parents. In the old days, we used to get a lot of anxiety expressed by parents and a lot of anxiety expressed by the Western Association of Schools and Colleges [regional accrediting association]. . . . I had to defend this as dean of faculty.

Even today, "when people . . . look at the way we do things," a faculty member relates, "the negative way to characterize [Pitzer] is [that] our procedures are sloppy, but I think they're . . . creatively flexible. I don't think you can have freedom without some sloppiness or slippage." It's all part of the process: the act of creativity and freedom of expression. The stereotyping has not only come from without. At The Claremont Colleges, Pitzer takes a lot of flack as the "quirky kid" in the family, one professor relates: "The Claremont Colleges . . . love to stereotype the other [Claremont] institutions. . . . The stereotype of Pitzer [in the early years] was pretty much a barefoot, longhair, dope-using, radical [institution]—about the only thing that lent some credence to that was Pitzer's incredible openness."

Faculty Retirements and Generational Differences

Fifth, there is widespread concern about the forthcoming retirements of the founding faculty at Pitzer College. The "old guard," the pioneers, are nearly all gone, according to interviewees. (In 1995-96, just four of the 16 charter faculty remained on campus, and three of them were retired or emeritus professors.) Can the new generations of academics, even the spirited "like-minded" recruits, veteran faculty and staff wonder, carry on the spirit of innovation, the early visions that were so close to the hearts of the pioneers? One psychology professor describes the dilemma in this way:

The original faculty who started at the college are just starting to retire now and the question that always comes up is can that second or third generation hold that core value? . . . [A] whole array of [innovative] institutions that were founded [in the 1960s] have gone out of business. . . . [The founders] were looking for alternative kinds of structures of institutions. And then as the second generation of faculty moved in, they didn't share those values and so what was distinctive about the institution [was lost].

A professor who has been at the institution for 30 years observes that the faculty cohorts today tend to be more research-oriented and careerist than their old guard counterparts, and less concerned with governance issues: "We . . . tend to recruit individuals with an eye to their scholarship in a way that we didn't in the early years." "Although Pitzer has always prided itself on attracting [a] faculty that is different," a former professor relates, "they're not faculty who are necessarily . . . challenging the status quo [or] the disciplines. . . . It's a more academic, scholarly faculty than it had [been] in the past and so you have an ambiance of Pitzer that is less eccentric, that is less funky, that is less different."

A professor who has been at the college for 22 years offers a different perspective:

Some senior faculty say that some of the junior faculty are more interested in their research and so forth and certainly some are very cosmopolitan in their orientation. But I find that the younger faculty are quite innovative in teaching and eager to get involved [in] very interdisciplinary, innovating programs. . . . I really believe that the younger faculty are quite interested in the social responsibility and intercultural, interdisciplinary strength that we have. So, I am not worried about the future of the college, losing this kind of direction that we've traditionally had.

The future is in good hands, she believes.

Innovative or Innovating?

Finally, one of the deeply rooted tensions, which emerges time and time again in the interviews, is the question of whether there is a necessary trade-off between innovation (in terms of the preservation of the early distinctive ideals of the institution) and institutional change (the embracing of new "innovating" ideas or advances in education and technology). In the words of one charter professor,

The real danger of being a founding father . . . is that it's very easy to develop a proprietary view of what you think the college ought always to be. . . . Pitzer was founded to be a college which would be responsive to shifts in society. . . . And you simply have to say, whether you like the change or not, "That's what we designed the college to be." I have some colleagues, one in particular, who was a founder along with me, and he takes some of those changes very hard, indeed. It wasn't *his* view of the college as a changing entity. [But the college] is going to be what it's going to be. It's living! How else could it be? It can't just stay in one place. It can't stand there like a rock in the middle of a stream, trying to stop the waters as they rush by saying, "This is where it's at; go no further."

"Life does not stand still," a former faculty member agrees, "and there are economic and cultural factors affecting Pitzer, and Pitzer cannot live in a vacuum." As life around us changes, we, too, have changed, a top-level administrator confirms. "You know, we're not dead yet!" she declares, and this is, in part, because Pitzer has embraced and moved into the 1990s with an appreciation of the global society, with a somewhat "different look and feel." "That doesn't mean that we're any less innovative," she explains, "in fact even more so. I see the whole technological revolution as fascinating and [it] forces that openness" at the college. She goes on to discuss the campus' work in the community: "We are attempting to start the first study abroad program at home [in the city of] Ontario. . . . [O]ur students would live in the [Ontario] community with families."

Pitzer is still very much on the "cutting edge," an early alumna agrees:

> The college has evolved with what has happened [in the larger society, but] I really don't think it's changed that much. . . . [C]ertainly I'm not saying it's stayed static. I'm simply saying it has always been cutting edge. That's one thing about Pitzer. It's been on the cutting edge . . . of ideas in education and academics—a lot of interdisciplinary, cross-cultural studies, Pitzer's emphasis on social responsibility—a lot of things that some colleges now are just kind of waking up to—. . . community work, [our] wonderful programs in . . . Third World countries.

CONCLUSION: SUMMARY AND IMPLICATIONS

One of the "charges" of The Claremont Colleges group plan has been to found new institutions, to "experiment" with uncommon ventures in undergraduate and graduate education. With the opening of each new college, the consortium has fulfilled new hopes and new educational dreams. This case study has explored the visions of innovation that sparked the creation of Pitzer College, the sixth institution of the Claremont consortium. Pitzer came to life in the early 1960s as a pioneering academic experiment in community governance, student-centered education, faculty freedom and creativity, and cross-disciplinary collaboration.

For more than three decades, Pitzer College has persevered as a distinctive, participatory, student- and faculty-centered community. Creativity, imagination, a zest for teaching, and lively outposts in research breathe life into the campus today. Looking back over the life and lessons of this uncommon liberal arts institution, what are some of the implications or teachings of the Pitzer College case study and history?

- The first lesson to be learned from the Pitzer story is that the structure or organization of an institution is critical to long-lasting innovation. Participatory governance at Pitzer College is driven by a committee system that is roots-based, open, and involving. The nondepartmentalized faculty organization has been key to the campus' interdisciplinary orientation. The absence of budgeted departments has also enabled and empowered the faculty, over the past 31 years, to pursue creative outlets in scholarship and teaching.
- Second, it is crucial that an institution support and reward faculty who are engaged in distinctive educational endeavors. At Pitzer, interdisciplinary teaching and collaborative academic pursuits are taken into account in faculty tenure and review decisions.
- Third, this case study sheds light on the importance of faculty recruitment. Pitzer is at a turning point in its history. With the imminent departures of the charter professors, the faculty look to the future generations of academics to support and sustain the campus' distinctive founding values and visions.
- Fourth, institutional size affects the endurance of innovative traditions. As the student population at Pitzer has grown, the early close-knit community feel of the campus has faded. Gone are the days of the all-campus retreats and weekly town meetings, where the whole college could fit into one room and "Pitzer" away.
- Fifth, there is a spirit of bonding and togetherness that characterizes the founding epoch of an institution that can never be recaptured again. The founding mothers and fathers at Pitzer speak fondly of the pioneering decade when experimentation was in vogue and students and faculty were designing the educational blueprint for the institution. Innovators at this campus carry the past with them, but they also look to the future and constantly assess how the college can reshape its early ideals to keep pace with the changing times.
- Sixth, the Pitzer College story turns our attention to the significance of a consortium, or the physical connection and/or collaboration of a

distinctive campus with other, more traditional or established institutions.

- Finally, innovative institutions are likely to come up against points of pressure or tension with regard to their unorthodox approaches or philosophies. Pitzer College struggles with the dilemmas of faculty overwork and participatory governance processes, student recruitment to college committees, student attrition, faculty replacement issues, campus stereotypes, and the struggle to keep alive the ties to the past while moving forward to embrace educational or technological advances. Pitzer's commitment to an intercultural perspective, its outreach to the community, and the students' involvement in Third World nations, are all signs of an institution that is not only innovative but innovating, in embracing new and creative expressions of knowledge, human concern, and activity.

NOTES

1. There are other stories, however. According to a former Pitzer president, there is early correspondence that indicated a "need for a women's college" in Claremont "to provide wives" for the students at then-Claremont Men's and Harvey Mudd Colleges "and [that] this was a school that should provide secretarial and other *appropriate* skills for young women."
2. Pitzer College was named in honor of benefactor and orange grower Russell K. Pitzer and his wife Flora Sanborn Pitzer. Mr. Pitzer promised an initial gift of $75,000 toward the establishment of the college (Clary 1970).
3. Follow-up interviews were conducted with two of the interviewees. Four individuals who resided outside of the Southern California area, or whose schedules did not permit a one-on-one meeting, were interviewed by phone.
4. While nearly all interviewees were able to identify a host of "distinctive" or "innovative" features of early Pitzer College, there was a sense among a few participants that the campus was not truly "alternative" or "experimental" in the beginning. The college, for example, started out with a "rather stiff set" of general education requirements. Pitzer was also "conventional" in the sense that it was founded as a women's college with house mothers, dorm hours, and other parietal rules. In the end, all agreed that something different, unusual, had taken place in Claremont in the mid-1960s. The comments in this section reflect the interviewees' perspectives with regard to these different or unusual characteristics.
5. The freshman seminar was originally called The Fifth Course.
6. The early general education requirements were abandoned by 1970.
7. Academic budgets are now coordinated through the office of the academic dean.
8. There are a few interviewees who believe that it is the very entry of the newer generations of academics that has resulted in the loss of some of the early distinctive ideals of Pitzer College.
9. The new general education requirements were adopted in 1989 (and became effective in 1990).

10. Even in the earliest years of the college, few students (1 percent of the graduates in 1969 to 4 percent of the graduates in 1974) were graduating with custom-designed majors. Still, the opportunity for doing so was available to students and has been a constant at the institution for the past 31 years.
11. Longitudinal data on special concentrations are available only for Pitzer College *graduates*.
12. Proposals for student-designed concentrations are submitted to and approved by the college's Curriculum Committee. The committee reviews each proposal, following a rather strict set of guidelines to ensure that the concentration provides a "properly balanced" and rigorous academic program (S. Glass, personal communication, 26 March 1997).
13. According to this interviewee, Pitzer College started "on a shoestring" budget and had to borrow money from the government to build its first buildings.
14. The consortium link has been both a blessing and a constraint in the eyes of the founders. While the resources and reputation of The Claremont Colleges, they say, have enabled the campus to survive, the association has sometimes limited the types of innovations that Pitzer could undertake (e.g., innovations in the academic calendar— "We were bound to the lockstep of the . . . concrete scheduling, class scheduling of the other colleges," an emeritus faculty member explains).

REFERENCES

Bernard, R.J. 1982. *An unfinished dream: A chronicle of the Group Plan of The Claremont Colleges*. Claremont, Calif.: Claremont University Center.

Clary, W.W. 1970. *The Claremont Colleges: A history of the development of the Claremont Group Plan*. Claremont, Calif.: Claremont University Center.

Dillon, S. 1983. *Pitzer College and its origins*. Unpublished paper, Pitzer College, Claremont, Calif. Available through Pitzer College History and Archives Project.

Ganahl, A. 1995. Look at it this way: Interdisciplinary study at Pitzer. *Pitzer College Participant* 28 (1): 18–20.

Genesis: Pitzer College bulletin. 1970. Claremont, Calif.: Pitzer College, June.

Looking back: 30 years with the founding faculty. 1995. *Pitzer College Participant* 28 (1): 12–14.

Office of Communications. 1997. Claremont, Calif.: Pitzer College.

Pitzer College application for re-accreditation to the Western Association of Schools and Colleges. 1989. Claremont, Calif.: Pitzer College, June.

Pitzer College bulletin. 1963. I, no. 1 (September). Claremont, Calif: Pitzer College.

Pitzer College catalogue 1996-97. 1996. Claremont, Calif.: Pitzer College.

Pitzer College summary of discussions about academic programs and related matters. 1964. A summary of discussions carried on at Claremont between local and visiting members of the faculty and staff, Claremont, Calif.

Registrar's Office, Pitzer College. 1996. List of concentrations or combinations of concentrations, 1993, 1994, 1995; Special concentration figures for Pitzer College graduates, 1969-70 to 1974-75 and 1991-92 to 1995-96, Claremont, Calif.

CHAPTER

New College of the University of South Florida

Still a New College

BACKGROUND: SETTING THE SCENE

Pink marble mansions, palm trees, and the sparkling waters of the Sarasota Bay enchant the visitor to New College of the University of South Florida. On the bay-shore side of U.S. Route 41, an ornate archway marks the entryway to the main campus, which is situated on the former winter estate of Charles Ringling of the Ringling Brothers, Barnum and Bailey Circus.[1] As you pass through the gateway and make your way down a long, narrow driveway, you come upon the landmark buildings of this innovative public liberal arts campus. There is Charles and Edith Ringling's sprawling, pink marble neoclassical revival mansion, which at one time housed the college's library, and where in the first year, "students and faculty gathered . . . for candlelight dinners" (*Living While You Learn* 1995, 80). Linked to the mansion by a marble and concrete colonnade is Cook Hall, a Mediterranean-style villa that the Ringlings built for their daughter, Hester. A former carriage house and chauffeur's quarters serves as the home of the New College admissions and foundation offices. The old estate manager's house is the social sciences building. Behind the Ringling mansion is the Sarasota bay front, where pelicans, dolphins, and all sorts of wading, diving, and swimming birds commonly make their appearance—a soothing and contemplative place (Arthur 1995; Grant and Riesman 1978; *Self-guided Campus Tour* 1995).

The Founding: "A College Town without a College"

In the 1950s, local educators and citizens in Sarasota, Florida, longed for a college that they could call their own. Business and civic leaders described their Gulf Coast community as a "college town without a college" (Arthur 1995, 2). A campus, they felt, would invigorate Sarasota commerce and life. Local "movers and shakers" soon went to work to attract a regional junior college, a state university, and then a planned Presbyterian college to their neighborhood. Unsuccessful in their attempts, in 1959 the chamber of commerce struck a deal with Congregationalist leaders who were eager to help found a small, private, non-sectarian college of the liberal arts and sciences in the South (Burns 1994; *New College* 1994).[2]

In a "preamble to a statement of purpose" for the proposed campus, chamber manager Tod Swalm suggested that "'we propose to forge boldly ahead to establish a college in Sarasota,' and then added a defining line, 'but not just another college'" (Arthur 1995, 5). Citing the large number of existing colleges in the United States, Swalm explained, "The Sarasota College will be—must be—unique in many phases of operation and orientation, to the end that it will achieve national recognition and stature to attract outstanding students from the 50 states to come to Sarasota for their own college-level education." These may have been the words of a chamber official "looking to attract new dollars to the area," Furman C. Arthur notes in his compelling history of New College, but "it was an uncanny characterization of the college that was to develop" (5).

On October 11, 1960, the college town would finally get its college. Incorporation papers were filed at the state capital in Tallahassee, Florida, and "New College" was chartered. The name—originally a reference to New College of the University of Edinburgh, Scotland[3]—came to signify an emerging desire that the campus would be "distinctive and innovative" (*New College* 1994). Early leaders proposed that the institution would have rigorous academic standards, that it would be rooted in the educational traditions of Oxford, and that "complete freedom of inquiry was to be encouraged while the search for truth and insight would be the norm" (Arthur 1995, 25). With dreams of becoming Harvard-like, at the 1962 campus dedication, founding president George F. Baughman and other officials solemnly mixed a small amount of earth that was dug from the campus of Harvard with the soil of the New College campus "to symbolize the relationship between the oldest and finest of the nation's educational institutions and the newest one" (Arthur 1995, 35).

In September 1964, 101 students (from 30 states and three foreign countries) arrived in Sarasota to embark upon what promised to be an educational adventure. According to journalist and alumnus Susan Burns (1994), there was not much of a campus back then. The first students "were housed in the old 12-story Landmark, a luxury hotel on Lido Beach" while their dormitories were being completed (121). Imagine the wonderment of living in a resort hotel, Arthur (1995) says, with the richly carpeted lobby, the swimming pool, and balconies overlooking the broad white sand beaches. "'I thought, what a helluva way to go to school,'" relates charter class member John Cranor (in an interview with Burns 1994). "'It was almost surreal. We had astronomy classes on the beach. I remember making star plots with sticks in the sand'" (120).

According to a brief history of the college (*New College* 1994), not only did the unusual accommodations, elegant marble mansions, and bay shores appeal to the students' spirit of adventure, but the academic unorthodoxy of the place was captivating to the incoming students (and to the faculty). *Time* magazine hailed New College's opening by saying: "The atmosphere will be permissive; students are called 'colleagues' and rules are called 'expectations'" (Arthur 1995, 59). The original educational plan called for independent projects and tutorials as well as an absence of credits and letter grades. (There would also be interdisciplinary core courses and comprehensive exams—these were abandoned after the third year). The "personal freedom previously only dreamed of, and an opportunity to engage in deep conversation with each other and with their professors exceed[ed] anything most [students] had known before and anything offered at conventional colleges" (*New College* 1994, 3). They were drawn to it.

The Merger

Looming in the background of the euphoria of freedom, intimacy, and experimentation, however, was a "growing shadow" of financial crisis (*New College* 1994). The institution probably should not have opened when it did, states Arthur in an interview with Burns (1994): "'We didn't have enough money. We never had enough money'" (122). Rising inflation in the 1970s hit the college hard, and the expensive nature of the distinctive academic program had taken its toll. By the time Arland Christ-Janer assumed the presidency in 1973, the campus was on the verge of financial collapse. Enrollments had sharply decreased—there were 70 fewer entering students than expected that year, resulting in a $225,000 budgetary shortfall. "Christ-Janer found the financial picture almost terrifying," according to Arthur (1995, 120). The campus reportedly needed to raise a sum of $650,000 by the end of June 1975, or else New College would be no more.

Seeing no other way out, on July 1, 1975, Christ-Janer engineered a merger agreement with the state university system. The University of South Florida (USF), a comprehensive research university in Tampa with a branch campus in St. Petersburg, had been seeking a site for another branch campus in the Sarasota-Bradenton area.[4] Christ-Janer seized this opportunity to relieve New College of its financial burdens. Under the terms of this historic agreement,

New College would become part of the University of South Florida: All grounds and facilities of the former "private" New College would now become part of USF. The University of South Florida would use the facilities to start up a Sarasota branch campus that would serve local commuter students. The beauty of the bargain was that New College would remain academically separate from the USF branch program and "would be able to continue as a distinctive honors college within the university" (*New College* 1994). The state university system would fund "New College of the University of South Florida" at the same level as other state universities, Burns (1994) explains: "The hitch was that the trustees of the college had to come up with an annual $750,000 difference that it cost to keep the more expensive New College program alive" (122).

Enter the New College Foundation

With the private New College now defunct, the board of trustees of New College reorganized itself into the New College Foundation, an independent, nonprofit entity that would raise money so that New College could maintain its innovative academic program and low student-faculty ratio (and a low tuition) (Burns 1994; *Living While You Learn* 1995; *New College* 1994).[5] Through the work of the foundation, led since 1979 by three-star general Rolland V. Heiser, the college has gained financial stability and national recognition. For three consecutive years, New College was rated by Time Inc.'s *Money Guide* as the number one best college buy in the United States, "topping a list of 1,049 public and private four-year colleges and universities" (*New College Foundation* 1995, 3).

New College Today

Today New College remains a highly selective, public residential liberal arts college. The campus enrolls 596 undergraduates (323 women and 273 men). Six percent of New College students are Asian American, another 6 percent are Latino, 2 percent are African American, and 86 percent are European American. Fifty-eight percent of New College students are Florida residents and 55 percent live on campus (Office of the Dean and Warden 1997). In the fall of 1996, 65 percent of all entering freshmen at New College ranked in the top 10 percent of their high school classes; 89 percent ranked in the top 20 percent. The average SAT score for incoming students was 1339 and the average high school GPA was 3.90 (Admissions Office 1997).

There are approximately 29 administrators and staff members at New College. (There are an additional 91 staff members—in records and registration, financial aid, the library, the career center, etc.—who serve both New College and the USF program.) (L.B. Hill, director of administrative affairs, USF at Sarasota/New College, personal communication, 2 April 1997) The campus employs 53 faculty members (all full-time). Forty percent of the faculty are female and 60 percent are male (Office of the Dean and Warden 1997).

There are three academic divisions at New College—humanities, natural sciences, and social sciences—and interdisciplinary programs in environmental studies, gender studies, and medieval studies that draw from the three areas of inquiry. The curriculum is still nongraded and there are no academic credits or distribution requirements. Each student negotiates an educational contract each term with a faculty member to design an individualized course of study. The educational contract is a written agreement outlining the student's short- and long-term academic goals, the educational activities that he or she plans to undertake for the semester, and the criteria for the satisfactory completion of the activities and projects that are specified in the contract. Seven academic contracts, three independent study projects, and a senior thesis are required for graduation from New College. The student must also pass an oral examination to complete the baccalaureate degree, and declare a major in a liberal arts discipline, joint disciplines, or an interdisciplinary field.

ORGANIZATION OF THIS CHAPTER

This chapter takes the reader to the shores of the Sarasota Bay, to the old winter retreat of the Ringlings, up the staircases of the mansions, past the arched windows and elegant nooks and into the faculty's, students', and administrators' haunts and retreats, to explore the history of innovation at New College of the University of South Florida. The case study begins with a demographic profile of the interview participants. From there, it describes the distinctive educational concepts that guided the founders' visions for the college. Then it traces the evolution of the distinctive ideals, focusing on where and how the campus has kept alive its innovative philosophies and where and how the institution has changed or transformed itself. The next section examines the key issues or challenges to innovation at New College. The chapter concludes with a summary and a reflection on the New College story and its implications for reform and innovation in higher education.

INTERVIEW PARTICIPANT PROFILE

To explore the history and current status of innovation at New College, 23 semi-structured interviews were conducted in late October and early November 1995. Each interview lasted about 50 minutes. The participants included 11 faculty members (six of whom who had been at the college for 22 years or more), 15 administrators (including the current dean and warden, two former provosts, the president at the time of the merger, all academic division chairs, and the coordinators of environmental studies), five alumnae/i (two of whom were students in the charter class), one student, and the president of the New College Foundation. (Some individuals occupied more than one role at the institution.) The interviewees included 17 men and six women spanning several different "generations" of the New College community: Six of the participants joined New College in its first four years (1964–1967), three came to the institution in its 10th year (1973), four found their way to the college in its 14th or 15th year (1977, 1978), and 10 joined New College in its 16th year or later (1979–1994). Excluding the student and alumnae/i, the "tenure" for the interviewees at New College ranged from three to 31 years, with an average length of stay of 16.8 years at the institution.[6]

DISTINCTIVE EARLY IDEALS AT NEW COLLEGE

In the late 1950s and early 1960s, campuses across the country were beginning to experiment with programs driven by "excellence and innovation." Independent study, year abroad, and calendar revision, Arthur (1995) reports, had become necessities for attracting good students. A consortium of institutions—Amherst, Mount Holyoke, Smith, and the University of Massachusetts—had just come out with *The New College Plan*, proposing a nonconventional institution with no departments, no faculty hierarchy or ranks, no intercollegiate or fraternal activities, and a reduction in the number of courses offered.[7] Dissatisfied with the conventional structures and styles of American higher education and with this new air of educational innovation and excellence in mind, "it seemed to the founders [of New College] that the time had come for purposeful changes in [the] educational program" (*Bulletin of New College* 1964, 65).

The pioneers of New College set out to design an institution that would provide distinctive approaches to teaching and learning in an atmosphere of intellectual rigor and excellence. In the first catalog (a pocket-sized booklet that students "could fit into their jeans pocket and share with friends"), the founders spelled out their early imaginative principles for the institution. First, the educational program was to be centered on the individual interests of the students and students would be given the responsibility for shaping their own academic lives. Second, the planners believed that there should be an absence of departments and that faculty should be free to experiment with new ideas. Third, there would be an egalitarian emphasis—students would work side by side with faculty as "colleagues" and competition based on accumulating credits and grades would be minimized. These three themes (individualism, faculty freedom, and egalitarianism) would form the foundation of the early innovative design of New College. Each theme is discussed in greater detail in the following sections.

Individualism: Student-Centered Education

First, at the heart of the early New College educational conception was the idea of individualism, or students actively shaping or taking charge of their own academic lives. According to the first catalog (*Bulletin of New College* 1964), the founders believed that the "best education" was one in which the undergraduate would be granted "maximum flexibility" and freedom to take responsibility for his or her own learning process. A profile of the college that was published for prospective students before the campus opened lists, as a "basic assumption" of the curriculum, the idea that "Each student is responsible, in the last analysis, for his own education" (*A Profile of New College* 1963). Further, "Students should have from the very outset opportunities to pursue in depth studies of areas that interest them." The planners emphasized that "the ideal curriculum is the one which takes into account as completely as possible the unique interests and talents of each student." The notion was that "the best that a college can do for the student is to teach him to learn on his own" (*Bulletin of New College* 1964, 65).[8]

One of the ways in which the college tried to encourage students to follow their own learning pathways was to offer independent study periods for research, travel, or off-campus projects between the regular academic terms. According to Arthur (1995), off-campus education was popular among early New College students and students were traveling all over the world to conduct their research. Tutorials were another means of enabling students to direct their own learning. The student would work closely with a faculty tutor to undertake intensive study of a particular area that fell outside the bounds of the curriculum (Arthur 1995; Institutional Self-Study 1970).

Perhaps the ultimate embodiment of the early ideal of individualized learning—what one long-time professor refers to as the "heart and soul" of the New College tradition—was the educational contract. Initiated in 1969, the New College contract put the education in the hands of the students. It was an agreement drawn up by the student and negotiated with a faculty advisor or "sponsor," in which the student outlined his or her program of studies and related activities for the term. As then-president John Elmendorf wrote in a letter to consultant David Riesman, contracts satisfied the wishes of the student generations of the late 1960s and early 1970s to "do their own thing" (Arthur 1995). The college "'initially presented itself to [students] as a place where they would have a great deal of freedom to pursue their own interests in their own way,'" Professor David Dykstra, editor of the 1970 Institutional Self-Study, wrote. "'Now with the contract system, students seemed to have found the promise they felt the college had held out to them for determining their own educational destiny'" (Arthur 1995, 98).

Not only did the early curricular options provide pathways for independent, student-centered education, but the culminating project at New College, the senior thesis, was often heavily focused around the unique personalities, intellectual interests, and "eccentricities" of the students. A former provost recalls some of the more creative thesis topics in the 1960s: "Dead Sea Scrolls . . ., seventeenth-century French witchcraft. . . . They were all over the map. . . . I remember one young man who did a really brilliant thesis on anti-Semitism in Voltaire and another fellow [who] did a thesis on time."

The early spirit of "do your own thing" was apparent even in campus ceremonies. At the first New College graduation on July 22, 1967, students crossed the stage to receive their diplomas in "regalia" of their own choosing: The class had voted not to wear caps and gowns (Arthur 1995). They were graduating in the same way that they had studied: as individuals.

Faculty Freedom and Undergraduate Teaching

The New College faculty were granted a tremendous degree of freedom in directing their own academic lives. The college's founding mothers and fathers set out to recruit teachers who would be willing to take risks, to "walk off of the end of the dock with us," in the words of the first academic dean, John Gustad. The planners rejected the idea of traditional academic departments in the belief that "true liberal education requires an appreciation for the unity of knowledge [and that] the largely arbitrary divisions of knowledge into departments is misleading" (A *Profile of New College* 1963). The college would be organized around three broad divisions (humanities, natural sciences, and social sciences). ("Some faculty members even cringe at the [idea of the] 'divisions,'" noted one journalist in 1964.) (Hudson 1964) This paved the way for faculty freedom.

"Relieved of the stifling departmental structures of most colleges," Arthur (1995) reveals, and "without even a formal curriculum committee, faculty could teach what they wanted. . . . No one had to 'second guess a dean'" (99). "'You could decide what constituted a passing grade, what went into a course, and what didn't,'" long-time professor David Smillie asserts in an interview with Arthur (99). "'Not only that but you had to make those decisions; no one would tell you.'" The interviewees in this study agree: The faculty back then were living out their dreams, a professor who has taught at the college for 28 years explains. "They were *free* to do whatever they wanted to do! . . . There wasn't any dictate. They were of a character—the kind of people that wanted to try different things and the opportunities were here." Many of the academics who joined New College in its pioneering years were young and rebellious, one long-time administrator relates. They "were criticizing the academic traditions that they were educated in" and "they wanted to do their own thing."

The result was a lively blend of energetic and engaging classroom communities with a diversity of teachers and teaching styles, from the more traditional lecture format to the free-flowing classes led by faculty members such as controversial professor of Religious Studies William Hamilton in the late 1960s. Gerald Grant and David Riesman (1978) report:

> William Hamilton, a theologian who had been one of the leaders in the Death-of-God discussion, offered a course simply entitled Monday Nights, in order, as he put it, to be able to discuss with students whatever he felt like on that particular Monday. . . . Hamilton gave students their [course] evaluations signed by him at the opening of the course so that they could fill in whatever they cared to say about themselves. . . . Both the course title and the self-evaluations went down without alteration on the students' transcripts. (235)

"The idea [was] that professors were there to teach, not to publish," an alumnus from the charter class recalls. Faculty back then would reach out to students, he says:

> [I had Professor] Doug Berggren in [my] first class in philosophy. [His classes] could excite you. I'd call him at home and say, "I'm stuck on this problem with Kant or Nietzche . . ." and I'd hear "click," his cigarette lighting, at 10 o'clock at night and he'd start talking and we talked and I'd have to hang up on him an hour later, say, "I've gotta go now," because he was getting into it. That was *wonderful*.

Egalitarianism

New College was conceived of as an egalitarian community in which students and faculty would meet as "colleagues in the pursuit of truth and wisdom" (Burns 1994, 119). The founders wanted to break down the barriers that traditionally separated students and scholars. The idea was that students and their professors ought to work side by side and that "the best education results from the active confrontation of two first class minds" (*A Profile of New College* 1963). The earliest documents stressed that although "faculty members are more advanced in their work than the students, [that] the student is just as actively and directly engaged in the search for truth as the teacher. Each is there to help the other" (*Bulletin of New College* 1964, 15–16). Thus, the role of the faculty member would be that of a co-learner: a colleague, a tutor, a guide.

It was a reciprocal process, one founding faculty member recalls: "The spirit [at] the beginning of the college . . . was a sense of not just the faculty member teaching whatever the faculty member wanted to teach, but the faculty member opening up and listening, being aware of what students might be interested in learning and then teaching them." He says that "the idea was to get the professor out of the center [of the classroom], de-center the professor, and get the students to be more actively involved in presenting things to the class." The faculty would be learning from the student as much as the student would be learning from the faculty.

In the spirit of co-learning and free inquiry, New College's founders also rejected the practice of assigning academic credits and grades. According to the 1970 Institutional Self Study, grades were "thought to foster ignoble motives and unwholesome competition" (18). The belief was that "student progress should be based on demonstrated competence and real mastery rather than the accumulation of credits and grades" (A Profile of New College 1963). John Gustad, who devised the original academic program, "felt that normal grading systems were unreliable in measuring student performance" (Arthur 1995, 45). Gustad also "believed that assigning course credits as a measure of student or faculty work loads was 'very largely meaningless' and he did away with the practice" (45). Students would receive written evaluations of their academic performance.

Perhaps most importantly, Gustad "believed that grades and credits, rather than learning, too often became 'the ultimate goal of the students'" (Arthur 1995, 45). Thus, "What strikes you about the place over time," one long-time administrator reveals, is the degree to which "learning for learning's sake" operates here. Education (rather than the accumulation of grades or credits) was to be an end in and of itself. Former New College president John Elmendorf (1975) points out in his discussion of the "new" elements in New College's program: "Within the college, processes would be emphasized rather than content, discovery rather than direction" (9). In the words of one charter class alumna, "The thing I remember most about [New College] was the idea that education is important in its own right, not as a road to a degree or to a job and I think that and the ability to have some choice in the kinds of things that we did is what attracted a lot of my classmates to a nonexistent college."

ENDURANCE AND TRANSFORMATION OF THE DISTINCTIVE EARLY IDEALS AT NEW COLLEGE

Flash forward to the 1990s. The guiding principles or missions of the campus and the unorthodox strategies and styles of education remain remarkably unchanged. In fact, the very same "principles" that the founders envisioned for the college some 30 years ago are spelled out, nearly word for word, in the catalogs and brochures that are published by the campus today. According to the current viewbook, "The principles [of the founders] became part of New College, and they guide students and professors at New College today as surely as they did when the college opened in 1964" (New College n.d., 1).

This section draws upon the voices of the interviewees, the archival materials, and histories to examine the endurance of New College's original innovative educational themes (individualism, faculty freedom, and egalitarianism). It then explores the longevity or "survival" of the institution and presents a summary of the key reasons for the preservation of the distinctive founding themes.

Individualism: Student-Centered Education

The ideal of individualism or student-directed learning remains a hallmark of the New College educational program. The college still firmly holds to the belief that "Each student is responsible in the last analysis for his or her own education." This is one of the guiding principles of the institution today (*General Catalog* 1995, 9). The independent study period remains a core feature of the curriculum along with the student-designed tutorial. The senior theses continue to be centered on the individual interests of the students, and the educational contract system, so much a part of the original learner-centered philosophy, remains at the heart of the New College curriculum. As associate professor and alumnus Aron Edidin asserts in the campus viewbook, "'Since I was a student here, fashions in higher education have changed, but New College has remained true to its uncompromising vision of students as the agents of their own education'" (*New College* n.d., 12).

Examples abound in the interviews. A second-year student who transferred to New College from a large state university explains that he is designing his own classes on twentieth-century feminist readings and postmodern theory: These are "two things [subjects] that I'm *really* interested in, two things that aren't offered [in the regular curriculum], but [that] I invented, so now [they] exist." A psychology professor describes a student several years ago who completed a thesis on navigation skills among Australian aborigines: "We don't have an Australian program here, and faculty don't have a lot of contacts with Australia, but the student set up her thesis and made all the arrangements to go to Australia. . . . I thought, 'This is amazing. This is a person who goes halfway across the world, sets up a project on her own.'" Another student of his "wanted to study learning in honeybees. We don't have a laboratory or anything for studying honeybees," he says. "I sent her off to a colleague . . . at the University of Hawaii who does study honeybees. She worked with him for a summer, came back, set up a lab, recruited assistants . . . , conducted her thesis research here, which she published, . . . left a laboratory that now serves other students." A spirited professor who has taught at the college for 30 years marvels,

> I graduate a lot of people in fields that don't exist [at this institution]! I graduate people in modern and postmodern [studies]. I graduate people in nineteenth-century studies because you always have the right to write a special program. I just had a student who . . . want[ed]

to do a combination of art history and Latin-American art and culture.
. . . Everything is negotiable with me because I do very much believe in
the contract system.

It is this very belief in the value of student-centered learning among the
faculty members (veterans and newcomers alike) that, according to a majority
of interviewees, has sustained the rich tradition of individualism at New
College. "No matter whether the school [was] private or public, merging with
the state, no matter whether there was money to do it or not, or whether there
were classrooms to do it or not or technology to do it or not," one administrator
points out, the academics here "have continued in that tradition [of individualized education]." During the period of the merger, an alumnus and professor
agrees, the New College faculty "was very fiercely committed" to the contract
system "and very determined to preserve it against any sort of contrary pressures from the state." They refused to let the learner-centered approach fade
away.

The students, too, with their nonconformity and rebellious spirit continue
to keep the original ideal of student-directed learning alive. In the words of a
founding faculty father, "the students are the ones to a large extent responsible
for sustaining . . . the unique, sort of nonconformity of the institution," the idea
that education should be relevant to the lives of the learners. He asserts, "If it
weren't for the students, then [the early innovative] vision would be in more
jeopardy than it is because the students have not changed in the sense of
becoming more conventional or less willing to move in a variety of directions
[and] take risks or be independent." (There are contrary opinions, however, as
is discussed later in this chapter.)

Interviewees also cite the absence of a rigid administrative structure or
hierarchy at the institution. "USF is a kind of vertically oriented traditional
bureaucratic structure," a top-level administrator says. "New College is anything but vertical; it [has] a very horizontal, community-based town meeting
[organization and] ethos." This facilitates individualized learning. There are
fewer barriers imposed on the students. Students do not have to jump through
so many hoops to try out new ideas or academic interests, as an academic
division chair states:

> There are students at University of South Florida and University of
> Florida [whose experiences] might parallel the kind of things that we
> do here, but the *barriers* that they have to go through to get special
> credit for this, to go off campus to do that, to get a topical major or an
> interdisciplinary major approved [are tremendous]—there's a lot more
> bureaucracy and they have to find faculty who will go to bat against
> the inertia of a large place for them.

While all agree that the early distinctive principle of individualized learning remains a major feature of the New College curriculum, some interviewees believe that the ways in which students are going about designing their custom-made programs have changed since the early years. The contracts today tend to be somewhat less imaginative, they report, more centered on course work rather than interesting or engaging non-curricular or off-campus experiences. In the words of a 1974 graduate and current administrator,

> When I was a student, I wrote a lot of contracts that didn't involve course work. I did one whole semester . . . where a friend of mine and I just studied energy, . . . the movement of energy through biological systems. . . . [T]here were no courses. We'd do readings and we would share our notes. I think, theoretically, that's still possible today, but my suspicion is that very few students or faculty work that way right now.

Another early graduate recalls a fellow student who "spent a semester . . . in San Francisco working through geometry, doing different kinds of sketches, and trying to understand [how] three-dimensional objects . . . were composed and sent [her] notebook [back to her professor] and that was satisfactory completion of the term. People don't do that kind of thing here anymore." According to the alumnus who studied energy, "People are doing a lot more contracts with just three courses, four courses, five courses, six courses, and [fewer are] taking advantage of maximizing the contract system [with non-course-related activities]." A professor of 22 years agrees: "I don't think the contract system is used anywhere near to the power that it allows. . . . What I'm most worried about . . . is that contracts are becoming standardized to support courses and that's it."[9]

Why the tendency toward the more "standardized" educational contracts? "I think both faculty and students are responsible for that," an alumnus and current administrator remarks. "Faculty are reluctant to sponsor contracts that seem odd or out of the ordinary, and students are either reluctant to propose them or reluctant to think of them." An academic who has taught at New College since 1965 believes that some professors—especially those who were hired in the "middle generations" of the institution—"came to New College . . . not because of the distinctive attributes of the institution, but because it was a job and therefore their sense of the institution is radically different from the earlier generation's. . . . [For] one [thing], there's less trust of students fundamentally, so [there's] less interest in and willingness to let students pursue a program of study that interests them." (She does, however, credit the newer cohorts of faculty arriving from graduate schools today for inspiring creative approaches to teaching and learning—very much in the spirit of the early days.)

The students, themselves, are of a different character today, according to one faculty veteran: "When I came here, a *fair* majority of the students chose to come to this college because it was an adventure. They didn't have to come here [because it was] the best buy for them." Students today, he says, tend to be less adventurous and they want more of a sense of structure—i.e., "'How am I doing, teach?' The response to that is that more and more teachers here have been inclined to say, 'Do what I tell you.'"

Back then, faculty and students were founding an institution, creating a college from scratch, he explains. "In the early years, we had people who were in the process of trying to *build* something from nothing and that was part of the dream." Everybody was terribly romantic and dreamy, and there was a greater interest in experimentation and doing away with the traditional structures of academe. It was a new institution and faculty and students were willing to take risks and to try new things.

Finally, the affiliation with USF seems to have played a role in the standardization of the educational contracts. Since the merger with the university, a long-time professor remarks, the college has had to develop a series of equivalencies for the contract to meet the requirements of the state university system: "What's happening is that educational activities are construed to be, one, courses [or], two, tutorials or independent reading projects. If someone were to develop a contract under 'other activities' . . . it would not fare very well."

Although the nature of the student-centered endeavors may have changed since the early years, interviewees overwhelmingly agree that the college remains committed to a learner-centered educational mission, a free and individualized academic climate. Visit the campus on commencement day, for example, and you will still witness an absence of caps and gowns: Graduates "dress up in many ways," declares a high-ranking administrator. "That's the ultimate expression of individualism."

Faculty Freedom and Undergraduate Teaching:
Still "Letting Them Loose"

A second dimension is that New College faculty continue to enjoy a tremendous amount of freedom and control over what they teach. "Teaching here is in that respect sort of a faculty member's paradise," a professor of philosophy marvels. There is still no curriculum committee, no departmental structure or rigid administrative hierarchy imposing rules and restrictions on what professors may teach: "I talk to professors at other institutions who have to propose a new course, and after a while maybe it will be approved and it gets on the books. There's nothing remotely like that here. If I decide to teach a course the day before I have to hand the copy in for the next term's course catalog, I can write a course description [and get it put in]." "We decide what we teach," an academic division chair affirms. "That's one of the hardest points for me to get across to job applicants because they're used to being *told* what they teach. We don't have course numbers. We have general areas [here] that [faculty] are responsible for covering, but how they do that, what the reading list is, is all up to them. There's no curriculum committee that screens anything."

A professor of 22 years echoes: "Faculty members are . . . to a very large extent, free agents. . . . There's no curriculum committee that tells me what I can teach or what I should teach. There are checks and balances, but basically you have to be responsible and you can do what you want." And a long-time professor of art history declares, "I think fundamentally why I can survive at New College is that there *is* no curriculum committee saying, 'What do you *mean* you're going to teach a course in Madness and Modernism?!' and saying, 'Well, we don't approve of that. You have to do more work in straight art history courses.'"

The key to the preservation of faculty autonomy at New College, then, is the absence of a rigid hierarchy. Faculty here have always been granted "the freedom to teach what they teach in whatever way they want" to teach, a professor who has worked at New College for 28 years asserts, because "of the minimal types of formal rules and regulations." "We don't have a whole slew of deans and assistant deans" regulating what we do, a division chair agrees. An administrative official puts it this way: "We [at New College] locate and recruit talented students and we keep a highly professional talented faculty and then we try to get out of the way. . . . [W]e try to bring good people on board—both students and faculty—and then let them loose and we hope good things happen." New College is still bringing good people on board and letting them loose.

Along with the continuing ethos of faculty freedom, teaching remains at the heart of the New College community. In the words of a professor who has been at the college for 30 years, "My generation of faculty came to the institution because it promised the opportunity to be teachers, not publishers. . . . We were committed to program development and working out good course structures that were going to excite students and we pretty much still hold to those kinds of notions." A professor who won a number of teaching awards at a research university before coming to New College five years ago states: "I'll probably never win an award [for teaching] here [because everyone is such a good teacher] and it doesn't bother me at all, because to be an average teacher here makes me feel really good. And if I hadn't won those awards, I doubt I would've gotten the job here, either."

While faculty do retain a tremendous degree of autonomy at this institution, at least one long-time academic believes that since the merger with USF, the institution has grown somewhat more bound to rules and regulations and that tends to restrict faculty freedom. Several interviewees indicate that the academic divisions have become more specialized and departmentalized: "Today, students and faculty . . . speak of a division of natural sciences and a *department* of biology," a long-time faculty member relates:

> [In the opening days,] we didn't have departments. We had three divisions. . . . But now, each discipline within [each division] has been construed as a little department . . ., setting up their own criteria for what they want to do, subject to approval at higher and higher ranks. . . . This movement from the early free-wheeling days . . . has brought us back operationally to the edge of a conventional liberal arts institution.

At the same time, some interviewees report that that there is more of an emphasis on publication today rather than innovative or creative teaching. In the early years the development of new courses was a way to advance, a charter professor explains:

> [Back then, faculty] could get tenure and promotion . . . in one of two ways: one, that they were competent in teaching and they had published a lot or [two,] that their publishing may not be so much, but they had developed a variety of new courses. Nowadays, the sense is that if you want to get tenure and promotion, you better publish. . . . That's one of the things that has . . . made the place a little more in danger of approaching conventionalism. . . . [I]n the original era, . . . [y]ou had to keep up with your field, you had to engage in scholarly thought, but how it manifested itself could be [in a number of ways].

"Research was not being emphasized as it is today," a veteran faculty member agrees, "because [now] you're in a state university system." An administrator explains: "After the merger, . . . scholarship standards for faculty were elevated. USF is a research institution, . . . not a small liberal arts college and our faculty go through the tenure and promotion process in the same way that faculty at this larger research institution are going through the process."

Even so, the general feeling is that teaching remains the key activity of New College professors: "Faculty [that we hire] have to enjoy working with students," says a professor who has taught at the college for 18 years. "If you spend most of your time on research, if your idea of [being a faculty member is] lots of traveling to conferences and you occasionally show up on campus to check on your students," then you will probably not survive here. Although there may be more research-centered criteria for evaluation today, and perhaps less faculty freedom in comparison to the pioneering days, New College remains a teacher- and teaching-centered community.

Egalitarianism

Finally, the college has preserved its early egalitarian ethos. The institution continues to adhere to its founding principle that "The best education demands a joint search for learning by exciting teachers and able students" (*General Catalog* 1995, 9). Learning is still conceived of as an active process, whereby students and professors work side by side as co-learners. In the words of a former top-level official, the college "started out [with] an approach to education which had to do with drawing the student into the whole adventure [of education] as a colleague, almost like a peer." "That still exists," he says. The college "has not swerved from its original intention in terms of what it set out to be and to do." An administrator agrees: "Our faculty [today] view this place as a community of learners. They feel less like teachers than just fellow learners with students." The de-centered classroom lives on at New College, as this charter professor reveals:

> In my classes, I have a different student or student group start the discussion each time. . . . In order to *not* simply be lecturing all of the time or for them simply to be absorbing what I think, I try to put [students] in the position of having to present something about the text or some question to start the discussion going. . . . [S]tudents are . . . actively involved . . . in deciding how [the course] is going to be run, what texts are going to be read, how the discussion is going to [proceed].

While active learning and cooperative classroom environments remain the norm at New College, not all faculty members are willing to allow students to decide how a course is structured—at least not at the very outset. When asked whether students shape what gets taught at New College, for example, one former provost replies,

> They don't shape shit! . . . There are lots of kids that are as smart as or smarter than I am here. They don't know as much as I do. They can't structure what's in a course that they haven't taken. . . . As far as I am concerned, if you haven't read Hobbes, I'm not interested in you telling *me* how Hobbes ought to be structured in my classroom. Who cares! I don't care. If you've read Hobbes, you can come back to me and say, "Hey, do it this way." Then I'll listen. That's cool.

Along with the continuing emphasis on active and egalitarian classroom environments, New College has preserved its trademark nongraded curriculum. The institution still holds to its original principle that "Student progress should be based on demonstrated competence and real mastery rather than on the accumulation of credits and grades" (*General Catalog* 1995, 9). According to an administrator, the students who come to New College "are really looking for somewhere where they don't have to compete with other students for grades. They simply want to enjoy learning for learning's sake. This nongraded contract system frees students from that competitive grade-mongering feeling that you have at institutions with grades . . . . [New College is still] a very cooperative, collaborative environment."

Why has New College remained true to its early egalitarian ethos? Interviewees indicate that it is, once more, the veteran faculty members and the students who keep the founding dreams of learner-centered and competition-free education alive. "The original faculty," a former top-level official reveals, are "a constant poke in the back to remind everybody why we got together up there in the first place. That, I think, ha[s] a lot to do with the maintenance of the [innovative] atmosphere. They provid[e] the aura, and new people coming in sort of catch onto that. . . . [T]he [charter faculty] who are still there, are sort of the conscience of the place."

The students, too, help to sustain this structure of an egalitarian, grade-free community. It is what draws them to the college. A second-year student who was enrolled at a comprehensive state university before transferring to New College, for example, says that at New College, "you work just for yourself and you're competing with yourself . . . not against other people. A lot of schools are set up to [have students] competing against [each] other [for grades]. That seems really artificial and not really helpful to actual learning processes." Learning for learning's sake remains a guiding principle at this college.

The Survival of New College as an Innovative Institution

More than three decades later and New College carries on with its original distinctive principles largely intact. Given the shifts in the economy since the 1960s, the changes in contemporary attitudes toward education (what some characterize as a conservative shift in public attitudes about reform in education), and the short lives of many of New College's counterparts in the 1960s and 1970s, what has kept this innovative institution healthy and alive? Taking a different turn on the topic, interviewees were asked to comment on New College's longevity—i.e., to share, if they could, some of the reasons why this distinctive college—unlike so many of the alternative campuses in the 1960s and 1970s—has survived.

The Merger with the University of South Florida

First and foremost, interviewees single out the affiliation with the University of South Florida. It saved the college's life, veteran faculty and staff agree. "In 1975, we were probably two hours from closing the institution and firing everybody," a charter professor recalls. "[T]hen, President Arland Christ-Janer . . . convinced the State of Florida that they could get the world's best real estate deal [if USF merged with New College] and also have, as he . . . phrased it, 'a jewel in the crown of the state university system' . . . . That [merger] . . . saved our little fiscal butt." An alumnus and current faculty member confirms, New College "was going to cease to exist." It was headed in the direction of the innovative colleges that closed in the seventies. "Had it not come to [the merger], I don't think there would be a New College."

It was a good "marriage," that union with the state, an administrator agrees. The merger "has . . . made it possible for people to go to a first-class, independent school for the cost of a state university," a charter class alumnus explains. In the eyes of one former top-level official, "The college is essentially a private college in the public sector, and everybody behaves [as if it is private]. The state has poured money into it like nobody." Students still enjoy a small student-faculty ratio (11 to 1) for the price tag of a public institution. According to the student handbook, "If New College were private, your [a student's] annual college bill would be about $25,000 and you probably wouldn't be here!" (*Living While You Learn* 1995, 49). (In 1995-96, the New College tuition for Florida residents was $2,066.40—including a January independent study term.)

What's more, the state has essentially kept its hands off the New College academic program. Written into the merger agreement, Arthur (1995) indicates, was a proviso "that the educational programs of the private college would be continued 'at no cost to the state' while preserving the 'identity and the unique concepts and quality' of the college" (128). This hands-off policy continues. In the words of an alumnus and faculty member, "Over the years, the people in positions of power in the state . . . have been convinced that they had a good thing down here and haven't been inclined to take a very active hand in how [the college] was run. They have been happy to leave that to . . . the faculty of New College." "Many people feared, myself included, that the merger would be the death of anything innovative or experimental [at New College]," a charter professor reveals. "That's just not been true." Geographic distance—the fact that USF is headquartered some 50 miles away in Tampa—has also been an advantage in preserving the college's autonomy. Despite the limitations imposed by a large state university system, the overriding message at New College was that USF "lets us do our own thing."

The New College Foundation

A second integral factor to the college's survival has been the New College Foundation. The foundation raises money to fund the differential between the amount that the state provides to the college and the actual costs of the New College program—which amounts in current dollars to some $1,400 per student per year. In this way, the foundation helps the college to maintain its small student-faculty ratio and to keep its tuition and fees low. Without the support of the foundation, interviewees say, New College would never have been able to carry on as a distinctive campus within a large state university.

The foundation's track record of financial improvements and resource building at New College is impressive. According to foundation literature, "the

New College Foundation has brought more than $60 million to the campus since 1980. Its corporate assets have risen from $1.9 million to more than $20.7 million during the period. The endowment has grown from zero to $19.5 million" (*New College Foundation* 1995, 2). "Many of the structures that you see on the campus, a foundation official marvels, "are a direct result of foundation initiatives." "Our physical enhancements," he says, "are unbelievable: [a] new fine arts complex, [a] $6.3 million natural sciences building which is being built purely with state funds, [a] $436,000 science teaching auditorium that's being built with private and public funds, [and] a [planned] $2.4 million . . . marine biology research center." More than half of the foundation budget is funded by endowment income and designated gifts; $1 million is raised each year through special events and annual giving. In 1994-95, direct support provided by the foundation to New College exceeded $2 million (*New College Foundation* 1995).

"Since its shaky start in 1975," Arthur (1995) concludes, "the foundation has made it possible, through financial support, for New College to continue within the state's university system. . . . Its continuing goal is to increase endowment to $36 million, nearly double its present size, and thereby to extend its support role" (175). The fact that New College exists today is a testimonial to the success of the campus' partnership with the State of Florida and to the fund-raising achievements of the New College Foundation.

Academic Innovation and Excellence: "Not Only Different, but Better"

A third key factor in the college's longevity has been the institution's emphasis on educational excellence. According to interviewees, many of the alternative campuses that were founded in the 1960s and 1970s went "overboard" with regard to the touchy-feely, "let's all go out into the woods" idea. In the voice of one charter academic,

> Some of the innovative places in the sixties *so* emphasized relevance [that they] substitut[ed] something else for anything that could be thought of as academic rigor. Those are the places that went by the by because they weren't really delivering the goods educationally. . . . The fact that [New College] carried . . . a sense of academic excellence all the way through [has] kept us alive, and now when we get ranked in *Money* magazine as number one, partly that's because of the [student-faculty] ratio and partly that's the foundation, but partly it's the level at which we work. . . . [W]e operate almost at the graduate level for undergraduates [and] *that's* kept us alive because we really have been not just different, but better.

There has always been a strain of intellectualism and academic rigor here, a long-time administrator agrees. "I think the colleges that went *way* over into the counterculture . . ., where everybody went into the woods, [disappeared].

That [radical egalitarianism] *seemed* to capture the times, but it was . . . an ephemeral thing, and . . . *that* didn't root in the society." Even in the late 1960s, at the height of the student activist movement, researchers Gerald Grant and David Riesman (1978) were struck by an intellectual "intensity" about New College. The faculty and students, they observed, were serious, "high-quality" thinkers who stretched themselves to the limits. The authors cite a letter from New College alumnus Charles McKay, who wrote: "'God, did we read! And did we absorb! I sometimes felt that New College, at least in 1968, was a speed-reading class that had somehow developed hysteria!'" (239).

"One way of encapsulating New College is that we demand a great deal of rigor in a very liberal environment," a professor of 22 years relates. The college offers students a tremendous amount of freedom in designing their own programs, a but "there are still requirements,"[10] a faculty member explains. "Even if somebody makes up a [major] that doesn't exist here like Folklore Studies, you have to do work in all sorts of disciplines. . . . It isn't just a matter of hanging out for four years. It's a very rigorous program. . . . You're expected to work hard." "The fact of the matter is," a former provost declares, "the reason we've survived is because we are a good intellectual institution . . . and that means a confrontation with books, with ideas." The intellectual foundation, he insists, "is the core."

Summing Up the Key Reasons for the Endurance of the Distinctive Early Ideals at New College

New College, then, is a true survivor of the alternative higher education movement of the 1960s and early 1970s. Over the past 31 years, the institution has kept hold of its founding visions in the face of financial crisis, near closure, a merger, and a changing social, political, and economic climate. What, in summary, are the key factors that have enabled this campus to sustain its pioneering principles? First and foremost, there is the continuing commitment to the innovative vision among the founding and veteran faculty. The incoming cohorts of academics, too, share the visions of the pioneers and keep the spirit and spark of innovation alive. Then there are the students who come to the college year after year in search of unorthodox and individualized educational experiences, and whose energy and resourcefulness renew the founding visions. All of this occurs in the context of an open and decentralized academic and administrative organizational structure (e.g., where there are no departments, no curriculum committees, and no complex hierarchies). Despite the "red tape" and rules imposed by the state university system, interviewees believe that the affiliation with the state (in conjunction with the work of the New College Foundation) has been essential for the institution's survival. In the end, it is the enduring commitment of the people here, the lively spirits who breathe life into the place, and the very unique organizational structures and partnerships between college and state, that keep this innovative college healthy and alive.

ISSUES AND CHALLENGES TO INNOVATION

Like any creative entity or community, however, New College has come up against pressures or tensions in its continued existence. This section of the case study explores the key issues and challenges to innovation at New College. These are student attrition, breadth versus depth, and issues associated with narrative evaluations.

Student Attrition

One of the most pressing concerns at this campus has been student attrition. "We don't graduate 90 percent of our students or even 75 percent of our students," an administrator reveals. Arthur (1995) reports: "The average number of students graduating during the life of the college is only forty six per cent of those entering" (175). There is "significant attrition at the upperclass ranks, even in the seventh semester and after," according to one campus administrator.[11]

Why the high rate of student turnover? First, not all students are prepared to handle the amount of freedom and responsibility that they are granted in designing their own educational programs. You need a high degree of self-discipline, enterprise, and motivation to survive at this college, an administrator explains. "It is easy to wash out here," a professor in the social sciences agrees. "If I had come here as an undergraduate, I don't think I would have lasted. I don't think at the time that I was an undergraduate that I had the focus or motivation to last." The intellectual and emotional demands of this place can be overwhelming for the 17- or 18-year-old student, an administrator in student affairs agrees. "Students . . . are not going to find a whole lot of formal structure here. They need to make their own structure and that can be a drawback for a student [just] coming out of high school."

"The curriculum does not always serve to prepare students for the [senior] thesis," an administrative official remarks. "Some students," he says, "seem to stumble along, semester-by-semester, without gaining a level of competence and a degree of focus that enables them to complete the thesis." The January independent study term, which is supposed to enable students to prepare for the thesis, remains an extremely unstructured element of the academic program, according to one academic division chair, and has failed to produce a high level of student development and achievement. Although there is a high rate of student success on the baccalaureate examination (more than 95 percent of New College students "pass" the final oral examination), the senior thesis process appears to be a barrier to student retention.

At the same time, the New College environment can be socially isolating, interviewees report. Students often live and work in solitude and there is not a common sense or feeling of shared community. A top-ranking official observes that building community is "a bit of a challenge here because our traditions of autonomy are so strong that sometimes it's not clear [that] we have enough shared experience to think of ourselves as a small collegiate, residential community." A professor who has taught at the campus for 30 years candidly shares, "We have a lousy social environment that is *very* draining, *very* socially isolated." Without a strong sense of connection to the larger campus community, and engaged in the solo work of individualized educational pursuits, students at New College may flounder or drift.[12]

Breadth versus Depth

Second, there is the issue of over-specialization. New College has no distribution requirements and undergraduates may find themselves focusing too narrowly on one particular topic or field at the expense of a more well-rounded educational program. "I've had students who got a liberal arts degree having never done *anything* in the . . . natural sciences," a founding faculty member relates, "people [students] in the natural sciences who have never done anything in the social sciences. . . . We have people in the natural sciences doing pre-med who do, in effect, nothing but that. Day and night they live in their own special world, which is very bad for intellectual exchange and cross-fertilization of ideas."

This is one of the trade-offs of the highly specialized, graduate school–like environment at this college, a professor in the sciences remarks. "Students [in the sciences]," he says, "would like to take foreign languages." They would "like to take the arts and all of this, but, then, in the sciences, they have all these things to do and on top of that, if you want to work in *my* lab, you have to take a couple of courses in neurobiology so that you have a pretty good idea of at least what's going on." Students' academic plates are, in other words, full. Undergraduates are frequently "burned out" and there is just no time to pursue other academic areas or interests.

In the end, things tend to balance out, one thoughtful administrator believes: "Students do make the wrong choices and will take an overly specialized course of study; they won't distribute across the full [curriculum]; and other kinds of bad choices are made. Over time, it has been clear that the quality of the choices that we make possible is so high that it more than offsets some of the [issues or problems]" with over-specialization. It is all part of life and learning in the individualized educational community.

Issues Associated with Narrative Evaluations

Finally, narrative evaluations bring with them their own host of issues and problems. First, written evaluations pose difficulties for professors who are teaching large classes (up to 50 or 60 students). In this case, the narrative evaluation becomes sort of mechanistic, an academic division chair explains. It tends to lose its meaning:

> I am not sure that in . . . large classes the written evaluation is a major benefit over just giving [out] grades. In the smaller classes, I think the written evaluations [are] a little bit more meaningful in that you have an opportunity to have talked with students to get some greater understanding [of their work]. [In these evaluations,] you can talk in more depth about what they know and what they may not know.

At the same time, he says, written evaluations "are not designed for communicating with the outside world very well." There may be interpretation problems for potential employers or graduate school admissions committees:

> These evaluations can be quite deceptive if they're sent to people outside of the college because the course here might be the equivalent of a graduate level course. The feedback I give to a student will say, "You did well in such and such an area, but you need to do more work on this particular topic." This could be interpreted by some outside person as, "Oh, this person is rather weak in this area" without the reader really understanding, "Oh no, if this were a regular undergraduate course, this person would have an A or an A+." All I'm doing is identifying for the student some further areas where they might advance their knowledge. But it's not meant to be a criticism in the sense of, "you *failed* in this particular area."

One student says that although he values the noncompetitive, nongraded curriculum at New College, he worries about whether attending a nongraded institution will affect his chances for admission to graduate school: "Sometimes without grades it's hard to know where you [stand]. . . . I wonder if that's going to affect me for grad school sometimes. I think some grad schools know this school so that helps, but [for] the ones that don't know, it's kind of a disadvantage." An alumnus and current administrator frames the issue in this way:

> Students . . . get to a point where they're applying [to graduate school] and people start asking questions like, "What was your grade point average?" And you say, "Well, we don't have grades." And they say, "Well, what was your course load?" And you say, "Well, we didn't have to take courses." And after a while, the school that you're trying to get into sort of throws up its hands and says, "We can't process you as an

applicant because you don't conform to enough of the criteria that we normally evaluate to know whether we want you or not."

According to one alumnus and professor, however, "[T]he specific lesson of New College is that graduate schools will still accept your students, and the record of New College students going on to graduate schools indicates that pretty clearly." In the end, the true measure of the institution's success with the nongraded curriculum may be its students. According to a top-level official,

> New College is recognized as the sixth highest Ph.D. producer per capita graduate in the country. In the social sciences, it's the number one per capita graduate Ph.D. producer and among women, it's number seven. So, apparently, the As, Bs, and Cs don't make any difference and what we find is that the New College students set their goals and either achieve their goals or don't rather than competing against each other for As, Bs, or Cs. . . . We find that this tends to produce entrepreneurs and leaders.

There is no reason why other schools should be afraid to pick up on this noncompetitive style of student assessment and achievement, a former provost agrees:

> The lesson [is] that the [nongraded system] works [for students]. Their heads don't blow up. They get into medical school. Everybody— parents and faculties—fear [that they won't]! They go to the best graduate schools in the disciplines I know about so all those conventional fears of what happens when inhibitions of that sort are stripped away [are invalidated].

CONCLUSION: SUMMARY AND IMPLICATIONS

Throughout its history, New College has held to a distinctive core group of values that separate it from the mainstream of academe. The college has carried forward its pioneering visions of student-centered education and individualism, of faculty freedom and imaginative teaching. The campus has maintained its egalitarian ethos and its nongraded, competition-free curriculum. While the early spirit and adventure of creating a new institution may have faded, while the students today may be engaging in fewer off-campus learning experiences, and while the merger with USF may have imposed some bureaucratic structures on the institution, New College has, for the past three decades, retained its visionary founding characteristics. Looking back over the life and lessons of this nonconventional college, what are some of the implications or teachings of this case study and history?

- The first lesson to be learned from the New College story is that hierarchical structures may constrain innovation. At this college, it is the freedom from academic departments, rigid administrative structures, and curriculum committees that has enabled and empowered the faculty and students to experiment with imaginative approaches to teaching and learning. If innovative campuses are to succeed, hierarchical or bureaucratic structures should be minimized. An open and decentralized organizational design appears to be key to nurturing freedom, flexibility, and creativity.

- Second, if innovative institutions are to preserve their founding principles, they must look to the people who created those visions—the founding and veteran faculty, the charter staff—who keep the spirit and traditions of academic innovation and excellence alive in their administrative service, advising, and teaching. The vision is passed along to incoming cohorts of faculty and students and is cherished and sustained by the entire community.

- Third, the students keep alive the distinctive missions of an innovative institution. Nonconformity is a trait of the New College student. Undergraduates come here from across the United States in search of a nonconventional higher education. They are a powerful force and a voice for preserving the founders' visions.

- Fourth, the New College case study turns our attention to the significance of forging partnerships or affiliations with other systems or institutions. It is clear from the New College story that there would be no New College today had it not been for the affiliation with the University of South Florida. Careful consideration to the terms and conditions of a merger agreement—including a provision that the distinctive campus would maintain its autonomy—appears to be crucial if the "experimental" character of the campus is to be preserved.

- Fifth, this investigation underscores the importance of financial support and fund-raising. The New College Foundation has been essential to New College's survival as a distinctive public liberal arts college. The campus' unique blend of public and private funding may serve as a model for other institutions.

- Sixth, to persist in a changing social and economic climate, an experimental or innovative institution should emphasize both academic innovation and academic excellence. What singles out New College from many of its ill-fated counterparts of the alternative higher education movement of the 1960s and 1970s appears to be its continuing emphasis on both educational rigor and innovation. New College's reputation as a distinctive, high-quality liberal arts institution has won the campus national recognition.

- Seventh, students who are fresh out of high school and who are not accustomed to self-discipline–style learning programs may flounder or drop out of innovative colleges. To facilitate student progress and to boost retention rates, campuses with student-centered or individualized programs should consider initiating first-year student seminars and/or other community-building activities to ease the transition to the autonomous learning environment. At the same time, it is critical that innovative institutions, such as New College, examine the role of academic advising and the ways in which students may be encouraged and guided in completing their course work and thesis requirements.

- Eighth, grades are not the sole means of evaluating student progress. The success of New College alumnae/i in graduate schools and in the professions indicates that alternative modes of education and student assessment are viable options to the traditional practices of assigning letter grades and academic units. Individuals with an entrepreneurial spirit are the "products" of this human-centered curriculum. Members of Congress, authors, journalists, Rhodes scholars, college presidents, and presidents of national corporations, Arthur (1995) reports, are all New College graduates. They are the legacy of the founders' vision some three decades ago to create a college that would be not only different, but imaginative, and, indeed, New.

NOTES

1. There are three properties that encompass the 140-acre New College campus: The Ringling campus; the Caples Fine Arts Campus (which includes a 12-acre estate with manor and carriage house on the bay shore); and the East Campus, across U.S. Route 41, where dormitories designed by famed architect I.M. Pei, a student center, and a lecture and conference center are located.

2. The Congregationalists had an impressive record of founding institutions of higher education, including Harvard, Yale, Dartmouth, Amherst, Smith, and Oberlin (Burns 1994).

3. Later, the college would make reference to New College of Oxford University as the inspiration for its name and as a model for its early Oxford-style tutorials (Arthur 1995; New College 1994).

4. Today there are four branch campuses of the University of South Florida (Fort Myers, Sarasota, Lakeland, and St. Petersburg). The branch campuses provide upper division course work and graduate-level studies; the central campus in Tampa offers lower and upper division undergraduate programs as well as graduate education in a variety of fields. More than 36,000 students are enrolled at the University of South Florida (and its branch campuses) and some 1,860 full-time faculty members are employed at the institution (University of South Florida 1996-97 Undergraduate Catalog 1996). The USF-Sarasota branch enrolls 1,343 students (Office of the Dean and Warden 1997).

5. Other changes coincided with the merger. As a college within USF, the top official on campus would be the provost (today, "dean and warden"—the "warden" part of the title was derived from the corresponding post at New College, Oxford) (Arthur 1995).

6. Three interviewees had more than one period of employment at New College. In these cases, the total number of years employed was determined by taking the sum of the number of years employed in each position at New College. Calculations for the year of arrival to the institution are based on the individual's earliest position at the college.

7. The institution outlined in the plan would become Hampshire College (see chapter 4).

8. Although the early college catalogs and brochures make reference to students having a great deal of freedom in designing their own academic programs and proceeding at their own pace, there was, in fact, a fairly rigid required core curriculum in place at the very beginning that limited the possibilities for "truly individualized" learning (Arthur 1995). Under pressures from students, and with the entry of a new president and a new cohort of faculty who "were questioning their own disciplines [and] the academic system," the core courses, as noted earlier, were abolished in 1968. (The faculty also voted to end an 11-month calendar, senior seminars, a foreign language requirement, and comprehensive exams.)

9. As early as 1973-74, James Feeney and Gresham Riley (1975) documented that the educational contract system was not producing the number of experimental ventures that had been anticipated at the college.

10. Although New College has no general education requirements, there are requirements or course guidelines for majoring (or "concentrating") in a particular discipline (*General Catalog* 1995).

11. There is some evidence that retention may be improving. According to one top-level official, in the past year, the "student body grew from 540 . . . to 587 . . ., and most of the growth was in retention, which really, really pleased us." James Feeney, director of special project development, reports that "retention of students to graduation has gone from under 50 percent to 60 percent in just over a decade. But a cohort generally does not see all active contenders graduate until seven years from graduation" (J. Feeney, personal communication, 7 January 1997).

12. The college has recently made strides to increase retention by initiating a series of team-taught, interdisciplinary seminars for first-year students to integrate students into the life of the college and to provide a forum for a shared community experience (Michalson 1995).

REFERENCES

Admissions Office. 1997. Sarasota: New College.

Arthur, F.C. 1995. *New College: The first three decades*. Sarasota: The New College Foundation.

Bulletin of New College, 1964–1966. 1964. Sarasota: New College.

Burns, S. 1994. The New College chronicles: Marketing, miracles and mindpower underlie the smashing success of this 30-year-old Sarasota institution. *Sarasota* (October): 46–47; 118–20; 122–23.

Elmendorf, J. 1975. *Transmitting information about experiments in higher education: New College as a case study*. New York: Academy for Educational Development.

Feeney, J., and G. Riley. 1975. Learning contracts at New College, Sarasota. In *Individualizing education by learning contracts*, edited by N.R. Berte, 9–30. *New Directions for Higher Education* no. 10 (summer).

General catalog, 1995–1997. 1995. Sarasota: New College of the University of South Florida.

Grant, G., and D. Riesman. 1978. *The perpetual dream: Reform and experiment in the American college.* Chicago: The University of Chicago Press.

Hudson, D. 1964. No 'fact factory': UR alumnus relates New College premise. *Richmond Times Dispatch* (2 October).

Institutional self-study. 1970. Sarasota: New College.

Living while you learn: A New College student handbook. 1995. Sarasota: The Office of Student Affairs, New College of the University of South Florida, June.

Michalson, G.E., Jr. 1995. *Report to the faculty of New College of the University of South Florida.* Sarasota: New College of the University of South Florida.

New College Foundation. 1995. Brochure. Sarasota: New College Foundation.

New College of the University of South Florida: A brief history. 1994. Sarasota: New College of the University of South Florida.

New College of the University of South Florida. n.d. Viewbook. Sarasota: Office of Admissions, New College of the University of South Florida.

Office of the Dean and Warden. 1997. Sarasota: New College of the University of South Florida. Campus demographic information provided by James Feeney, director of Special Project Development.

A profile of New College, Sarasota, Florida. 1963. Brochure for prospective students. Sarasota: New College.

Self-guided campus tour from Robertson Hall, 1995-96 edition. 1995. Sarasota: New College of the University of South Florida.

University of South Florida 1996-97 undergraduate catalog. 1996. Tampa: University of South Florida.

CHAPTER 4

Hampshire College

An "Innovating" College in the Pioneer Valley

Late one night, . . . I was wandering through an apple orchard on the grounds of Hampshire College. The air was soft and misty, and somewhere over the outline of the Holyoke Range, I could see a faintly luminous moon.

Bill Vance, Amherst Record, *30 September 1970*

BACKGROUND: SETTING THE SCENE

Rolling countryside, grazing sheep and cows, old barns, and autumn foliage are sights to be seen on the road to Hampshire College in Amherst, Massachusetts. Carved out of an apple orchard and farmland in the Pioneer Valley of western Massachusetts, Hampshire College sits on 800 acres of former meadows, woods, and farmland and is shadowed by a low strip of mountains called the Holyoke Range. Following a long, curving driveway into the main entrance of the campus, you reach the circular "hub" of the college and catch your first glimpse of Hampshire's landmark brick and concrete buildings. On the right, there is the Harold F. Johnson Library with its art deco Robert Crown Athletic Center extension. Next to the library is the Charles W. Cole Science Center, which features a two-story, 2,600-square-foot "bioshelter" greenhouse and two floors of open, wall-free laboratories. Walking paths through the woods lead to Franklin Patterson Hall (an academic building named in honor of Hampshire's first president), the Longsworth Arts Village (named for the second president), and the college residence halls or "houses." Towards the periphery of the campus, there are modular apartments (or "mods" as they are affectionately known), and spread over some 175 acres of college land is a farm and agricultural research center that includes a three-acre organic vegetable garden.

Hampshire College is one of five institutions of higher education in the Pioneer Valley of Massachusetts. One mile up the road are the ivy-covered halls of Amherst College, a private liberal arts college that was founded in 1821 and enrolls some 1,590 undergraduates. Within walking distance of Amherst College is the University of Massachusetts at Amherst, a large public research university that was started in 1863 and serves more than 17,000 undergraduates and 5,800 graduate students. Nearby South Hadley is home to Mount Holyoke College, a liberal arts college for women that was founded in 1837 and has a student population of 1,950. Several miles away, in Northampton, is Smith College, another women's college that was founded in 1871 and enrolls 2,600 students. Together, these campuses form one of the most famed consortia in American higher education: the Five College Consortium (or Five Colleges, Inc.). The five colleges carry out cooperative programs and share resources and library facilities. There are intercollegiate faculty exchanges and students may enroll in courses at any of the consortium institutions. Altogether, the Five Colleges enroll more than 25,000 students, employ some 2,000 faculty members, and offer more than 5,000 courses (*Hampshire: Freedom* 1994).

The Founding

The story of Hampshire College begins in the 1950s when faculty members from the University of Massachusetts at Amherst, Smith College, Amherst College, and Mount Holyoke College drafted a proposal for a fifth college in the Pioneer Valley that would offer distinctive approaches to higher education. The result was *The New College Plan: A Proposal for a Major Departure in Higher Education* (Barber, Sheehan, Stoke, and McCune 1958). According to Charles R. Longsworth (1992), the founding vice president and second president of Hampshire College, the plan "was prepared at a time when imminent growth in the college-age population put demands upon American colleges and universities to provide space and opportunity for a vastly enlarged body of students" (109). The existing campuses in the Pioneer Valley felt the pressure to grow, but did not want to sacrifice their small college character. At the same time, the four presidents "found their institutions resistant to change." In the words of Longsworth, "They were successful, prestigious, conservative, and happy. Yet there were faculty and administrators and students who were restless, and who thought there might be better ways to educate, . . . that traditions should be challenged and broken" (109).

The New College Plan created quite a stir in higher education, recalls Longsworth (1992): "It promised to unleash faculty initiative and student imagination—all on a balanced budget" (110). Former associate dean of faculty Richard M. Alpert (1980) relates that the plan "was a strong attack on the conventional college as overly rigid, authoritarian, and inefficient. This plan sought to free the faculty and students from the grip of unnecessary structures and requirements and, by doing so, to tap the wellspring of talent and creativity that comes from unfettered faculty and student choice" (503).

Although the authors were cautious about proposing radical departures in the content of the liberal arts curriculum, and warned that the campus not become "too experimental" for fear of "intellectual slovenliness" and the loss of serious faculty and students (Astin, Milem, Astin, Ries, and Heath 1991; Weaver 1989), in the eyes of Longsworth, the plan was, indeed, a radical departure for its time.

Seven years passed and *The New College Plan* lay dormant. It was not until 1965, when Amherst College alumnus Harold F. Johnson pledged a generous gift of $6 million towards the establishment of the new institution, that Hampshire College was chartered by the Massachusetts legislature. The presidents of the four Valley institutions joined Johnson on the board of trustees, and hired Franklin Patterson, then director of the Lincoln Filene Center for Citizenship and Public Affairs at Tufts University, as president of the new college.

The board commissioned Patterson and Longsworth to write a revision of the 1958 document that would serve as a "blueprint" for the campus. The result, *The Making of a College: Plans for a New Departure in Higher Education* (Patterson and Longsworth 1966), would become the planning document for the institution-to-be. According to Alpert (1980), *The Making of a College* carried forward the basic commitment to student and faculty independence and freedom of choice that was set out in *The New College Plan*. It proposed student-led seminars and students educating themselves, faculty contracts (rather than a tenure track—a change from the 1958 plan), and little or no student financial aid[1] (Astin et al. 1991; Birney 1993; Frazier 1977). The authors introduced "modes of inquiry" (the processes or methods of intellectual inquiry) as "the central organizing principle in the college curriculum" (Patterson and Longsworth 1966, 86) and declared that there would be no required courses, no credit hours or units, and no grades. "From the start," Hampshire College admissions literature points out, "this college was designed to be different" (*Hampshire: Freedom* 1994, 2).

Campus construction, planning, and recruitment of the faculty and staff occupied the next several years of the newly chartered college's life. In 1968, on the old orchard land, the ground was broken for three college buildings—the library, Patterson Hall, and a dormitory (Merrill House) (Stiles 1965). On

September 14, 1970, the campus would open its doors to an entering class of 251 students and 51 faculty members (Birney 1993; *Hampshire College* 1970). The new departure—in the works for some 12 years—had finally arrived to the Pioneer Valley.

Hampshire College Today

Today this youngest sibling of the Five College Consortium enrolls some 1,068 undergraduate students, 602 (56 percent) of whom are female and 466 (44 percent) of whom are male. Five percent of Hampshire students are African American, 3.4 percent are Asian American, 3.3 percent are Latino, 0.6 percent are Alaskan Native or Native American, 74.1 percent are European American, and 13.8 percent are international students or members of other (or unknown) ethnic groups. Ninety-five percent live on campus and 17 percent are residents of the state of Massachusetts. Of the 1,942 students who applied for admission to the college in the fall of 1996, 1,291 (66 percent) were admitted (L. Beede, associate dean of faculty, personal communication, 25 March 1997).

There are 238 administrators and staff members at Hampshire College. The faculty is comprised of 84 full-time and 10 part-time academics. Forty-four percent of the faculty are female, 56 percent are male, and 17 percent are persons of color. The student-to-faculty ratio at Hampshire is 11 to one (L. Beede, personal communication, 25 March 1997).

The college is organized into four interdisciplinary Schools: Cognitive Science and Cultural Studies, Humanities and Arts, Natural Science, and Social Science. Courses are nongraded (students receive written evaluations), and there are no credits or curricular requirements. Students progress toward the bachelor of arts degree by completing three divisions of study (or "divs"). Division I ("basic studies") is designed to expose students to the conceptual ideas and methodological tools (modes of inquiry) of the college's four academic Schools. Students complete an "examination" in each School that is either project- or course-based[2] (Astin et al. 1991; *1995-96 Catalog* 1995).

In Division II ("the concentration"), students develop and carry out individualized programs of study (similar, in some ways, to college majors). The concentration involves independent projects, courses, reading programs, internships, and/or field studies (*Non Satis Non Scire* 1995). There are two required components of the Division II program: Students must demonstrate evidence of "intellectually substantive engagement" with multicultural or Third World perspectives and students must perform community service work.[3] At the end of Division II, the student compiles a portfolio consisting of papers, independent projects, course and/or field study evaluations, artistic products, and/or other work that he or she has completed in conjunction with the concentration. The student also prepares a retrospective analysis of the "Div II" process and the learning experience (*1995-96 Catalog* 1995).

Once the student has successfully "passed" Division II, he or she begins the final phase of his or her Hampshire education: Division III ("advanced studies"). In Div III, the student enrolls in advanced, integrative seminars and undertakes a major independent study project (the equivalent of a senior thesis or artistic project). The Div III project is completed under the guidance of a three-member committee. (Two of the committee members are Hampshire faculty members; the third may be a professor at one of the four neighboring institutions, a professional working in the student's chosen field, or another advanced student.) (*1995-96 Catalog* 1995) To commemorate the completion of the divisional sequence, after the final Div III committee meeting, students gather friends to celebrate and ring the "Div Free" bell: a Hampshire tradition.

ORGANIZATION OF THIS CHAPTER

This chapter examines the history and endurance of educational innovation at Hampshire College. The case study begins with a demographic profile of the interview participants in this study, the current and past generations of the Hampshire College community who shared their voices and memories of the campus. The next section draws upon the early documents and the data gathered in the interviews to describe the original distinctive educational ideals of Hampshire College. The chapter then traces the evolution of these beginning ideals, focusing on where and how the campus has kept alive its innovative philosophies and where and how the institution has changed or transformed itself. The next section focuses on the key issues or challenges to innovation at Hampshire. The case study concludes with a summary and a reflection on the Hampshire College story and its implications for reform and experimentation in American higher education.

INTERVIEW PARTICIPANT PROFILE

To explore the history and current status of innovation at Hampshire College, 26 semi-structured interviews were conducted with 33 founding and/or current faculty members, administrators, and students in early November 1995.[4,5] Each interview lasted about 50 minutes. The participants included 15 faculty members (10 of whom had been at the college for 23 years or more), 12 administrators (including the current president, vice president, and dean of faculty), nine students, three alumnae/i (all of whom graduated in the first six years of the college), and one former trustee. (Some individuals occupied more than one role at the institution.) The interviewees included 17 men and 16 women spanning several different "generations" of the Hampshire College community: Nine of the participants joined Hampshire in either its preopening or opening year (1969, 1970), five started in years two to five (1971–1974), two arrived at

Hampshire in the college's sixth or seventh year (1975, 1976), three came to the institution in its ninth through 11th year (1978–1980), and 14 joined the college in its 14th year or later (1983–1995). Excluding the students, alumnae/i, and the former trustee, the "tenure" for the interviewees at Hampshire College ranged from four to 26 years, with an average length of stay of 19.2 years at the institution.

DISTINCTIVE EARLY IDEALS AT HAMPSHIRE COLLEGE: KNOWLEDGE AS "THE POET OF OUR DREAMS"

"No major departure, no new or consequential venture, is made without a context and a vision," write Patterson and Longsworth (1966) in *The Making of a College*. "The general context of Hampshire College," they relate, "is an experimental society faced by great constraining tendencies which are in need of redress by new alternatives. The particular context for Hampshire is a time of difficulty for undergraduate education when new possibilities are needed and being sought" (44). Patterson and Longsworth, whose ideas shaped the original visions of the college, believed that liberal arts education had "lost a vision of itself. It has lost what Whitehead called 'the atmosphere of excitement' that marks education capable of transforming knowledge from cold fact into 'the poet of our dreams . . . the architect of our purposes.' Perhaps this is to say it has lost what it all too seldom had: a soaring imaginativeness in its consideration of learning, which connected knowledge with the zest of life" (44).

Hampshire College was designed to bring a "soaring imaginativeness" and a "zest of life" into its "consideration of learning" by experimenting with the ways in which the private liberal arts college could serve as a "vehicle for the realization of self in society" (Patterson and Longsworth 1966, 46). Student initiative or self-directed learning was one of the hallmarks of the newborn college. Also central to the founding mission was the campus' egalitarian community ethos—an emphasis on student participation in campus governance and students as "teachers" or colleagues with the faculty in the classroom arena. Third, Hampshire embraced the ideals of undergraduate teaching and creativity and freedom for faculty, and had a non-tenure system for academic appointments. Fourth, the college would promote interdisciplinary education through an absence of departments, team teaching, and cross-disciplinary student projects and divisional work. These four themes—individualism, egalitarianism, undergraduate teaching and faculty freedom, and interdisciplinary education—are woven throughout the early documents on Hampshire College and emerged time and time again in the interviews that were conducted with the campus' founding and long-time faculty, administrators, and alumnae/i. Each innovative theme is discussed in greater detail in the following sections.

Individualism: Student-Directed Education

First, at the very heart of the Hampshire College educational conception was the notion of student-directed learning or placing students in charge of their own educational lives. "What we want to create is independent initiative and intellectual enterprise," state the authors of *The New College Plan* (Barber et al. 1958, 9). "Hampshire's constant intellectual goal is to enlarge the capability of each student to conduct his own education," affirm Patterson and Longsworth in *The Making of a College* (1966, 48). "Since 1966," Patterson declared in a speech delivered to the first class of students, "a deliberate attempt has been made . . . 'to equip the student as best we know to learn how to make his own way as a learner, as a student and as a whole person,' in a changing age" (President Patterson 1970, 3).

The idea was to teach students how to teach themselves. In the words of one early alumna, "I think that Hampshire as an institution ask[ed] you to concentrate on asking the questions and not what the answers were. And that way of asking questions. . ., the process of *how to find* those answers more than the answers themselves, resulted in a product for me that was very different from a body of knowledge. What it resulted in for me was a way of being in the world" [emphasis added]. Another alumna, who transferred to Hampshire from Mount Holyoke in the early 1970s, relates:

> At Mount Holyoke, I felt as if I was being asked to put a funnel in the top of my head and pour in the facts and spit them out. At Hampshire College, the faculty asked very probing and deep and difficult questions, and really let the students struggle with not only finding out the answers, but finding out how to find the answers. In my law classes, I was shown how to do original legal research in a law library, in my divisional exam in Natural Science . . ., I presented my calculus proofs. . . . The emphasis here is not just on pouring in factual knowledge, but understanding the processes by which a scientist, a historian, a humanist, a social scientist thinks about problems.

Students would not be held "to a rigid formula of required course sequences." Instead, they would proceed through a consecutive series of academic divisions (the same three divisions that are in place today) at their own pace to "achieve increasing independence and responsibility for their own education" (*Hampshire College* 1970, 156). "'Dethrone the course' was one of the mottos that people had back then," one long-time professor explains. "You know, 'We don't want to have this thing [called a course].' 'We don't do grades.' Courses are resources, ways you get information. You [students] basically [did] all of your work independently." "You didn't graduate from Hampshire by accumulating credits," echoes a founding faculty member. There were no course credits. "There [were] no course grades. Courses [were] merely one option for learning, but the expectation was that students would be doing independent projects, that they would be off on field studies, doing things."

One of the most important ways in which students were encouraged to direct their learning experiences was to design their own concentrations (or majors) in Division II. "This is another of the freedoms Hampshire gives its students," note the authors of the 1970 college catalog (*Hampshire College* 1970, 38). They explain: "In serving as associate architect of his own program of concentration . . ., the student engages in a process which is in itself a self-education. It substitutes a program of studies adapted to the special needs and interests of the particular student for the usual uniform requirements of a 'departmental major' predesigned to fit all cases" (38). Hampshire College was not designed to shape students into a common mold. It was created to provide an educational arena for the individual to chart his or her own educational pathways. The fundamental idea was "progressive self-education" whereby the student "learns the value and the joy of gaining his [or her] own wisdom" (Educational Advisory Committee 1966, 11).

Egalitarianism

Second, there was a spirit of egalitarian community at early Hampshire College. Faculty and students—everyone—was on a first-name basis, and "socializing easily crossed status lines," according to former staff member Joel S. Meister (1982, 29). There was a degree of informality between faculty and students that was uncommon at most colleges and universities. Students at Hampshire were encouraged to become active participants in the classroom. The planners envisioned students serving as "teachers," and believed that "the best teaching tends to bring students into a colleague relationship with faculty, where students and faculty alike are learners, and alike share on occasion in the act of teaching others" (Patterson and Longsworth 1966, 70). At the same time, self-motivated students would be seeking each other out as "teachers," thereby broadening the definition of both teacher and learner. "Faculty would be guides, facilitators, resource persons, mentors" (Meister 1982, 30).

Undergraduates at Hampshire College were not only freed from the formality and authoritarian relationships that typically separated students and professors, but were encouraged to take an active part in college governance, including appointment and promotion decisions for faculty. "Students were on the committee that hired me," marvels a faculty member who started in 1974. "It was students who came to me in 1973 and recruited me." Although some of the original plans for the college called for an incorporated, nonprofit institution with a "hierarchy of strong, experienced leadership," Robert C. Birney (1993), founding dean of the School of Social Science, points out that "from the outset, there was a strong challenge to this model, which emphasized community spirit, an open process of decision making, and the necessity of maintaining high levels of consensus" (18).

Why the open structure? Patterson and Longsworth (1966) believed that "administration ha[d] come to be a massive component of American collegiate and university education" (188). They insisted that "a deliberate effort will be made to avoid a centralized bureaucracy" at Hampshire (188) and "to permit active participation in processes of planning and operation by faculty, students, trustees, and administrators" (189)—all without being "inoculated" by an "anti-leadership vaccine." "Over-administration, as well as over-committeefication," Patterson and Longsworth declared, "will be avoided like the plagues they are" (xx).

Undergraduate Teaching and Faculty Freedom

Next, the pioneering planners of Hampshire College sought to restore the centrality and status of undergraduate teaching (Alpert 1980). The new campus was seeking free-spirited individuals to engage students in lively classroom discussions and activities. As the authors of *The New College Plan* emphasized, "The . . . College curriculum requires people who are vitally interested in teaching, ready to devote time and imagination to attending to the *students'* thinking, not just their own" (Barber et al. 1958, 31). Patterson and Longsworth (1966), similarly, proposed that "Hampshire will build a faculty devoted as much to teaching in the terms the College stands for, as to scholarship and art" (xix). And President Patterson declared in his speech to the first class of students that one of the overriding goals of this institution would be "'to restore at the undergraduate level, attention to the status of teaching as a fundamental matter,' a guideline in planning the present [group of] 'fine faculty'" (President Patterson 1970, 3).

At the same time, the college would grant faculty members the freedom to decide what they wanted to teach: "Each of the . . . faculty will be free to decide what he will teach, in consultation with his colleagues and in response to his own interests and those of the students" (Patterson and Longworth 1966, 11). "The goal is free development of the curriculum in response to changing intellectual interests'" (Patterson and Longsworth 1966, 282). Patterson and Longsworth explained: "Within the College's general framework of purposes and its accent on the centrality of method in disciplines of inquiry and expression, faculty will have unusual freedom to teach in terms of their own principal intellectual or artistic interests" (xix).

There were no academic departments at early Hampshire College, no rigid curricular structures or requirements dictating what or how a faculty member could teach. Just as the students were to be set free to pursue their own individualized learning paths, so, too, were the faculty liberated from the confines of traditional curricular structures and techniques.

Teaching had, in fact, become such a driving force in the early life of the college, that, according to Alpert (1980), a large proportion of the faculty had come to view research as a threat to good teaching, "and especially to the faculty's primary mission of serving the students." "In some cases," Alpert reports, "this commitment to teaching went so far as to generate outright hostility to research and to make a virtue of avoiding publishing and the pursuit of other broad professional goals" (505).

To ensure a continuing vitality in faculty teaching, the college adopted what Alpert (1980) terms "perhaps Hampshire's most striking departure from the dominant forms in the academic profession" (505): a system of faculty employ- ment by contract rather than tenure. Professors would be employed by renew- able contracts of either three, five, or seven years, and reviewed two years before the expiration of the contracts—with input from the entire campus community (students, faculty, administrators, etc.). The founders of the col- lege believed that the absence of a tenure system would keep alive an atmo- sphere of creativity and experimentation in teaching. In the words of Birney (1975), "The history of new and innovative institutions strongly suggested that, with the settling in of permanent faculty, the spirit of innovation is often lost. It was especially appealing, therefore, to test the contract system as a device for maintaining vitality and a spirit of renewal among the faculty" (104).[6]

Interdisciplinary Education

Finally, the early planners of Hampshire College embraced the idea of interdis- ciplinary education. "The most *crucial* distinguishing factor at Hampshire at the outset," says one charter faculty member, "is the way in which interdiscipli- nary work [was] the very basis of the place." The faculty were not willing to define themselves as narrow specialists, Alpert (1980) reports, "nor depart- ment-based disciplinarians" (504). The founders rejected the idea of disciplin- ary departments—the college was organized into three multidisciplinary Schools: Humanities and Arts, Natural Science and Mathematics, and Social Science.[7]

Cross-disciplinary teaching was prized from the college's inception, accord- ing to interviewees. "As I look back at the emergent programs and courses that I taught [in the early days]," a professor of American Studies recalls, "I often co-taught with a cultural anthropologist, with a cultural historian, with a psychoanalyst, with a geologist, [and] with a natural scientist." Imagine biolo- gists rubbing shoulders with mathematicians, physicists collaborating with chemists and other scientists, offers a professor of 23 years. That was what it was like back then. There were English professors working with social scientists, mathematicians teaming up with historians. "I think [interdisciplinarity] was a sort of genius piece of the experiment," a former dean of faculty and long-time professor marvels, "that by breaking down departmental organizations and putting faculty into different kinds of situations, it unleashed a lot of energy and a lot of creativity that otherwise might not have happened."

The absence of departments and the emphasis on interdisciplinary education unleashed a spirit of faculty creativity in crossing disciplinary boundaries. There was a "sense of openness about, 'Well, here's a program in environmental studies. Let's put it together this way,'" remembers one charter faculty member. The feeling was that "you're not immediately faced with the rigidity ... of an entrenched department that says, 'Well, that's all very nice, but that would have to be part of just an experiment, you know, because we already have our curriculum, we already know what history is.' So in those early years, you [were] involved in a kind of open-ended idea of forming and reforming intellectual pursuits that often combine disciplines in ways that in conventional departments are not permissible or at least are frowned upon." The interdisciplinary, student-centered nature of the divisional projects, too, brought faculty members together from different Schools and disciplinary backgrounds who would advise students and sit on project-based examination committees.

ENDURANCE AND TRANSFORMATION OF THE DISTINCTIVE EARLY IDEALS AT HAMPSHIRE COLLEGE

Now, step forward into the 1990s. "Morale is high, excitement continues," states Longsworth (1992), "and the fundamental ideas on which Hampshire was built are still in place" (123). Based on the findings of this study, Hampshire has, on the whole, kept alive its innovative founding missions. This section draws upon the voices of the interviewees, the archival materials, and campus histories to examine the endurance and/or transformation of Hampshire's original distinctive educational themes (individualism, egalitarianism, faculty freedom and teaching, and interdisciplinarity). It then explores the longevity or "survival" of the institution, and offers a summary of the key reasons for the preservation of the innovative founding ideals.

Individualism: Student-Directed Education

"Freedom from the boundaries of traditional academic disciplines. Freedom from the stultifying effect of letter grades. . . . Freedom to create a life that is seamless, in which your work has meaning—to you and to others" (*Hampshire: Freedom* 1994). These are some of the freedoms that Hampshire College offers its students that are outlined in the current viewbook and that have stood the test of time. The early structure of student-centered academic divisions, for example, remains at the core of the academic program. The college is still without academic credits, course requirements, and letter grades. Undergraduate concentrations remain highly individualized, and learning how to learn continues to be an integral feature of the educational program.

In the words of one founding faculty member, Hampshire College "was designed to try to give students greater initiative in planning their own academic programs than did traditional colleges and universities, and it still does that." A staff member who has worked at the college since its second year agrees: "One of the distinctive things about Hampshire is that it [still] engages students in the process of creating knowledge rather than just viewing [students] as a kind of an empty vessel into which you pour [knowledge. The college] says, 'You, yourself, can make a contribution to whatever discipline,' and really some Division III's do that."

"This is a place where students who are interested in studying the Cuban Revolution can *really* open up and get at it," explains a long-time faculty member in economics and history. It is a place where individuals can study AIDS education, as one current student has done, or the Nuremberg Trials. Here undergraduates can initiate seminars on classical philosophers or Marxist theories. In the words of a founding professor,

> I feel [that] Hampshire's operating at its best when students come to me and say, "We're required to take an advanced course or seminar for Division III. There's nothing being offered in the catalog that looks good to us, but a bunch of us think that we would like to do this [independent seminar]". . . . The last one I [sponsored] was a Kafka seminar. . . . The students put it together themselves. . . . One of my fields is anarchist theory. Sometimes students will come and say, "We are forming . . . an anarchist study group and will you help us." Some years ago, there were some students who wanted to study Foucault and they [wanted to] form a Foucault study group. That's some of the best stuff that happens.

Whether it is anarchist theory, the Cuban Revolution, or Foucault, Hampshire students are still designing their own courses of study and curricular themes. How has Hampshire College been able to preserve its distinctive student-centered learning mission? "We haven't had very much turnover of [faculty] who came here early," explains a 24-year professor, "and to some extent that means that there has been a consistency and a kind of retention of original values" (including the individualized learning mission). Over the past 10 years, the average rate of faculty turnover has been about 2 to 3 percent per year (L. Beede, personal communication, 26 March 1997).

"We are *continually* discussing whether this [potential change] does or does not meet with what was laid down in *The Making of a College*," a professor of 19 years relates. "We have senior faculty who have been here since the beginning who have a certain vision and who constantly voice that in faculty meetings and in public. . . . [Change] is a hot item. People *really* take it seriously and students and alums take it *enormously* seriously." A faculty member who has taught at the institution for 25 years confirms: "You even talk to students and students who then graduated just last year and they have a lot of vested interest in seeing Hampshire keep up [its founding ideals] to be different."

Students and alumnae/i, are, in fact, a constant source of support for the preservation of the original individualized vision of the institution—not only in their firm commitment to the ideals of the founders, but in their success in life and work as graduates. A top-level official explains that Hampshire is "producing a kind of graduate who is, in our opinion, and the opinion of a lot of the rest of the world, well educated for the kind of world [in which we live]—[educated] to think for [him- or her]self, to be creative and also efficient, to be self-disciplined as well as to take risks." "The alums who come out of Hampshire," she reports, "are people with the potential to make a difference in the world. I think that's at the core of the institution's commitment to its original mission. That's a pretty driving force."

Although students are still free to direct their own education at Hampshire College, interviewees point out that the campus has now established policies or guidelines to assist students in making progress toward their degrees. That is, there is now a stricter set of rules governing the length of time in which students may complete each of the academic divisions. There were no such rules in place in the early days.

An early alumna and current administrator explains: "There's a little bit more structure in place to help gauge student academic status, which is I think healthy. I think there used to be too much of a period in which [students] could fall through the cracks and just not get their footing at all and then leave. So, there's a little bit more structure in place and more frequent advising. But that hasn't altered the fundamental premise of Hampshire of every student having an individualized program."

"There are some who really still believe that the best way to get a Hampshire education is sink or swim," says an administrator. "You let the student do what the student wants and you hope for the best, so that anything like deadlines or deadlines for progress are inhibiting of the students' own unique process." In the end, although at least two interviewees were quite vocal about the new requirements (including the two-course option) representing a "backsliding" from the original vision, most interviewees believed that the changes have been healthy for the institution as a means of guiding students through the divisional program and increasing retention.

Egalitarianism

What of the early egalitarian ethos? Do undergraduates still have a voice in campus governance procedures? Are students still as actively engaged as partners with the faculty in the classroom arena? First, "Very much in keeping with the original model concept of the college," says a communications professor of 23 years, "students are involved at all levels of decision making roles [at the institution]. For example, we're still one of the few colleges that has students who have decisive votes on search committees and also who vote for reappointments in the Schools and also serve on the College Committee on Reappointments and Promotions and this is something we take a great deal of pride in." When it comes time to review the files of faculty who are seeking promotion to full professor, a long-time economist agrees, "everyone [still] contributes to a file." Students contribute, faculty colleagues contribute, colleagues from the Valley institutions contribute, "and those files are open to the members of the School, which includes students."

At the same time, active learning remains a central feature of the college's teaching and learning community. "Students participate in a lot of the teaching," offers one long-time professor in the social sciences. "Third- and fourth-year students serve as co-teachers and teaching assistants with less advanced students. Students serve as the second member on committees that supervise Division I projects." "Last Friday," she adds, "we sat around all day and had this curriculum planning meeting. There were almost as many students as faculty present in the meeting." The ideals of participatory governance and student co-teaching have been with the college "since the beginning." Moreover, "Here at Hampshire, faculty members are still on a first-name basis with students," an early graduate and current staff member remarks. "The idea is that respect is not based on some formal status," an administrator explains. "Greg [Prince, the college president] is Greg to all his students, [and to] the faculty. . . . Penina [Glazer, the vice president] is Penina. . . . Students work with faculty and not sort of against them or for them. . . . I really like that here."

This is one of the things that "I find exhilarating" about the place, a charter faculty member exclaims, that is:

> the relation between teachers and students. . . . On occasion, I'll teach a course at Mount Holyoke or Smith and I'll get "Oh, Professor _____ this," and "Oh, Professor _____ that." And they'll say, "Do we need to know this for the final exam?" kind of question and [there is] that *whole* power relation, which is much less here [at Hampshire] than at other schools. We can talk to [students] more directly.

There is a sense of being involved in a partnership with students. In the words of an administrator who has worked at the institution for 12 years, the faculty at Hampshire are the "guides on the side instead of the sages on the stage."

It is, again, these "guides on the side," these spirited faculty members—especially those from the founding years, who continue to inspire students to take part in teaching and governance, who carry forward the ideals of community governance and nonauthoritarian faculty-student interactions. "Some of the old school professors are a little more relaxed about [forming close relations with students]," a current student shares in an interview. "I know . . . John Reid takes kids on these huge trips to Cape Cod and then, if you're going to do an independent project or do your Div I with him, he'll go, 'Get in my car, we're going to the dinosaur tracks, kids, let's go, let's go!' And he throws you in his Jeep Cherokee and you go!"

While many interviewees believe that the campus continues to adhere to its original participatory governance ethos, there are some faculty who argue that the college has grown more bureaucratic over the years and that there is less opportunity for student involvement in campus decision making. "There's much more of an attempt to curtail [student participation in governance]" these days, one charter academic reports. With the exception of the School of Natural Science, he says, "the other Schools [now] specify very clearly *which* students can be [voting] School members and attend School meetings . . ., whereas [in] the School of Natural Science, it has always been the case [that] anybody who wants to come [to a School meeting] can come and participate as a full member in the discussion and in the decisions."

There is "more centralization of power in the administration," a professor of 16 years explains, "and less faculty [and student] participation and voice in institutional decision making." "There's a *lot* more administration than there was 21 years ago," another long-time faculty member relates. "There are a lot more deans, there's a lot more staff in development, admissions, business, etc. The faculty hasn't grown very much, but the administrative . . . staff [has] gr[own] enormously in the last couple of years." This has impacted the role and voice of the community in campus decision making. In the end, although opinion varies with regard to the participatory governance ideal, most interviewees report that Hampshire students continue to have more of a voice and input into the affairs and governance at their institution than in their perception do their counterparts at almost any other college or university in the United States.

Undergraduate Teaching and Faculty Freedom

Next, the college has carried forward its pioneering principle of faculty freedom and creativity in undergraduate teaching. In the words of a professor of communications,

We [faculty members] still [can] take an impulse and say [to a colleague], "Hey, let's do a course"... We do this *a lot*. And we teach stuff we're really *vitally* interested in, so I think the general level of teaching is very, very good here, because we're teaching stuff we really care about.... You don't have to wait until you're 55 before you get to teach "the course" that so-and-so's been teaching until he croaked. We are very good about working on our colleagues a lot, saying, "Do you want to try this? . . ." I think that's [one] thing that I would highlight as being a carryover from the old days.

A long-time faculty member in the sciences agrees:

The [Hampshire] system is exciting to teach in because [faculty are] continually creating new courses. . . . If somebody wants to create a course on the science and politics of AIDS, there's no committee that's going to say, "No you can't do that until two or three years from now." They just go ahead and *do* it, keeping the structures very loose so that you can teach according to your interests.

"If I have an idea for a new course, I just teach it," declares a founding faculty member. "I don't have to submit a proposal to any curricular committee or anything. I can just go off and design it and students will come and take it. And I can try it out and modify it."

This is the key to the endurance of faculty creativity in teaching: Hampshire College has remained free of disciplinary departments. A long-time professor explains:

This business of [faculty] staking out turf is a function of departmental structure, where some [professor] who's been there longer says [to the new faculty], "Well, look, I teach Medieval English. That's what I do. . . . And by God, you young faculty can teach Introduction to Literature, you can teach this, you can teach that, and we have a set curriculum and you guys fit into it as best you can." I think [the absence of departments is] one of the big reasons for [the preservation of the faculty freedom].

The system is also self-sustaining, according to interviewees. Hampshire faculty model this type of creativity in teaching to their students and to each other. In the words of one long-time professor,

We get new faculty and they look around and see what their colleagues are doing, and they catch on. They take to it real fast that "Oh, okay, well I should be creating new classes." And one of the things we do routinely when we interview people, is we ask them to do a couple quickie drafts of courses they'd most like to teach. So, we're both checking them out and also telling them something about the institution. So, some of [the reason why the teaching mission persists] is momentum.

Interviewees also credit the existence of the other consortium institutions. Faculty at Hampshire College are able to develop new kinds of courses and interdisciplinary curriculum with the assurance that basic or introductory level courses will still be offered at the other Valley institutions. In the words of one faculty veteran,

> It has to be a fact that it's a privilege to have been created by the other four colleges, as a brainchild of the planning of the other four colleges, and that we have full rights and privileges for ourselves and our students. We're not, like, in an Iowa cornfield, where we're just all alone trying to do our thing with interdisciplinary co-teaching. Any of my students . . . are free to sign up for conventional courses at Smith, Amherst, Mount Holyoke, or University [of Massachusetts, Amherst] and with the best teachers.

At the same time, the college has never established a tenure system for faculty. Today, "it is a 10-year system," explains one administrative official:

> The first [faculty] contract is three years, second contract is four years, and then it's a series of 10-year contracts, but it's [still] not blank tenure: [Even] at the end of 10 years, there is a review. . . . Halfway in the middle of each of these contracts, is a mid-contract review. So, people are reviewed all the time by their colleagues. And faculty are very strong about keeping it that way.

The non-tenure system helps to keep alive a spirit of faculty vitality in teaching.

While faculty freedom and creativity remain hallmarks of academic life at Hampshire College, interviewees point out that there is more of an emphasis on scholarship and publication in faculty promotion and reappointment reviews today than in the early days. "Increasingly, [when] we're evaluating faculty for promotion," one long-time professor observes, "what we've relied on are much more traditional measures—publications." "External research has become much more a criterion for reappointment and promotion at this campus than it was," a charter academic explains.

> Us old guys [sit] there [in meetings] and say, "Hey, wait a minute. Teaching is the principal criterion [for promotion]." But the deans and the president encourage faculty to go out and get grants to do research and encourage faculty then to take a day off during the week to pursue their research, so that a hell of a lot of the faculty are only on campus or visible to the students four days a week. And so we're gradually, gradually, gradually getting closer to what I think is just a standard liberal arts college.

As early as 1980, Alpert was reporting that "The value of research and publishing has . . . gained support and the faculty now exhibit the kind of tension around the teaching-research conflict that is found at many other teaching-oriented colleges" (505). "Hampshire," he explained, "has tried to build its faculty reward system mainly on teaching. Nevertheless, there is an increasing pressure for faculty to be engaged in some form of professional development that has meaning in a broader professional community" (515). The reason? "The nature of the academic profession leaves little other choice if an institution wants to continue to recruit high-quality faculty and students. Hampshire could not recruit a high quality faculty, talented students, and gain institutional prestige while at the same time preserving a definition of faculty performance and student achievement radically at odds with the definition that dominates the rest of American higher education" (515).

A faculty member who has taught at the campus for 20 years agrees:

> I don't think the college would have survived to this point on the notion of it being [solely] a teaching institution—meaning little schol- arship and no rewards [for scholarship]. We had to sort of rethink some of the structures and incentives [for faculty review] and it was difficult, because there were disagreements. But, I think what's hap- pened is [that there is] a kind of new consensus . . ., a sense that "Yeah, we are primarily a teaching institution, but we do expect faculty to be involved with ideas and shaping ideas and working beyond the [Hamp- shire] community."

Interdisciplinary Education

Finally, interdisciplinarity has remained at the heart of the Hampshire educa- tion for the past two and a half decades. The college remains free of depart- ments and disciplinary majors, and collaborative team teaching is ever-present at the campus today.

Interdisciplinarity is a very "marked feature of Hampshire," a staff member of 21 years maintains. "A *lot* of courses are team taught and they're taught by people in very disparate disciplines." "At one time or another," a founding professor in mathematics remarks, "I've taught with geologists, I've taught with ecologists, I've taught with biologists and physicists. I regularly teach a course with one of the English professors. We teach a course on nature writing and natural history literature and that's exhilarating."

A long-time administrator, likewise, relates, "One of the things about Hampshire [is that] this business of sort of the sacred walls between disciplines is just out the window. I've taught public health (I'm a medical anthropologist) with a medical sociologist. We feel that those disciplines and techniques are perfectly appropriate for teaching public health. There's a lot of cross-disciplin- ary teaching." That emphasis on co-teaching and interdisciplinary education, in the words of one founding faculty member, "has remained unchanged throughout the whole [life of the college]."

For several of the faculty interviewed, interdisciplinary teaching has been transformative in their lives and careers. A long-time professor of economics reveals:

> I teach with historians and I teach with a geographer often enough so that the way I see my own discipline has been transformed, and I don't realize how much until I'm actually working with other economists ... and realize I . . . have assumed [that] sociology, geography, history, anthropology, psychology, law, and politics would be a part of [our work]. It's only when I sort of step back and work with other people that I begin to realize just how much I *assume* and just how much co-teaching over the years with various people means. . . . It's changed my scholarship. . . . I've just gotten used to not sort of living in that narrow way. I think that's the way we've probably most been committed to what [the founders of the college] *dreamed* would happen.

The key to the "staying power" of the cross-disciplinary design of Hampshire College has been the absence, again, of academic departments. In the words of a charter professor, "The [college's] decision to be department-less in the beginning . . ., in retrospect, was crucial [to the maintenance of interdisciplinary education]. Departments can be fiefdoms of control and recruitment and so on, and they tend to want to perpetuate themselves." A long-time faculty member of politics affirms: "I think one lesson [of Hampshire College] is that if you're serious about getting your students engaged in intellectual life early on, you should abolish your departments. They're unnecessary intrusions on the natural inquisitiveness and interest in the world that students come to college with."

Faculty recruitment, too, has been key to the preservation of the interdisciplinary mission of the institution. One long-time academic explains:

> We continue to attract, both in hiring and students, people who see themselves as marginal—sort of at the fringe of their graduate department and they've already transgressed somewhere; they've trespassed into other fields and they find it hard to define themselves by the typical slots that are available in departments. We *want* people like that because we expect them to be generalists, to follow their own interests, and collaborate with other faculty, to be able to serve a wide range of students.[8]

In the words of one founding faculty father, "The place has an infectious vision—it tends to attract people who are infected by the vision or [are] susceptible to infection, and has gotten an *enormous* amount of very hard work from people over the years." The support of the board of trustees and the leadership of the institution has also been crucial to the endurance of the college's early interdisciplinary and distinctive missions.

A faculty member of 24 years credits the interdisciplinary nature of the student divisional work, whereby students will still recruit faculty from different fields to advise on their projects and sit on their committees. The divisional structure *"requires* [faculty] to work collectively," he says. "It's a way of keeping in touch with a whole range of issues and ideas and we like it!" A high-ranking administrator explains that in the divisional projects,

> Three faculty will be brought together by the student who may never have worked together on anything before. A year later . . ., *they* may have discovered a whole set of ideas from their colleagues that they never saw in relationship to their work and, then, in turn, will say "There'd be a really interesting course here. . . ." And so they're constantly changing, being stirred, being forced to do new things.

The Survival of Hampshire College as an Innovative Institution

Twenty-five years later and Hampshire College carries on with its original distinctive missions largely intact. Given the shifts in the economy since the late 1960s and early 1970s, the changes in contemporary attitudes towards education (what some characterize as a conservative shift in public attitudes about reform in education), and the short lives of many of Hampshire College's counterparts in the 1960s and 1970s, what has kept this innovative institution healthy and alive? Taking a different turn on the topic, interviewees were asked to comment on Hampshire College's longevity; i.e., to share, if they could, some of the reasons why this distinctive college—unlike so many of the alternative campuses in the 1960s and 1970s—has survived.

The Five College Consortium

First and foremost, interviewees single out the Five College Consortium as the key to Hampshire's longevity. The access to resources, they say, is unparalleled. Hampshire students can enroll in more than 5,000 classes, study with some 2,000 faculty members, and enjoy the facilities and library resources of three other distinguished liberal arts colleges in Massachusetts and a research university. "In a sense," a faculty member marvels," we have a richness of resources, that if we were trying to do this all by ourselves in the middle of a cornfield in Iowa we wouldn't have." Location and collaboration have been key.

As a member of the Five College Consortium, Hampshire College can continue to offer an unusual assortment of courses and seminars that are centered on faculty interests and student needs. The campus does not necessarily have to cover the full range of traditional academic subjects because those subjects are offered by the fine teachers and staff of the neighboring institutions. Like Pitzer College, then, the presence of the four other autonomous Valley institutions not only enables Hampshire College to survive, but to survive with its distinctive philosophies intact. "It's a kind of cushion in a sense," states a professor of politics. "It allows us to do somewhat unusual courses, themes." (The affiliation is also beneficial to the four other Valley institutions, which have access to the distinctive curricular resources and programs of the Hampshire College community.)

At the same time, the interinstitutional collaboration serves to enhance Hampshire's marketing potential. "To be associated with Amherst and Smith and Mount Holyoke—three distinguished private colleges," a charter academic maintains, "and then the University of Massachusetts—a huge state university, has meant that people take us seriously and they have from the beginning, even though we've got this program which is very, very different." The consortium has always been a draw to potential students and faculty.

Late Start-Up Date—Lessons Learned from Other Innovative Institutions

Second, Hampshire College has benefited from its later start-up date. The campus opened in 1970, at the tail end of the alternative higher education movement of the 1960s and 1970s. By the time the campus had come to life, the college's planners and faculty had already witnessed the successes and failures, the dreams and the dangers of other experimental institutions of the same era. "We've . . . watched places [other experimental colleges] go under for various reasons," states a faculty member of 23 years. "I suspect more faculty here probably are more aware of [the experiences of these other innovative colleges] than the average faculty member because I think we see it as something we need to pay attention to." Several of Hampshire's faculty members also spent time at the other alternative campuses. We try to learn from those [other distinctive institutions'] experiences, a faculty member relates.

Hampshire College as "Innovating"

Next, a number of interviewees single out the college's lifelong emphasis on "experimenting" or "innovating," that is, the institution's openness to changing with the times, to testing and trying out new teaching methods and curricular contents and themes (e.g., a Third World Expectation). The campus was founded to be an "experimenting" college, according to Patterson and Longsworth (1966), and "not to be tied to a narrow or doctrinaire 'experimental' orthodoxy. . . . It plans to sustain an experimental mood as far forward in time as it can" (34).

"What was fortunate," an administrator relates, "was that [the planners of the college] put in place a structure that could easily absorb [new] things [feminist studies, environmental studies, etc.], that faculty could easily shift on the courses, that students could by designing their education around certain problems that were very, very central to them, *push* for certain kinds of directions, and the existence of the five colleges could also enable the college to move in certain directions."

In the words of an administrator who has worked at the institution since 1983,

> I think every college that started out as being different has to be careful of a kind of conservative digging into "This is the way it was and this is the way it's gonna be," and I think Hampshire actually prides itself on being quite responsive to the changing demographics and the kinds of students that we get and the changing needs of faculty, etc. That's what we think is one of our main strengths, is our responsiveness, flexibility to change, ability to regroup, and to question ourselves as we ask our students to question themselves.

Hampshire College has remained not only innovative, but innovating.

Summing Up the Key Reasons for the Endurance of the Distinctive Early Ideals at Hampshire College

Nearly 40 years after the writing of *The New College Plan*, Hampshire College carries on as a distinctive institution of higher education. Looking back over the life and lessons of this unorthodox college, what, in summary, are the key factors that have enabled this campus to sustain its pioneering principles? First, interviewees single out the dedication to the original vision among the founding and long-time faculty. The Hampshire vision, most say, is "infectious" and is passed along to the latter generations of students and academics who keep alive the early missions of the founders. The decentralized organization of the institution, too, with its multidisciplinary Schools and absence of academic departments, has paved the way for long-lasting interdisciplinary innovation and spirited teaching and learning. Above all, it may be Hampshire's association with the Five College Consortium in the Pioneer Valley, the cross-campus collaboration and coordination, that has enabled this one-of-a-kind institution to carry on as an innovating institution for the last two and a half decades.

ISSUES AND CHALLENGES TO INNOVATION

Like any creative entity or community, however, Hampshire College has come up against tensions or pressures in its continuing existence. This section of the Hampshire story explores some of the timeless issues and challenges to innovation at the college. These are student attrition, faculty overwork, founding faculty retirements and generational differences, and issues associated with an absence of tenure.

Student Attrition

One of the most critical issues that the college has faced over the years is student attrition. Early on, institutional planners discovered that the highly individualized educational program at Hampshire "worked increasingly well for those [students] who understood it and were drawn to it," but worked against those who were not accustomed to directing their own educational lives or who were not certain of their intellectual interests (Birney 1993, 14). Initially, the dropout rates "were a treacherously high 40 percent," Birney points out. Back then, attrition was so commonplace that students had invented a word for it: "creative floundering" (Bloch and Nylen 1974). With the adoption of the two-course option and other guidelines to assist students in moving through Hampshire's divisional programs, retention rates have improved. Still, the college continues to face the departure of a number of students "who cannot adapt to this nontraditional approach to college education" (Birney 1993, 14).

Many students are overwhelmed by the degree of freedom and independence that they are granted in shaping their own education. In the words of a former trustee and faculty member, "It [is] hard for [students for] the first year and a half [at Hampshire] because students have been told for 12 years what to do with their education." At Hampshire they hear, "'You know, it's your baby, now do something with it." In the words of a fourth-year student,

> No one here is telling you what you need to be doing all the time. If you don't take responsibility and talk to professors, then it's not a good idea for you [to be at this college]. I mean, you can get really lost. . . . You'll be miserable and you'll feel like you're floating most of the time. Nothing will make sense. I went through a period like that where I was between a bunch of advisors, not really sure what I wanted to do. And it was a struggle. But at the same time, I'm glad I'm here and I think about other schools I was thinking about going to and I'm really happy I'm here now.

"Education is so personal," offers another student. "I know that there are just some people who need structure; they need to know where they stand and have the grades, just be able to know [that they] need to do this and this specifically in order to [do this]. . . . That's one of the reasons why I would hesitate to agree that Hampshire offers the 'best' for every student because I don't think that it does. You really do have to [be a person who can] take initiative."

The campus' highly individualized program can also be an isolating experience for students. In a 1981 report written in conjunction with the college's 10-year review, Ann M. Woodhull noted that one of the problems with the present system of Division I examinations is that the program is too individualistic. Division I, she found in student interviews, is "a lonely process for students." Students who are engaged in highly individualistic programs may not have a feeling of common purpose or shared experience with their peers. This may lead to floundering or dropping out. Grant and Riesman (1978) reached similar conclusions in their study of experimental colleges and universities. At Hampshire, they noted that the lone student-scholar, working on intense, independent academic pursuits, often becomes detached or disconnected from others. The campus, they wrote, has been described as a "friendly place without friendship, 'almost like a commune, yet with people being isolated'" (361).

Faculty Overwork

Second, there is the issue of faculty burnout. "At crucial moments in the semester," faculty members Frank W. Holmquist, Laurie Nisonoff, and Robert M. Rakoff (1984) point out in their report on the labor process at Hampshire College, "the faculty may be working over one hundred hours a week, reading and commenting upon [student] portfolios and preparing for formal oral examinations, while continuing to teach classes and advise" (192). "Office hours," they write, "are long and crowded, the phone is active, governance work requires attention, recommendations are requested, colleagues are evaluated, classes need preparation and co-teaching requires coordination, exam meetings are scattered throughout the week, lunches are often the working variety, and the to and fro of communication with the professional world requires attention" (199–200). In this arena of chronic overload and "emotionally draining mental gear-shifting," academics become burned out, used up, frazzled, exhausted. "By Thursday," Holmquist et al. observe, "many faculty members simply look bad — and sometimes act bad—due to progressive lack of sleep over the week" (199).

The same holds true for professors today, according to one long-time academic: "We are basically doing college work seven days a week. We're writing those [student] evaluations over Christmas and we're writing them in June. And I think the feeling is that if you team teach, it's less work, but actually if you team teach, it's as much work or more work." "Faculty work their asses off," a former professor agrees. "It's very labor intensive."

The participatory governance processes also contribute to faculty burnout: "Because everything is done in this very democratic way," a professor of economics explains, governance is "extremely time consuming. [And] you're constantly doing the same things over and over again because there's always new faculty, there's always new students. . . . One of my friends . . . who was here when I got here said that this [campus] was the circle of Dante in hell, reserved for those student radicals of the sixties and seventies who believed in democracy . . . because we have to do things over and over and over again" to ensure that all voices are heard. Governance, she sums up, "is just never ending, and we're all doing far too much of it."

Founding Faculty Retirements and Generational Differences

Third, there is concern among several long-time faculty and staff members at this college that the spirit and ideals of the original vision will diminish as the founding and veteran faculty retire. Speaking for his "generation" of academics, a professor of 24 years explains,

> One of the problems is that we're all getting older. . . . We haven't had very much turnover of [faculty] who came here early. And to some extent that means that there has been a consistency and a kind of retention of original values. And I think if we got more young people, there'd be more change, more change in the program [and] people who weren't committed to the initial principles and the whole Franklin Patterson idea.

A founding professor, likewise, remarks:

> The philosophical system we established is in danger due to pressure mostly from the faculty hired in the past 10 years who have much more traditional goals. We have to take into account society over the past 15 years, and they [these junior faculty] all grew up and graduated during [the] Reagan and Bush [years], and so they are, in fact, more conservative than I am, and I am not a radical, educationally.

The college, he says, maintains its uniqueness, however, and is gaining more recognition for its distinctiveness today than ever before, "and as long as I'm around, *I'm* going to be part of that uniqueness."

Issues Associated with an Absence of Tenure

Next, there are issues associated with the absence of tenure at Hampshire College. At most colleges and universities, a professor of 25 years points out, "faculty are granted tenure" and "you're kind of secure for the rest of your academic life. But, at Hampshire, there's always that [feeling of] uncertainty" because all faculty members are reevaluated over the course of their academic careers. "I've been here a very long time," he adds, "and I've been through that thorough-going review system three times, myself. The reappointment system is anxiety ridden "because you're constantly on review, you're never off the treadmill."

A founding administrator notes that "there have been modifications to the faculty contract system [e.g., 10-year contracts], which make it a little less threatening than it used to be." In the early years of the institution, she says that "the [faculty] contracts were for shorter periods and there was no guarantee that you could not be let go within five years of retirement age. Essentially, the college could keep you on through your 30s, 40s, and 50s, and then let you go. I don't know how much that [change] has affected things."

CONCLUSION: SUMMARY AND IMPLICATIONS

It is now nearly 30 years since the writing of *The Making of a College* and some four decades since *The New College Plan*. Experimental colleges have come and gone, but Hampshire College has lived on with its "signature" student-centered program well intact. The college has, for the most part, held to its foundational ideals of participatory governance and active learning. Although the campus has increasingly begun to emphasize scholarly research and publication, Hampshire College remains a teacher- and teaching-centered institution where free-spirited classes and faculty creativity are unleashed. Finally, there remains an unparalleled commitment to interdisciplinary modes and approaches to liberal arts education. Disciplinary departments do not exist at this institution, and faculty and students regularly delve into unknown fields or create new areas of inquiry.

In the words of one long-time administrator, the college "hasn't gone to the idea that we really need to do grades. We haven't gone to the idea that accumulation of courses is the way to go. . . . We've kept this progress by the exam system going all along. And so we're 25 years into it, and it's still working fine." Looking back on the life of the college and the recollections and voices of the founding faculty and pioneers, what are some of the teachings or lessons of this case study and story?

- The first lesson to be learned from the Hampshire College study is that traditional academic structures may inhibit innovations in teaching and learning. At Hampshire College, it is the very absence of a rigid hierarchical system of administrators, disciplinary departments, course credits, and grades that has enabled and empowered teachers and students to engage in multidisciplinary educational endeavors, co-teaching, and creative learning experiences.
- Second, this study underscores the importance of the core group of founding faculty members in sustaining the original distinctive visions of an innovative institution. At Hampshire College, the early dreams of the pioneers are cherished and modeled by the charter faculty and staff who continue to undertake imaginative approaches to teaching and work and pass along their "zeal" and creativity to the incoming generations of academics.
- Third, affiliation with other institutions appears to be vital to the success of an unorthodox institution. Hampshire College's connec-

tion with the four other Valley institutions has been the critical element in the college's survival. The Five College Consortium thrives because each campus has remained autonomous and self-governing.

- Fourth, to endure as an innovative institution in a changing social and economic climate, distinctive colleges should remain open to testing and trying out new ideas and unexplored areas of knowledge and inquiry. Innovating education is integral to the Hampshire College history. By incorporating new educational themes, the campus has carried forward its distinctive ethos into the present day.

- Fifth, innovative institutions are likely to come up against points of pressure or tension with regard to their unorthodox principles or philosophies. At Hampshire College, as at so many other innovative colleges from this era, there are the issues of attrition and faculty burnout, concerns about the forthcoming retirements of founding faculty, and issues associated with the absence of a tenure system. Still, nearly all individuals interviewed said that they could not picture themselves at any other institution. The real joy at Hampshire comes from living and learning in the midst of an imaginative community of creative scholars and students.

NOTES

1. In the words of one long-time faculty member, "the campus was as much a financial experiment as an educational experiment." The notion that the college could be tuition driven, however, proved to be unrealistic and unworkable, and was abandoned in the campus' first year (Birney 1993).

2. An "examination" at Hampshire is not a "test," like a midterm or final exam, but an independent research study or creative project that is proposed and carried out by the student under the supervision of a faculty member (1995-96 Catalog 1995). In Division I, there is a course-based examination option (the "two-course option") whereby students may fulfill divisional requirements, in part, by successfully completing two designated courses within a School. This option was adopted by the college in 1985 (Non Satis Non Scire 1995).

3. Although there are no course requirements at Hampshire College, the campus does require students to perform community service and to fulfill a Third World Expectation in Division II.

4. The interviews included one group interview with eight students who were enrolled in Hampshire's independent study class on alternative education.

5. One interviewee, who was not available to meet during the week of the campus visit, was interviewed by phone.

6. In the original plans for the college, the institution was going to train a group of "master teachers" who would go on to teach at other institutions of higher education. This never came to be.

7. In 1972, the School of Language and Communication (now the School of Cognitive Science and Cultural Studies) was added (Alpert 1980).

8. Although many interviewees singled out the commitment to innovation among the incoming academic cohorts at Hampshire College, a few long-time academics and administrators indicated that the more recent generations of faculty did not share the same spark or spirit of rebelliousness as the founders of the institution. (See the discussion of "Founding Faculty Retirements and Generational Differences" in the "Issues" section of this chapter.)

REFERENCES

Alpert, R.M. 1980. Professionalism and educational reform: The case of Hampshire College. *Journal of Higher Education* 51 (5): 497–518.

Astin, H.S., J.F. Milem, A.W. Astin, P. Ries, and T. Heath. 1991. *The courage and vision to experiment: Hampshire College, 1970–1990.* Los Angeles: Higher Education Research Institute, Graduate School of Education, University of California, Los Angeles.

Barber, C.L., S. Sheehan, S. Stoke, and S. McCune. 1958. *New college plan.* Amherst, Mass.: Committee for New College.

Birney, R.C. 1975. Employment by faculty contract. Amherst, Mass. Hampshire College Archives CG3.S8 #2. Johnson Library Center [In *A documentary history of Hampshire College: 1965-1975*, edited by S.A. Dayall, 1992, 104–5. Amherst, Mass.: The Trustees of Hampshire College].

———. 1993. Hampshire College. In *Important lessons from innovative colleges and universities*, edited by V.R. Cardozier, 9–22. *New Directions for Higher Education* no. 82 (summer).

Bloch, P., and N. Nylen. 1974. Hampshire College: New intents and old realities. *Change* (October): 38–42.

Educational Advisory Committee. Report of the Educational Advisory Committee to the President of Hampshire College, 13 April. 1966. Amherst, Mass. Hampshire College Archives CG3.S2 #1. Johnson Library Center [In *A documentary history of Hampshire College: 1965–1975*, edited by S.A. Dayall, 1992, 11–13. Amherst, Mass.: The Trustees of Hampshire College].

Frazier, N. 1977. Freedom and identity at Hampshire College. *Change* (November): 14–17.

Grant, G., and D. Riesman. 1978. *The perpetual dream: Reform and experiment in the American college.* Chicago: The University of Chicago Press.

Hampshire College 1970. 1970. Catalog. Amherst, Mass.: Hampshire College.

Hampshire: Freedom to demand more of yourself than any college could. 1994. Viewbook. Amherst, Mass.: Admissions Office, Hampshire College.

Holmquist, F.W., L. Nisonoff, and R.M. Rakoff. 1984. The labor process at Hampshire College. In *Against the current: Reform and experiment in higher education*, edited by R.M. Jones and B.L. Smith, 183–214. Cambridge, Mass.: Schenkman.

Longsworth, C.W. 1992. A brave new world: Hampshire College. In *Five colleges: Five histories*, edited by R. Story, 105–31. Amherst, Mass.: Five Colleges, Inc., and Historic Deerfield, Inc.

Meister, J.S. 1982. A sociologist looks at two schools—The Amherst and Hampshire experiences. *Change* (March): 26–34.

1995-96 Catalog and Course Guide. 1995. Amherst, Mass.: Hampshire College.

*Non satis non scire (*not to know is not enough) 1995-1996. Hampshire College* [Student] *Policy handbook*. 1995. Amherst, Mass.: Hampshire College.

Patterson, F., and C. Longsworth. 1966. *The making of a college*. Cambridge, Mass.: MIT Press.

President Patterson: "Your experience . . . not someone else . . . but you." 1970. *Hampshire College Section, Amherst Record* (30 September): 3; 7. Available through Hampshire College Archives, Johnson Library Center.

Stiles, R. 1965. *The planning and beginning of Hampshire College*. Amherst, Mass. Hampshire College Archives TR3.2.S2 #1. Johnson Library Center [In *A documentary history of Hampshire College: 1965–1975*, edited by S.A. Dayall, 1992, 29–30. Amherst, Mass.: The Trustees of Hampshire College].

Vance, B. 1970. Excitement pervaded the atmosphere. . . *Hampshire College Section, Amherst Record* (30 September): 3. Available through Hampshire College Archives, Johnson Library Center.

Weaver, F.S. 1989. Liberal education, inquiry, and academic organization. In *Promoting inquiry in undergraduate learning*, edited by F.S. Weaver, 3–16. *New Directions for Teaching and Learning* no. 38 (summer).

Woodhull, A.M. 1981. *Modes of inquiry: A report on Division I at Hampshire College*. Amherst, Mass. Hampshire College Archives CG.S2 #1. Johnson Library Center [In *A documentary history of Hampshire College Volume 2: 1975–1985*, edited by S.A. Dayall, 1995, 20–25. Amherst, Mass.: The Trustees of Hampshire College].

CHAPTER 5

The University of
Wisconsin-Green Bay
"Eco-U" in the 1990s

BACKGROUND: SETTING THE SCENE

Nestled against the shore of a long inlet of Lake Michigan, with the Fox River winding through its wooded hills, is the city of Green Bay, Wisconsin, a Midwestern community of nearly 200,000 residents that is known for its Green Bay Packers football team, its paper manufacturing plants, and its dairy industry. Green Bay is like a winter wonderland in November, at the time of this campus visit. The rooftops are quilted with snow, and snowmen are standing guard in the yards of the homes on the southeast shore of the bay. You drive through these snow-covered residential streets to reach the main entrance to the university, off of Nicolett Drive. There, overlooking the waters of the bay, on some 700 acres of gently rolling, wooded terrain, is the University of Wisconsin (UW)-Green Bay (or UWGB). The university is situated on the former grounds of the Shorewood Country Club— on the north edge of campus, there is a nine-hole working golf course that doubles as a cross-country skiing course in the winter (Switzer 1970; *Undergraduate Studies Catalog 1994-96* 1994).

There are 13 major academic and support buildings at UW-Green Bay, most of which are connected by a network of large underground tunnels (to ease the chill of the Wisconsin winters and, some say, to connect people from across the disciplines). The original architects and planners of the campus incorporated "people pockets" (small gathering spaces) into these connecting corridors, along with windows with views of garden scenery (where the tunnels rise above the ground) (Fischer 1971). The architects also took advantage of the natural beauty of the wooded campus environment. Along the periphery of the campus, there is an arboretum with streams, ponds, prairie land, and trails that are linked to the bay shore.

The Founding

The story of the University of Wisconsin-Green Bay begins in the 1960s, a decade of social, political, and educational change. These were good years for public higher education. There was a new mood of expansion and experimentation in the air as enrollments soared in colleges and universities, and state appropriations for public higher education reached unprecedented levels (Weidner 1994).

In the state of Wisconsin, enrollments at the University of Wisconsin-Madison had spiralled upward in the 1960s, and at some of the former Wisconsin State University campuses "enrollments incredibly went from around a thousand to around 10,000 by the end of the decade" (Weidner 1994, 23). To accommodate the waves of incoming students, to expand and strengthen the University of Wisconsin System (which, at that time, had only two undergraduate degree-granting institutions—Madison and Milwaukee), and to stimulate community growth and development, the University of Wisconsin System moved to establish two additional universities. On September 2, 1965, just nine months after taking office, Governor Warren Knowles signed into law a bill authorizing the establishment of two new campuses of the University of Wisconsin (one to serve the citizens of northeastern Wisconsin, and one to serve the residents of the southeastern area of the state) (Brown 1974; *Undergraduate Studies Catalog 1994-96* 1994; Weidner and Kuepper 1993).[1]

When citizens, business leaders, and local officials in Green Bay learned of the University of Wisconsin's interest in adding a new four-year institution in the northeastern area of Wisconsin, they organized a grassroots movement to try to persuade UW officials to establish the university in their hometown. Discussions and meetings were held with members of the State Coordinating Committee for Higher Education (CCHE) and with then-UW president Fred Harvey Harrington and other key officials to make the case for a new UW campus in Green Bay. Citizens of other nearby counties and cities (e.g., Appleton, DePere) also rallied to try to persuade the state to establish the university in their communities.

In early February of 1966, it was official. After years of fierce battles and heated controversies over the location of the new UW campus in northeastern Wisconsin,[2] the State Site Selection Committee "unanimously recommended the new 535-acre site north of [Highway] 54-57 five miles from downtown Green Bay—the Shorewood site—as 'by far the most aesthetically pleasing site proposed in the Northeast,' and predicted that a university built there could become 'one of the most attractive campuses in the nation'" (Brown 1974, 15). By June 13, 1966, state officials had approved initial plans and surveys for the new University of Wisconsin-Green Bay (Lane et al. 1968).[3]

Edward W. Weidner, director of the Center for Developmental Change at the University of Kentucky and former head of the political science department at Michigan State University, was appointed chancellor of the new university on October 7, 1966. In his remarks at a welcome reception, Dr. Weidner promised that the University of Wisconsin-Northeast (as it was then called)[4] "would be 'unique—not a copy of any other university'" (Brown 1974, 16). The initial academic plan that evolved over an intense 17-month period emphasized interdisciplinary learning, student-initiated education, and problem-focused "theme" colleges rather than traditional academic departments. The central organizing theme of the University of Wisconsin-Green Bay was to be the environment (in the broadest sense—physical, social, and aesthetic). In the early years, the campus was dubbed the "Environmental-U" or "Eco-U."[5]

On a harsh, cold, and windy day in November 1967, some 300 community members, faculty members, the founding chancellor of the new University of Wisconsin-Green Bay, legislators, and other representatives of UW-Green Bay and the UW System "gathered in the stubble of an alfalfa field to break ground for the first buildings" of the university (Brown 1974, 20). Two years later, on September 2, 1969, with the chancellor's office still located in a farmhouse, the vice chancellor's space in the former pro shop of the golf club, and several deans situated in a cottage along the bay, the university would come to life, welcoming its first class of 1,900 students to the Shorewood site (Weidner 1975). "The dream that some had cherished for a decade," historian Betty D. Brown writes, "had come true" (24).

The University of Wisconsin-Green Bay and the University of Wisconsin Today

Today UW-Green Bay is one of 13 public four-year institutions of higher education in the University of Wisconsin System. In 1974, the University of Wisconsin merged with the then-Wisconsin State University (WSU) System, incorporating the nine former public comprehensive universities in the state. Today there are 26 institutions in the University of Wisconsin System: 13 four-year UW campuses and 13 two-year campus centers. The center campuses offer first-year and second-year collegiate-level education that is transferable to the baccalaureate degree programs at all UW System institutions.

The University of Wisconsin-Green Bay currently enrolls 5,530 students (5,318 undergraduates and 212 graduate students). Of the 5,530 students, 3,499 (63 percent) are female and 2,031 (37 percent) are male; 1.6 percent of the students are Asian American, 0.9 percent are African American, 0.8 percent are Latino, 1.9 percent are Native American, and 94.8 percent are

European American or members of other ethnic groups. Twenty-two percent of UW-Green Bay undergraduates are over the age of 25, and 95 percent are Wisconsin residents (61 percent hail from either the local county or contiguous counties in northeastern Wisconsin; 77 percent are from counties in northeastern Wisconsin) (Office of Institutional Research 1997).

There are 524 administrators and staff members at the University of Wisconsin-Green Bay. The faculty is comprised of 159 full-time and 120 part-time academics. Thirty-two percent of the full-time faculty are female, 68 percent are male, and 9 percent are persons of color (Office of Institutional Research 1997).

The University of Wisconsin-Green Bay offers both interdisciplinary and disciplinary programs of study spanning four general areas: humanities and fine arts, natural sciences and mathematics, social sciences, and professional studies. Undergraduates may pursue majors in traditional disciplinary fields (e.g., English, biology, chemistry, economics, psychology) or interdisciplinary programs that apply knowledge from several academic disciplines (e.g., communication and the arts, humanistic studies, environmental science, human biology, environmental policy and planning, human development, social change and development). Students who major in a discipline must also complete a minor in an interdisciplinary program. Undergraduates must complete a minimum of 120 credits to receive the bachelor's degree, including general education requirements and major and/or minor program requirements.[6]

Along with the baccalaureate degree programs, the university offers an associate of arts degree and provides preprofessional training in fields as diverse as agriculture, architecture, and theology, to chiropractics, counseling, and mortuary science. The University of Wisconsin-Green Bay also awards master's degrees in administrative science and environmental science and policy that are interdisciplinary and problem focused. The institution offers four cooperative master's degrees (in the areas of education and business administration) in conjunction with UW-Oshkosh and UW-Milwaukee (*Undergraduate Studies Catalog 1994-96* 1994). (Graduate degrees were introduced at UW-Green Bay in the fall of 1974.)

ORGANIZATION OF THIS CHAPTER

This chapter examines the history and endurance of educational innovation at the University of Wisconsin-Green Bay. The case study begins with a demographic profile of the interview participants in this study, the current and past generations of the university community who shared their voices and memories of the campus. The next section draws upon the archival documents and the data gathered in the interviews to describe the early distinctive educational ideals of UW-Green Bay. The chapter then traces the evolution of these beginning ideals, focusing on where and how the university has kept alive its innovative philosophies and where and how the institution has changed or transformed itself. The next section examines key issues or challenges, pressures or tensions to innovation at UW-Green Bay. The case study concludes with a summary and a reflection on the UW-Green Bay story and its implications for reform and experimentation in American higher education.

INTERVIEW PARTICIPANT PROFILE

To explore the history and current status of innovation at the University of Wisconsin-Green Bay, 26 semi-structured interviews were conducted with 34 founding and/or current faculty members, administrators, and students in mid-November of 1995.[7] Each interview lasted about 50 minutes. The participants included 21 faculty members (13 of whom had been at the college for 25 years or more), 15 administrators (including the current chancellor, the founding chancellor, and the current and the former provost), three alumnae/i (two of whom graduated in the early 1970s), and four current students (the president and vice president of the student government association, and chair and vice chair of two student policy committees). (Some individuals occupied more than one role at the institution.) The interviewees included 25 men and nine women spanning several different "generations" of the UW-Green Bay community: Thirteen of the participants joined the university in its opening or preopening years (1966–1969), six started in years two to three (1970–1971), three arrived at UW-Green Bay in the university's fifth to seventh year (1973–1975), another three came to the institution in its 10th or 11th year (1978,1979), and nine joined the campus in its 16th year or later (1984–1995). Excluding the students and alumnae/i, the "tenure" for the interviewees at UW-Green Bay ranged from less than six months to 27 years, with an average length of stay of 21.4 years at the institution.

DISTINCTIVE EARLY IDEALS AT THE UNIVERSITY OF WISCONSIN-GREEN BAY

In the 1960s, innovation was in the air, marvels founding chancellor Edward W. Weidner (1994) in a recent retrospective on UW-Green Bay. Political protest, calls for "relevance" in the university, and criticisms of the impersonality of the large research university brought issues of social and educational change to the forefront of American higher education. All across the nation, new experimental programs and institutions were being founded to accommodate student demands for increased "relevance," interdisciplinary options, and learner-centered approaches in education. "The result of this positively charged atmosphere," Weidner writes, was an academic plan for the University of

Wisconsin-Green Bay "that was creatively different and notably idealistic" (38).

The planners and pioneers of UW-Green Bay believed that the university had an obligation to try out different ideas, concepts, and patterns that the established University of Wisconsin (at Madison) would not be able to embrace. "The new University [in Green Bay] was to be experimental and innovational in spirit," Weidner (1973) explains in an unpublished paper on the origins of the institution (20). "Appointed on 7 October [1966]," he relates, "I already had a number of ideas of what was wrong with higher education, and a determination to see if UWGB could not become an institution that would move in a new direction" (20).

What kind of new direction would the university take? Based on Weidner's various writings about the founding years and early academic plans of UW-Green Bay, along with the interview data and archival analyses, there appear to be five distinctive educational characteristics that formed the heart of the mission of the new university. First, the campus would break away from traditional disciplinary structures—interdisciplinary concentrations would replace conventional academic departments; teaching and learning would be centered around multidisciplinary perspectives and orientations. Second, experiential learning and outreach to the community would be integral to the early educational programs of UW-Green Bay. Third, there would be a strong emphasis on student-initiated education or students actively shaping or taking charge of their own learning processes. Fourth, there would be a tremendous amount of freedom and creativity for faculty, and undergraduate teaching would be the academic's primary activity. Fifth, the campus would foster close-knit relationships between professors and students in a caring, egalitarian community. These five themes (interdisciplinarity; experiential learning; student-initiated education; faculty freedom and undergraduate teaching; and close-knit, egalitarian community) would form the heart of the early innovative vision for the University of Wisconsin-Green Bay. Each theme is discussed in greater detail in the following sections.

Interdisciplinary Education: "The Land of Lost Christmas Toys"

First, interdisciplinary education was a hallmark of the new university. "Interdisciplinarity became the bedrock of the academic plan early on," writes Weidner in a 1993 article with former vice chancellor William G. Kuepper. "Professors at Green Bay were advised by their counterparts at Madison to emphasize interdisciplinarity, which was difficult or impossible to achieve on the Madison campus" (25). One faculty pioneer who was interviewed in this study explains:

The tendency in education, which was very strong in the sixties, . . . was a tendency toward increasing specialization and narrowness of programs, of faculty, of students, [and there] was a great deal of discontent about that! So, one general aspiration [of UW-Green Bay] was to provide an educational experience that had some breadth, that gave students the opportunity to discover how much linkage there is among different fields of knowledge.

The university planners broke away from the "sacrosanct" structure of the academic department. "The most ingenious defiance of The System is the way Green Bay is organized," wrote *Harper's Magazine* editor John Fischer in a 1971 report on UW-Green Bay. "It [the university] has no departments of the conventional kind, controlling budgets, hiring, promotions, and courses of study" (22). Instead, interdisciplinary departments (called "concentrations" or "units") would be the "central organizing mechanisms" at early UW-Green Bay, with authority over academic budgets, curriculum, and faculty appointments and promotions. (Initially, the problem-focused theme colleges at UW-Green Bay—environmental sciences, community sciences, human biology, and creative communication—were to be the central organizing structures at the university. Soon, it became clear that the interdisciplinary departments, rather than the theme colleges, should take center stage—i.e., have authority over academic budgets, appointments, and curricular policy) (Weidner and Kuepper 1993). "Literally revolutionizing—turning upside down—the usual institutional arrangement by which disciplinary departments support (or, more often, fail to support) interdisciplinary programs," professor Sydney H. Bremer remarks in a 1994 address to the Association of American Colleges, UWGB put the interdisciplines in control" (Rice and Bremer 1994, 12).

In all cases, Weidner and Kuepper (1993) report, the "disciplines were to be subordinate and supportive" (26). Students would major in an interdisciplinary concentration, although they could "co-major" in a disciplinary field. Instead of conventional general education requirements, University of Wisconsin-Green Bay would offer a series of interdisciplinary, problem-focused Liberal Education Seminars (LES) that integrated the issues and ideas of various academic fields. In the words of one founding high-ranking administrator, "We originally eliminated distribution requirements as general education. And the reason was, of course, that if you had a distribution requirement, all [that] the students would do, is take a beginning course in a discipline in various areas, and they'd be trapped into a major in the disciplines. So, we had an interdisciplinary general education program" in mind from the very beginning.

Even the names of the interdisciplinary concentrations were new (Rice and Bremer 1994). In the early campus catalogs and communications, you come across programs with such creative and unusual titles as Communication-

Action, Ecosystems Analysis, Human Adaptability, and Analysis Synthesis (a program that was unofficially called "Anal Syn").

Cross-disciplinary teaching was also a fixture of the new university. A charter faculty member, now a dean, recalls that "in the early years, . . . there was a considerable amount of team teaching. . . . [T]here was a lot of cross-fertilization, a lot of sharing and so on." The "professor whose formal training had been in biology," Weidner (1977) observes, "might be working side by side with a colleague trained in sociology, and a mathematician might find himself laboring beside a music professor. The possibilities were nearly limitless, and experimentation in many combinations was to be encouraged" (67–68).

Even the architectural design of the university reflected the interdisciplinary mission and spirit of the place. Campus buildings were connected inside at the lower level and outside at the upper level to encourage a mixing of students and faculty from the different concentrations and disciplines. "Building interconnections and patterns of layout," Weidner wrote in 1977, "help prevent the kind of isolation that exists in a more traditional setting, where a chemistry building, for example, is an independent structure and becomes, in effect, the property of the chemists. . . . The chemists or members of other disciplines at Green Bay have no similar kind of isolated facility" (78). "We started out with the theory that the faculty should be scattered," relates a founding administrator, "and [that] the classrooms should be scattered so that students would be taking classes in all sorts of buildings, walking through the hallways. It was just one pavilion of learning if you wish."

It was this early ambiance and newfound sense of freedom and interdisciplinary expression that drew many of the original and dreamy academics to the university. In the words of Professor Bremer, the first faculty members "came [to UW-Green Bay] eager to try something new, many of us uncomfortable in the usual disciplinary boxes and happy to find our way to what one of my colleagues called 'the land of lost Christmas toys. . . .' We embraced a university where we felt, as academic outsiders together, we could belong" (Rice and Bremer 1994, 9–10).

Experiential Learning and Outreach to the Community

Second, the early visionaries of the University of Wisconsin-Green Bay embraced the ideas of experiential learning and outreach to the community. "Experiential education was [an] underlying principle of the UWGB Academic Plan from the very beginning," reveals Weidner (1973). The campus adopted a 4-1-4 academic calendar with a January interim to encourage students to undertake off-campus work, practica, or VISTA or Peace Corps experiences. The Liberal Education Seminars also involved students in real-world problems and environmental issues or themes. In the sophomore seminar, for example, the student would undertake an off-campus, supervised project in northeastern Wisconsin. He or she might work in a local paper mill, a day care center, or poverty program (Fischer 1971). In the junior seminar, the student would venture into another culture in the United States or abroad to study the same problem or topic in a different sociocultural context (*The University of Wisconsin Green Bay Catalog* 1969). He or she might spend several months on a campus in another part of the country, on an Indian reservation, or traveling through Europe or Latin America with a small group of faculty and students. "The purpose, in both years," Fischer explains, was "to make sure that [students'] academic work [was] intimately related to the outside world" (27).

The idea of community service was hailed by the planners of UW-Green Bay. According to Weidner (1973), they were all very much aware of the university's regional obligations to serve the residents of the Northern Great Lakes region. The planners believed that the outside world was the university's great laboratory, an arena for exploration, outreach, and discovery. "It was a true communiversity approach," notes Weidner (1973). In his remarks at an informal meeting of the founding faculty, Weidner (1969) proclaimed:

> The community and the university must be related to one another. If we are going to have a relevant curriculum, then we cannot ignore the community. Some people think they can save the world by ignoring the world. . . . We must bring the community to the campus and the campus to the community, not just through extension, but in all of our activities including classroom teaching, research, and curriculum building. (1)

Individualism: "Student-Initiative" Education

A third feature lay at the heart of the early distinctive vision for UW-Green Bay: an emphasis on student-initiated education or students taking charge of their own educational lives. A founding professor recalls that one of the "big themes" of the university early on "was the idea that we could have an educational institution that respected students and involved them more actively in their own education." Students were expected to be "full participants in their education, not mere passive occupants of classroom chairs," according to the authors of the 1968 *Comprehensive Development Plan* for UW-Green Bay (Lane et al. 1968, 5). "Detailed requirements were to be few," Weidner (1994) indicates, "checklists of courses to be completed for a particular major were to be discouraged or non-existent. Students were to work within broad guidelines and with an advisor to develop their own educational contracts for a degree" (37).

We called this "student-initiative education," a founding father remembers. "The nature of our majors—especially initially—was such that students were given an opportunity to develop their own majors if they wanted to. . . . We prohibited any mimeographed list of requirements for a degree. Each student was to develop his or her own [academic program]. . . . There aren't many universities where that would [have] be[en] possible." "We had all sorts of crazy ideas!" an emeritus professor of humanistic studies agrees. There were these "student-generated courses—students could make up their own courses— and . . . independent studies."

A veteran professor of sociology and current administrator explains: "It was a very radical academic plan. This was the era of relevance, and [so] students had a lot of control over putting together their academic plan." And from this 1974 graduate: "We were an innovative campus, [and] people had very, very strong opinions about . . . Vietnam [and] individual rights. . . . [T]hat 'do your own thing' philosophy . . . was alive and well [at Green Bay]."

Undergraduate Teaching and Faculty Freedom: "Feasts of Blood and Gore" and "Tales of Derring-Do"

Fourth, undergraduate teaching thrived at early UW-Green Bay, and faculty were granted a tremendous amount of freedom to create their own courses and curricular themes. One dynamic faculty pioneer recalls that in the early days, "We had seven courses to teach [during the year]." And "no repeats! . . . Most of us didn't like that, but, hey! It was innovation. It was initiative. We made up our courses! . . . Most of us taught three different courses . . . each semester, plus we had a January interim." The January interim, he says, became an arena for curricular experimentation and creativity for the early academics at Green Bay: "I loved it! I made up two courses [for the January term], one called Feasts of Blood and Gore, a study of gothic fiction. Then Tales of Derring-Do. It was a come-on for the students and I had 108, 110 students in a four-week intensive [course]."

Teaching was an obsession in those days, according to a professor who was hired in the late 1970s: "I came here and I was really impressed by the fact that there was this *really* strong emphasis on teaching. . . . It was *very*, *very* unusual. It wasn't just that people were supposed to be teaching a lot, which is charac- teristic of a second tier state university. It's that people were *constantly*, *constantly* reflecting on teaching. It was an *obsession*."

A Close-Knit, Egalitarian Community

Fifth, the campus was designed to offer a more personalized approach to higher education, to nourish close and lasting ties between faculty and students. As Chancellor Weidner remarked to the first UW-Green Bay faculty at a 1969 breakfast meeting,

> If we are going to be a relevant university, we must give up the comfort- able old idea that professors meet their classes and post office hours (two

or three hours a week) and then hide the rest of the week. . . . We are at a time when we have to be available, all of us. . . . If a month goes past and you have not had *any students to your home*, then there is something wrong in your approach to students. And if a week goes past and you have not had *coffee* with some students, if you have not got lost in some of our new *people pockets* with some students, then there is something wrong. . . . To meet the demands of the 1970's, we must be with students outside the classroom just as much as inside the classroom. (Weidner 1969, 6)

One of the predominant concerns of higher education in the late 1960s, Weidner (1973) explains, was the relationship between professor and student. Faculty-student relations, especially at the larger college or university, were increasingly distant and impersonal. The University of Wisconsin-Green Bay wanted to bring the student and the faculty member into closer contact and to nourish individualized learning and student-centered teaching. "Ideally," Weidner (1977) relates, the thought was that "professor and student would work as co-learners, with the professor acting as group leader rather than as the traditional authority" (67). In sum, Weidner writes, "the context of the problem-based departments was to be egalitarian rather than elitist" (67).

In some cases, early professors and students engaged in a close-knit, intensive family-like living and learning community. One faculty founder looks back nostalgically:

The *glory* of the place [back then] was there was a kind of looseness and a sense of excitement and continually trying new things. . . . Dave [Galaty] and I and a couple of other faculty members started the Experimental Learning Community [at UW-Green Bay] back in the seventies. . . . We had 60 students the first year . . . and all of their course work [took place in the basement of one of the student apartments on campus]. We had four faculty members and it was a community . . ., an innovative opportunity to learn in small groups . . . and we were very much into consensus. . . . [It was] incredibly exhilarating. . . . I remember sunny afternoons in which the whole group would chip in and we would go out and buy half gallons of ice cream of every imaginable flavor and everybody would be sitting around in a circle out on the grass holding a spoon and these half gallon containers would just pass around—chocolate chip, tutti-frutti—and just enjoying the sunshine and eating ice cream with 60 students that you knew better than your own kids!

ENDURANCE AND TRANSFORMATION OF THE DISTINCTIVE EARLY IDEALS AT THE UNIVERSITY OF WISCONSIN-GREEN BAY

And what of the campus today? Are Green Bay faculty and students still engaging in collaborative, interdisciplinary education? Is student-centered, experiential learning and faculty freedom still a hallmark of the university? What about the early close-knit community spirit? Are students and professors still forming familial-like bonds and sharing ice cream on sunny days? While long-time faculty and administrators admit that much of the original, distinctive vision for the campus has faded (gone, for example, are the theme colleges, gone is the unusual nomenclature, and gone is the environmental, Eco-U focus), UW-Green Bay continues, at least in part, to honor its roots of experimentation. This section draws upon the voices of the interviewees, the archival materials, and campus histories to examine the endurance and transformation of innovation at UW-Green Bay in each of the five theme areas (interdisciplinarity; experiential learning; student-initiative education; faculty freedom and undergraduate teaching; and close-knit, egalitarian community). It then explores the longevity or "survival" of the institution and presents a summary of the key reasons for the preservation and/or transformation of the distinctive founding themes.

Interdisciplinary Education

First, interdisciplinarity is a longstanding feature of the University of Wisconsin-Green Bay. The interdisciplinary departments remain the central organizing units of the university, with authority over academic budgets, faculty appointments, and curriculum. "Despite all threats of retrenchment," a longtime professor of anthropology proclaims, "budgets have stayed put in the interdisciplinary units. Those are the units that hire, that review and tenure people. And that's where curricula comes from." If the disciplines ever become budgetary units, a long-time professor of social change and development warns, "you can kiss the [interdisciplinary] mission goodbye." He is reminded of some advice that he received from former chancellor Edward Weidner: "The first chancellor, Edward Weidner, told me as he was retiring that the *fundamental* thing if you want to hold onto the original mission [of this institution is that] it . . . matters . . . where the budgets go. And right now it remains the case that budgetary units are interdisciplinary units. They are not disciplines."

And so today, as in the beginning, artists and historians are still teaming up to make decisions. Theater and philosophy professors are sitting side by side in interdisciplinary faculty meetings. "If I were in a traditional psychology department," a professor of psychology marvels, "most of the colleagues that I would interact with would be psychologists, and the big distinction would be whether they were clinical or experimental psychologists. But, here, you're as likely to be interacting on a daily basis with a biologist, an artist, an actor, as you are with other psychologists."

Even the hallways and office areas remain interdisciplinary. Although "we do tend to sort ourselves into the more traditional academic clusters," Bremer reports (Rice and Bremer 1994), faculty from different disciplines still share conference rooms and office space. Bremer, for example, who is an English professor, is "'officed' between colleagues in theater and history, with faculty in Native American studies, mass communications, psychology, Spanish, French, German, and philosophy also along the same hallway" (8). This unique physical arrangement helps to sustain the founding spirit of cross-disciplinary teaching and collaboration at UW-Green Bay.

Most interviewees believe that if the university ever tried to abolish the interdisciplinary academic organization, the faculty (especially the veterans and founders) would resist it. Just "try to suggest that we change in some way," a top-level administrator proposes, "that we eliminate the interdisciplinary focus; we go with straight discipline focuses, and look at the reaction that you would get! It would be like trying to strip somebody's identity away from them. The faculty and staff would resist that incredibly. [Interdisciplinarity is] part of the culture [of the campus] and it's part of the individual's identity." A professor of 25 years agrees: "Part of the reason that [interdisciplinarity has] been maintained is because of the desire on the part of those faculty to preserve what it is they spent a good part of their lives building. . . . I truly think that that's one reason why some of [the interdisciplinary, distinctive structure] has been maintained. . . . Those faculty stayed and didn't leave."

The students, too, continue to value and support the "interdisciplines." Although the university introduced disciplinary majors in 1984, and all students must at least minor in an interdisciplinary field, more than half of all undergraduates today still choose to pursue an interdisciplinary major. In 1995-96, for example, of the 875 majors of graduating seniors at UW-Green Bay, 345 or 39 percent were completed in a disciplinary area, while 530 or 61 percent were completed in an interdisciplinary field. The trend has been steady. In 1990-91 and again in 1991-92, the figures were 41 percent and 59 percent, respectively; in 1992-93, 39 percent and 61 percent; in 1993-94, 42 percent and 58 percent; and in 1994-95, 40 percent and 60 percent (Office of Institutional Research 1997).[8]

While interdisciplinarity is a longstanding and cherished tradition at UW-Green Bay, according to interviewees, not all academic units or personnel are as fully immersed in interdisciplinary approaches as the pioneering faculty and staff of the early days. In the beginning, a professor of social change and development recalls, the *entire* university was dedicated to interdisciplinary approaches. "When I got here," he says, "there was a real strong sort of intellectual, ideological commitment to the idea of interdisciplinarity and problem-focused education." Today, a faculty veteran who teaches in communication and the arts agrees, "you're pointing to pockets and particular programs [at UW-Green Bay] and particular courses [that are interdisciplinary] rather than to the length and breadth of the institution." "If I look around the campus," he continues, "and ask, 'Where are genuine interdisciplinary programs in place, strongly supported, and so on?' you would see an uneven landscape. We've been forced to make some compromises."

Perhaps the most significant compromise that the institution has made has been the introduction of disciplinary majors. Enrollment bottomed out in the late 1970s, a charter professor and former high-ranking administrator explains. Back in the "dark days" of the 1970s, he recalls, "it was hard to recruit students." Prospective students—mostly first-generation college students from the surrounding region—"would look at these [interdisciplinary] degrees [in] Humanistic Studies, Urban Analysis/Regional Analysis, . . . Communication in the Arts," and say, "'I'm really looking for a degree in music.' Or 'I'm really looking for a degree in sociology. You don't have that major at UW-Green Bay.'" "In the seventies, we tried to maintain what we had been doing," he explains, "we tried to hang onto that global academic plan that had been built early on and we were just failing."

"We were having terrible enrollment problems" in the middle to late 1970s, an academic dean and long-time professor relates:

> Every year, we would not hit our target enrollment goals because the students who were coming to this university [were] first-generation college students. They wanted to major in business or they wanted to major in geology or . . . economics. What is Analysis-Synthesis to them? . . . What was Communication in the Arts to someone who wanted to major in music? So, how do we get around that? Very simple. . . . Ultimately, near the early eighties, . . . students were allowed to major in disciplines. They were still required to minor in interdisciplinary units, and that's true to this day.

According to data provided by the Office of Institutional Research (1997), in the five-year period between 1975 and 1980, fall semester enrollments at the University of Wisconsin-Green Bay did not rise above 3,900. In the 1980s (and during the era that disciplinary majors were introduced at the university), enrollments at the institution steadily increased (from 4,164 in 1980 to 4,906 in 1984 to 5,221 in 1988). Since the late 1980s, enrollments at the institution have been more volatile but have generally been on the upswing (see figure 2).

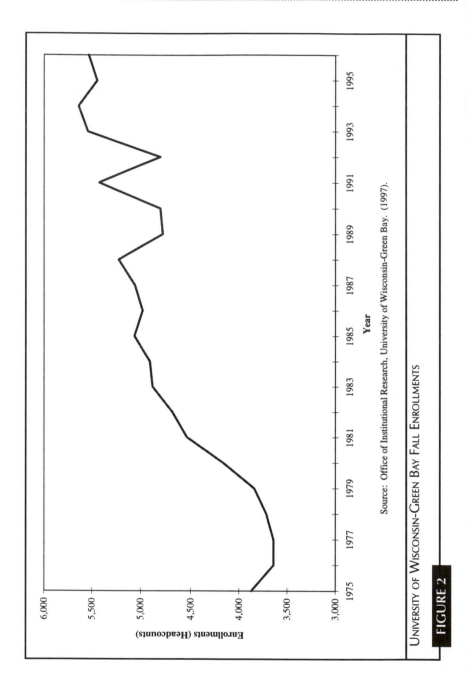

Source: Office of Institutional Research, University of Wisconsin-Green Bay. (1997).

UNIVERSITY OF WISCONSIN-GREEN BAY FALL ENROLLMENTS

FIGURE 2

The interdisciplinary educational mission of early UW-Green Bay was also jeopardized by the merger of the University of Wisconsin and Wisconsin State University in 1974. "As I reflect on our history," a charter academic and former administrator remarks, "one of the reasons that we were not able to protect everything was because of the dramatic change that took place in Wisconsin higher education in the seventies with merger." Prior to the merger, he says, there was a "strong sentiment that . . . innovation was necessary" and that "Green Bay should be sort of the innovating, cutting edge institution [of the University of Wisconsin]." In its opening years, UW-Green Bay was granted preferential funding based, in part, on its distinctive interdisciplinary features. All of that changed, he says, with the departure of the president of the UW System (Fred Harvey Harrington) who "supported us back in the early days [and with] the subsequent merger of the Wisconsin systems. . . . Just about the time when we were getting going, the earth shifted under our feet rather dramatically. It became clear that if we just kept plowing ahead . . ., then we were going to be in desperate straits."

During the merger, budget cuts were instituted at all of the former UW System institutions in order to bring the costs of the UW campuses closer to those of the old Wisconsin State University institutions (Weidner and Kuepper 1993). Soon, UW-Green Bay lost its preferential funding as the interdisciplinary, environmental campus of the University of Wisconsin. As Bremer in 1994 explains, "That merger, in the mid-70s, just a few years after UWGB opened, set in motion forces toward centralization, bureaucratic regularization, and even curricular homogenization" (Rice and Bremer 1994, 11). "Merger [was] probably the biggest external disaster to strike this place," a professor of communication and the arts relates: "We were thrown into political competition with all of the other state university campuses who had already established consistencies." The institution, veteran faculty and administrators agree, had to change.

Along with the merger of the Wisconsin higher education systems, some long-time faculty indicate that UW-Green Bay's interdisciplinary character was compromised by the hiring of academics over the years with a more narrow or specialized disciplinary orientation. A founding faculty member states:

> One mistake that's happened here is that as the disciplines started to become majors, some units started to hire people pretty narrowly. . . . They started to think too narrowly—you know, "We need this kind of organic chemist," or "We need a demographer that can do this little thing over here," rather than "We need an organic chemist that can talk to a demographer. . . ." [P]art of the younger generation of faculty here has been hired too narrowly and I think that's a danger for the place.

"When I applied [for this position in the late 1970s]," a professor of social change and development relates, "the job was advertised as political economy. They would take an historian, a sociologist, or an economist. . . . Now, when we post a position, the deans are insistent . . . that we indicate a single discipline in most instances."

The early interdisciplinary team-teaching emphasis, according to interviewees, has also faded. "There's very little team teaching that goes on now," says one charter professor and current academic dean. A founding faculty member in biology observes: "We do less [team teaching] now perhaps than we used to. . . . Budget has not allowed us to continue that kind of [activity]."

In the end, despite some feelings of loss and betrayal over the modifications in the early interdisciplinary vision, most of the faculty and staff interviewed still value the interdisciplinary opportunities that do exist at this institution. It is the interdisciplinary academic organization (the budgeted interdisciplinary units), they marvel, still in place after 26 years, that keeps this university vital and different.

Experiential Learning and Outreach to the Community

Second, over the years, the campus has witnessed the loss of the experiential education component of the early university. Gone is the 4-1-4 calendar and the January interim. Gone are the experiential Liberal Education Seminars where students would venture out into the Northern Great Lakes region or journey across the world to study environmental problems or themes. The senior seminar—the only surviving element of LES—has recently been eliminated.[9]

What brought about the demise of the Liberal Education Seminars and the creative January interim period? "The goal of having significant numbers of students engaged in off-campus projects," Weidner and Kuepper (1993) report, "was the first component of the Liberal Education Seminars to be seriously compromised. Costs were high, and student enthusiasm was mixed" (30). A founding high-ranking official admits: "It [the Liberal Education Seminar] was a good idea and we gave it a good try, but . . . part of the program kind of fell apart because people couldn't afford to go overseas. . . . It was too dreamy. Neat idea, but just didn't work." Most of the students at UW-Green Bay were (and still are) working their way through college, and could not afford to travel abroad.

"The January interim," too, "was regarded as a pearl of great price," according to a charter faculty member and former dean. He says:

> The students couldn't afford in many instances to take advantage of
> the January interim. If you look around the country, you'll discover

very quickly that schools that have January interim programs that are well subscribed are residential colleges, usually with a population that isn't obliged to work part-time in order to stay in school. . . . Seventy percent of the students who graduate from [UW-Green Bay] graduate with significant debt. . . . People who are working part-time and are in debt do not go meandering off on January interim programs.

"The January concept was an excellent one," an administrator in public relations agrees, but "watching the enrollment numbers every year, . . . January would go up to 1,000, 1,500 students and we had 3,000, 4,000 [students enrolled] and it would slide back down. It was always a low percentage of the students [taking part]." Sometimes, she says, the campus would lose contact with students following that long interim period:

I'd see the students who worked in my office or who I knew. . . . They'd be here [on campus] through December and I wouldn't see them again until mid-February. Occasionally, I'd run into [them] downtown and say, "I haven't seen you." [They'd say,] "Well, I got a job [and] it's really paying well," "My boyfriend and I decided to get married," or "I went to Appleton for a job . . . and it's too far to commute." Now, would those students have stayed if they had come back in [before mid-February]? A lot happens in a young person's life in that time frame and our calendar never caught them and kept them in. . . . Because we have a high percentage of working students, they seemed to [use that time] to really [save] some money for second semester.

While the campus no longer engages all students in intensive kinds of experiential learning programs, applied or problem-focused education is still a central mission of UW-Green Bay, and community outreach remains first and foremost in the minds of the university leadership. With the recent addition of a performing arts center that attracts citizens from across the state, and a Division I athletic program, the university has revitalized the concept of "communiversity" by strengthening ties between campus and community.

Individualism: "Student-Initiative" Education

When it comes to the early, free-spirited individualized programs and student-designed majors at UW-Green Bay, here, again, the times and the academic procedures have changed. Although students can still come to the university and customize their learning experience through independent study and a personalized degree, according to interviewees, the curricular pathways are not as flexible as they used to be. "Things have tightened up quite a bit since I was a student here," an early alumnus and current professor explains. He recalls:

When I was a student, you could almost literally take any set of courses that you wanted and graduate. [The] personalized major [at UW-

Green Bay] was really loosely defined in the late sixties and early seventies. . . . You could design your own program. It could be almost anything. . . . It was to the point where I don't think any two students ever took the same set of courses to satisfy their general education requirement. That's tightened up quite a bit. . . . Students are getting a lot less flexibility now in terms of the courses.

Why the tightening up? It was a matter of efficiency in a time of budgetary cutbacks, according to this alumnus and professor. "For the last number of years," he says, "we've undergone budget reductions and we just can't afford to offer the same [range] of courses that were offered in the mid-seventies. [Institutions] have to make some decisions on how [they are] going to be more efficient in terms of delivering curriculum and I think that's one way that it has happened."

The early individualized curriculum was also to become more and more of a burden on the UW-Green Bay faculty—there were increasing demands on faculty time as enrollments grew and no additional faculty were hired. A founding professor recalls:

Some [faculty] actually took on independent study courses on top of doing seven courses [a year]. Well, you can't keep doing that or you've gotta be very young and energetic and you've gotta have a different reward system than the one that we have. . . . [W]e still are responsible for seven courses [per year] although there's no January term to take up that slack for the one course.

And from this early alumna:

[In the 1970s,] you would say [to a professor], "This is the kind of thing I would like to study and these are my objectives and this is what I intend to do." That still exists to some extent, but as more demands were placed [on faculty], and as the graduate program opened and . . . additional faculty [were not hired], there . . . wasn't as much of an opportunity to . . . do independent study. . . . [The student-designed course and independent project] still happens [here], but not to the extent that it used to—because of the greater number of students and diminishing number of faculty.

In a recent article in the *Times Higher Education Supplement*, UW-Green Bay professor Harvey J. Kaye (1995) reports: "In my first year here [1978] there were 150 faculty for 2,500 students; today, the same number of faculty are responsible for 4,500 students" (14). According to the Office of Institutional Research (1997), since 1985, the student-to-faculty ratio at the university has remained at about 22 to 1—a significant increase over the 15 or 16 to 1 student-to-faculty ratios of the earlier years.[10]

At the same time, the student generations have changed. "Initially, it was almost required [that students design their own academic programs]," a founding father remembers, "because this is what students 'around the country wanted.' There are now checklists of requirements to graduate in X, Y, or Z," he explains. "You have to file a program with the registrar, [but] that program can be very individualistic. . . . And there are students that do that [today], but it isn't done nearly so frequently as previously. . . . I think the students at this university still have as many choices as at any other university in the country—if they want to exercise them." Indeed, there are still those students who follow their own pathways very much in keeping with the spirit of the opening days: A recent alumnus, who completed nearly 30 credits of his course work in internships and independent study, says: "You have the ability to write your own major [at UW-Green Bay], the ability to write your own courses, [to] do independent studies where you actually design the course work, you identify the material, you pick the textbooks, you write the syllabus, you go before a faculty advisor and he or she says 'EEEEHHHH' and you change it." It is just up to you.

Undergraduate Teaching and Faculty Freedom

Next, are the faculty still engaging in creative and experimental curricular approaches in undergraduate teaching? With the loss of the January term, some interviewees believe that the early spirit of creativity in teaching has faded.

It is a different period in the history of the institution, veteran faculty explain. The freewheeling founding era is over. We are no longer at an institution where there is a blank slate, says one academic pioneer. When UW-Green Bay opened, he remarks, "we had a few senior faculty, but mostly the place was run by us young Turks. Part of the excitement was that there was very little in place, so we could do it all, pretty much!" Faculty could invent course after course, and experiment with unusual methods and processes of teaching. While the institution remains committed to teaching and faculty freedom— "It's pretty easy to devise courses here and get them into the catalog," says a founding father—increasing enrollments and faculty workloads have constrained innovative teaching.

At the same time, an emeritus professor relates, the faculty reward system has been "conventionalized" such that creativity in teaching is no longer valued above publishing and research:

> In the early period, some [faculty] would concentrate on teaching, which is really what I was interested in. . . . [W]e had . . . a very free and loose way of looking at criteria for promotion, but that became conventionalized. . . . All that looseness, all that marvelous creative

disorder and chaos—we had to organize that. You have the people who came in and said, "This [set of creative teaching experiences] is just too wishy washy."

These days, he says, "you get promoted by publishing books or articles." Yet, still, he "loves" to invent classes and seminars, adding "I'm the last of an old breed":

I've devised more than 30 courses over the years. Then I [have] devised techniques, which you could not possibly do [at another institution]—I created a religious studies program, I created a course in the classical worlds of Greece and Rome . . . and I would never have been able to do that at another university. So, that was a marvelous opportunity for me. That's been preserved.

A Close-Knit, Egalitarian Community

Finally, as student-to-faculty ratios have increased, the early close-knit community spirit of UW-Green Bay has diminished. With heavier time constraints on the faculty and increasing enrollments, it has become more and more difficult, interviewees say, for faculty to meet with their students and to develop close and personal relationships with undergraduates. "When we were a smaller department years ago," says a long-time professor of human development, "we had closer relations with students and we did more things together with students collectively [such as] picnics and volleyball games. We just don't have the time for that sort of thing anymore. A lot of us had closer relationships with students who remained lifelong friends from those earlier years. It's a different setup now because it is a much larger number of students and we [faculty] have much more complicated obligations—committee work, etc." "Those were the days," a founding faculty father in the humanities recalls. We had experimental learning communities with students, "but that doesn't happen anymore." The faculty-student ratio is "completely out of line," a long-time professor explains:

When I got here, my introductory level courses were probably 75 students. . . . My introductory courses five years ago were 200. . . . Now, you tell me how I'm gonna deal with 200 students effectively. . . . It just doesn't work. I have no time to see students. I used to require my students to visit me at least once in a semester so I knew who they were. I wouldn't dare invite them in now. There's just no time in the day.

The Survival of the University of Wisconsin-Green Bay as an Innovative Institution

Two and a half decades later, and the University of Wisconsin-Green Bay carries on. Given the shifts in the national economy, the merger of the Wisconsin state university systems, and budgetary cutbacks in Wisconsin higher education (in the 1970s and today), it is remarkable that UW-Green Bay has remained open and sustained at least some elements of its early innovative visions. Taking a different turn on the topic, interviewees were asked to comment on UW-Green Bay's longevity—i.e., to share, if they could, some of the reasons why this historically distinctive university—unlike so many of the alternative colleges and universities of the 1960s and 1970s—has survived.

Adaptability and Change

First, the institution has remained flexible and adaptable to change. Over the years, a founding professor and former top-ranking administrator explains, "We've had to make some tough decisions" to eliminate some programs, to add conventional degrees. It was a very painful process, he says, to watch some of those early programs fade away, but had we not sacrificed some of the early dreams, I am not certain that there would still be a UW-Green Bay.

A long-time professor and academic dean puts it this way:

> My view is that had [UW-Green Bay] not changed in the mid-eighties to allowing outright majors and disciplines . . ., that we would not be surviving very well. There are just too many students that come out of high school that want a major in biology or psychology or one of the traditional disciplines. . . . [I]f all [this campus] had were co-majors [in disciplinary fields], I don't think [students would want to come] here. They'd go somewhere else.

The very reason that the campus has survived, she says, is because it *did* change: "I think if [the university] would have kept its head in the sand and kept some of the more arcane language and not created disciplinary majors, ...it would be in deep trouble."

Community Support

Second, good community relations and public support have been key to the survival of UW-Green Bay. While early on there were tensions between the environmental, "Eco-U" campus and the local conservative, paper manufacturing community, with the changes in the academic program and with the addition of Division I athletics and a regional performing arts center, the campus has gained the respect of the local citizenry. Green Bay residents today take pride in their local university and want their sons and daughters to attend

UW-Green Bay. They fill the stands during basketball season and root for their home team.

"Some of our survival had nothing to do with academics," an administrator in public relations points out. "Some of our survival has been related to a divisional basketball program that excited the local community." She explains:

> This is an NFL town [with the Green Bay Packers]; it's very sports-minded. After football season, there's this gap of things you can do unless you ice fish or ski and you can only ski so much! . . . People on the street see my UWGB sticker on the window [of my car] and they'll talk about basketball; that's our common ground. . . . [O]ur student athletes are good students and they don't get into too much trouble. [The community can] relate to them. . . . And for the people who go to the arena, who aren't UWGB people, aren't college graduates . . ., it's important that they can see somebody that they know [out on the basketball court]. If people on the street are excited about the campus, the business community will be excited about the campus.

A former top-ranking official, likewise, indicates that although UW-Green Bay's distinctive interdisciplinary education is certainly a draw for students, we all "know that freshmen [don't] pick colleges because of their academic plan ... We are on the sports pages during basketball season all over the state. Our performing arts center attracts citizens from throughout Wisconsin. Our student housing is probably the best in the state"—every room is equipped with its own private bathroom. A founding professor in the humanities agrees:

> A lot of the reason we survived and we got the backing of the people is not because they liked us so much academically, but, hey, we would have a Division I team that won its conference, went to the NCAA. We had good coaches. . . . We put in dorms, apartments. We got the performing arts center, which is one of the jewels now. . . . And that's why the people liked us! Not necessarily because they liked our innovative academic program, but over the years, we've had successful basketball teams, successful soccer teams, . . . and then we have now this performing arts center. No one's gonna close us down!

"I think that questions of viability . . . are behind us," a founding faculty member and former administrator concludes. "We're not in that category anymore of 'Are they gonna close that place down.' [UW-Green Bay is] too much an integral part of northeastern Wisconsin now and it really has begun to and will continue to reestablish itself as an institution of choice for students."

A Public Institution

Third, the University of Wisconsin-Green Bay is a public institution. "Once you have [established] a state school in a certain area which politicians are proud of," a founding professor relates, "it's very difficult to close it down. . . .

[T]he people will remember that." "In the seventies," he says, "no one closed us down because we had too much . . . support at the very highest levels. We had a lot of rich guys who wanted us to succeed. . . . Weidner had a lot of contacts in Washington. . . . We had . . . people [supporting us] who were young politicians and now who are judges—Supreme Court Judges." And "besides that," he remarks, "the University [of Wisconsin] had committed itself to us—so, we had a lot of support down in Madison" (where the UW System office is located).

A long-time professor of human biology agrees: "One of the things that was helpful initially . . . was the fact that we were part of a system and that we had tremendous support . . . from the [UW] System in terms of getting [the campus] off the ground. How do you [get that support] if you're all by yourself, if you're just a single institution? I don't know. Most of the campuses that were innovative" and that survive, were part of a system.[11]

"Why did we survive and others not?" an administrator of 25 years begins. "We're a public institution. Public bureaucracies tend not to allow institutions to fade away and die when they've invested a lot of money. And so, if anything, they would force change on us, rather than see us close."

Summing Up the Key Reasons for the Endurance and Transformation of the Distinctive Early Ideals at the University of Wisconsin-Green Bay

The University of Wisconsin-Green Bay, then, is a bold survivor of the alternative higher education movement of the 1960s and early 1970s. Over the past 26 years, the campus has kept alive its distinctive interdisciplinary struc- ture despite budgetary cutbacks, a merger, and a changing social and political climate. Looking back over the life and lessons of this remarkable institution, what, in summary, are the factors that have enabled UW-Green Bay to preserve, where it has, its early pioneering principles? What are the factors that have been linked to the changes or transformations in the original innovative designs?

When it comes to the endurance of UW-Green Bay's distinctive founding ideals, interviewees single out the institution's unique academic organization. They emphasize over and over again the importance of the interdisciplinary budgeted departments as the key to the endurance of the interdisciplinary educational mission at UW-Green Bay. At the same time, they cite the presence of a critical mass or core group of founding faculty and administrators who have remained at the institution and who keep the founding spirit of interdisciplinarity and educational innovation alive in their creative leader- ship, scholarship, and teaching.

When it comes to the changes or transformations in the founding distinc- tive philosophies, interviewees point to shifts in the attitudes and interests of the student generations, increasing student-to-faculty ratios, and institutional efforts to accommodate the disciplinary and professional needs of the local community. They also refer to the budgetary cutbacks imposed by the state, and UW System–wide pressures to conventionalize.

ISSUES AND CHALLENGES TO INNOVATION

Throughout the years, UW-Green Bay has faced pressures and tensions as an innovative university. This section of the case study explores some of the key issues and pressures to innovation that have impacted the lives of the students, faculty, and administrators at this institution. These are innovation in a state university system, faculty immobility, and founding faculty retirements and generational differences.

Innovation in a State University System

First, UW-Green Bay faces the pressures of innovation as a public institution of higher education. Although affiliation with the University of Wisconsin has ensured the survival of UW-Green Bay as an institution, funding is desperately low for Wisconsin state universities, interviewees explain, and there is often no room for interdisciplinary, student-centered, and experiential programs. "The governor is robbing us of hundreds of thousands of dollars a year!" a faculty member in anthropology asserts. "The lack of funding has really hurt us over the years," a music professor agrees. He says that his department may not be able to hire the necessary adjunct faculty to teach in several major fields. "I'll tell you how bad things are," he confesses. "One of the scientists [I know] will talk about, 'Well, today I've got to work on equipment, get it ready for a lab.' They can't afford to send it out [to be fixed], so he repairs it. . . . I repair piano benches. . . . I have a desk full of parts and some tools and I repair piano benches. I take apart the piece of wood that needs work. I take it home to my workshop, bring it back here, screw it together."

"While I was chair [of] Humanistic Studies," a veteran professor responds, "we lost 26 people and we never got replacements, which we're suffering for now." His message to future innovators in a public system? "You've gotta remember that the funds are going to dry up someday. You're subject to the vagaries of the economic system. In this political climate, education is not a high priority; it's cutting taxes [that is]."

And from this top-ranking UW-Green Bay administrator:

> To presume that an institution's destiny is in its hands is a fallacious assumption! And you need to be sure that in your study you get that one in big bold print! Public institutions in larger systems do not set their tuition. We [the institution] don't approve our programs, and [we don't] control our enrollment levels. So, we do not have the

throttles on the three major variables necessary for quality and innovation. . . . That's a very important issue: whether or not there's room in America for difference.

The funding and support for innovation in a public institution is always a problem, remarks a former high-level official at the university:

> In a public university, no one should ever be so idealistic as to think they're going to get money for innovation. They aren't going to get one penny for innovation in the long run. Maybe [they will be funded] for five years. . . . Most public institutions today are in systems, and if they're going to be innovative, they've got to do it within the current financial parameters and . . . in such a manner that they can put stuff into the computers and the [data] tables spill out in the central administration and to the regents satisfactorily. [The central administration is] not going to develop special tables for you. My own experience in Wisconsin is they're happy to give you freedom to innovate, but not the funds. And it's their tables and not your tables that are presented to the regents.

Faculty Immobility

Second, there is the issue of faculty immobility. For the professors who come to an innovative campus to build a university, to be part of an educational "dream," the experience can be so consuming that professional interests (research and publication) are often abandoned or set aside. Eventually, the academics who devoted themselves to the institution may lose their marketability. This is what happened to some of the early faculty at Green Bay. "A lot of people gave their hearts to this place," says a long-time professor of humanistic studies, "and then got clobbered, in the sense that they wound up, six years in[to the campus's life], not doing well with their publications and either they were given tenure here and then they still maintained their associate professorship without going on, or they couldn't move [to another campus] because the bottom dropped out [of the faculty market]. And they feel betrayed."

"I'm glad that I came to Green Bay," a charter professor in psychology offers. "It was a fulfilling experience. It was also a professional dead end. This is something . . . that affects innovative institutions. Faculty members after a while become very much aware that they're likely to be heading into a blind alley as far as professional advancement is concerned [because of their lack of research]."

And then there really aren't others in your discipline with whom you can exchange ideas, he says, because UW-Green Bay is an interdisciplinary institution. "Sitting around the department where I did my graduate work . . ., you'd sit around the coffee room there talking to other psychologists. . . . That's been lacking here [at UW-Green Bay] and it affects professional development . . ., the absence of somebody to talk to if you have an idea."

Founding Faculty Retirements and Generational Differences

Third, there is widespread concern over the forthcoming retirements of the core group of founding faculty at the university. Long-time professors and administrators wonder whether the early dreams and innovative ideals of the institution will be lost when the founding mothers and fathers retire. A veteran professor of communication and the arts relates: "A lot of us now are in our mid-50s or late 50s or early 60s. All [of us] . . . sank very deep tap roots into this institution. . . . I'm anxious . . . because a lot of us are very similar in age [and near retirement]. That could be a problem in the long term." "We're getting to the point where a lot of [faculty and staff] are going to be retiring in the next 10 years," a long-time staff member agrees. "I'm real worried about what's going to happen here. I don't know if the young professors coming in have the commitment or the dedication. . . . I think it will be a big change."

In Environmental Science, a founding faculty member warns, a majority of the faculty "are going to retire within a five- to eight-year window. So, depending upon how much of the culture carries over, how much the old timers who remain try to encourage that, it will almost be like starting all over again in the sciences."

Veteran faculty members wonder whether the new generations of academics at UW-Green Bay will be able to carry forward the early innovative missions of the founders of the institution. A professor who has been at the institution for 21 years observes that the faculty cohorts today tend to be more research oriented, more focused on their own careers than the generation of professors who came before them: "They [new faculty] have come out of graduate programs that are highly research oriented. They have more publications now than faculty had 20 years ago and they're committed to the life of scholarship. . . . I think the faculty who came here [in the] late sixties, early seventies came here *really* with a pretty strong commitment to this place." It is questionable whether or not the new generations of academics, he says, will uphold the founding heritage of their predecessors.

Interviewees do, however, express hope in the new administration of UW-Green Bay for the preservation and revitalization of the founding visions. The current chancellor, Mark L. Perkins, and his leadership team have developed a series of guiding principles for the twenty-first century of the University of Wisconsin-Green Bay that incorporate many of the distinctive missions of the early days (e.g., interdisciplinarity, campus and community partnerships, creativity, collegiality, cooperation, and innovation) (*Guiding Principles for the 21st Century* 1994-95).

CONCLUSION: SUMMARY AND IMPLICATIONS

In the end, UW-Green Bay has moved from the 1960s to the 1990s with some compromises, but with a revitalized commitment to the community and with the heritage of the pioneers still, to some extent, in place. Although the individualized, student-centered approach, for example, has faded as the university has "tightened up" its requirements and budgets have been cut, there are still opportunities for independent study and personalized majors at UW-Green Bay. The experiential Liberal Education Seminars may have vanished, along with the close-knit, egalitarian community spirit of the early days, but the problem-focused mission is still upheld, and the university's ties to the community have been strengthened. Although the campus has introduced disciplinary majors—perhaps the most significant compromise since the early years—the institution remains free of conventional disciplinary departments because budgetary and curricular authority still resides in the interdisciplinary units. Finally, while the founding spirit of creativity in faculty teaching has diminished, there are still opportunities for academics to invent new courses and to engage in interdisciplinary program development without the pressures of a large and unwieldy campus bureaucracy.

Although the university has witnessed much of the early visions of the pioneers fade away with the budgetary cuts and statewide pressures to homogenize, the innovative heritage of UW-Green Bay is kept alive and celebrated not only in the hearts and minds of the old guard faculty, but in the new leadership on campus and in the continuing interdisciplinary organization of the institution today. In the words of a long-time faculty member, "Rather than throwing in the towel and saying, 'We'll go back [and become] a traditional institution,' for better or for worse, we have compromised certain things while holding on to other things." Looking back over the life and lessons of this distinctive university, what are some of the lessons or implications of the University of Wisconsin-Green Bay's three-decade story?

- The first lesson to be learned from the UW-Green Bay experience is that innovation may be a risky venture in a public university. System-wide measures or standards of quality and budgetary appropriations often do not take into account distinctive teaching or learning approaches. Although affiliation with a public university system may ensure the longevity of an innovative institution, it will not necessarily ensure the longevity of *innovation*.
- Second, adaptability and flexibility appear to be critical if a public innovative institution is to meet the changing needs of its local community and campus constituencies. Building good community relations via athletics and performing arts facilities may also strengthen town-gown relations and promote institutional viability.

- Third, academic structures that support cross-disciplinary interaction and collaboration are essential for preserving interdisciplinary approaches in higher education. At UW-Green Bay, curricular and budgetary power resides in the institution's interdisciplinary academic units. In this way, faculty from diverse disciplinary backgrounds are constantly interacting and making joint decisions.
- Fourth, the presence of a founding core group of charter faculty is critical to the endurance of the original missions of a distinctive institution. It is the founding faculty and staff at UW-Green Bay who have, in large part, kept alive the early spirit of educational experimentation and creativity. When those charter faculty and staff begin to leave in large numbers, the challenge of clinging to early ideals will intensify.
- Fifth, increasing student-to-faculty ratios affect the longevity of innovative traditions. High student-faculty ratios tend to limit opportunities for student-centered education, close-knit interactions, and co-learning between faculty and students.
- Sixth, academics who join an innovative campus in its freewheeling charter years may face problems with professional advancement or mobility. Faculty who devote their early academic lives to developing distinctive curricular programs may find that they have little time for research or publication and, as a result, are no longer marketable in academe. At the same time, institutions with strong interdisciplinary missions may not provide opportunities for professors to interact with members of their disciplinary community. This may inhibit professional exchange, publication, and mobility.
- Finally, the UW-Green Bay story turns our attention to the variations of institutional change in distinctive colleges and universities. The University of Wisconsin-Green Bay has not "given up" the dreams of its founders or turned away from its charter missions. The university has remained true to the visions, in part, while transforming and evolving in other ways. While this early northeastern Wisconsin "Eco-U" campus is a more mature and much-changed institution today, it is heartening to realize that the dreams of the founding mothers and fathers are still present in kindred pockets and venues all across campus. This is perhaps what is most remarkable about the University of Wisconsin-Green Bay.

NOTES

1. The southeastern UW campus would become the University of Wisconsin-Parkside.
2. Propositions and resolutions regarding possible sites for a new UW campus in northeastern Wisconsin had been submitted and debated for several years prior to the election of Governor Knowles.
3. The University of Wisconsin-Green Bay was originally intended to serve as a multi-campus institution, incorporating the two-year UW campuses (or "centers") at Marinette, Manitowoc, and Menasha (Fox Valley), and absorbing a former two-year UW campus in Green Bay. In the mid-1970s, the Marinette, Manitowoc, and Menasha centers were separated from UW-Green Bay at the time of a merger between the University of Wisconsin System and the former Wisconsin State University campuses (Brown 1974).
4. The name "The University of Wisconsin-Green Bay" was formally adopted in November 1966.
5. According to founding faculty member Michael W. Murphy (M.W. Murphy, personal communication to Chancellor Mark L. Perkins, 14 January 1997), in its earliest years, UW-Green Bay was famous for its ecological focus. The first Earth Day ("E-day") in the nation, he comments, "had one of its biggest celebrations right here on this tiny campus, and by the next year we had Senator Gaylord Nelson and Buckminster Fuller [maverick architect, poet, and ecological engineer] both together here, filling the arena for the E-day celebration at Eco-U." Murphy, himself, organized a multimedia poetry reading for the event, including music and slides and live narration, which he "took on the road" for three years (*Universities: Tearing Down the Ivy* 1972).
6. At the time of the campus visit, students were also required to enroll in a capstone senior seminar that was organized around interdisciplinary themes and contemporary issues and problems. As part of the university's recent comprehensive academic program evaluation (CAPE), the faculty senate voted to eliminate the senior seminar program beginning with the graduating class of December 1997 (M.L. Perkins, chancellor of UW-Green Bay, personal communication, 23 January 1997; Registrar's Office 1997).
7. Group interviews were conducted with members of the University Leadership Team (the chancellor, provost, and assistant chancellor for planning and budget); representatives of the University Committee (a policy-making committee of the faculty senate); and officers of the Student Government Association.
8. These figures include graduates who completed multiple majors at UW-Green Bay. The figures exclude students who enrolled in the university's Extended Degree Program (a program that enables students to complete most of their baccalaureate degree requirements off campus).
9. Some of the former January interim courses and Liberal Education Seminar studies and travels are now conducted during the May-June intersession at UW-Green Bay.
10. Exact figures for student-to-faculty ratios are not available prior to 1985.
11. This is not to say that innovative institutions in the public sector are free from pressures or constraints that are imposed by a public university system. This issue is taken up in the next section of this chapter.

REFERENCES

Brown, B. 1974. *The founding of the University of Wisconsin-Green Bay*. Green Bay: University of Wisconsin-Green Bay.

Fischer, J. 1971. Survival U is alive and burgeoning in Green Bay, Wisconsin. *Harper's* (February): 20, 22–23, 26–27.

Guiding principles for the 21st century: A report on strategic planning 1994-95. 1994-95. Green Bay: University of Wisconsin-Green Bay.

Kaye, H.J. 1995. Start all over again. *The Times Higher Education Supplement* Opinion section (8 September): 14.

Lane, C.D., F.T. Nugent, D.J. Tulos, J.D. Hess, J.E. Ruiz, and D.I. Snyder. 1968. *Comprehensive development plan: The University of Wisconsin-Green Bay*. Green Bay, Wisc.; Grand Rapids, Mich.: University of Wisconsin Green Bay Campus; The State of Wisconsin Department of Administration Bureau of Engineering; and Daverman Associates, Inc., Architects-Engineers-Planners, November.

Office of Institutional Research. 1997. Green Bay: University of Wisconsin-Green Bay. Institutional data is also available on-line in the UW-Green Bay electronic factbook. http://www.uwgb.edu/~furlongd/factbook/toc.html

Registrar's Office, University of Wisconsin-Green Bay. 1997. *Undergraduate studies catalog 1996-98, University of Wisconsin-Green Bay*. http://www.uwgb.edu/www/acad/WWW-PLAN-GE.HTM#GE

Rice, E., and S.H. Bremer. 1994. *Institutional environments for innovation: Comparing the Antioch and UW-Green Bay experiences*. Paper presented at the Association of American Colleges Conference, Washington, D.C., 22 January.

Switzer, L. 1970. University program stresses man's natural, social and scientific environment. *College and University Business* (April): 83.

Undergraduate studies catalog 1994-96, University of Wisconsin-Green Bay. 1994. Green Bay: University of Wisconsin-Green Bay.

Universities: Tearing down the ivy. 1972. Film features several experimental colleges and programs of the early 1970s, including Hampshire College and the environmental, communiversity projects at UW-Green Bay. Available through Media Services at the University of Wisconsin-Green Bay, Green Bay, Wisc.

The University of Wisconsin Green Bay catalog 1969-1970. 1969. Green Bay: University of Wisconsin-Green Bay.

Weidner, E.W. 1969. Chancellor's informal remarks to the faculty: "The academic plan: At the starting post." Green Bay: University of Wisconsin-Green Bay, September 6.

———. 1973. Origin of the University of Wisconsin-Green Bay. Unpublished paper. Green Bay, February 15.

———. 1975. *Problem-oriented education: The University of Wisconsin - Green Bay as a case study*. Paper presented at Linköping University, Sweden, 29 May.

———. 1977. Problem-based departments at the University of Wisconsin-Green Bay. In *Academic departments: Problems, variations, and alternatives*, D.E. McHenry and Associates, 63–85. San Francisco: Jossey-Bass.

————. 1994. Inventing a university: The University of Wisconsin-Green Bay, 1965–1969: Up against the clock and entrenched rivals. *Voyageur* 23–33, 36–37.

Weidner, E.W., and W.G. Kuepper. 1993. University of Wisconsin-Green Bay. In *Important lessons from innovative colleges and universities*, edited by V.R. Cardozier, 23–35. *New Directions for Higher Education* no. 82 (summer).

CHAPTER

University of California Santa Cruz

A Collegiate University

BACKGROUND: SETTING THE SCENE

Sunlight gleams through towering redwoods as you walk along secluded pathways through the woods to reach the main buildings of the campus. Deer frolic in the hills and meadows, and signs warn of mountain lions in a setting where "nature was left to dominate artifice," where a limestone quarry has been preserved as a natural amphitheater, and dells once provided a "natural backdrop for performances of Shakespeare's *A Midsummer-Night's Dream*" (College by College, 1972; Von der Muhll, 1984, 58). High in the foothills overlooking Monterey Bay and the Pacific Ocean is the University of California, Santa Cruz (UCSC), a public university with a breathtaking landscape and a distinctive emphasis on undergraduate education.

The Santa Cruz campus is set on 2,000 acres of redwood forest and meadowland on the grounds of the former Cowell Ranch. An old cookhouse, granary, ranch house, and horse barn (now an admissions office, child care center, women's center, and theater) mark the entrance to the university. On the hilly slopes to the west of the main entrance, there is a 25-acre organic farm, and on the hills above Cowell College (one of UCSC's residential Colleges), there is a four-acre garden, once presided over by Englishman Allen Chadwick, a "philosophical gardener" who planted seeds by the phases of the moon (Grant and Riesman 1978).

At the core of the campus, in the middle of the forest, there are the McHenry Library, science hill, art studios, lecture halls, a performing arts center, and athletic facilities (*UC Santa Cruz General Catalog 1995-96* 1995). In the surrounding hills, there are eight residential Colleges, each with a unique architectural flavor and curricular theme—e.g., from the wood and tile roofs of Cowell College, with its emphasis on the humanities, to the Mediterranean village style of Crown College with its focus on science and technology (College by College 1972). The Colleges were designed to provide the warmth and intimacy of a small campus in a large university setting. Each was built on a human scale, within an easy walk of forest solitude. The College buildings, according to researchers Gerald Grant and David Riesman (1978), were designed to honor the natural environment: No building was to be higher than two-thirds the height of a redwood tree. "On every bridge, at every bend in the pathways," writes Professor George Von der Muhll of the beauty of the Santa Cruz campus, "students were implicitly invited to dream new dreams, far from the busy haunts of man" (Von der Muhll 1984, 58).

The Founding

The story of UC Santa Cruz begins in the late 1950s, a time of rapid population growth in California. The census reported the state's population at 6,907,387 in 1940, 10,586,223 in 1950, and 15,717,204 in 1960 (McHenry 1977). There had been a net increase in state growth averaging about 500,000 annually since the end of World War II (McHenry 1993). A study by the California State Department of Finance projected that unless new University of California campuses were built, enrollments at UC Berkeley and UCLA might swell to 35,200 and 39,900, respectively, in no more than a decade (McHenry 1977; Von der Muhll 1984).

In October 1957, the regents of the University of California elected Clark Kerr, former chancellor of UC Berkeley, as president of the UC System and authorized the establishment of three new campuses of the University of California: one in the San Diego area; one in Los Angeles-Orange County; and one in Northern California in the "south central" coastal region, below the San Francisco Bay area (Carter 1971; McHenry 1977).[1]

After an extensive and careful survey of possible sites for the Northern California campus, in March 1961, the regents selected the 2,000-acre scenic Cowell Ranch site in Santa Cruz. In this glorious forest setting above the ocean, the first faculty and students would take their places as the charter members of the new university in Santa Cruz.

The Colleges: The "Best of Both Worlds"

The academic plan for UCSC was a product of the imaginations of Clark Kerr and his graduate school roommate, the late Dean McHenry, a political scientist from UCLA who was appointed the first chancellor of the Santa Cruz campus in 1961. Back in their graduate school days at Stanford, Kerr and McHenry had argued about who had the better undergraduate education (Kerr at Swarthmore with its intense, personal community or McHenry at UCLA with its research focus and university facilities). The two men concluded that the ideal campus would be one that combined the resources and research faculty of a large university with the student-centered intimacy and community of a small liberal arts college (Grant and Riesman 1978). This vision would come to life and flourish in the founding plans for UC Santa Cruz.

Kerr and McHenry sought to create a "collegiate university" at Santa Cruz, one that would run counter to the isolation and impersonality of the large, monolithic "multiversity" (McHenry 1977; Von der Muhll 1984). Although the Santa Cruz campus would offer graduate programs and sponsor research activities, and would grow to the size of the giant research universities (accommodating a projected enrollment of 27,500 students by the end of the century), Kerr hoped to sustain the community feeling of a small liberal arts college through clusters of theme colleges. The idea, in Kerr's legendary words, was to "make the campus seem small as it grows larger."

The essence of the Santa Cruz plan was the residential College. Under the guidance of McHenry, the university would develop a series of small undergraduate Colleges in the Oxford-Cambridge tradition, that would foster a sense of belonging and close-knit community in the university (McHenry 1977, 88).[2] In the words of founding Kresge College professor Michael Kahn in a 1981 essay, "The hope was to obtain the best of both worlds: each college would be sufficiently unique and autonomous to offer the advantages of intimacy. . . . [The university] would provide the facilities and excellence of a major university" (63).[3]

The early campus plans called for the establishment of three residential Colleges with a gradual expansion of up to 20 Colleges (Thelin 1977). Each College would have, on average, 40 faculty members and 600 students (McHenry 1966). The College was conceived of as a "scholarly village" that would be headed by a provost (a tenured member of the faculty) and a group of "academic preceptors" (academic and student life advisors) in the English tradition. Every faculty member would be a "fellow" of one of the Colleges, and the fellows would be drawn from an interdisciplinary mix of academics. The College provost (and his or her family) would live in residence at the College, along with several of the faculty fellows (Carter 1971; McHenry 1964, 1977; Undergraduate and Graduate Bulletin 1966).[4] Each faculty member would hold a joint appointment with his or her College and a disciplinary group called a "board of study." Academic appointments and promotions would be based on the joint recommendations of the College and the board.

In the fall of 1965, with the buildings of Cowell College still under construction, 46 charter faculty and 652 students gathered in trailers to inaugurate the first classes of UCSC (*UC Santa Cruz* n.d.; Von der Muhll 1984). Cowell College, the first College, opened in October of 1965, and a "new and quite different college" would follow for each of the next seven years (Grant and Riesman 1978). Stevenson College (named for Adlai Stevenson) was started in 1966 with a curricular focus on the social sciences. Crown College opened in 1967 with an emphasis on the natural sciences. Merrill College started in 1968 with a focus on international affairs and Third World issues. Porter College (formerly College Five) began in 1969 as a fine arts college. Kresge College was launched in 1970 with a physical sciences focus and then an ecological and humanistic psychology theme. Oakes College opened in 1971 with an emphasis on minority populations, and College Eight began in 1972 with a focus on environmental studies (McHenry 1977; Sinsheimer 1994).

An adventuresome and pioneer-minded group of faculty would join the innovative campus in Santa Cruz in 1965. The earliest academics were captivated by the distinctive university environment, with its emphasis on undergraduate teaching in the collegiate setting. Students, too, were drawn by the idea of a new experimental university. In the beginning, the campus attracted the top 5 percent of high school graduates. At the height of its popularity in the 1960s, McHenry marveled in a recent retrospective on the university, UCSC had four times the number of qualified applicants that could be accommodated (McHenry 1993). Back then, UCSC was the most popular campus of the University of California System, attracting the "best and the brightest" applicants. Students vied for the chance to enter UCSC, turning down admissions offers from the prestigious flagship state campuses of UC Berkeley and UCLA.

University of California, Santa Cruz, Today

Today UC Santa Cruz enrolls 10,215 students (9,159 undergraduates and 1,056 graduate students). Of the 10,215 students, 5,987 (59 percent) are female and 4,228 (41 percent) are male; approximately 11 percent of the students are Asian American, 3 percent are African American, 15 percent are Latino , 3 percent are Filipino, 1 percent are Native American, and 61 percent are European American or members of other ethnic groups. (Ethnicity data are not available for approximately 7 percent of UCSC students.) Nearly half (48 percent) of Santa Cruz students live on campus (Office of Planning and Budget 1997).

There are 2,326 administrators and staff members at UC Santa Cruz today. The faculty comprises 389 full-time and 167 part-time academics. Forty-one percent of the faculty are female and 59 percent are male. Twenty-one percent of the "ladder-rank" faculty at UCSC are persons of color and 95 percent hold doctorates (Office of Planning and Budget 1997).

The University of California, Santa Cruz, has 43 boards or "committees" of studies (now called "departments"), offering majors under four general divisions (arts, humanities, natural sciences, and social sciences). Undergraduates are required to complete a minimum of 180 credits (including campus-wide general education requirements and major requirements) to receive the baccalaureate degree. In their senior year, students must pass a written and/or oral comprehensive examination, or complete a senior thesis or an "equivalent body of work" (*UC Santa Cruz General Catalog 1995-96* 1995).

The collegiate structure remains integral to the undergraduate experience at UCSC. The campus never reached the scale envisioned by the founders. (The projected enrollment of 27,500 and the expansion of up to 20 residential Colleges proved to be unrealistic in the fiscal and demographic climate of the state in the 1970s.) In fact, no new College has been opened in the quarter century since College Eight in 1972. Even so, the university remains unequivocally committed to the cluster college organization. Between 1,000 and 1,300 students and 30 to 100 faculty members from diverse disciplinary fields are affiliated with each of the eight residential Colleges at UCSC, and construction is underway for Colleges "Nine" and "Ten" (*The Colleges* 1995). Most first-year students live in residence at their College and all first-year students are required to complete an interdisciplinary core course in their College that focuses on writing, discussion, and critical reasoning, and an orientation to the education and culture of UCSC.

One of the most innovative features of the Santa Cruz campus is the grading system (established by the founding faculty members in the 1960s). All students receive narrative evaluations (accompanied by a "Pass" or fail ["No Record"] notation). Only "passed" courses and accompanying evaluations are included on the undergraduate student transcript, although courses assigned a grade of "No Record" may affect a student's class standing.[5] Undergraduates have the option of receiving a traditional letter grade (A, B, C, or No Record), accompanied by a narrative evaluation, in most lower division and upper division classes at the university.[6]

In addition to a full range of undergraduate majors, the Santa Cruz campus offers 22 graduate programs in fields spanning anthropology, computer engineering, environmental studies, marine sciences, and the history of consciousness—an interdisciplinary Ph.D. program that centers on the history of cultural organizations and artistic expression; the analysis of ideas of human nature, society, and the community; and theories of representation and identity formation (*UC Santa Cruz General Catalog 1995-96* 1995). Graduate students, like undergraduates, receive narrative evaluations (rather than letter grades) in all courses taken for credit at UCSC. (The evaluation is accompanied by a "grade" of "Pass," "Fail," or "Incomplete.")

ORGANIZATION OF THIS CHAPTER

This chapter examines the history and endurance of educational innovation at UC Santa Cruz. The case study begins with a demographic profile of the interview participants, the faculty, administrators, and alumnae/i who shared their voices and impressions about UCSC. The next section describes the distinctive educational concepts that guided the founders' visions for the university. The chapter then traces the evolution of the distinctive opening ideals, focusing on where and how the university has kept alive its innovative philosophies, and where and how the institution has changed or transformed itself. The next section examines the key issues or challenges to innovation at Santa Cruz. The chapter concludes with a summary and a reflection on the UC Santa Cruz study and its implications for future reform in American higher education.

INTERVIEW PARTICIPANT PROFILE

To explore the history and current status of innovation at UC Santa Cruz, 27 semi-structured interviews were conducted with founding and/or current faculty members, administrators, and students in January of 1996.[7] Each interview lasted about 50 minutes. The participants included 20 faculty members (12 of whom had been at the university for 25 years or more), 16 administrators (including the founding chancellor, the current chancellor, the executive vice chancellor, and four College provosts), the mayor of Santa Cruz (who is a lecturer and field studies coordinator at UCSC), and two alumni who graduated in the early years of the university. (Some individuals occupied more than one role at the institution.) The interviewees included 23 men and four women spanning several different "generations" of the UCSC community: Eight of the participants joined UCSC in either its preopening years or opening year (1961–1965), 10 started in years two through five (1966–1969), six arrived at UCSC in the university's seventh through 10th year (1971–1974), and three joined the university in its 16th year or later (1980–1991). The "tenure" for the interviewees at UCSC ranged from four to 34 years, with an average length of stay of 22.9 years at the institution.

DISTINCTIVE EARLY IDEALS AT THE UNIVERSITY OF CALIFORNIA, SANTA CRUZ

The University of California, Santa Cruz, was designed to avoid the bureaucratic confusion, impersonality, and specialized and highly fragmented research focus of the large American university (Carter 1971). The campus came to life at the height of the free speech movement in the 1960s, when college and university students were seeking refuge from the impersonal structures and fiercely competitive, factory-like atmosphere of the Berkeleys and other research universities. Clark Kerr and Dean McHenry sought to respond to the demands of the student generations and to fulfill their graduate student dreams, by creating a collegiate university in the country's largest public university system. In the words of one administrator and veteran professor, "This campus tried to be an eccentric component of [the UC System]. It tried to step to its own beat and its own drummer."

How did UCSC challenge or rebel against the conventions of the mainstream university? Based on the interviews conducted with founding and longtime faculty, administrators, and alumni (along with campus archival research and historical document analyses), there appear to be four key themes of educational innovation that guided the early missions of UCSC. First, the campus would promote interdisciplinary teaching and learning through College-based courses and faculty co-teaching. Second, the planners sought to achieve a balance between faculty research and undergraduate teaching; teaching would be prized at the institution and faculty members would be granted a tremendous degree of freedom to create new and innovative courses. Third, individualized learning was embraced by the founders—UCSC students would be encouraged to take charge of their own learning, to pursue individualized majors, and to design their own courses and independent studies. Fourth, the collegiate organization of the university would nourish close-knit relations between students and faculty within a large-scale research university. Together, these four themes (interdisciplinary education, faculty freedom and undergraduate teaching, individualized education, and close-knit community) would form the heart of the pioneering missions of UCSC. Each theme is discussed in greater detail in the following sections.

Interdisciplinary Education

First, UC Santa Cruz was designed to resist traditional disciplinary structures and departmental frameworks. "Dean McHenry [and] Clark Kerr had done a lot of thinking about what was wrong with the University of California," one veteran faculty member and current administrator explains. "UCSC was structured in such a way that it would break up or disempower the old vertical disciplinary, departmental kinds of structures, and it was intended to ... create a multidisciplinary . . . mix, and to enable . . . faculty to form clusters of interdisciplinary interests, without necessarily eliminating the traditional degrees."

The fundamental mechanism for interdisciplinary education at UCSC was the collegiate system. Each College was designed to be an interdisciplinary community with faculty from the sciences, social sciences, arts, humanities, and natural sciences. Academics would devote half of their time to teaching in the courses in the Colleges, and half of their time to the classes offered through disciplinary groupings of faculty or boards of studies at UCSC.

McHenry and the other early planners of the university insisted that the term "board" be used instead of "department" since UCSC would run counter to the traditional and powerful departmentalized university. Instead of having a "chair" of a department, one founding professor explains, there would be "conveners" of the boards of studies. And some of the boards would transcend the bounds of a single discipline, offering interdisciplinary majors (such as environmental studies—which started out as a committee of study—and a graduate degree in history of consciousness, which blended the social sciences and the humanities).

The "original idea" of the board, according to one College provost and long-time professor, "was that you would have students who would concentrate in the area of sociology and for the purposes of final exams, you would need to bring together a board of examiners in sociology to see if [the student] had learned sociology. So, these groups of faculty would form themselves into boards more or less for the purpose of examining students. That was it." "The boards were [present] only to make sure that there were enough course offerings through the Colleges that students in various disciplines could get what they needed," an early alumnus and now a current faculty member agrees. "They really were not departments in the classic sense at all."[8]

According to McHenry (1977), the early administration of UCSC "took several precautions to prevent [the] boards from emerging as departments" (102). Administrative and budgetary authority for the boards was vested in vice chancellors (later called deans) of three divisions (humanities, social sciences, and natural sciences).[9] Half of a faculty member's salary would come from the College and the other half from the academic division. Faculty appointments and promotions would be determined by the joint recommendation of the interdisciplinary faculty of the College and the disciplinary board of studies (Ring 1971).

For the students, creative interdisciplinary courses would form the heart of the early undergraduate education at UCSC. According to the 1965–1975 academic plan for UC Santa Cruz, undergraduates would take most of their lower division and some of their upper division course work in the classes offered through their College. All entering first-year students would enroll in an interdisciplinary core course at their College that would center around the College's unique interdisciplinary theme (e.g., Cowell's core course on Western Civilization, Stevenson's core course on Self and Society, Crown's core course on Technology and Society). Several Colleges offered interdisciplinary majors, and students could design their own interdisciplinary major program under the guidance of faculty members or faculty committees.[10]

The collegiate organization released an outpouring of creative and interdisciplinary team-taught classes at early UCSC, according to Von der Muhll (1984). "Sometimes," he says, "it permitted the flowering of a long-suppressed desire to teach outside one's professional field" (65). A psychologist and an astronomer, for example, offered a course on enology, the science of wine making (Ring 1971); a philosopher, a literary critic, and a biologist offered a class on death; and a political scientist and a biologist taught a course about chickens. (The "chicken course," ridiculed by some, resulted in a serious book on the topic that received widespread acclaim.) (Smith and Daniel 1975)

Early faculty were drawn to UCSC by the interdisciplinary emphasis and connectedness of the university. "Instead of being at a university where I was in the English department with nobody but English people," a charter professor in English recalls, "I was in a College with everybody and it was *really* interdisciplinary and we all taught together in the core course that all of the freshmen took for the whole first year and then it continued for the whole second year. What was really fabulously wonderful about those early years was that the College was a scene in which *everybody* was participating."

Faculty Freedom and Undergraduate Teaching

A second foundation was that teaching was prized at early UCSC. The founding plans for the university called for a balance between faculty research and undergraduate teaching, and faculty were encouraged to develop creative courses in the College curriculum. While the boards of studies would emphasize disciplinary research, the Colleges, McHenry (1977) writes, would be devoted to undergraduate teaching.

"I think in the beginning there was the notion that you could be a great teacher and get tenured here," explains a professor who has taught at the institution since 1969. A founding faculty member recalls: "We were . . . challenging the whole conventional tenure system in the sense that this was supposed to be a place where undergraduate teaching would count more than it did in most places."

"Most of the [early] classes were very small (12 to 15 students), [with] almost no lectures," an early alumnus and faculty member relates. "There were a lot of faculty members who saw the role that they had as more like facilitators. [Teaching was] more of a dialog with students than a lecture format." This was a reaction, again, to the large lecture halls of UC Berkeley. The University of California, Santa Cruz, "wanted to be a little bit more humane," says an emeritus professor in the sciences, so that "students [would] not [be] treated so much as if they're like cogs in a machine." We paid attention to the quality of undergraduate instruction, he says; we wanted to involve students so that they would feel a part of their education.

There was a sense of passion for creative undergraduate teaching in the start-up years of UCSC. A professor of 26 years remembers, faculty "could undertake all kinds of experiments in college teaching." He recalls an anthropology professor whose class was studying the Native Americans of the central

California coastal region. The students in the class built a Native American pit house—a "big, semi-subterranean house essentially built into the earth." Bob Durling, a literature professor, "built a maze up in the woods [on campus], . . . and the purpose of the maze was to give students a sense of construction and the problems . . . and the intricacies [involved in maze construction]. There was a literature on that subject." "People were doing all kinds of weird and unusual things," he adds, "and it was incredibly stimulating. It was one of those things where you said to yourself, 'Well, I can work within my discipline, I can work in a whole new area, . . . and if I get weird ideas I can put together a class, an experiment,' and that made the place very, very attractive."

Individualism: Student-Centered Education

Students, too, were granted a tremendous degree of freedom to shape their own academic programs at early UCSC. There was a strong commitment to student-centered or individualized learning. Course requirements were kept to a minimum, and students were "whole-heartedly" encouraged, in the words of one early brochure, to undertake independent studies "once they have found their academic feet" and to pursue a personalized degree (in coordination with a faculty sponsor or committee) (*So You're Thinking* 1969). The campus founders believed that "in the university, as outside it," the individual must be responsible for his or her own education; "therefore individual initiative must have an important place in determining the conduct, pace and content of a student's work" at Santa Cruz (*Undergraduate Program* 1965, 5–6).

Students would "put together their own majors," an early graduate and current faculty member recalls—"things like peace and economic transformation—where they [would be able to study] whatever they were interested in." Personalized majors, he reports, typically cut across disciplinary fields, and were pursued by at least one-fifth of the students in the first few years of UCSC. There were also a number of student-directed seminars at early UCSC.

The students who came to Santa Cruz in the 1960s and early 1970s wanted to "do their own thing," a veteran faculty member and administrator observes. Going to "UC Santa Cruz in 1968 was like going to Haight Ashbury," he proclaims. "My first [big] class was 250 students and I walked in with a suit and a tie and here's this room full of the brightest, but some of the most individualistic students that I'd ever encountered . . . , primarily what we would have called flower children–looking [students]. People had dogs and long hair and sandals and no shirts and here I was" fresh out of graduate school.

Perhaps the most daring departure at UCSC, one that also honored the early idea of individualized learning and inquiry, was the narrative evaluation system. Instead of conventional letter grades, students would receive written evaluations of their course work (accompanied by a grade of "Pass" or "Fail").[11]

In this way, undergraduates at UCSC would be competing only against themselves. There would be no "grade grubbing" or competition for the top scores. Students would focus on their own unique skills and learning processes in an environment that valued the individual learner.[12]

Close-Knit Community

Finally, the new university would foster a spirit of bonding and close-knit community. Undergraduates would take nearly all of their courses in the Colleges, where they would live and learn and form close ties with fellow students and faculty in their "familial" corners of the redwood forest. The pioneering planners of Santa Cruz organized the university around the collegiate system, once again, to foster a more humane and friendly environment than the "mass production, assembly line kind of education" at the large research university. The idea for Santa Cruz was that students would "feel part of a smaller, more intimate group of people," says one veteran professor in the sciences, that undergraduates would form bonds with fellow students and faculty both inside and outside the classroom setting.

"Education [was to be] an intimate, interactive process," an emeritus faculty member agrees. Professors and students often developed personal relationships, especially since faculty offices were located in the Colleges and some professors lived in residence at the College. The faculty-to-student ratio was about 12 to 1 in the early days. Students and faculty would get to know each other on a first-name basis. An early alumnus fondly recalls: "Classes would meet at the professor's house or they'd meet out in the meadow somewhere."

"In the earliest years, there was a tremendous effort to break boundaries between faculty and students," a founding faculty member and former provost remembers, and "a great emphasis on eating together in the dining hall, and that continued for many years." "You got to know the students," remarks a professor of 27 years. "We had the [core course at Cowell] with field trips every week for three or four hours and I used to spend an incredible amount of time [with those students]. Some of them I still know very well because we were at a time when I was 25, and the students were 20, so it became almost like [we were friends]. In fact, I think the Cowell College motto was 'The Pursuit of Knowledge in the Company of Friends.'" We all "just knew each other" back then, a veteran professor of psychology agrees. "I know that if I saw someone [on campus] that I didn't recognize, I would say, 'Who's that?'"

Creative College events, such as College Nights, poetry readings, Culture Breaks, and performances, offered additional opportunities for community togetherness, intellectual nourishment, and celebration. One nostalgic faculty pioneer remembers the spirit and bonding at early Cowell College:

[Professor] Norman O. Brown did a reading of *Finnegan's Wake* and it went on all night! [Students and faculty] read sections. It just kept going and going and going. . . . This was in the courtyard [of Cowell College], and anybody who wanted to could come and listen. It was just one event after another [in those days]—political events, cultural events, riots. It was exciting in that sense.

Cowell College, he marvels, "moved as a whole community. When I think of the early College, I think of the whole student body sitting down at lunch, everybody there, moving up the hill from the residences together to the same [core] course. . ., and at the end of it walking back. . . . That was really an amazing thing: faculty and students all moving together."

At early Kresge College, which drew its inspiration from the human potential movement, the whole College was modeled after a personal growth group and a caring, familial community. One "innovative thing about Kresge College," a Kresge administrator remarks, "that gives us a touchy-feely [reputation], is that [at the start] we had the entire College—faculty, staff, and students (and this includes the custodians and the night watch people)—all divided into family groups, kin groups."

Early students and their kin groups were integrally involved in the planning and design of the College through participation in a course called Creating Kresge College. When it came time to move into their newly built dwellings (which included octet-shaped communal structures with no inner walls or partitions), Grant and Riesman (1978) observe, "each of the kin groups stood in a circle around a bonfire holding hands while they burned their unwanted possessions. When the fires died, they walked single file, holding hands, up through the woods to their new home. They were silent, their faces enraptured" (89).

ENDURANCE AND TRANSFORMATION OF THE DISTINCTIVE EARLY IDEALS AT THE UNIVERSITY OF CALIFORNIA, SANTA CRUZ

After more than three decades, the early dreams and visions for UC Santa Cruz have faded. The founding hopes and ideals for educational experimentation were threatened by enrollment shortfalls and budgetary cutbacks in public higher education in the 1970s. (Table 2 depicts how enrollments steadily increased from the mid-1960s to the mid-1970s, and then declined and leveled off in the late 1970s and early 1980s.) As the countercultural era came to an end, and the student generations changed, pressures to conventionalize intensified. Alas, the new and dreamy venture in the redwoods of Santa Cruz began the long march back to the mainstream.

TABLE 2

THREE-QUARTER AVERAGE ENROLLMENTS AT UC SANTA CRUZ

Academic Year	Undergraduate Enrollment	Graduate Student Enrollment	Total Enrollment
1965-66	637	0	637
1966-67	1,247	26	1,273
1967-68	1,856	61	1,917
1968-69	2,464	96	2,560
1969-70	2,937	154	3,091
1970-71	3,446	267	3,713
1971-72	3,903	306	4,209
1972-73	4,351	282	4,633
1973-74	4,740	292	5,032
1974-75	5,223	327	5,550
1975-76	5,587	323	5,910
1976-77	5,695	319	6,014
1977-78	5,545	331	5,876
1978-79	5,417	337	5,754
1979-80	5,565	388	5,953
1980-81	5,901	463	6,364
1981-82	6,203	516	6,719
1982-83	6,200	521	6,721
1983-84	6,189	530	6,719
1984-85	6,416	578	6,994
1985-86	6,874	623	7,497
1986-87	7,700	709	8,409
1987-88	8,031	754	8,785
1988-89	8,507	727	9,234
1989-90	8,577	879	9,456
1990-91	8,787	933	9,720
1991-92	8,922	939	9,861
1992-93	9,021	968	9,989
1993-94	8,970	925	9,895
1994-95	8,766	980	9,746
1995-96	8,548	1,004	9,552

Source: Office of Planning and Budget. University of California, Santa Cruz. (1997).

The turning point came in the late 1970s when, under the leadership of Chancellor Robert L. Sinsheimer, the campus was radically reorganized. Amidst falling applications for admissions, increasing disciplinarization, and tensions associated with the dual structure of Colleges and boards of studies, the Colleges, in the words of William Adams (1984), were essentially stripped "of all curricular authority and any real leverage in the personnel process" (24). The early intellectual emphasis of the Colleges was sacrificed as faculty appointments and promotion decisions were placed in the hands of the boards, and faculty moved their offices away from their interdisciplinary collegiate faculty fellows to be closer to their colleagues in the disciplines. The College provost (once akin to a small college president) was now primarily a student affairs administrator. The theme Colleges, once rich curricular environments, became primarily residential life communities.

The reorganization of UC Santa Cruz marked the end of much of the early utopian spirit of innovation of the founding era and signaled the start of a new, more conventional phase in the campus's history. This section examines, in more detail, how the reorganization and other pressures and changes over the years at UCSC have impacted the four early distinctive educational missions of the university (interdisciplinary education, faculty freedom and undergraduate teaching, individualized education, and close-knit community). It then explores the longevity or "survival" of the campus, and offers a summary of the reasons for the transformation of the innovative founding ideals of UCSC.

Interdisciplinary Education

First, the interdisciplinary character of the Santa Cruz campus has faded. Gone are the days of the philosophers, literary critics, political scientists, and biologists teaming up to offer courses on death, wine making, or chickens. Today, UC Santa Cruz faculty are deeply immersed in their disciplines. One indicator is that, gradually, nearly all of the boards of studies became conventional disciplinary departments.[13] And today all "boards of studies" at UCSC are officially called "departments," the name change having been adopted in the summer of 1996 (R.M. Tanner, executive vice chancellor, personal communication, 13 March 1997).

Undergraduate education at UCSC is now primarily confined to the disciplines. The campus has moved away from the free-spirited opening days when some of the Colleges were offering up to 50 interdisciplinary courses. A glance through the 1995-96 UCSC catalog reveals that most of the Colleges today sponsor no more than four or five such courses,[14] many for only one to three units. (In the early years, College courses carried a weight of five units.)

"What happened in the reorganization," a professor of 22 years explains, "is that [the Colleges] were completely gutted of their academic piece." The University of California, Santa Cruz, faculty who devoted themselves to creative, interdisciplinary teaching and program development in the Colleges, found that they were not being recognized in tenure and promotion decisions. (The academic reward structure was based on the conventional, disciplinary research and publication criteria established by the UC System.)

At the same time, the dual structure of Colleges and boards of studies proved to be inefficient. "The Colleges took an *enormous* amount of work from the faculty, particularly on personnel cases," explains one veteran professor and College provost. "When we hired people, we had to meet as a board and then a different group of [faculty] would meet in the College, and then you would have to negotiate between the board and the College—not only for hiring, but for promotion." "In the University of California," he adds, "you come up all the time [for review] and everything had to go through the board and it had to go through the College. . . . It was an *enormous* amount of work and [there was] a lot of acrimony because the boards had goals and the Colleges had goals and they were different."

Next, there were the changes in the academic labor market and the pressures and standards of the national academic disciplinary communities. In the words of a professor who has taught at the campus since 1968,

> One of the . . . things that drives disciplinarization is [the labor market]. . . . The new [faculty] that were being hired [in the late 1970s] were people who would not have any of this "'College' bullshit." . . . "Teaching the core course?! Forget about it! College advisees?! Forget about it!" [The feeling was,] "I'm here to write my book, get myself promoted. Insofar as I invest my energies in this place, they will be invested primarily in my [department]." The job market changed the climate such that a lot of the newer faculty had a different perspective on [higher education] and . . . the task[s] of being a faculty member. This is very different from the more open, somewhat utopian [job market] of the people that were in my cohort, for whom interdisciplinarity was a new thing and was an exciting thing.

This campus is really "a child of the late sixties" a long-time professor of economics agrees, "and it's hard to find [faculty today] who really want to divorce themselves from their disciplines and throw themselves into interdisciplinary programs." Many of the economics faculty, for example,

> viewed the College system in the late seventies as actually harmful to them because we had economists scattered all over the campus. They could never talk to each other. . . . This structure . . . discourage[d] collegiality [in the disciplines] because the [faculty] you would see next door to you were people you could talk about the weather with, but they had no academic interests in common with you.

To this long-time faculty member, as well as others, the reorganization was an unfortunate but necessary outcome for UCSC.

Finally, the early mission of interdisciplinarity at UCSC was jeopardized by enrollment shifts in the 1970s and changes in the student generations. In the words of a founding professor, "There was a terrible period in the seventies in higher education [when] there just weren't enough students. There wasn't enough money. Whereas we originally got the top 5 or 10 percent of students in the UC System, very soon we were competing for the bottom. . . . We couldn't afford to be picky." Incoming students wanted to enroll in disciplinary courses, so the campus moved to accommodate their needs.

"When I first came to Santa Cruz" in the late 1960s, an emeritus professor explains, "the kind of students that were attracted here were highly creative individuals." They were interested in unusual, interdisciplinary courses and innovative studies. They were "incredible!" "By the late seventies," he says, "that was gone. The economy was in terrible shape. . . . Students were job-oriented. . . . The campus suffered because we had the reputation of being a hippie-dippie campus and parents would say to their kids, 'You ain't going to Santa Cruz; you're going to go somewhere where you'll get trained [for a career].' So, that produced change." The result was an increased emphasis on the conventional, straight and narrow disciplinary majors and degrees.

With the exception of a few surviving interdisciplinary majors, perhaps the only remnant of the founding epoch of interdisciplinary education at UCSC are the College core courses. The core courses, some of which disappeared for a time in the 1970s, have reemerged as an interdisciplinary component of the first-year undergraduate curriculum. (All first-year students are required to complete a core course at their College.) Most of the core courses, however, are one-quarter seminars, in contrast to the year-long and sometimes two-year-long offerings of the early years. Many are taught by teaching assistants or lecturers, whereas full-time, ladder-rank faculty members led the core courses in the opening years.

There have been some recent efforts to restore the academic emphasis of the Colleges. In 1991, the academic senate of UCSC approved a report of the Joint Subcommittee of the Committees on Educational Policy and Planning and Budget that recommended that the Colleges be recognized as "social and intellectual entities" at the university with responsibilities to mount courses taught by senate (tenured or tenure-track) faculty. The report recommended that there be additional rewards for faculty members who provided extraordinary service to the Colleges, and called for all tenured and tenure-track professors to teach a one- to three-unit course in the Colleges every three years or to provide "comparable service to undergraduate education" (McHenry 1993). These new policies, interviewees relate, have encouraged faculty to become more involved with the Colleges and the core courses.

Faculty Freedom and Undergraduate Teaching

Second, the early spirit of undergraduate teaching has largely vanished. The days of the small, intensive seminars, the creative classes where students and faculty would build mazes in the woods or construct Native American pit houses, are but a fond memory at UCSC. While Santa Cruz retains its reputation as an institution devoted to undergraduate teaching, since the reorganization, the College courses (with their central emphasis on undergraduate education) have largely disappeared, class sizes have grown, and the faculty reward structure has increasingly emphasized research and publication.

What happened to the early spirit of engagement and commitment to undergraduate teaching? Once again, UCSC was hit hard by the budgetary shortfalls in the 1970s, a dynamic charter staff member explains: "California absolutely has gone through hell [with the budget constraints], and I think what happens is that when you start getting these horrible, horrible cuts, some of the really wonderful stuff goes and what you are left with are the bones, the bare skeleton of what passes as liberal arts education."

"We have been pushed by the legislature," a long-time professor agrees, to boost enrollments in order to receive state funding and resources. "Everything," she adds, "is enrollment driven," and this means larger and larger class sizes. This campus, she says, was not designed for teaching lecture courses of 500 students: "If you look at the rooms in the Colleges that [were intended for the purposes of] teaching, they are small. We have *very* few lecture halls, very few places where we can teach large classes, which is a source of frustration to many. We try really hard to still do the small seminar experience for students," but it has become more and more difficult.

"Our faculty-student ratio," a charter professor reveals, is now "approximately twice that of a place like Stanford. They are about 10 to 1; we are about 20 to 1!" In the early years, Santa Cruz prided itself on its low 12 or 13 to 1 faculty-to-student ratio. That was part of the campus' appeal.

Perhaps more than any other single factor, the early plans and dreams for creative, undergraduate teaching at UCSC have been jeopardized by the faculty reward system, which is, again, based on the standards established by the University of California. A long-time professor in the sciences explains that in the early years, faculty at UC Santa Cruz

> were being [evaluated for promotion in] the same way as people at Berkeley and UCLA . . ., but we were being asked to participate in this . . . College enterprise. . . . Everybody began to realize you're not going to get promoted on the basis of your College teaching because when you go up for tenure, it's your research, it's your publications [that count]. . . . So what began to happen was that [sciences faculty] began to draw back from the Colleges and the scientists began to kind of fall into a more conventional, [research-centered] university system.

This was true for nearly all disciplines. A veteran professor of history explains:

> [In the mid-1970s,] many faculty, particularly the careerist faculty, could see which side their bread was buttered on, and they said, "To hell with Colleges. I don't want any part of it. Put me in my department and let me write my books and get my promotions. . . ." Those of us who didn't do that, who kept on doing things like [engaging in creative teaching and] trying to dream up new programs . . ., by and large paid quite a heavy price in terms of academic advancement.

This was the fate of an early professor who devoted himself to teaching and to developing the Garden Project (four acres cultivated for flowers and vegetables) at UCSC:[15]

> The literal term that they use when you're denied tenure is that you're "dead." And, in fact, when the [faculty] voted against me [for tenure], a colleague came down to tell me, and I was in a meeting . . . at the time, and . . . he whispered in my ear, "You're dead." And that was really the case. . . . I was never again invited up [to campus] or acknowledged in any way whatsoever. Even going up to the garden, which I started and *poured* myself into, an *immense* effort on my part, there was a reverse magnetism even there. So, it was real bitter.

"The pressures of conformity are enormous in a public university," a top-ranking administrator points out. The University of California, Santa Cruz, over time, he says, "couldn't resist the pressures of the other UC campuses, or, more than that, the pressures across the country [to emulate] the model of the Carnegie Research . . . university." In 1970, UC Santa Cruz was classified by the Carnegie Foundation for the Advancement of Teaching as a liberal arts college. Today, UCSC is categorized as a Research II university (or an institution that awards 50 or more doctoral degrees each year, places a high priority on research, and receives federal support for scientific research totalling $15.5 million to $40 million per year) (*A Classification of Institutions of Higher Education* 1994).

Finally, the early spirit of undergraduate teaching at UCSC has been impacted by the retirements of many of the faculty pioneers who devoted their lives to the original dreams and missions of the institution. In addition to the reorganization, a founding father explains,

> the other thing which has made *enormous* changes in our campus happened just a couple of years ago: The [early] retirement incentive plans. . . . The last plan, which was called VERIP 3, is the one that I took advantage of. It provided incentives like additional years of service. . . . It was essentially impossible to turn down. It was simply too good. I essentially kept my salary, and that's incredible.

Individualism: Student-Centered Education

Third, the student-centered educational programs and ideals of early UCSC have, for the most part, disappeared. While the university retains its personalized narrative evaluation system (perhaps the campus' single greatest achievement in long-lasting innovation), and while students still have the opportunity to pursue individualized majors, fewer undergraduates at UCSC today are creating their own degrees and independent study programs. Over the last two decades, there has been a fairly steady drop in the percentage of students who complete a baccalaureate degree in a self-designed major. According to data provided by the Office of the Registrar (1996), in 1975-76, 8.1 percent of all undergraduate degrees awarded at UCSC were conferred upon students with individual majors; in 1981-82, this figure had dropped to 4.1 percent; in 1989-90, the percentage had decreased to 2.9 percent; and in 1994-95, the figure had fallen to just 1.6 percent.[16]

The founding commitment to individualized education, and the energy and enthusiasm for student-centered learning, interviewees report, has declined over the decades as curricular requirements have increased and have become more rigid and structured. A long-time professor explains:

> Our breadth [or general education] requirements [in the late 1960s], were that students would take three courses each from the natural sciences, the humanities, and the social sciences. Now, there are 11 or 13 different general education requirements. You have to take a quantitative course . . ., you have to take three particular kinds of courses in each of the disciplines. There are a lot of little detailed rules.

In the early years, a charter professor points out, the institution placed a "greater premium on students finding their own individual ways." "What has changed," he remarks, "is that [in the beginning], students . . . were encouraged" to pursue individualized programs. Now, students "can do [an independent major], but you really have to be fanatically determined to do it, and most students wouldn't even know that it can be done. The university is not anxious to further that kind of thing. It seems to me that is symptomatic of a kind of education [here] that is simply more conventional."

And again, the students, themselves, have changed. "The sixties are over," one veteran professor relates:

> [The] concern [now among students is] with getting a job. They did some surveys—the students' highest priorities [at UCSC] in 1969 or 1970 were (1) to better the world and (2) to develop my complete self and become a complete citizen. Maybe number (5) [on the list] was to make a lot of money. . . . That began to change [as the sixties ended and] the campus brought in [transfer] students [in order to maintain enrollments]. These students were much more focused on a job and

the next step in their lives rather then "let's go out in the redwoods and meditate. . . ." [The presence of transfer students] probably removed some of that [early] enthusiasm and spontaneity.

Close-Knit Community

Finally, over the years, the early feelings of faculty-student collegiality, the lively spirit and togetherness of the Culture Breaks and the all-night readings of *Finnegan's Wake*, have faded. While the Colleges at Santa Cruz have remained strong residential communities, with core courses, dinners, and College Nights (and nearly all first-year students living on campus), since the reorganization, faculty connectedness to the Colleges and to students has diminished.

The reorganization, in essence, broke the bonds and affiliation of the full-time professors with the Colleges. A professor of 27 years explains that the reorganization "eventually led to the transfer of something like 130 faculty from one office in one College to another office in another College." With the increasing emphasis on faculty research in the boards of studies, student accessibility to professors was limited. Growing class sizes and budgetary con-straints also resulted in the breaking up of the early close-knit faculty-student communities in the Colleges at UCSC.

Faculty "don't have time to stop and chat in the courtyard and have a cup of coffee with a student" like they used to, a veteran academic confesses. Profes-sors, he says, have become more and more burdened with teaching large lecture classes and taking on research responsibilities, and so there is less time for informal interactions with students: "It used to be that the faculty would have lunch in the dining hall. The faculty don't do that [anymore]. They don't show up at College Night, even though they're invited. . . . I'm speaking of Crown College in particular. Stevenson has probably maintained the collegial spirit more than some other Colleges. Perhaps Porter, too."

In the late 1960s, an early alumnus who now teaches at UCSC reveals, "you didn't know all of the 1,800 students on campus, but you couldn't walk around campus without sensing that you had seen all of these people before. You knew them all on that level of small-scale stuff, whereas now with 10,000 students, I clearly don't recognize the vast majority of people I pass on a path on campus. So, that's a major change."

A long-time professor and also an early alumnus observes:

> There are still a lot of faculty here that care about students. You still see faculty members having classes at their houses and out on the lawns when the weather is good. But you can't take 530 students out on the lawn! It's not like a little seminar where you could do that. And so that has changed. There are now an awful lot of larger classes at the expense of small seminars. . . . The separation of . . . academic life and

student life is a real division now that never used to exist in the early years.

Even Kresge College, with its early kin group organization and intensive familial-like bonding, has suffered the consequences of the reorganization and other tensions and constraints. Professors were becoming burnt out from the intensive interactions with students and colleagues. "Faculty members felt that they were asked to do too much," one long-time Kresge employee recalls, "that the emotional load on them was too heavy, that the amount of work that they had to do on the campus was too much. They wanted to have a greater sense of participation in their professional lives, and maybe a little less in the lives of the students." Today, she says, "you can come to a faculty meeting [at UCSC] and look at what's on the agenda, and have a discussion about that. You don't have to tell anybody what your true inner feelings are and why you were thinking that perhaps we should move in this direction [as in the early encounter group days at Kresge]. It's a much more business-like approach."

The Survival of the University of California, Santa Cruz, as an Innovative Institution

Thirty-one years later and the University of California, Santa Cruz, carries on as a collegiate public university. Given the shifts in the national economy, the budgetary cutbacks in California higher education (in the 1970s and today), and the short lives of many of UCSC's experimental campus counterparts from the 1960s and 1970s, what has kept this innovative institution alive? Taking a different turn on the topic, interviewees were asked to comment on UCSC's longevity—i.e., to share, if they could, some of the reasons why this distinctive university—unlike so many of the alternative campuses in the 1960s and 1970s—has survived.

Adaptability and Change

First, like the University of Wisconsin-Green Bay, UC Santa Cruz has been willing to reassess its original, 1960s-centered philosophies and to adapt its missions to serve the changing interests and needs of the student and faculty populations. While the reorganization of the campus was a radical and somewhat painful shift from the original distinctive ideals of the university, many professors and administrators believe that without this widescale restructuring, UCSC would not have survived the economic and enrollment downturns of the 1970s.

When applications were dropping in the 1970s, one administrator and long-time professor reveals, there was some concern that UCSC would be closed. University of California, Santa Cruz, had to sacrifice some of its early College-based programs to stay afloat in a changing social, political, and economic climate. Santa Cruz had to reinvent itself as a more conventional university.

A Public Institution

Second, others believe that for all of the pressures and constraints imposed by the University of California, UCSC probably would not have been able to survive had it not been a part of a large-scale public university system. In the words of an emeritus professor of physics, UCSC's survival is "partly [related to] the UC System. [UCSC] is endowed with a *huge* amount of guaranteed resources as compared to a small private college, which is *very* dependent upon students coming and on the external reputation" of the institution.

As former chancellor Robert L. Sinsheimer observes in his 1994 autobiography, "UC Santa Cruz was one of a group of colleges and universities launched in the 1960s . . . to 'reform' higher education. All fell on hard times. Santa Cruz survived only by virtue of its lifeline to the UC system" (272). While the University of California may have imposed pressures for change or standardization at the Santa Cruz campus, it seems to have also provided the institution with a sense of stability and security as a member of a larger family of highly acclaimed institutions.

Combining the Innovative with the Traditional

Finally, the early emphasis on both interdisciplinary, student-centered teaching and learning, and traditional disciplinary majors and research, seems to have "saved" this institution from collapse. The Santa Cruz campus was designed to offer the "best of both worlds" (the innovative education and close student-faculty collaboration of a small college community, and the research and scholarly resources of a large university). While the early free-spirited and interdisciplinary curriculum associated with the Colleges has faded, the collegiate university ideal (still thriving in the residential College structure) continues to attract students and faculty who are seeking an alternative to the conventional public university.

At the same time, UCSC's strong disciplinary programs, especially in the sciences, interviewees point out, have earned the campus national recognition and a following of high-ranking faculty. In a recent survey of more than 200 top research universities, UCSC was ranked 15th in the nation with regard to the quality of its research productivity (Graham and Diamond 1997). A veteran professor of history explains:

> One feature of this campus that doomed some of the other early utopian experiments [in higher education] [was that] they didn't have really first-class science, and you must have first-class research science as a university . . . if you're going to survive. We have had numerous Nobel laureates and members of the National Academy of Sciences on

this campus and continue to place in the top 10 in large numbers of categories in terms of graduate education, . . . publications, etc. . . . The sciences here have always been the straw that stirs the drink. They're far and away the largest earner of overhead moneys on grants and so on.

It is UCSC's grounding in both the conventional, scholarly disciplines (such as the sciences), and the student-centered innovations of the original collegiate ideals and dreams, that has guided this campus into the future and has helped to ensure a long life for UCSC.

Summing Up the Key Reasons for the Transformation of the Distinctive Early Ideals at the University of California, Santa Cruz

More than three decades since its opening day, UC Santa Cruz survives as a historically distinctive university in a conventional public higher education arena. Looking back over the life and lessons of this uncommon university, what, in summary, are the key factors that have affected the endurance and transformation of the original pioneering missions of UCSC?

Nearly all interviewees point to the changes in the economy, severe budgetary cutbacks, the faculty reward structure, and shifts in the attitudes and interests of students and faculty. They report that the tensions implicit in the dual organization of the early Colleges and boards of studies, the enrollment downturns of the 1970s, and pressures and standards imposed by the UC System, all resulted in the radical restructuring of the campus in the late 1970s. With the reorganization of UCSC, the academic emphases of the Colleges largely vanished, and the undergraduate teaching and interdisciplinary approaches of the university diminished. The University of California, Santa Cruz, today is an institution of excellence and high standing, according to interviewees, but it is not the campus of which its founders dreamed.

Despite its transformation, UC Santa Cruz still, in many ways, stands alone in the larger higher education community. The campus today, with its distinctive narrative evaluation system, its breathtaking forest setting and residential College communities, offers a unique alternative for students and faculty who are seeking a different kind of public university.

ISSUES AND CHALLENGES TO INNOVATION

Since its inception, UCSC has come up against pressures or tensions as a distinctive educational institution. This section of the case study explores some of the timeless issues and challenges to innovation that have impacted the lives of the students, faculty, and administrators at UCSC. These are campus stereotypes and image problems, founding faculty retirements and generational differences, and issues associated with narrative evaluations.[17]

Campus Stereotypes and Image Problems

Like many of the alternative campuses of the 1960s and 1970s, UC Santa Cruz has come up against negative stereotyping—e.g., misperceptions and bizarre mythologies about the campus as a haven for radicals, hippies, and "dope-smoking" students in the redwoods. "Because of its innovative programs and communal atmosphere," Adams (1984) writes, "Santa Cruz has always struggled against the perception that it is a haven for hippies and incompetents" (20).

"Santa Cruz always, always had this goofy kind of image that it was always fighting against!" a charter staff member reveals. "It was always trying to convince people that we [at UCSC] are really serious, we're doing wonderful things! I always felt that because we were state supported, we've had a certain kind of scrutiny and a certain kind of negative feeling about 'Oh, people in Santa Cruz, they live in teepees. They do this and that.' People didn't take us seriously and that *always* disturbed me."

Particularly damaging are the stereotypes that have emerged from within the UC System. A 24-year faculty veteran explains:

> A sometimes magnificent and sometimes foolish radical educational experiment such as this was embarrassing to the University of California. . . . Talk to a Berkeley faculty member, and he will somehow convey to you that Santa Cruz is some kind of a loony bin or there's no serious intellectual work [here]. This is very galling because UC Santa Cruz, especially now, is quite a respectable university, has many distinguished faculty people—Angela Davis or Norman O. Brown, Hayden White. . . . Even in our maturity, people at Berkeley can sort of make fun of us and not take us seriously. That translates into allocations of resources.

Founding Faculty Retirements and Generational Differences

Second, there is widespread concern over the recent wave of retirements among the core group of founding faculty at UCSC. Virtually all of the early faculty members that McHenry assembled in the 1960s have now retired under one of the recent (and highly attractive) retirement incentive packages offered by the university. In 1995-96, for example, only 2 of the original 46 faculty founders remained on the full-time faculty at UCSC. Veteran academics wonder whether the early spirit of the campus will vanish when the last of the pioneers retires.

"I'm one of the last handful [of founders] out of some 40 or 45 people who started!" proclaims one veteran professor. "A new generation has taken over," he relates, "and many of the younger faculty are much more professionally organized and much less interested in institutional reform. . . . That's a disappointment."

"I think the faculty memory of the early years is fading," a long-time professor in the sciences agrees. "From the first four years [of the university], probably 90 percent of the original faculty have now retired." Unless the founders can successfully "pass the baton" to the next generations of academics, he fears, the original identity of the institution may disappear.

In the heartfelt words of a founding administrator, "When those early retirements happened, that was very traumatic for this campus . . . and the loss was very seriously felt, and I don't think people have recovered from some of that. . . . It contributes to that feeling of loss" of experimentation and the spirit and vitality of the early years.

Issues Associated with Narrative Evaluations

Finally, there are issues associated with UCSC's narrative evaluation system. Narrative evaluations often present an unbearable burden for faculty who are teaching large lecture classes of several hundred students. A professor of 26 years explains:

> There are . . . faculty who have to write these [evaluations], who are saying, "Well, my colleagues [in other institutions], just sit there at the end of the quarter and go, 'A, B, B, C, B, A.' Meanwhile, I spend my Easter and Christmas laboriously entering this stuff." [While] some [faculty] believe very strongly [in the narratives], and have fought successfully to retain . . . evaluation[s], [others] are saying, "You're making me teach 100 students and you want me to write a narrative evaluation for 100 students?!"

Professors often have difficulty personalizing evaluations in a large class where they cannot get to know several hundred students. A College provost explains: "The increasing class size [at UCSC] has . . . jeopardized the narratives. How can you get to know the students well when there are large classes?" An emeritus professor in the social sciences, likewise, declares: "If you're going to write something sensible about a student, you have to know that student. If you're lecturing to 250 students, you ain't gonna know anything about any of them, except maybe two or three or four [students]." And a top-ranking official admits:

> The truth is, in large classes . . ., the narrative evaluation system just doesn't work. You can't do a narrative evaluation of 200 kids in a big lecture course. . . . We have tens of thousands of outstanding narrative evaluations that have never been [completed]. That's like taking a course and not getting a grade, and that's not a good thing.

"I have students who, spring quarter in their freshmen year, have never seen an evaluation from a course," a long-time professor agrees. "And it's very unsettling when you're just starting your first year, like 'How am I doing? I know I passed all of my classes, but how am I doing?'" He says that every two years,

> the faculty have to turn all their evaluations in, or they don't get a promotion. And so you'll see this scrambling. [The administration will say], "You've got 35 outstanding evaluations [and] we're not going to consider your case for tenure until you do them." So they will go back and produce these lost evaluations. That's unacceptable and that may kill yet the narrative evaluation system.

In addition to the amount of time that a faculty member must devote to writing the narrative evaluations, narrative evaluations are expensive for the university to produce and to maintain. A recent study at UCSC indicated that the total cost of the narrative evaluation system in 1989-90 was approximately $304,000 and in 1991-92 $437,000 over and above the cost of a traditional grading system (*Affirmation of Accreditation* 1994).

Finally, some have expressed concern about the narrative evaluation system and graduate school admissions. A founding staff member explains that in the early days,

> there was a lot of negativity [about the narrative evaluation system], a lot of challenging of it [such as:] "Oh my God. When our grads go out there in the world, what's going to happen to them? Will they get admitted to graduate school . . . if they [have only] evaluations?" It was proven over and over and over again, that when our graduates went out into the world, they became some very interesting, accomplished people who had lived through the Santa Cruz experience, had *thrived* on it.

Most colleges and universities around the country today are familiar with and accept UCSC's narrative evaluation system. According to UCSC admissions literature, "most UCSC graduates go on to advanced study, and 90 percent of those who apply to graduate schools are accepted. Medical and law school placement rates are well above State and national averages" (*UC Santa Cruz* n.d., 11).

CONCLUSION: SUMMARY AND IMPLICATIONS

In the end, the life and history of the University of California, Santa Cruz, is a remarkable story of struggle, innovation, and transformation. In the 1960s, UCSC in many ways revolutionized American public higher education by dividing the megaversity into smaller collegiate units, by promoting undergraduate teaching, interdisciplinary learning, and student-centered education in a close-knit, egalitarian community. Today, although you can still wander through forest solitude and follow paths through the redwoods to reach the eight residential Colleges at UCSC, the academic life of the institution revolves around the disciplines and departments at the university. The creative undergraduate teaching and individualized learning programs of the early years have faded.

To visit UC Santa Cruz today is to visit a much changed institution from the opening era. But it is also to experience a campus that is still set apart from the mainstream of higher education in several remarkable ways: the anti-competitive narrative evaluation system of grading, the integrating College core courses, and the residential cluster college communities in the breathtaking redwood forest. Looking back on the life of this uncommon university and the recollections and voices of its founding faculty and pioneers, what are some of the teachings or lessons of the Santa Cruz case study and history?

- The first lesson to be learned from the UCSC study is that inventive educational approaches and practices may be ill-fated in a public university system. At UC Santa Cruz, state enrollment formulas, UC appointment and promotion criteria, and budgetary pressures have all taken their toll on the campus' early distinctive educational missions.
- Second, it is critical that an innovative institution support and reward faculty members who are engaged in distinctive educational endeavors. If interdisciplinarity and creativity in teaching are to flourish in a research university, then the faculty reward structure must take into account excellence in interdisciplinary education, teaching, and program development.
- Third, external factors or forces (changes in the economy, shifting student and faculty attitudes and interests, changes in the job market) may have serious consequences for the longevity of educational innovation in a public college or university.
- Fourth, higher education institutions are people-centered environments and it is often the spirited pioneers who keep the original dreams of experimentation alive. Veteran academics at UCSC fear that when the last of the charter group of professors retires, the founding missions of the institution will be lost.
- Fifth, core courses or first-year seminars offer possibilities for innovation in a larger or conventional university. Narrative evaluation systems and residential college communities (that are architecturally and thematically distinct) may provide opportunities for cross-disciplinary connection and community building in a mainstream university.

- Finally, institutional flexibility and adaptability appear to be vital if a distinctive public institution is to meet the changing needs of its student and faculty populations. The University of California, Santa Cruz, has carried on with a sense of its heritage, but with new visions and new dreams. At the age of 31, UCSC has reinvented itself.

NOTES

1. The campuses were to become UC Irvine, UC San Diego, and UC Santa Cruz.
2. In planning the collegiate system at UCSC, McHenry was also influenced by Woodrow Wilson's proposed reforms for Princeton University, the house system at Yale and Harvard, and the cluster college organization of the University of Pacific and The Claremont Colleges (Duke 1996; McHenry 1977; Von der Muhll 1984).
3. Some veteran faculty believe that Kerr and McHenry decided to break the campus into smaller colleges to avoid the student demonstrations that were taking place at the multiversities like UC Berkeley, which had a central plaza. "The whole initial format [of UCSC] was a little hokey," one early professor reveals. "McHenry and Clark Kerr thought that to get away from the student protests at Berkeley, and the whole megauniversity, they'd break [UCSC] up into small colleges so that the students would have a hard time getting together to protest anything. The cover story was that [UCSC] would mimic the British system of colleges."
4. The faculty in astronomy, which did not offer an undergraduate major and whose primary base was some 50 miles away at the Lick Observatory, were not affiliated with a College (Von der Muhll 1984).
5. In the initial years of the university, both "Pass" and "Fail" grades were recorded on the student transcript. Since the winter quarter of 1972, only passing grades have been recorded on the transcript (Ring 1972).
6. At the time of the campus visit, the grade option was available in most upper division courses, but only in selected lower division courses at the institution. Today, UCSC undergraduates have the option of receiving a letter grade in any upper or lower division course at the university. This new policy—adopted by the UCSC academic senate in the spring of 1996—includes a "clause" whereby a faculty member or department can challenge a student's decision to receive a grade in any particular course.
7. One telephone interview was conducted in the summer of 1995 with the founding provost of Cowell College, the late Page Smith. Both Page Smith and the late Dean McHenry were true pioneers at UCSC and leading figures in the early educational innovations at Santa Cruz. I am grateful to have had the opportunity to talk with both of these legendary and guiding spirits of UCSC.
8. In the original plans for the university, "there weren't even to be departments," says a professor of 27 years. Soon after the campus was founded, however, the faculty found it necessary to organize themselves into disciplinary groupings for the purposes of providing graduate study and disciplinary programs and examinations for students.
9. In 1990, arts became the fourth division at UCSC (McHenry 1993).

10. The Colleges began to develop their own interdisciplinary majors around 1970, according to McHenry (1977). By 1975-76, he reports, there were six College majors (Arts and Crafts and Their History, and Western Civilization at Cowell; Modern Society and Social Thought at Stevenson; Latin American Studies at Merrill; Aesthetic Studies at College Five [Porter College]; and Women's Studies at Kresge College).

11. While most undergraduates received a grade of "Pass" or "Fail" in the early years of the university, students could request a letter grade in upper division courses that were required for the completion of a major in that field (*Undergraduate and Graduate Bulletin* 1966). To demonstrate mastery of the curriculum, all students were required to complete either a comprehensive exam or senior thesis.

12. There were other innovations at early UCSC that promoted the anticompetitive ethos. The university, for example, refused to establish big-time sports. Campus leaders favored intramural and club sports that stressed participation rather than competition (Adams 1984). The campus mascot was, and continues to be, the banana slug.

13. There are a few exceptions (e.g., the environmental studies, women's studies, ocean studies, and history of consciousness departments all offer interdisciplinary programs and approaches).

14. Porter College, which offers a variety of music, dance, theater, and arts seminars and practicums, is the exception.

15. The Garden Project was part of the spirit of the opening period of UCSC. According to Grant and Riesman (1978), "Students literally transformed the campus as they planted flowers along college pathways, grew vegetables, and cultivated the hillside above Cowell College where free bouquets were placed on stands each morning" (260–61).

16. Longitudinal data on individualized majors are available only for graduates of UCSC beginning in the 1975-76 academic year (degrees conferred between the summer of 1975 and the spring of 1976).

17. The issues associated with innovation in a large public higher education system are discussed throughout this chapter and, therefore, are not taken up here.

REFERENCES

Adams, W. 1984. Getting real: Santa Cruz and the crisis of liberal education. *Change* (May-June): 19–27.

Affirmation of accreditation self-study report. 1994. Santa Cruz: University of California, Santa Cruz, March.

Carter, L.J. 1971. U. of California at Santa Cruz: New deal for undergraduates? *Science* (15 January): 153–57, 171.

A classification of institutions of higher education 1994 edition. 1994. Princeton: The Carnegie Foundation for the Advancement of Teaching.

College by college, a public university in Oxford style is evolving at Santa Cruz. 1972. *Sunset Magazine* (June): 94–98.

The colleges: Living at the University of California, Santa Cruz. 1995. Santa Cruz: UCSC Publications and the Office of Admissions and Housing, August.

Duke, A. 1996. *Importing Oxbridge: English residential colleges and American universities.* New Haven: Yale University Press.

Graham, H.D., and N.A. Diamond. 1997. *The rise of American research universities: Elites and challengers in the postwar era.* Baltimore: Johns Hopkins University Press.

Grant, G., and D. Riesman. 1978. *The perpetual dream: Reform and experiment in the American college.* Chicago: The University of Chicago Press.

Kahn, M. 1981. The Kresge experiment. *Journal of Humanistic Psychology* 21 (2): 63–69.

McHenry, D.E. 1964. The University of California, Santa Cruz. In *Experimental colleges: Their role in American higher education,* edited by W.H. Stickler, 133–44. Tallahassee: Florida State University.

———. 1966. The problem of impersonality and size. An address given to the Utah Conference on Higher Education, Salt Lake City, September. Available through UC Santa Cruz Special Collections.

———. 1977. Academic organizational matrix at the University of California, Santa Cruz. In *Academic departments: Problems, variations, and alternatives,* D.E. McHenry and Associates, 86–116. San Francisco: Jossey-Bass.

———. 1993. University of California, Santa Cruz. In *Important lessons from innovative colleges and universities,* edited by V.R. Cardozier, 37–53. *New Directions for Higher Education* no. 82 (summer).

Office of Planning and Budget. 1997. Santa Cruz: University of California, Santa Cruz. See also the Institutional Research and Policy Studies World Wide Web page at: http://planning.ucsc.edu/irps/

Office of the Registrar. 1996. Institutional data on the number of degrees awarded to undergraduate students with individual majors. Santa Cruz: University of California, Santa Cruz.

Ring, L.J. 1971. *Innovation at Santa Cruz—more than tinkering.* Paper presented at the 1971 Conference of the American Association for Higher Education, Chicago, March. (ERIC Document Reproduction Service No. ED 056 667)

———. 1972. University of California, Santa Cruz. In *Innovations in undergraduate education: Selected institutional profiles and thoughts about experimentalism,* edited by N.R. Berte, 45–63. Tuscaloosa: The University of Alabama.

Sinsheimer, R.L. 1994. *The strands of a life: The science of and the art of education.* Berkeley: University of California Press.

Smith, P., and C. Daniel. 1975. *The chicken book.* Boston: Little, Brown.

So you're thinking of coming to Santa Cruz. 1969. Brochure. Santa Cruz: University of California, Santa Cruz, June.

Thelin, J.R. 1977. California and the colleges. *California Historical Quarterly* LVI, no. 2 (summer): 140–63.

UC Santa Cruz. n.d. Viewbook. Santa Cruz: Office of Admissions, University of California, Santa Cruz.

UC Santa Cruz general catalog 1995-96. 1995. Santa Cruz: University Advancement, University of California, Santa Cruz.

Undergraduate and graduate bulletin. 1966. Catalog. Santa Cruz: University of California, Santa Cruz.

Undergraduate program. 1965. Catalog. Santa Cruz: University of California, Santa Cruz.

Von der Muhll, G. 1984. The University of California at Santa Cruz: Institutionalizing Eden in a changing world. In *Against the current: Reform and experiment in higher education*, edited by R.M. Jones and B.L. Smith, 51–92. Cambridge, Mass.: Schenkman.

CHAPTER 7

The Evergreen State College

"No Carbon Copy of Other State Institutions"

*I had no intention of living in the Northwest! I'm an East Coast, snow
and sun person. . . . I didn't unpack for seven years. I said, "I can't live
here!" . . . But, I'm telling you, when I came to work, it was like I
couldn't* imagine *spending the majority of my day at any other place
where the values were so strange. It just felt like I needed to be here.
The values were clear. They were mine. They were what I believed in.*
An Evergreen faculty member of 23 years

BACKGROUND: SETTING THE SCENE

Nestled on 1,000 acres of forest land that extends upward from 3,300
feet of beachfront on Eld Inlet of Puget Sound is The Evergreen State
College, an innovative public liberal arts college in Olympia, Washington. The campus is located just 20 minutes from the state capitol in
downtown Olympia and is a one-hour drive from the Olympic Mountains and
Mount Rainier on the Cascade Mountain Range. At the edge of the campus,
there is a 13-acre organic farm and a cozy farmhouse where students and
faculty gather for potlucks, retreats, and suppers. Hiking trails and paths
through the forest lead to Geoduck beach,[1] where students can rent canoes or
kayaks and explore Puget Sound.

At the heart of the campus there is a red-brick plaza (Red Square) that
Evergreeners must pass through to reach most campus buildings. On one side
of Red Square, there is the College Activities Building ("the CAB"), a campus

hub that houses campus eateries, the bookstore, student organization offices, and the college radio station (KAOS-FM). During the lunch hour on a chilly winter's day, the CAB comes alive with energy and activity: Groups of students in a unique assortment of self-styled garments gather in circles on carpeted floors and in chairs near the deli area to share ideas about their classes and to talk about life, dreams, and politics. Vendors sell earthy-looking hats and jewelry at the entryway to the CAB, and posters and banners advertising campus events hang from the second-floor balcony and catch your eye.

Adjacent to the CAB is the Library Building, a multi-purpose structure that houses the main library, admissions office, advising center, and college administrative offices. Inside the building, there are murals designed by students as class projects, including a three-story dragon mural in the library stairwell that was designed by the members of the Man and His Art program in the opening year of the college (Clemens 1987). A short walk across Red Square is the Lecture Halls building ("significantly, the smallest structure in the center of campus") (Tommerup 1993, 88), the Lab I and Lab II (arts and sciences) buildings, and an arts annex. The newest addition to the Evergreen campus is the Longhouse Education and Cultural Center, a wooden structure that is modeled after the historical longhouses of the Northwestern Coastal Native American communities. The Longhouse serves as a nucleus for multicultural studies and activities at Evergreen (*Evergreen Self-Guided Tour* n.d.; *The Evergreen State College 1997-98 Catalog* 1997; Lyons 1991).

The Founding

The story of The Evergreen State College begins in November of 1964 when the Council of Presidents of the five state-supported colleges and universities in Washington (the University of Washington, Washington State University, Central Washington State College [now Central Washington University], Eastern Washington State College [now Eastern Washington University], and Western Washington State College [now Western Washington University]) issued a report examining the status and future of higher education in the state of Washington. The report, titled "A Plan for Public Higher Education in Washington," noted that the population of western Washington was rapidly increasing and recommended that the state legislature establish a new public college in order to accommodate projected enrollment increases (Clemens 1987; *Grounds for Greatness* n.d.; *The Making of the College* n.d.).

Acting on the council's recommendations, the 1965 legislature assembled a Temporary Advisory Council on Public Higher Education composed of legislators, state college and university presidents, community college representatives, and public leaders. The Temporary Advisory Council was charged with the task of determining whether a new college was needed in western Washington and, if so, where the campus should be located and what kind of institution it should be (Clemens 1987). The Advisory Council utilized the services of a consulting firm (Nelson Associates, Inc., of New York) to investigate the issue of population growth and the future demand for higher education in western Washington.

"Not blessed with a crystal ball," Mark Clemens (1987) points out in his 20-year profile of The Evergreen State College, the consulting firm concluded that higher education enrollments would rapidly expand in the 1970s and that Washington's existing public and private campuses would not be able to accommodate a projected applicant pool of nearly 17,000 students by 1975 unless new institutions were built. "At the earliest possible time," wrote Nelson Associates in their 1966 report, "a new four-year college should be authorized." The campus, they said, should be prepared to enroll 10,000 students by 1975.[2]

In October 1966, the Temporary Advisory Council submitted its final report to the state legislature, supporting the consulting firm's recommendation that the state open a new four-year college as soon as possible. The Advisory Council proposed that the college be located in Thurston County, within a 10-mile radius of Olympia, and that the site incorporate at least 600 acres. On March 1, 1967, the 40th legislature "voted Evergreen into being," authorizing the founding of a four-year campus that would be located in the Olympia area. Evergreen would be the first public four-year college to be founded in the state of Washington since 1896 (Clemens 1987; *Washington's Newest State College* n.d.; Youtz 1984).

The legislature proposed three major objectives for the new "Southwest Washington State College" (as it was then known): (1) to serve the needs of southwest Washington; (2) to provide services to the Washington State government and its employees; and (3) to develop an innovative structure that would not duplicate existing academic resources in the state. Gordon Sandison, the state senator who chaired the Temporary Advisory Council on Public Higher Education, was instrumental in encouraging this third mission of educational innovation. At the first meeting of the newly formed board of trustees, Sandison announced: "It was not the intent of the Legislature that this be just another four-year college; it is a unique opportunity to meet the needs of the students of today and the future because the planning will not be bound by any rigid structure of tradition as are the existing colleges, nor by any overall central authority, as is the case in many states" (cited in Youtz 1984, 95).

On August 15, 1968, the board of trustees "definitely made a commitment to nontraditional education" in selecting Dr. Charles McCann, dean of the faculty at Central Washington State College, as founding president of The Evergreen State College[3] (Clemens 1987). Charter faculty member Byron L. Youtz (1984) reports: McCann was an "articulate spokesman for individualizing the college learning experience" (95). At his very first press meeting,

McCann proclaimed that Evergreen "would be 'no carbon copy' of other state institutions" (Clemens 1987).

The Washington State legislature provided the funds so that The Evergreen State College would have a year (1970-71) to plan and to prepare for the opening of the institution. A pioneering group of 18 faculty members, three academic deans, and a provost was hired to design the curricular programs, the governance structures, and the initial policies and procedures for the new college (Youtz 1984). The planners represented a unique mix of educational philosophies and pedagogical approaches, including advocates of Great Books programs, proponents of self-paced and collaborative learning, supporters of cooperative and wilderness education, and advocates of independent study. Many of the charter academics and administrators were drawn from other educational experiments, such as the State University of New York (SUNY), Old Westbury; Prescott College in Arizona; New College in Florida; University of California (UC), Santa Cruz; the General Program Experiment at San Jose State; and the Interdisciplinary Science Program at Oregon State.

Perhaps the most influential of these early visionaries was Mervyn Cadwallader, one of Evergreen's three founding deans and the former director of the San Jose State College experimental program (1965–1969). Cadwallader was a disciple of Alexander Meiklejohn, the educational reformer who led the Experimental College at the University of Wisconsin (1927–1932) (Meiklejohn 1932). Cadwallader had modeled his San Jose program around Meiklejohn's interdisciplinary experiment and Joseph Tussman's Meiklejohn-inspired Experimental College at UC Berkeley (1965–1969) (Cadwallader 1984; Tussman 1969). As a founding dean at Evergreen, Cadwallader seized the opportunity to transport the ideas of Meiklejohn to Evergreen and its planning faculty team. As Youtz (1984) writes, "Much of the curriculum planning effort of the first year was devoted to detailed design of the strongest possible and most diverse set of Meiklejohn-like interdisciplinary programs we could conceive. We called them 'Coordinated Studies'"[4] (97).

Coordinated Studies drew on the structural and pedagogical features of Meiklejohn's general education reforms at Wisconsin. They were conceived of as year-long, team-taught, multidisciplinary academic programs involving four to five faculty members and 80 to 100 students. Each program would offer a common reading list and schedule, program retreats, small seminars, and cooperative projects. Students would receive narrative evaluations rather than letter grades (Clemens 1987; Youtz 1984). The faculty team would hold weekly faculty seminars to exchange curricular ideas and to discuss the reading list and the interdisciplinary instruction. Each Coordinated Studies program would be bound together by a "covenant"—a written agreement that would set forth the duties and expectations of program participants and define the basis upon which credit was to be awarded to students.

Along with the Coordinated Studies programs, the planning faculty and administrators of Evergreen instituted several other key components of the first-year college curriculum (all of which remain intact at the campus today): Individual Learning Contracts (independent study contracts that would be negotiated between a student and a faculty member); Group Contracts (20 to 40 students and a faculty member [or two] "would agree to study a particular field or subject in depth, full time, for one or more quarters") (Youtz 1984, 99); and internships and cooperative education programs. Early on, the founders decided that there would be no majors, no departments, no faculty ranks, and no educational requirements at Evergreen.

While the planners worked day and night to complete the educational designs for the college, and the buildings began to emerge, Clemens (1987) reports, "the town watched and waited." On October 4, 1971, The Evergreen State College would open its doors, welcoming an entering class of 1,178 students and 55 members of the faculty. (The planning faculty had selected 37 faculty members out of more than 7,000 applicants to join the innovative campus in the first year.) (Jones 1981) It was a spirited time in the life of the college. The first courses were held in temporary classrooms, faculty homes, churches, legislative chambers, state parks, and even on an island until the campus buildings were completed in late October. After months of intensive preparation and planning, The Evergreen State College had come to life.

Evergreen Today

Today The Evergreen State College enrolls 3,625 students (3,410 undergraduates and 215 graduate students). Of the 3,625 students, 2,067 (57 percent) are female and 1,558 (43 percent) are male. Five percent of Evergreen students are Asian American; 4 percent are African American; 4 percent are Latino; another 4 percent are Native American; and 83 percent are European American or members of other ethnic groups. Sixty-seven percent of the entering classes at Evergreen hail from Washington State, and 27 percent of all Evergreen students live on campus. Thirty-eight percent of Evergreen students are age 25 or older (The Evergreen State College 1997-98 Catalog 1997).[5]

There are 423 administrators and staff members at The Evergreen State College. The faculty is comprised of approximately 205 full-time and 75 part-time academics (B.L. Smith, personal communication, 12 March 1997). Forty-one percent of the faculty are female, 59 percent are male, and 25 percent are persons of color. Eighty-one percent of the faculty hold the Ph.D. or other terminal degree. The instructional student-to-faculty ratio at the college is 22 to 1 (The Evergreen State College 1997-98 Catalog 1997).

The college continues to honor the distinctive early ethos of the founders of the institution. There are still no majors, no general education requirements, no disciplinary departments, no faculty ranks, and no grades at this uncommon college. Undergraduates receive narrative evaluations of their academic work and are required to complete 180 quarter credit hours to receive a baccalaureate (B.A. or B.S. degree). In nearly all cases, students enroll in one full-time Coordinated Studies program or contract of study per quarter. Faculty, likewise, devote themselves to full-time teaching in a single program or contracted study area each term.

In addition to a diverse range of Coordinated Studies programs, the college offers Core programs (originally called Basic Programs) that introduce first- or second-year students to Coordinated Studies as a foundation of knowledge and skills for more advanced work at Evergreen. Evergreen today offers three types of Contracted Studies: Individual Learning Contracts, Group Contracts, and Internship Learning Contracts (an independent plan for conducting an internship that is negotiated between a student [usually a junior or senior], faculty sponsor, and field supervisor at an internship site—e.g., a business, social service agency, or nonprofit organization) (*The Evergreen State College 1996-97 Catalog* 1996; *Student Advising Handbook* 1995).

There are five general "foci" of the Evergreen curriculum (identified in internal strategic planning documents in the mid-1980s) that reflect the core values of the institution. These are: (1) interdisciplinary study; (2) personal engagement in learning; (3) linking theoretical perspectives with practice; (4) collaborative/cooperative work; and (5) teaching across significant differences (a commitment to gender, ethnic, and cultural diversity in the curriculum and in admissions and faculty and staff hiring procedures) (*Constancy and Change* 1989).

All curricular offerings at Evergreen today are organized within five interdisciplinary curricular areas or "Planning Groups" (formerly called Specialty Areas): Expressive Arts; Environmental Studies; Scientific Inquiry; Social Science; and Culture, Text and Language. All Evergreen faculty members are affiliated with one of the Planning Groups.[6]

The campus today offers graduate studies leading to the degrees of master of environmental studies, master of public administration, and master in teaching. The college also provides part-time studies and evening and weekend programs that are team taught and interdisciplinary, and geared toward the schedules of working adults (*The Evergreen State College 1997-98 Catalog* 1997).

Today, The Evergreen State College is known far and wide for its interdisciplinary, collaborative Coordinated Studies programs. There are a number of distinctive public service centers at the college that are funded by the state legislature to carry out the campus' educational service mission. The Washington Center for Improving the Quality of Undergraduate Education at Evergreen was founded in 1985. It is committed to higher education reform and to sharing resources with other institutions to support the development of interdisciplinary learning community programs. The center facilitates faculty exchanges, coordinates workshops and conferences, and provides technical support to assist other campuses in providing high-quality, interdisciplinary approaches to teaching and learning. There are currently 46 colleges and universities participating in Washington Center programs, including all of Washington State's public four-year institutions and community colleges, 10 independent colleges, and one tribal college (*The Evergreen State College 1997-98 Catalog* 1997).

ORGANIZATON OF THIS CHAPTER

This chapter explores the history and endurance of educational innovation at The Evergreen State College. The case study begins with a demographic profile of the interview participants in this study, the current and past generations of the college community who shared their voices and memories of the campus in this investigation. The next section draws upon the archival documents and the data gathered in the interviews to describe the early distinctive educational ideals of Evergreen. The chapter then traces the evolution of these beginning ideals, focusing on where and how the college has kept alive its innovative philosophies and where and how the institution has changed or transformed itself. The next section examines key issues or challenges, pressures or tensions to innovation at Evergreen. The case study concludes with a summary and a reflection on the Evergreen story and its implications for reform and experimentation in American higher education.

INTERVIEW PARTICIPANT PROFILE

To explore the history and current status of innovation at The Evergreen State College, 22 semi-structured interviews were conducted with founding and/or current faculty members, administrators, and students in late January and early February of 1996. Each interview lasted about 50 minutes. The participants included 15 faculty members (including six members of the planning year faculty), 10 administrators (including the current president, the founding president, and the academic vice president), four alumnae/i (three of whom graduated in the first eight years of the institution), and one student. (Some individuals occupied more than one role at the institution.) The interviewees included 13 men and nine women from several different "generations" of the Evergreen community: Eight of the participants joined Evergreen in either its preopening years or planning year (1968–1970, 1970-71), another eight started in the first three years of the institution (1971–1973), two arrived in the college's eighth or ninth year (1978, 1979), and four joined the college in its 19th year or later (1989–1995). Excluding the current student, the "tenure" for the interviewees at Evergreen ranged from four to 28 years, with an average length of stay of 21.3 years at the institution.[7]

DISTINCTIVE EARLY IDEALS AT THE EVERGREEN STATE COLLEGE

"The Midnight Oil Burning Society," Clemens (1987) reports, "is how the campus *Newsletter* referred to the three deans and 18 faculty members who worked days, nights and weekends pulling dreams out of thin air and transforming them into real programs that would be offered to real students." Arguments, thoughts, ideas, conferences, reports—a kind of chaos—McCann said at the time, were "hammered into a positive, creative force by imaginative, determined people." What resulted in this year-long, intensive "act of creation" was a vision for the new institution that embraced a "list of negatives" (no departments, no ranks, no requirements, no grades) accompanied by a "vaguer list of positives" (collaboration, interdisciplinary study, individualized education) (McCann 1977). The planners and early faculty members fleshed out an original curricular scheme for Evergreen that included the following key distinctive ideals: (1) interdisciplinary teaching and learning; (2) individualized or student-centered education; (3) undergraduate teaching and faculty freedom; (4) egalitarianism (an absence of faculty ranks and grades; students and faculty as co-learners; participatory governance); and (5) experiential learning (internship and practical engagement in issues, social problems, and professional fields). Each of these early unique attributes of The Evergreen State College is described in the sections that follow.

Interdisciplinary Teaching and Learning

First, interdisciplinary education was the heart and soul of the early Evergreen curriculum. Collaborative, team-taught Coordinated Studies programs were intended to be the cornerstone of the teaching and learning experience, offering multidisciplinary exploration of diverse fields of study and inquiry. The idea, according to an early informational brochure, was that in "small, cooperative learning communities, usually involving 100 students and five faculty from different fields," students would "study common topics or problems from a variety of academic perspectives" (*Once Over Lightly* 1971, 2). The opening year catalog instructed prospective students: "Instead of studying, for example, Sociology, Economics, or Psychology as disparate, self-justifying fields, you will study central problems or themes by learning to make use of appropriate techniques from these several disciplines" (*The Evergreen State College Bulletin 1971-72* 1971, 19).

The first-year curriculum offered a lively blend of Coordinated Studies programs. A sampling of the titles from the 1971-72 academic year includes

Causality, Chance and Freedom, a program that integrated philosophy, history of science, mathematics, computer science, neuropsychology, psychology, and biology; Contemporary American Minorities, which offered perspectives from African American studies, Native American education and organization, and American literature; Human Development, which linked psychology, education, history, comparative literature, biology, philosophy, and anthropology; and Space, Time, Form, which combined physics with visual arts, "physical science aesthetics," political science, and history (*Once Over Lightly* 1971).

The Evergreen planners decided that there should be no academic departments, no specialized groupings of faculty preserving the "sacred" walls between the disciplines. Faculty members would teach outside of their fields of expertise and work side by side with students in multidisciplinary learning communities. President McCann (1977) recalls:

> We [the founders of Evergreen] were committed to exploring interdisciplinary study as far as it could be taken with undergraduates . . ., to study phenomena from as many angles simultaneously as the expertness of the faculty would supply. We expected a side effect, in that as an expert becomes occasionally a learner in interdisciplinary study, a student benefits from the powerful example of a faculty member in the art of learning. When interdisciplinary—our term is *coordinated*—studies work at their best, faculty members begin to uncover new ways of knowing, new angles of pursuing and widening their own areas of study. (151)

A long-time faculty member in art reveals the thrills and challenges of engaging in cross-disciplinary teaching at early Evergreen:

> The . . . thing [about coming to Evergreen] was that I was going to teach with people outside of my discipline. I would get an opportunity to teach with people in philosophy, in science, things like that. . . . Scared me to death! . . . The first program I was in was called Words, Sounds, and Images. [The faculty team] all took turns presenting each week and designing things . . . that everybody did. So, when [faculty member] Robert Gottlieb said we would all learn to sing a [German piece] by Beethoven and learn to read music, I couldn't just say, "While my students are doing it, I'm gonna go out for a cup of coffee." And I had such a block about singing. I had to get out my terrors just as the [students] all did and it was hard—I had to read all of these books and be able to talk about it with these students. . . . But, as tiring as it was, as difficult as it was, it was a *world* that I couldn't believe was happening. . . . The students couldn't believe it. Nobody could believe it.

Individualism: Student-Centered Education

Second, the pioneering planners of Evergreen embraced the idea of individualized learning and placing the student at the center of the educational process. While Coordinated Studies emphasized the interdisciplinary connections of academic fields in a collaborative learning community, Contracted Studies allowed for independent study of a particular subject or interest area. A founding academic dean explains: "So on the one hand, you would have this [Coordinated Studies] group which could get as large as four or five faculty members and over 100 students who would be doing nothing else but be a little college by themselves for a whole year. Then, on the other hand, quarter by quarter, individual research projects."

"Many of us [early faculty and administrators]," writes McCann (1977), "believed that learning occurs best when the learner takes responsibility for the program of study" (151). In preliminary campus announcements, the planners stressed that the student would "contribute actively to his own learning and that of other students through discussions and presentations. He will not merely receive facts and ideas from his teachers; he will be constantly encouraged by them to learn for himself and to make his work count by improving his skills as a communicator" (*The Evergreen State College* 1970). In the words of the first Evergreen catalog, "Instead of listening passively to lectures most of the time, you will be responsible for engaging actively in regular discussion" (*The Evergreen State College Bulletin 1971-72* 1971, 21).

Through Contracted Studies and highly engaging, student-centered Coordinated Studies programs, students would be free to design their own academic plans and to direct their own academic lives. In the words of a planning faculty member, "We wanted students to understand that they played an active role in their education, that they were responsible for the kinds of decisions and choices that they made, and to learn *how* to be responsible for them." Youtz (1984) explains: "'Learning how to learn', that is, helping students to become independent of their teachers, was one of our principal educational goals" (98).

There would be no educational requirements and no majors at Evergreen so that each individual student could design and follow his or her own learning pathway. The planners also did away with grades to ensure that students would be evaluated on the basis of personal achievements and individual growth and development. Professors would write narrative evaluations of each student, commenting on the individual's unique attributes and skills. An alumnus who attended Evergreen in the 1970s comments: "I went to Washington State University my freshmen year and I was disillusioned by the fact that I found myself working for a grade rather than working for knowledge. [Evergreen] allowed me to come alive intellectually. I had ownership over my education. ... I came away with an incredible sense of empowerment."

Undergraduate Teaching and Faculty Freedom

Third, teaching was to be the heart of faculty life at the college. In the words of one of the planning faculty members,

> We [charter faculty] were interested in making a place that would keep undergraduate teaching and learning in the center of activity, rather than faculty publication, athletics, student politics, [etc.] and to have everything flow from that and back to that. [Teaching] was the end-all and be-all that we thought ought to animate the place. And so that's what we tried to do. That was the main thing. That was first and last what we thought we were about.

There were no academic departments and no curriculum committees dictating what or how a faculty member could teach. Academics had the freedom to engage in creative teaching styles and to invent new courses. A faculty member who was hired in the 1970s reports:

> One year, [all] I did [was individual student] contracts. I said to students that I didn't want to ever come to campus, that I will do a contract with you, but I have decided that this quarter, I don't want to be on campus. I don't want to think of myself as somebody who goes to an office. I'll meet you anywhere you want. I'll meet you in restaurants.... I'll come to your house. I will "be teacher, will travel." So, I had this whole mess of students and I used to go to all of these different places.

To ensure that teaching was kept fresh and alive at Evergreen, the early faculty members decided not establish a tenure system. A veteran academic in the sciences explains:

> [The faculty] decided that there wouldn't be tenure [at Evergreen] because we wanted to avoid the old "yellow pages syndrome" that we all knew from our own college days. You know, the old yellow page of lecture notes! The old guys that work like hell the first seven years of their [academic] life and then have an early retirement and do the same thing [in their classes] over and over forever! That happens in tenured institutions. . . . We thought that tenure was an unnecessary thing.

Evergreen faculty would receive three-year contract appointments and would be evaluated on the basis of cumulative portfolios of their teaching activities, including evaluations that were written by students, faculty colleagues, and academic deans. The portfolio would also include self-evaluations and evaluations submitted by the faculty member to students, colleagues, and deans. In the words of one charter academic, it was decided that "the faculty [would be] required to write self-evaluations [and that] students would evaluate faculty so that faculty could understand what they needed to do to be better teachers, to continue to grow."

At the same time, the founders believed that the curriculum should be constantly changing or "self-destructing" from year to year to ensure a continuing sense of vitality and excitement about teaching. In the words of the 1972-73 Evergreen catalog, "In order to keep abreast of the changing world and to capitalize quickly on our own experience, we do not simply carry forward to the next year's catalog the listings in the previous year's. . . . This arrangement insures a degree of freshness and the benefits of a thoughtful review of the opportunities for learning that Evergreen represents" (11–12). An alumnus and current member of the faculty reports: "When the campus first started, [the faculty] had this rule . . . that you're not allowed to repeat anything you'd done previously. The reason [for this] was there was a big fear amongst faculty initially that we'd slide back into a traditional mode of teaching . . ., that [teaching] could get stale here, and there was an idea that we don't want things to get stale here."

Egalitarianism

Fourth, the campus was devoted to participatory, egalitarian community ideals. As Jack H. Schuster (1989) reports in his site visit report for the Carnegie Foundation for the Advancement of Teaching, the planners of Evergreen set out to build something "akin to a 'classless society.' This was a conscious effort. First names were universally used by faculty, staff, and students" (7).

The dividing lines between students and faculty and between faculty cohorts were knocked down at early Evergreen. There was no faculty rank, no seniority system creating artificial distinctions among teachers. Charter faculty member Byron L. Youtz explains:

> At the outset of our curricular planning in 1970, it became clear that academic rank would be a serious impediment to the team teaching methods of Coordinated Studies. Members of a team could best work as co-equals so that the subject area expertise could pass from one member of the team to another as required by the study plan rather than by some seniority system. (Youtz 1984, 109)

This meant that young, new faculty members were equally as likely to facilitate a Coordinated Studies program as were the more experienced academics at Evergreen. "In teaching a Coordinated Study Program," Youtz says, "all faculty [would] learn from one another independent of seniority" (109).

A historian who was hired in the very first years of the campus puts it this way:

> We [early faculty] were going to be asking people to come here and give up certain professional directions and take a risk professionally.

> We didn't want there to be artificial levels, so we did away with rank.... And [it was hoped that] there would be honest communication back and forth between faculty and students, and that we would get rid of the artificial categories and the titles. You'd be on a first-name basis [with students].

Coordinated Studies programs would be collaborative ventures with students and faculty working in partnership in the learning process. As Kenneth G. Gehret observed in a 1972 article about Evergreen, "the distinction between students and teachers is played down [at Evergreen]; professors are thought of as co-learners with their classes" (17).

Evergreen's cooperative, anticompetitive ethos was also fostered through the absence of traditional letter grades. An early faculty member explains that the founders wanted "to get rid of the grading system . . . to create an equity amongst students, to get rid of the competition in the classroom." Student evaluation would, again, center on the individual accomplishments and growth of the learner (as captured in the narrative evaluations).

Campus governance structures, too, reflected the early egalitarian mission of Evergreen. Rather than having a few officials at the top making all of the decisions for the college, Evergreen sought to involve all campus constituencies in governance, with "a broad base of participation and from points of view that are shared and that represent college-wide concerns" (*The Evergreen State College Bulletin 1972-73* 1972, 13). There would be open and honest communication (what one planning faculty member referred to as "good faith") in decision making. Students would have a great deal of input in campus governance.

To prevent power-wielding structures from "penetrating" the campus, the college also created temporary ad hoc committees (called "Disappearing Task Forces" or DTFs) that involved students, faculty, and staff in consensus decision making (*The Evergreen State College Bulletin 1972-73* 1972). According to Youtz (1984), "The planners had an abhorrence for the lethargy and inertia which they had experienced elsewhere with standing committees, to say nothing of the power (and hence the politics) which such committees vested in a few members of the academic community" (98). The DTFs would address a single problem or task, and when the work of the group was completed, the task force would disband, disappear.

In addition, the academic deans at Evergreen would serve rotating, temporary appointments, and would be drawn from the faculty. "That [was] real healthy!" a founding academic exclaims. "Administrators," in general, he says, "were going to be locatable and accountable for their decisions." This *included* the president of the institution:

> Charlie McCann was *totally* committed to democratic procedures. By the time I got to Evergreen [in 1970], I was not madly in love with

academic administrators, but one of the things that blew me away about Charlie was that he *always* went to democratic procedures. So, when we were getting down to something like, say, salary [or] when we had to develop governance policy for the college, we had everybody from the hardest core bureaucrat on the one hand to the secretaries on the other on that team. And we, the team, made the policy. Charlie would make input if he felt like it, but he did not intrude. . . . And that's a *hell* of a statement about him! There have been very few academic administrators who didn't just verbalize that democracy. [Charlie] never once violated it. . . . Charlie would come to seminars. His door was always open. I could walk into his office any time if he wasn't with somebody, and I could talk to him. From my point of view, for a college president, that was just astonishing!

Experiential Learning

Finally, experiential, out-of-classroom learning was integral to the distinctive educational philosophy of Evergreen. Internships relating to both career learning (professional or job skills) and service learning (social or community service) were available to students through the Individual Contract system—an Office of Cooperative Education was established in the college's first year to assist with field placements and supervision (*The Evergreen State College Bulletin 1972-73* 1972; Youtz 1984). The campus was committed to providing relevant, out-of-classroom learning experiences to students. An early brochure stated:

> Traditionally, students have left the "real world," entered college to advance their education and, four years later, returned to that "real world." Since the world changes so rapidly . . ., reentry after four years can be a harrowing, even irrelevant experience for students. Consequently, Evergreen's programs place great emphasis on student participation in off-campus community activities—as tutors in local schools, as companions to psychiatric patients, as aids in hospitals, as participants in community events, as information gatherers for various groups, as interns in business and governmental agencies and other experiences. (*Once Over Lightly* 1971, 6–7)

Internships, apprenticeships, and field placements were integrated into the campus' curricular offerings. According to the 1972-73 *Evergreen State College Bulletin*, the idea was to "couple experience of the real world with reflection. Although sophisticatedly informed and rational habits of thought may be acquired and strengthened through campus-based efforts, those reflective capabilities are not likely to prove most useful unless they are engaged with direct experience of the institutions and the people through whom the larger society conducts its business and empirically reveals itself" (13–14).

In the eloquent words of one charter academic, "Our belief was that the future would belong to people who were able to fuse their life and learning.... What we achieved was trying to create a learning environment which would challenge students to see that there's no effective separation between the way you live your life and the things that you learn and the things that you're asked to apply out of that learning."

ENDURANCE AND TRANSFORMATION OF THE DISTINCTIVE EARLY IDEALS AT THE EVERGREEN STATE COLLEGE

More than 25 years later, and the dreams of the founders are alive and flourishing at Evergreen. The guiding missions or ideals of the campus planners, the unorthodox strategies and styles of education remain remarkably well preserved. In fact, the very same principles that the founders envisioned for the college some 25 years ago, are ever-present in the catalogs, brochures, planning documents, and reports that are published by and about the campus today (e.g., *Constancy and Change* 1989; *The Evergreen State College* 1995; *The Evergreen State College 1997-98 Catalog* 1997; Lyons 1991; Tommerup 1993). The five curricular foci of the institution are a testament to the staying power of the original distinctive educational ideals and the institution's increasing commitment to diversity and to serving the needs of the educational community both within and beyond the southwest Washington region. In the words of a high-ranking administrator,

> Evergreen has remained remarkably true to [its early visions] over time and it *remains* an extraordinarily *internally consistent* institution in that sense—[in] the way [the campus] grades and the way students organize themselves, the way academic programs are organized, the way the curriculum is constructed *remains consistent with* that founding theory of knowledge. I've never been at an institution that's so clear about what it's about.

This section of the case study draws upon the voices of the interviewees, the archival materials, and campus histories to examine the endurance and evolution of Evergreen's early distinctive educational themes (interdisciplinary teaching and learning, individualism, undergraduate teaching and faculty freedom, egalitarianism, and experiential learning). It then explores the longevity or "survival" of the institution, and offers a summary of the key reasons for the preservation of the innovative founding ideals of Evergreen.

Interdisciplinary Teaching and Learning

First, interdisciplinarity remains a centerpiece of the Evergreen curriculum. Cross-disciplinary educational programs are at the heart of the academic experience today, and interdisciplinary learning has been singled out as one of the five educational foci of the institution. According to the 1996-97 campus catalog, one of the fundamental ideas that sets Evergreen apart from other colleges and universities is the view that "connected learning—pulling together different ideas and concepts—is better than teaching separated bits of information" (*The Evergreen State College 1996-97 Catalog* 1996, 5). The college is firmly committed to the belief that "it is impossible to isolate bits of learning and present them as if they had no connection to other learning and to other parts of the world" (6).

This commitment is perhaps best symbolized in the interdisciplinary, collaborative Coordinated Studies programs, which remain a fixture of the Evergreen curriculum. Today there are 46 Coordinated Studies programs at the college, comprising 61 percent of the regular, full-time curricular offerings;[8] group contracts and core programs account for the other 39 percent of curricular programs at the college. What kinds of interdisciplinary programs are being offered at The Evergreen State College today? A review of the titles of the Coordinated Studies efforts in 1995-96 reveals a rich array of cross-disciplinary programs: Political Economy and Social Change: Race, Class and Gender (an exploration of race, gender, and class relations through the lenses of history, feminist studies, theories of racism, and international political economy); Hispanic Forms in Life and Art (an integration of the history and literature of medieval Spain and colonial Spanish America, and contemporary Latin American literature and culture); Shakespeare and Chaucer: Experience and Education (a study of the poetry of Shakespeare and Chaucer, along with philosophies of education, aesthetics, and literary criticism); and Mythic Reality: Imaging the Goddess (which explores the connections between theater, literature, Third World feminism, and goddess myths) (*The Evergreen State College 1995-96 Catalog* 1995). Two and a half decades since the opening of the institution, and interdisciplinarity thrives at Evergreen.

What keeps the spirit and tradition of interdisciplinary teaching and learning alive at Evergreen? First and foremost, there is the absence of academic disciplines (and majors) and conventional academic departments at Evergreen. In the words of one veteran academic, "I think it's the lack of departments, the lack of, in a sense, internal organization—one body of faculty—that has helped the cohesion of the faculty. . . . One of the strengths of Evergreen is that we never had any [confrontations like,] 'You are in this department and not in any other and you're loyalty is to this and so on.' There really is a desire to have folks teach across the curriculum."

Although Specialty Areas (now called Planning Groups) were introduced in the 1980s to "set up more predictable, better sequenced year-to-year program patterns," the faculty in the groups were not given budgets or hiring authority—this was to guard against the areas taking on the traditional roles of departments (*Constancy and Change* 1989, 23). "Even when we went to divisions [Specialty Areas]," a faculty member explains, "we kept all of the budget central. We kept all the faculty hirings central. I served as the budget dean for more than five years and there was no 'department' out there that was defending its turf or the amount of money they got [and] whether or not they retained faculty positions."

Second, a remarkable number of the founders have remained on the faculty at Evergreen. In 1995-96, 30 of the 58 original faculty members and academic deans (more than 50 percent of the first-year faculty) continued to teach at Evergreen. Forty-one percent of all regular, full-time faculty in 1995-96 had been employed at Evergreen for at least 25 years. The founding president of the college, Charles J. McCann, also continues to serve as an emeritus member of the faculty (*The Evergreen State College 1996-97 Catalog* 1996).

As one dynamic charter academic explains, "The fact that so many faculty have stayed for so long—that there's been very little faculty turnover in this institution . . .—can't help but cause some of the attitudes and values and behaviors [interdisciplinarity, etc.] to persist." A fellow faculty pioneer relates: "We [founders] all have been very committed to developing and maintaining and nurturing the things that we came up with in the first couple of years. I think that speaks quite directly to the ability to maintain ourselves" (i.e., the interdisciplinary, student-centered traditions of the institution).

Third, faculty recruitment has been critical to the continuation of interdisciplinary approaches at Evergreen. A faculty member of 24 years reports: "One of the things that new faculty are looked at for is not only their disciplinary expertise. They are often hired into a particular vacancy, but they are also looked at for their ability to teach more broadly across the curriculum." Another long-time academic responds: "We try to be very careful in the way we hire people. . . . We try to be sure that we get people who are very broadly trained, and who have interdisciplinary interests and they're not going to just wanna be a physicist or a chemist or a political scientist, that they're going to want to do the kind of work that we do." And from this top-level academic administrator: "We set up a hiring system [in the beginning] that was very clearly nondepartmental and tilted towards interdisciplinary people. That maintained that [interdisciplinary] thrust."

The students, too, support and strengthen the interdisciplinary mission of the institution. A faculty member in urban planning points out: "The strongest spokespeople [for the institution] have been the students. There is a natural selection by and large. . . . Virtually every student who comes and stays here, comes because they want to do this type of education. So, they're engaged in it."[9]

Individualism: Student-Centered Education

Second, there is a long-lasting commitment to student-centered learning at Evergreen. Students take charge of their education through active participation in Coordinated Studies seminars and Individualized Learning Contracts.

The campus remains free of educational requirements and letter grades. Curricular programs are centered around the individual interests and concerns of the learner, and narrative evaluations focus on the personal accomplishments and growth of each student. An excerpt from the Evergreen State College 1989 campus self-study accreditation report perhaps best captures the enduring ideal of personal engagement in learning (one of the five curricular foci of the institution today):

> Students at Evergreen are required to make their own choices about their educational objectives and their courses of study. This empowerment and self-consciousness about ends is enhanced by full time (16-credit) study in one program, the lack of major requirements for graduation, and the realities of an evaluation system which requires students and faculty to judge and be judged on the basis of their unique experience and accomplishments. The intensity demanded by the structure of many Evergreen programs creates a situation where students feel responsibly engaged not simply in a dyadic relation with the teacher, but in a community of learners within the program. (*Constancy and Change* 1989, 15–16)

How has the early distinctive emphasis on individualism been maintained at Evergreen? Long-time faculty and staff indicate, again, that the presence of a core group of founding faculty members and the absence of disciplinary departments, majors, and major requirements has provided Evergreeners with the encouragement and the opportunity to continue to design and direct their own learning. In the words of an Evergreen student, "The system of interdisciplinary studies, not having any requirements to graduate, and having the space to learn in the manner that you want to allows for people to come out of here with an extreme sense of themselves and an extreme sense of being able to accomplish things, self-motivation."

Undergraduate Teaching and Faculty Freedom

Third, teaching remains at the heart of the Evergreen curriculum. "Teaching is what Evergreen is all about," the 1996-97 campus catalog proclaims, "so the college's entire curriculum, from Core programs to advanced and independent study, is designed to enhance the student's ability to learn. . . . Faculty are drawn to Evergreen because they love teaching—they are interested in the process of teaching and learning, and they want to work with students in an environment that rewards that interest" (6).

There is a continuing sense of creativity and excitement about teaching at Evergreen. An emeritus faculty member in the sciences reports:

> The faculty have maintained an incredible amount of academic freedom at Evergreen. You don't even have to teach your field! So oftentimes, people get out of their field and try other things. The

academic freedom is just outrageous! In my later years, I got very interested in natural history and thought that natural history should be taken more seriously as opposed to science. . . . I don't know of any other school where I could have taught natural history in anything other than maybe a leisure ed. program or something. . . . But here, . . . I've spent whole quarters with students doing nothing but bugs! And they learn a lot about bugs! And birds and stuff like that. And I think that's probably pretty rare. You can do that here. It's true for all the faculty. They can really branch out.

Another veteran academic puts it this way: "Faculty . . . come here and find that they can explore some of their own interests and develop some of their own talents, and because there is no template model for Coordinated Studies programs, they have a lot of flexibility to try out [new ideas] and be creative in certain kinds of ways."

And still, the curriculum is always being reinvented at Evergreen (Kuh et al. 1991). Although some academic programs may now be repeated from year to year, the programs are constantly changing as new teaching teams take over and new groups of students participate. A faculty member of 25 years reports:

Early on, we used to *never* teach the same thing twice because everybody was experimenting. If you offered it twice, [we used to think] you might be starting to get into a rut. Now, it does happen [that programs are offered more than once,] but oftentimes you're with a different team, or even when you're with the same team, you have new ideas, and [the class is] never quite the same.

The founding spirit of creativity in teaching is also reinforced by the absence of seniority and departmental structures at Evergreen. "The . . . thing that keeps the [teaching] mission alive," a veteran faculty member relates, "is that we have no rank! There's nobody that's the boss that says 'You can't do that! You better talk to so and so because they have to approve this.' It's not true. There are no departments" and no curriculum committees. "We can create our own quarters!" she continues, "our own calendar! We can say we're only going to work on Saturdays; we just have to do the equivalent of a certain number of hours. We can do anything we want! We have our own budget" in each teaching program.

Perhaps most important, teaching has remained the primary criterion for academic review and reappointment at Evergreen (*Faculty Handbook* 1997). Faculty today are still required to maintain a portfolio including course syllabi, evaluations from students, evaluations from faculty colleagues in teaching teams, and self-evaluations spanning a teacher's career. A charter professor and former academic dean explains:

When you go up for promotion at most other campuses, they . . . know about your publications, but nobody really knows how good a teacher

you are. . . . We [at Evergreen] know because when I am teaching in
these [Coordinated Studies] programs, I am working with four other
faculty members, and they know whether I'm reading the book of the
week for our faculty seminar. When I give lectures [to the class,] they
know whether I'm prepared. [My portfolio includes] course evaluations, my evaluations of students, students' evaluations of me, colleagues' evaluations of me.

In the words of one academic administrator, the college has "set up a
culture" that supports innovation in teaching:

Evergreen does not have the dualisms about rewarding one thing [e.g.,
research] and saying you value something else [teaching]. . . . We
[always] said teaching mattered and that became the central value in
reappointment. As we hired [new faculty], we assessed for teaching
interests. [The candidates] even had to teach a class during the
interview and they had to write an essay of their educational philosophy as part of the application. All of that is a message to folks that's
pretty clear [about the value that is placed on teaching].

Since the time of the campus visit, Evergreen has changed its academic
reappointment policy: The campus now offers both term and continuing
contracts to faculty members. (Prior to the adoption of the new policy in the
summer of 1996, Evergreen faculty were hired for one-year, three-year, or
eight-year contracts. Evaluations took place at the end of a faculty member's
first year and second year at the college under the three-year contract; and
during the individual's second, fifth, and seventh year of employment under
the eight-year contract.) (Faculty Handbook 1988)

Today regular part-time and full-time faculty members are eligible for
continuing contracts up until the time of their voluntary departure, retirement,
or dismissal from the college. Academics are initially appointed to a term
contract, and after nine (but no more than 18) quarters of full-time teaching in
interdisciplinary programs with six or more faculty (at least four of whom are
regular faculty members on continuing appointments), they are eligible for a
continuing faculty appointment at the college (Faculty Handbook 1997).

According to Evergreen academic vice president and provost Barbara Leigh
Smith (personal communication, 21 February 1997), under the new policy all
Evergreen faculty members (on both term and continuing contracts) are
reviewed annually by their peers and students. Academics who are employed
under continuing contracts are also evaluated every five years during a three-
hour conference with all of the colleagues with whom they have taught. The
five-year evaluation is based upon a review of the faculty member's cumulative
portfolio of teaching experiences and evaluations from faculty and students,
along with a five-year self-evaluation that includes a retrospective on the
individual's work and a three- to five-year growth plan.

Why was the new reappointment policy adopted at Evergreen? According to a memorandum written by academic dean John Cushing to the Faculty Reappointment Policy Study Group (J. Cushing, memorandum, 7 January 1994), over the years, faculty and deans at the college had raised a number of concerns about the term appointment system. Cushing reports that academics who were employed under one-year or three-year contracts found the process to be threatening and feared non-reappointment, especially in times of budget cuts. In addition, the old policy stated that the three-year contracts provided the same amount of job security as the eight-year contracts, yet it was widely believed among faculty that only the eight-year contracts guaranteed a sense of long-term job security.

While some have compared the new reappointment policy to a tenure system (Is Tenure Evergreen? 1996), others indicate that the system differs from a traditional tenure process in a number of ways (B.L. Smith, personal communication, 21 February 1997). Since there are frequent reviews of faculty members who are employed under continuing contracts, and since evaluation is heavily based upon an academic's achievements and skills in interdisciplinary teaching, the system protects the centrality and vitality of teaching at the institution. It still guards against the "old yellow pages of lecture notes" syndrome and provides a continuing sense of vitality and freshness in teaching.

Egalitarianism

Fourth, Evergreen has kept alive its early egalitarian ethos. The campus remains free of hierarchical role divisions and status distinctions, such as faculty titles and ranks. Students, teachers, administrators, and college president all call each other by their first names, and formal boundaries between students and professors are minimized—faculty and students continue to view themselves as "co-learners," working in collaborative Coordinated Studies communities.

In the words of a faculty member in the arts, "Learning how to learn is a part of everyone's work who's a teacher [at Evergreen]. You learn how to learn together, with your students. It's not like you have all the answers." A current student agrees: "Interaction between students and faculty . . . is very important, that human contact. [Faculty are] not so separate from us and we're learning from them and they're learning from us. There's not a hierarchy of 'Oh, I'm the teacher and you listen to what I have to say.'" According to the 1989 institutional self-study report, "Collaborative and cooperative work has been a central feature of the Evergreen experience since the college opened" (Constancy and Change 78).

Campus governance structures also remain flexible and participatory. Although there are a few permanent standing committees in place at Evergreen today, the primary vehicle for college-wide decision making continues to be the

Disappearing Task Force or dissolving ad hoc committee, which is based on consensus. The campus also retains its distinctive system of rotating deanships (*Constancy and Change* 1989). "The deans are members of the faculty," one academic explains, "they're not outside administrators."

At the same time, students continue to have a great deal of input in campus decision making. In the words of a faculty member of 24 years,

> Our students here have . . . tremendous voice, . . . tremendous influence in terms of what gets offered [in the curriculum], and can influence significantly the design of a program even once it's underway. . . . In hiring of faculty, students serve on the [hiring] committees, the incoming faculty speak before classes, and we actively recruit the student input and that's taken very seriously. We'll have a visiting faculty member here and the students, by really being interested in her or his classes, will then have a significant effect on whether that person is hired or not.[10]

Finally, Evergreen remains committed to a non-competitive student evaluation system. One founding faculty member observes: "There's been a real strong defense of the written evaluation" as opposed to a standard grading system. In the words of the 1989 institutional self-study report, "Students find that this [nongraded] approach renders unnecessary the view of other students as competitors scrambling against each other for the few good grades" (*Constancy and Change* 79).

What keeps the egalitarian ethos alive at Evergreen? The structuring of the curriculum around full-time teams of faculty and students who are devoted to cooperative learning has, in essence, glued this feature of the Evergreen mission into place. The entire curriculum, the academic life of the faculty member, and the learning community of the student are centered in the collaborative Evergreen program of study. In the words of a long-time academic, "The particular program, group contract, or class that [students are] registered in is the *only* thing [students and faculty are] doing. I think that's been one of the reasons for [Evergreen's] success."

The values of cooperation and collaboration have also been passed down from one generation of Evergreener to the next through the long-lasting commitments of the veteran faculty who firmly believe that this type of education, and these antihierarchical, involving approaches to college governance, to use the words of one charter academic, are effective and "they're fun!" Egalitarianism has become a fixture of the campus culture.

Experiential Learning

Finally, there is enduring commitment to experiential learning at Evergreen. "Linking theory with practice" is one of the five foci of the curriculum today, and many academic programs continue to integrate internship experiences into the learning activities. Juniors and seniors may engage in individualized internship projects through the college's "Internship Learning Contracts." According to the 1996-97 college catalog, more than half of Evergreen's students complete one or more internships by the time that they graduate. (This compares to a national figure of less than 2 percent of all college students.)

One of the lessons to be learned from Evergreen, a faculty member in the arts explains, "is there's got to be a real affirmation of theory and practice" in education. At this campus, she says,

> you don't just sit around and talk about things. People have to do things; they have to get out. They have to make projects. . . . That's one thing that's wonderful about Evergreen. Our programs always have these big "doing" components. I can't tell you how many times I come [to campus] and in the traffic circle, there are buses and vans and trucks full of students going to *do* the thing they've been talking about. They're going to Indian reservations; they're going to visit the state capitol; they're going to the forest to look at trees. They're always going somewhere, doing things.

The dreamers and visionaries of early Evergreen designed a campus that would integrate life and learning, and according to charter faculty members, the college has lived up to this dream. Evergreen was recently singled out in a book by George Kuh and colleagues (Kuh et al. 1991) as one of the nation's 14 "involving colleges," campuses that foster student learning and development outside of the classroom, that integrate in-class with out-of-class life and learning experiences. During their visit to Evergreen, the researchers were struck by the "seamlessness" of in-class and out-of-class activity.

The enduring ideal of experiential learning has been sustained over the life of the college, once again, through the commitment of the veteran faculty (and like-minded recruits) and the students who self-select to attend Evergreen. According to interviewees, it is the continuing presence of the founders and the ever-present ethos of the "Evergreen way" that keeps alive the spirit and commitment to practical real-world learning experiences.

The Survival of The Evergreen State College as an Innovative Institution

More than 25 years later, and The Evergreen State College thrives as an alternative institution of higher education. This is a remarkable achievement for a public college. Over the course of its lifetime, Evergreen has faced several crises, including at least seven bills to close the college. Severe budgetary cutbacks in the State of Washington in the 1970s and a changing sociopolitical climate also threatened Evergreen's continuation as an alternative college (Clemens 1987; Kuh et al. 1991; Schuster 1989; Youtz 1984). Given the shifts in the economy since the 1960s, the changes in contemporary attitudes toward education (what some characterize as a conservative shift in public attitudes about reform in education), and the short lives of many of Evergreen's counterparts in the 1960s and 1970s, what has kept this innovative institution healthy and alive? Taking a different turn on the topic, interviewees were asked to comment on Evergreen's longevity—i.e., to share, if they could, some of the reasons why this distinctive college—unlike so many of the alternative campuses in the 1960s and 1970s—has survived.

Late Start-Up Date—Lessons Learned from Other Innovative Institutions

First and foremost, authors and interviewees single out Evergreen's later start-up date. The college opened in 1971, at the very end of the alternative higher education movement of the 1960s and 1970s. The campus planners thus had the advantage of learning from the earlier educational experiments of the period. When it came time to recruit faculty, they brought in individuals who had experience at other innovative institutions. "It is notable," write Richard M. Jones and Barbara Leigh Smith (1984), "how many Evergreen faculty came to Olympia via Old Westbury, Santa Cruz and similar institutions" (44). Youtz (1984) explains: "The war stories of these veterans considerably tempered our wilder dreams" (96). Charles Teske, Evergreen faculty member and founding academic dean of humanities and arts, asserts in a footnote to Youtz's piece:

> I cannot emphasize too strongly how important it was to have in our planning year the wisdom of those who came to us from "earlier educational experiments" which either had failed or were wavering.... Our veterans saved us from those pit-falls [of other institutions]. Indeed, it may not be all that wrong to maintain that we are still around because we were one of the last innovative colleges to open. (Youtz 1984, 96)

A founding faculty member at the campus today puts it this way: "A number of people who came here, came here with prior experience at places that had tried to do some of these [innovative] things. They came with a fairly vivid sense about what the structural mistakes that they'd made at those places were." And a long-time administrator at the college agrees that "people are a big ingredient" in Evergreen's longevity. In the beginning, she says,

> the college . . . hired people with a little more savvy than some of the other experimental schools of the time. We hired people away from other experimental schools. We hired people who'd been at Santa Cruz or had been at Old Westbury or had been at Oberlin, and we hired them in fairly large numbers the first two years, so they came I think with a little more reality about what it would take to run an institution. And that helped. It gives [the institution] an experience base.

An Autonomous Board of Trustees

Second, Evergreen has benefited from having its own board of trustees. Unlike many of the other state-supported innovative institutions of the era (e.g., UC Santa Cruz, University of Wisconsin-Green Bay), Evergreen has been granted relative autonomy and its own built-in system of support. Although there is now a Higher Education Coordinating Board in the State of Washington, there is no central governing board of trustees whose interests represent the norms of a large conventional public university system. This has been a key factor in the college's longevity.

Founding faculty member Richard M. Jones (1984) singled out Evergreen's autonomous board of trustees in a discussion of the factors that "bedeviled the growth of kindred ventures into alternative higher education" of the 1960s. He said that unlike most distinctive colleges and universities of the period,

> Our Board of Trustees is an autonomous governing body. . . . More-over, the particular trustees who saw us through our first year were among the most conservative, republican, successful business persons in the state. . . . They did not always understand what the planning faculty had planned, and did not always approve of what they did understand. But they did consistently support the plan in response to all forms of off-campus opposition. . . . [W]hen push came to shove on the several votes to close the college in its early years, the only politically significant eyeballs available for showdown confrontation were those of five white, conservative, republican successful business persons—and their political clout. No more effective protective parenting could have been planned for such an improbable infant as we were. (120)

Leadership

Third, institutional leadership also appears to be a key to Evergreen's longevity. The early trustees brought in a former state governor (Dan Evans) to serve as the college's second president "in one of the roughest periods" of the college's history (the late 1970s and early 1980s). An alumnus and current administrator relates:

> Evans . . . was a three-term governor and was very well regarded in the state legislature. . . . That helped a hell of a lot. At that time, we were under heavy fire from the legislature for underenrollment. The late seventies was a time when many of the alternative institutions that had been started up in the late sixties or early seventies were going under. So, we felt the same pressure, but we were fortunate in that with Evans here, the legislature grudgingly, but nevertheless, backed off. . . . It was savvy of the trustees at that time to be able to cut this deal with Evans to come in and take over the presidency and I think we're damn lucky that he did. It helped a lot.

Evans publicized the college's achievements to the world, Clemens (1987) reports:

> Evans mobilized the whole college in presenting its story. Early in his administration, he formed the Design for Enrollment DTF to reorganize and clarify its position in the competitive educational marketplace of the 1980s. He also employed his political credibility and skill as an orator in an ongoing campaign to inform the public and media that Evergreen was both a unique resource for present-day students and a modern heir to long-held educational values.

Summing Up the Key Reasons for the Endurance of the Distinctive Early Ideals at The Evergreen State College

By legislative mandate, The Evergreen State College was designed to be different. For more than 25 years the college has carried out that early vision. Looking back over the life and lessons of this remarkable campus, what, in summary, are the key factors that have enabled the college to sustain its pioneering principles? What has kept the innovative educational philosophies alive at Evergreen? First and foremost, there is the continuing presence and dedication of the founding faculty who sustain the distinctive early ideals in their commitment to interdisciplinary teaching, student-centered education, and experiential learning at Evergreen. The innovative principles and philosophies are passed down to new faculty cohorts who are recruited for their interest in collaborative, interdisciplinary teaching. Then there are the students who self-select to attend Evergreen, generation after generation, in search of an education that is centered around cooperative learning, individualism, and diverse fields of inquiry. At the same time, the campus remains free of rigid and hierarchical organizational structures, which allows for a continuing sense of vitality in teaching, an openness and freedom to experiment. Above all, it may be Evergreen's later founding date and its lively original planning teams, who were drawn from a family of innovative and experimenting institutions, that have enabled Evergreen to endure as a distinctive public institution.

ISSUES AND CHALLENGES TO INNOVATION

Like any creative entity or community, The Evergreen State College has come up against pressures or tensions in its continued existence. This section explores some of the key issues and challenges to innovation at Evergreen. These are innovation in a state-supported institution, faculty overwork and burnout, academic immobility, and the forthcoming retirements of founding faculty.

Innovation in a State-Supported Institution

First, Evergreen faces pressures and tensions as an innovative public institution. As indicated earlier, the college has had to do battle with the state legislature for years to preserve its alternative mission. "Every year since 1970," Youtz (1984) writes, "there had been at least one bill introduced into the Legislative hopper to close Evergreen, to turn it into state offices, or a police academy, or at least a southern branch of the University of Washington" (103–4). Long-time faculty and administrators speak of a "siege mentality" at the campus in the 1970s and early 1980s.

"From the beginning," a founding administrator relates, Evergreen "was fighting off attacks from people who really had no idea what we were doing here—or they had the wrong idea—you know, we were nothing but a bunch of hippies. I suppose [we] asked for it, but [we] wanted people from the very beginning to know what we intended to do and how we were going to do it, and from that moment, the arrows and the mud started [to fly]." An early alumnus and current administrator puts it this way:

> There have always been people in the legislature that have serious misgivings about the alternative nature of this [college]. I think that shared sense of being embattled all the time really brings people together and that people forged a common sense of what the place was about and an appreciation of each other because of that feeling that the outside was after us, that we were misunderstood and oftentimes abused.

"The standard rap against the place," he says, "is that this is now a holdover from the sixties where students get credit for basket weaving, where anything goes, that it's a center of leftist activity." In the last 10 years, however, he indicates that the college has gained increasing acceptance and recognition, both in the legislative arena and in the state in general. Several high-profile magazines and national reports have publicized the successes of Evergreen's graduates who often go on to assume leadership positions in industry and community organizations, and are very successful in graduate schools (Clemens 1987).

Still, the college remains in a precarious position as a state-supported institution. Budget issues have been an ever-present concern. A member of the planning faculty remarks:

> Budget cuts have really hurt. . . . Since [the planning year,] we've averaged a budget cut every two years. . . . The first year that we had students [1971-72], I coordinated a program . . . which had five faculty and 100 students, and my program budget for the academic year was $4,500. . . . This year, my program [has] three faculty, 66 students, and my entire program budget for the year is $760. We've learned to get along on next to nothing and still provide a high-quality product.

Faculty Overwork

Second, there is the issue of faculty overwork. "This is a very labor intensive place," an academic administrator explains, "and that's always a tension here. Faculty typically teach 16 hours a week here. The normal is more like nine [hours] in most other schools. That's a consequence of teaching full time."

Evergreen prides itself on its intensely personal approach to teaching and learning. Faculty often devote hours upon hours to crafting thoughtful narrative evaluations for each student and faculty colleague, and spend a great deal of time in preparation and reflection in writing their own self-evaluations, which become part of their cumulative teaching portfolios. A founding academic who recently retired from the college explains: "In some ways, it was a nightmare" writing those narrative evaluations. He says: "I'd write a small novel at the end of every quarter. Faculty members *dreaded* it! . . . I would put in 30, 40 hours writing evaluations at the end of each quarter. . . . You would want to get it right—to say what the student did and what was unique about the student's work."

A member of the planning faculty, likewise, observes that "burnout is a very, very real issue" at Evergreen. He says that "faculty need more time to get away," and that some of his colleagues take unpaid leave: "Those faculty that can afford it, like my teaching partner this year, will drop to one-quarter time in the spring [quarter]. . . . And the few of them that have been successful at writing books can get enough revenue from that to take unpaid leave and support themselves. . . . But, there's so much enthusiasm in most faculty for what we're doing that it offsets [the burnout]." There is always the excitement of teaching at Evergreen.

A veteran academic agrees: "Faculty members, especially at evaluation time, will grouse about having to write page-long narratives rather than doing alphanumeric grades, but whenever they think of the alternative and realize that that grading system, rather than a personally based narrative, would do away with the collaboration that we stress in our programs, everybody forgets about that." In the end, the vitality and excitement of teaching in the Evergreen community frequently outweigh the emotional and physical energy that is involved in this kind of education.

Faculty Immobility

Third, there is the issue of faculty advancement and mobility. Faculty members at Evergreen devote most of their time to teaching in the college's full-time, interdisciplinary programs. Often, there is little time to conduct research or to stay current in one's disciplinary field. A chemist remarks: "The work week is about 60 hours a week for a faculty member and there's little or no time for research. When I have done research is when I'm teaching an upper division program and I get a student project going. . . . So, I have done some publications here, but not nearly what I would do elsewhere because we put our time with the students in class."

Faculty "don't come here just because they're just looking for a job," an academic in urban planning says. She explains: "You . . . come here because you believe in the place, and there's a risk that you will get out of your field—the research, the publishing, and so forth. There are some risks [for faculty] depending on your field if you come here early in your career." A top-level administrator on campus sums up the dilemma in this way:

> Faculty . . . here . . . are always teaching in interdisciplinary programs where they are continually being pulled off of their disciplinary base. Because the intensity of the full-time instruction here is so great, very few of our faculty are able to maintain a research and publication life which keeps them current in their home disciplines. So, if you come here as a biochemist or an economist, by the time you've been here for a few years, you're a very weird kind of biochemist or economist, and it will be very hard for you to be employed in a conventional institution because you've lost your place in your discipline. . . . For faculty . . ., once you're here, you're here for life, and there is nowhere else. Partly there is nowhere else . . . because you have become a weird kind of economist. But, it's also that there's no place else for you because you can no longer conceive of teaching in that [disciplinary] way anymore.

Founding Faculty Retirements

Evergreen is at a turning point in its history. Like many of the innovative colleges and universities of the 1960s and early 1970s, Evergreen faces the forthcoming retirements of its founding faculty. "That's a challenge for us," an administrator remarks. "In another 10 years," she says, "there won't be any founders left. So, what will we be? How will we define ourselves? That's exciting. It's scary. It's threatening."

While the campus has been fairly successful in recruiting faculty who share the distinctive values of the founders of the institution, some academics fear that when the majority of the founding faculty members retire, the campus' distinctive heritage could be lost. A member of the planning faculty expresses his concern: "The question of generational continuity is *extremely* important and difficult and I don't know for sure what the answer to it is. I'm not sure anybody does. What that means is that in another 25 years, what used to be Evergreen may simply be in songs and old stories."

CONCLUSION: SUMMARY AND IMPLICATIONS

Vision. Flexibility. Spirit. And remarkable durability. Since the time of its pioneering creation in the late 1960s, The Evergreen State College has, in the words of its founding president, "been no carbon copy" of other state institutions. For two and a half decades, the college has continued to offer interdisciplinary, student-centered alternatives in education; cooperative, creative teaching opportunities; an open and participatory (and disappearing!) governance environment; and real-world, out-of-classroom learning experiences. Despite budgetary crises and threats of closure, Evergreen has carried on as an innovator in public higher education. Looking back over the life and lessons of this distinctive college, what are some of the implications or teachings of the Evergreen case study and history?

- The first lesson to be learned from The Evergreen State College study is that freedom from conventional academic structures sustains and nourishes educational innovation. At Evergreen, it is the very absence of departments, curriculum committees, faculty rank, competitive grading scales, and curricular requirements that has enabled this campus to engage in collaborative and creative processes of teaching and learning for more than 25 years.
- Second, an ever-changing or evolving curriculum or governance design may promote long-lasting experimentation and vitality in teaching, learning, and decision making. The "self-destructing" curriculum at Evergreen, the Disappearing Task Forces, and the rotating deanships all contribute to a sense of dynamism and creativity.
- Third, this analysis underscores the importance of the continuing participation and dedication of founding faculty members in distinctive institutions of higher education. At Evergreen, the dreams of the pioneers are kept alive and passed down to future faculty and student generations by the dynamic charter academics who remain at the college.
- Fourth, faculty recruitment is critical to an innovative institution's longevity. As Evergreen faces the forthcoming retirements of its charter academics, the institution looks to the future generations of faculty to carry on the distinctive traditions.
- Fifth, students often self-select to attend an innovative campus. At Evergreen, the distinctive spirit of the college is kept alive, in part, by the energy and interest of the Evergreen students.
- Sixth, faculty reappointment systems that reward teaching are a necessity if academics are to continue to engage in collaborative, interdisciplinary education. Portfolio assessment may provide one alternative (or supplement) to traditional forms of faculty evaluation.
- Seventh, new innovative educational ventures should look to the experiences of other distinctive campuses across the country as they develop their curricular plans and institutional policies. The recruitment of faculty with a background in alternative higher education may also be critical for a distinctive college's success or longevity.

- Eighth, innovative institutions in the public sector may be subject to intense scrutiny, budgetary cutbacks, and threats of closure. Campuses with their own independent boards of trustees and those that recruit presidential leaders from the public political arena may have a better chance of survival.
- Ninth, faculty members who are engaging in interdisciplinary programs at innovative institutions may find that their opportunities for professional mobility in academe are limited. Faculty burnout may also be a consequence of the intensive, collaborative full-time teaching-centered approaches at distinctive colleges.

In the end, however, it is the joy and excitement of cooperative exchange and nourishing dialog between faculty and students that captures the hearts and souls of the people at Evergreen. Human concern and passion for education is the essence of the place, the quality that continues to make Evergreen Evergreen.

NOTES

1. The campus' mascot is the Geoduck (pronounced "gooey-duck"), a giant clam native to Puget Sound.
2. Like many of the optimistic planners of innovative colleges and universities in the expansive 1960s era, Evergreen's founders did not foresee the economic and demographic turnarounds of the decade ahead. In the 1970s, the Pacific Northwest was hit with an economic recession that would reduce the number of college-bound students. The Evergreen State College has never reached the early enrollment projection of 10,000 students (Bergquist 1995; Clemens 1987; Youtz 1984).
3. The college's name, "The Evergreen State College," was officially adopted on January 24, 1968.
4. According to one founding faculty member, the planning faculty held a contest amongst themselves to see who could come up with the best name for the new interdisciplinary, team-taught programs that they had designed for the college: "The prize for the contest to name this particular interdisciplinary beast was a quart of Chivas Regal scotch! [Faculty member] Richard [Jones] won it with the term 'Coordinated Studies.'"
5. In addition to the main campus in Olympia, Evergreen has a campus in Tacoma, Washington, that opened in 1972 and that offers interdisciplinary, collaborative upper division Coordinated Studies programs designed primarily for working adults. The Tacoma campus also provides lower division course work (leading to the A.A. degree) in conjunction with Tacoma Community College. The lower division program is a Bridge Program—participants have priority placement in the upper division program of the Evergreen-Tacoma campus. The Tacoma campus currently enrolls 189 students (23 percent of whom are male and 77 percent of whom are female). Eighty percent of the faculty and 58 percent of the students are persons of color (B.L. Smith, personal communication, 21 February 1997; Bridge Program 1997; *The Evergreen State College 1997-98 Catalog* 1997).

6. At the time of the campus visit, the curriculum was organized into 12 interdisciplinary "Specialty Areas": Environmental Studies; Expressive Arts; Knowledge and the Human Condition; Language and Culture; Management Studies; Native American Studies; Political Economy and Social Change; Science and Human Values; Science, Technology, and Health; Master of Environmental Studies; Master of Public Administration; and Master in Teaching. All faculty members were affiliated with one or more Specialty Areas. In February 1996, the Specialty Areas were replaced by the five smaller interdisciplinary Planning Groups to provide a more balanced or representative distribution of faculty members across curricular groupings (Long Range Curriculum Disappearing Task Force 1996).

7. One interviewee had held more than one position at the college at different points in her career. In this case, the total number of years employed at Evergreen was determined by taking the sum of the number of years employed in each position at the college. Calculations for the year of arrival were based on the earliest position held at Evergreen.

8. When the college opened in 1971, albeit with far fewer students, the number of Coordinated Studies programs that were offered was 13 (*The Evergreen State College Bulletin 1971-72* 1971).

9. According to James W. Lyons (1991) and David Dodson (1991), the high proportion of adult learners at Evergreen helps to sustain the college's distinctive founding missions. "It must be acknowledged," writes Dodson, "that a certain portion of the institution's success has been attributable to the natural intellectual curiosity and educational persistence of its more mature student body" (205). A top-level administrator on campus today agrees: "I would say it has mattered a lot that a large proportion of our students are adult learners. They've set a tone for the classrooms, they tend to be more self-directed and they appreciate many of the aspects of the colleg[e] such as the emphasis on applied work."

10. Interestingly, Evergreen students have never formed a permanent student government body. According to interviewees, students' lives at Evergreen revolve around their academic programs, where they form close-knit, involving communities with fellow students and faculty. While there have been a number of proposals to establish a student government (most recently, in the fall of 1996), this remains a hotly contested issue at the college.

REFERENCES

Bergquist, W.H. 1995. *Quality through access, access with quality: The new imperative for higher education.* San Francisco: Jossey-Bass.

Bridge program: TESC-TCC 1996-97 academic year. 1997. An on-line description of The Evergreen State College Tacoma Campus - Tacoma Community College Bridge Program. http://192.211.16.13:80/individuals/younga/home.htm

Cadwallader, M.L. 1984. Experiment at San Jose. In *Against the current: Reform and experiment in higher education*, edited by R.M. Jones and B.L. Smith, 343–66. Cambridge, Mass.: Schenkman.

Clemens, M., ed. 1987. *Twenty years of making a difference: The Evergreen State College 1967–1987.* Olympia, Wash.: The Evergreen State College.

Constancy and change: A self-study report. 1989. A report prepared by The Evergreen State College for the Northwest Association of Schools and Colleges Commission on Colleges, August. Olympia, Wash.: The Evergreen State College.

Dodson, D. 1991. Evergreen: Prototype or dinosaur? In *The role and contribution of student affairs in involving colleges,* edited by G.D. Kuh and J.H. Schuh, 199–206. Washington D.C.: The National Association of Student Personnel Administrators.

Evergreen self-guided tour. n.d. Olympia, Wash.: The Evergreen State College.

The Evergreen State College. 1995. Viewbook. Olympia, Wash.: The Evergreen State College Office of College Advancement.

The Evergreen State College bulletin 1971-72. 1971. Olympia, Wash.: The Evergreen State College.

The Evergreen State College bulletin 1972-73. 1972. Olympia, Wash.: The Evergreen State College.

The Evergreen State College 1995-96 catalog. 1995. Olympia, Wash.: Admissions Office, The Evergreen State College.

The Evergreen State College 1996-97 catalog. 1996. Olympia, Wash.: Admissions Office, The Evergreen State College.

The Evergreen State College 1997-98 catalog. 1997. Olympia, Wash.: Admissions Office, The Evergreen State College.

The Evergreen State College: Preliminary announcement. 1970. Olympia, Wash.: The Evergreen State College.

Faculty handbook. 1988. Olympia, Wash.: The Evergreen State College.

Faculty handbook. 1997. Pre-publication copy. Olympia, Wash.: The Evergreen State College.

Gehret, K.G. 1972. Reports: Washington's Evergreen College. *Change* (May): 17–19.

Grounds for greatness. n.d. Olympia, Wash.: The Evergreen State College.

Is tenure Evergreen? 1996. ACADEME (November-December): 10–11.

Jones, R.M. 1981. *Experiment at Evergreen.* Rochester, Vt.: Schenkman.

————. 1984. Response to Youtz. In *Against the current: Reform and experiment in higher education,* edited by R.M. Jones and B.L. Smith, 119–25. Cambridge, Mass.: Schenkman.

Jones, R.M., and B.L. Smith, eds. 1984. *Against the current: Reform and experiment in higher education.* Cambridge, Mass.: Schenkman.

Kuh, G.D., J.H. Schuh, E.J. Whitt, R.E. Andreas, J.W. Lyons, C.C. Strange, L.E. Krehbiel, and K.A. MacKay. 1991. *Involving colleges: Successful approaches to fostering student learning and development outside the classroom.* San Francisco: Jossey-Bass.

Long Range Curriculum Disappearing Task Force. 1996. [Packet of materials, including recommendations and summaries of previous long-range curriculum planning reports. Provided by the Office of Institutional Research at The Evergreen State College.] Olympia, Wash.: The Evergreen State College, January 8.

Lyons, J.W. 1991. An eclipse of the usual: The Evergreen State College. In *The role and contribution of student affairs in involving colleges*, edited by G.D. Kuh and J.H. Schuh, 173–98. Washington, D.C.: The National Association of Student Personnel Administrators.

The making of the college: 1964–1967. n.d. Olympia, Wash.: The Evergreen State College.

McCann, C.J. 1977. Academic administration without departments at The Evergreen State College. In *Academic departments: Problems, variations, and alternatives*, D.E. McHenry and Associates, 147–69. San Francisco: Jossey-Bass.

Meiklejohn, A. 1932. *The experimental college.* New York: Harper.

Once over lightly: The Evergreen State College. 1971. Olympia, Wash.: The Evergreen State College.

Schuster, J.H. 1989. The Evergreen State College. Site visit report for the Carnegie Foundation for the Advancement of Teaching's Campus Community Project, Claremont, Calif., 27 June. Draft.

Student advising handbook, The Evergreen State College 1995-96. 1995. Olympia, Wash.: The Evergreen State College Academic Planning and Experiential Learning Office, June.

Tommerup, P.D. 1993. Adhocratic traditions, experience narratives and personal transformation: An ethnographic study of the organizational culture and folklore of The Evergreen State College, an innovative liberal arts college. *Dissertation Abstracts International* 54 (03): 1051. (University Microfilms No. AAC93-20067)

Tussman, J. 1969. *Experiment at Berkeley.* New York: Oxford University Press.

Washington's newest state college. n.d. Brochure. Olympia, Wash.: The Evergreen State College.

Youtz, B.L. 1984. The Evergreen State College: An experiment maturing. In *Against the current: Reform and experiment in higher education*, edited by R.M. Jones and B.L. Smith, 93–118. Cambridge, Mass.: Schenkman.

CHAPTER 8

Conclusion
Cross-Campus Results and Implications

INTRODUCTION

The 1960s ushered in a decade of reform and experimentation in American higher education. Hundreds of new and radically different colleges and universities burst onto the scene against a backdrop of social and political turbulence, heated and passionate student demonstration, enrollment and economic upswings, and countercultural lifestyle exploration. Although most of these new and unorthodox campuses thrived in the 1960s and early 1970s, attracting scores of interested and talented faculty members and students, few were able to survive the economic downturns of the 1970s, the severe drop-offs in the rate of enrollment growth, and the shifting student attitudes and increasingly careerist student aspirations. Many innovative institutions were forced to close their doors or to abandon their visions of educational innovation.

What has become of the alternative colleges and universities that remained open and survived the dramatic transformations of the 1970s? To what extent have these campuses been able to sustain their unorthodox founding missions in the 1990s? While previous researchers have tried their hands at explaining or accounting for why the innovative higher education movement lost its momentum, and why some innovative campuses abandoned their early visions or simply collapsed while others endured or succeeded, there have been no recent empirical investigations that have examined these phenomena across institutions.

This study attempted to fill this void in the research literature. Case studies were conducted at six innovative colleges and universities across the United States to determine how and why alternative institutions preserve their distinctive ideals or missions and survive in a changing social, political, and economic climate. The principal questions of the research were as follows: What keeps the founding dream, the spirit of reform alive at innovative colleges and universities? What are the keys to the survival or longevity of nonconventional higher education institutions? What leads to the compromise or abandonment of the distinctive early missions or ideals of an alternative institution? Finally, what do these distinctive campuses, their life cycles, stories, and experiences have to teach us about the processes of innovation and the preservation of reform efforts in American higher education?

This chapter synthesizes the results of the six case studies, responding to these questions and presenting cross-campus comparisons of the factors that affect the longevity of innovation at distinctive colleges and universities. The chapter begins with a portrait and summary of the endurance of the early innovative values and missions at the six institutions. The next section weaves together the findings of the case studies to describe the variables that have been found to facilitate long-lasting innovation at alternative colleges and universities. The following section examines the factors that have been found to enhance the survival or longevity of distinctive institutions. The chapter then discusses the variables that inhibit continuing innovation at the six sites and summarizes the key issues or challenges to innovation at these campuses. The chapter concludes with a discussion of the implications of the research findings for higher education and innovative institutions and offers suggestions for future studies of alternative colleges and universities.

ENDURANCE AND TRANSFORMATION OF THE DISTINCTIVE EARLY IDEALS ACROSS CAMPUS SITES

To what extent have the innovative institutions in this investigation been able to preserve their distinctive founding philosophies or early unorthodox principles? Table 3 presents a summary and cross-campus portrait of the enduring innovative features across case study sites. Looking at the patterns that are displayed in the table, the longevity of innovation among institutions is striking. With the exception of the two universities (University of Wisconsin-Green Bay and University of California [UC], Santa Cruz), every campus in this investigation has persevered with nearly all of its early principles or founding philosophies intact.

The persistence of particular distinctive traits or characteristics across institutions is revealing. All campuses that started without course requirements, academic units, and faculty ranks, for example, have remained free of structures. All sites that resisted departmental organization in the beginning (including the University of Wisconsin-Green Bay) continue to exist without traditional disciplinary departments. All campuses that offered individualized learning contracts and personalized major options in the early years have successfully retained these distinctive features. With the exception of the University of Wisconsin-Green Bay and UC Santa Cruz, all institutions in this study have remained committed to faculty freedom and creativity in undergraduate teaching. And all campuses that started with a narrative or non-graded evaluation system have resisted the establishment of a conventional grading approach (including UC Santa Cruz).

The only distinctive ideals that appear to have been sacrificed or compromised to some degree across institutions are the experiential education component (at New College and the University of Wisconsin-Green Bay), the participatory governance framework (at Pitzer College and Hampshire College), and the emphasis on undergraduate teaching as opposed to faculty publication and research (at the University of Wisconsin-Green Bay and UC Santa Cruz and, to some extent, New College and Hampshire College). On the whole, the cross-campus portrait of innovation in table 3 reveals a remarkable pattern of stability, especially among the smaller colleges (Pitzer College, New College, Hampshire College, and Evergreen). In general, it seems that the smaller liberal arts colleges (whether they be private or public) are more likely to keep hold of their distinctive founding heritage than the larger public universities.

These findings confirm and extend the results of previous studies of experimental colleges and universities (e.g., Grant and Riesman 1978; Townsend, Newell, and Wiese 1992), which indicate that public institutions are more vulnerable to external pressures and are less successful in maintaining their distinctiveness over time. The present study adds to the research literature by suggesting that certain *types* of public institutions—small "public liberal arts" colleges (like Evergreen or New College)—are more successful in sustaining their innovative founding missions than are the larger public universities (the University of Wisconsin-Green Bay, UC Santa Cruz). Autonomy or independence from a centralized state governing board or university system seems to be a key factor in this success. New College, for example, has benefited from its geographical distance from the University of South Florida and by having its own independent fund-raising foundation (the New College Foundation); Evergreen has been fortunate in having an autonomous board of trustees as opposed to a system-wide or statewide coordinating system of regents.

TABLE 3

ENDURANCE AND TRANSFORMATION OF THE DISTINCTIVE EARLY IDEALS ACROSS CAMPUS SITES

Distinctive Ideal[a]	Pitzer College		New College of USF		Hampshire College		U. of Wisconsin-Green Bay		U. of California, Santa Cruz		The Evergreen State College	
	Present at Start	Present Today	Present at Start	Present Today	Present at Start	Present Today	Present at Start	Present Today	Present at Start	Present Today	Present at Start	Present Today
Individualism												
No required courses					Yes	Yes					Yes	Yes
Student-centered education	Yes	Yes	Yes	Yes	Yes	Yes	Yes	No	Yes	No	Yes	Yes
Individualized learning contracts			Yes	Yes	Yes	Yes					Yes	Yes
Individualized major option	Yes	Yes			Yes	Yes			Yes	Yes*		
No academic units			Yes	Yes	Yes	Yes						
Egalitarianism												
Participatory governance	Yes	Yes*			Yes	Yes*					Yes	Yes
Students on appointment/ promotion committees	Yes	Yes			Yes	Yes						
Faculty & students as co-learners			Yes	Yes	Yes	Yes	Yes	No	Yes	No	Yes	Yes
No grades/Narrative evaluations			Yes	Yes	Yes	Yes			Yes	Yes[b]	Yes	Yes
No faculty rank											Yes	Yes

Table continues

TABLE 3 (continued)

Distinctive Ideal[a]	Pitzer College Present at Start	Pitzer College Present Today	New College of USF Present at Start	New College of USF Present Today	Hampshire College Present at Start	Hampshire College Present Today	U. of Wisconsin-Green Bay Present at Start	U. of Wisconsin-Green Bay Present Today	U. of California, Santa Cruz Present at Start	U. of California, Santa Cruz Present Today	The Evergreen State College Present at Start	The Evergreen State College Present Today
Faculty Freedom/Teaching												
Faculty freedom/creativity	Yes	Yes	Yes	Yes	Yes	Yes	Yes	No	Yes	No	Yes	Yes
No curriculum committee			Yes	Yes	Yes	Yes					Yes	Yes
Undergraduate teaching vs. publishing & research			Yes	Yes*	Yes	Yes*	Yes	No	Yes[c]	No	Yes	Yes
No tenure					Yes	Yes					Yes	Yes*
Interdisciplinarity												
Cross-disciplinary teaching	Yes	Yes			Yes	Yes	Yes	No	Yes	No	Yes	Yes
Faculty not housed by discipline	Yes	Yes					Yes	Yes			Yes	Yes
No academic departments	Yes	Yes	Yes	Yes	Yes	Yes	Yes	Yes[d]			Yes	Yes
Experiential Education												
Off-campus study/internships			Yes	No			Yes	No			Yes	Yes
Off-campus projects integrated into curriculum							Yes	No			Yes	Yes

Table notes follow on the next page

TABLE 3 (continued)

* = A qualified "yes," that is this ideal has been maintained to some extent or in certain areas at the institution.

[a] These categories are intended to serve as broad, all-encompassing descriptors of the core distinctive ideals that were found to be present across institutional sites. The terminology that is used to describe the ideals may vary to some degree in the individual case study chapters. Information regarding each ideal is provided only for those campuses that strongly adhered to the ideal at their inception.

[b] From the beginning, UC Santa Cruz students have had the option of receiving a grade (accompanied by a narrative evaluation) in selected courses at the university.

[c] The early planners of the Santa Cruz campus sought to achieve a balance between faculty teaching and academic research. The university embraced both ideals in its opening years.

[d] Although there are now both interdisciplinary and disciplinary academic units or departments at the University of Wisconsin-Green Bay, all budgetary, curricular, and hiring authority remains in the hands of the interdisciplinary units at the institution.

FACTORS THAT FACILITATE THE ENDURANCE OF INNOVATION ACROSS CAMPUS SITES

Despite pressures to become more conventional, most innovative campuses in this investigation have remained remarkably true to their early distinctive characteristics. What are the factors that have enabled these institutions to maintain their original unorthodox values in a changing social, political, and economic climate? Based on the findings of the case studies, there appear to be four key variables that facilitate the endurance of distinctive educational approaches at innovative colleges and universities. These are: the presence and support of founding faculty members; faculty recruitment strategies; an academic reward system that values innovation; free-flowing, nondepartmental organizational structures; and administrative support for innovation.

The Presence and Support of Founding Faculty Members

Across all campuses, interviewees single out the presence and the dedication of charter faculty members as integral to the success and longevity of innovation. The veteran scholars are often hailed as the faithful supporters and advocates of the original distinctive missions of the institutions. At Pitzer College, for example, the charter academics are viewed as the creators and innovators who fuel the visions and who keep alive the spirit and processes of community governance. At New College, the veteran faculty are considered to be the "conscience of the place," in the words of one administrator, "a constant poke in the back to remind everybody why we got together up there in the first place." The charter (and newer cohorts of) faculty have sustained the rich traditions of individualism and active and egalitarian classroom environments.

The presence of a large number of original faculty members at Hampshire College has also been fundamental to the preservation of the student-centered educational missions and the long-standing dedication to participatory governance at the institution. At Evergreen, the traditions of interdisciplinarity, individualized education, egalitarianism, and experiential learning are all kept alive, in part, by a dedicated core group of veteran faculty who continue to teach at the campus and who champion the ideals and visions of the early days.

Even at those institutions that have, for the most part, abandoned their innovative principles, it is, again, the commitment of the founding faculty that sustains the innovations that do remain in place. At the University of Wisconsin-Green Bay, for example, an institution that has in many ways succumbed to external, statewide pressures to conventionalize, the founding faculty and administrators are the guiding forces in preserving the campus' interdisciplinary organization. At UC Santa Cruz, a campus that has been radically reorganized since its freewheeling start-up era, there is still a sense that the veteran faculty (only a handful of whom remain at the institution) keep alive the early spirit and ideals, especially with regard to the narrative evaluation system.

In the end, the long-time faculty at innovative colleges and universities serve as models and mentors for other academics and voices for the preservation of the founding missions. In their lively and creative teaching, in their dynamic approaches to curriculum development and campus governance, and in their fond memories and storytelling about the cherished start-up years, they are the keepers of the dreams.

These findings are consistent with the results of previous research, including Burton Clark's (1970) study of three older distinctive colleges (Antioch, Reed, and Swarthmore). Among the "organizational elements" that "made the innovation [at the three colleges] durable and noteworthy," Clark singles out the development and power of a personnel core, which is commonly comprised of the senior faculty. This faculty "core," Clark notes, is a powerful source of continuing dedication and support for the institutional vision (or what he calls the "organizational saga") of the colleges.

Faculty Recruitment Strategies: Passing the Torch

The distinctive heritage of an institution is also perpetuated by the incoming cohorts of faculty who share the founders' passion and spirit for innovation and who have been drawn to the college or university because of its alternative mission. At Evergreen, for example, the campus' cooperative educational philosophies are perpetuated and passed down to new academic cohorts who are recruited for their interest in collaborative and interdisciplinary teaching. There is an "Evergreen way" that pervades the campus, and new faculty, working in close collaboration with veteran academics, come to appreciate and adopt the multidisciplinary, team-teaching approaches of the institution.

At Pitzer College, professors refer to a process of "like hiring like," or bringing in new faculty who share the college's basic commitment to interdisciplinary approaches and perspectives. At New College, too, the incoming cohorts of academics who share the basic values of the pioneers sustain the spirit and spark of individualized learning, faculty creativity, and egalitarianism. And at Hampshire College, academic recruitment has been key to the preservation of the interdisciplinary mission and the emphasis on undergraduate teaching and faculty freedom. Hampshire has been described as having "an infectious vision."

Clark (1970), again, describes something very similar to this "infectious" vision in his discussion of organizational saga, or a unifying vision of deeply cherished beliefs about the mission of an institution that sustains the distinctive educational characteristics of the campus. Clark points out that if the saga or distinctive ideology system of a college is to gain long-lasting support, then the institution must seek to recruit and retain faculty who "fit" the institution and who subscribe to the values, approaches, and beliefs of the campus. The results of the current investigation support and extend Clark's findings (about Antioch, Reed, and Swarthmore) to include the experiences of six innovative colleges and universities in the 1990s.

An Academic Reward System That Values Innovation

Next, academic reward structures that value distinctive or creative approaches in teaching or scholarly activity are critical for innovation to endure. Those campuses that have been most successful in sustaining their early interdisciplinary teaching approaches (e.g., Pitzer College, Evergreen) reward faculty for engaging in cross-disciplinary or creative teaching endeavors. At Pitzer College, for example, one of the key criteria in academic advancement and tenure decisions is successful joint teaching. At Evergreen, creative, team-taught seminars and interdisciplinary approaches are perpetuated by a faculty reappointment system that values excellence in teaching and interdisciplinary education.

At those campuses that have, for the most part, sacrificed their distinctive pedagogical approaches or teaching missions, it is often the case that faculty were not being rewarded for innovative teaching or curriculum development. At UC Santa Cruz, for instance, the interdisciplinary, student-centered teaching in the Colleges was abandoned, in large part, because academics were being evaluated on the basis of the conventional, disciplinary research and publication standards established by the University of California. At the University of Wisconsin-Green Bay, the early teaching mission was also sacrificed to some extent as the campus increasingly began to emphasize research and publication criteria in faculty promotion decisions.

Free-Flowing, Nondepartmental Organizational Structures

In addition, open or flexible organizational structures have been essential for ensuring long-lasting innovation. Antihierarchical, nondepartmental arrangements allow for curricular experimentation and pedagogic risk-taking. At Pitzer College, for example, professors are free to engage in creative approaches in teaching and research activity and to cross disciplinary boundaries without the constraints of traditional academic departments or a complex administrative hierarchy. At New College, the absence of departments, curriculum committees, academic deanships, and rigid bureaucratic structures has sustained a continuing sense of experimentation in teaching and learning. At Hampshire College, too, the freedom from departments, course units, and grades has helped to keep alive the campus' imaginative interdisciplinary approaches and educational programs. Evergreen has also resisted the establishment of departments, curriculum committees, course requirements, faculty rank, and competitive grading systems. The faculty and students at the college enjoy a tremendous amount of freedom in collaborative teaching and learning activities. Even the University of Wisconsin-Green Bay has been able to preserve, to some extent, its early interdisciplinary approaches by resisting the establishment of conventional budgeted disciplinary departments.

Administrative Support for Innovation

Finally, the commitment, vision, and dedication of campus administrators and trustees have been critical to the longevity of the innovative missions at a number of these alternative colleges and universities. At Pitzer, for example, interviewees praise the college's leadership for its long-standing support of innovation and its openness and willingness to encourage faculty to engage in creative, unexplored areas of scholarship and curriculum building. At Hampshire, the dedication of institutional leaders and the board of trustees is singled out as an integral factor in the preservation of the campus' distinctive interdisciplinary ethos. And at Evergreen, where the academic deans are drawn from the faculty of the college, there is a continuing level of administrative support for and commitment to the collaborative teaching and learning communities. Evergreen's presidents, including former Washington State governor Dan Evans, have remained strong advocates of the college's unique brand of higher education.

FACTORS THAT ENHANCE THE SURVIVAL OF INNOVATIVE INSTITUTIONS OF HIGHER EDUCATION

Given the rapid and dramatic shifts in the national economy, the changing social and political climate, and the short lives of many alternative colleges and universities of the 1960s and 1970s, it is remarkable that the six institutions in this study have managed to retain at least some of their early distinctive principles and to remain open in the 1990s. The previous section examined the factors that have been found to facilitate the longevity of innovative educational ideals at alternative colleges and universities. This section turns to the topic of *institutional* survival. Looking across case study sites, why have these six campuses managed to keep their doors open when the majority of distinctive colleges and universities of the era closed down? What has kept these imaginative ventures alive? Based on the results of the case studies, there appear to be four key factors that enhance the longevity of innovative enterprises in higher education. These are affiliation with a consortium or larger system of institutions, a late start-up date, adaptability and change, and community support.

Affiliation with a Consortium or Larger System of Institutions

First, affiliation with a consortium or larger group of institutions seems to prolong the life of an innovative college or university. Pitzer College, for example, has benefited from its association with five other solidly established liberal arts colleges and a graduate school in the Claremont Consortium. The campus would never have been able to overcome early financial difficulties and keep the doors of the college open, interviewees explain, without the tremendous resources and support of The Claremont Colleges. Hampshire College, likewise, has persevered because of its ties to a renowned consortium of institutions in the Pioneer Valley of Massachusetts. The surrounding campuses have served as a kind of buffer of support for the college, and students and faculty have access to other academics, students, and a wide variety of courses and programs at a neighboring network of higher education institutions.

Affiliation with a larger group of institutions has been vital even for those campuses that have been associated with a state university system. Long-time faculty and staff at New College, for example, believe that the merger with the University of South Florida "saved the college's life." Faculty and administrators at the University of Wisconsin-Green Bay indicate that for all of the constraints of affiliation with a public university system, the Green Bay campus survives, in part, because of the association with the University of Wisconsin. At UC Santa Cruz, interviewees also report that the campus probably would not have been able to endure in a rapidly changing socioeconomic and political climate had it not been part of a large-scale public university system. State university systems may seek to radically change or conventionalize an innovative institution, but, over time, they may form a kind of buffer of support for institutional survival.

A Late Start-Up Date: Lessons Learned from Other Innovative Campuses

Second, a later start-up date may increase the longevity of a distinctive institution. Hampshire College and Evergreen, for example, opened in the early 1970s, at the very end of the alternative higher education movement. The planners of these campuses were able to avoid some of the dangers that led to the downfall of earlier experimental colleges and universities. Both campuses recruited charter faculty members who had experience at other innovative institutions and who had special insight into the problems associated with alternative higher education. As Evergreen founder Byron L. Youtz (1984) explained, "The war stories of these veterans considerably tempered our wilder dreams" (96).

Adaptability and Change

In some cases, the key to the survival of a distinctive institution has been a campus' ability to reassess its original 1960s-centered philosophies, and even compromise or abandon its early ideals to adapt to the changing interests and needs of the student and faculty populations. As is discussed later in this chapter, UC Santa Cruz and University of Wisconsin-Green Bay were both radically restructured to accommodate the changing interests and values of the student generations of the 1970s. For these institutions, the sacrifice of early innovations was a difficult, often painful, decision, but a necessary outcome in the minds of the planners and faculty if the campuses were to endure.

Community Support

For state-supported institutions, gaining the support and respect of the public may also serve as a key to institutional longevity. At the University of Wisconsin-Green Bay, for example, the increasing sense of local pride and support for the university through the campus' athletic teams and a renowned performing arts center has been critical to the longevity of the institution. At Evergreen, once again, appointing a former state governor to serve as the college's second president was essential for gaining public support and moving the campus through one of the roughest periods in its history (the late 1970s). At a time when enrollments were shrinking and there were several threats to close the college down, Evans was a spokesperson for the college in spreading the word about Evergreen and in increasing public support for the innovative campus.

FACTORS THAT INHIBIT THE ENDURANCE OF INNOVATION ACROSS CAMPUS SITES

Just as there are certain factors or circumstances that promote the longevity of innovations, there are also variables that tend to inhibit the endurance of alternative ideals or practices. Based on the results of the case studies, there appear to be three major variables that limit or constrain long-lasting innovation in distinctive colleges and universities. These are affiliation with a public university system, shifts in enrollments and changes in the student generations, and increasing student-to-faculty ratios.

Affiliation with a Public University System

First, as indicated earlier, innovation may be ill-fated in a public university. While all public experimental ventures have come up against budgetary cutbacks and statewide pressures to conventionalize their distinctive practices, public universities have been particularly constrained by the policies and rules imposed by a large bureaucratic higher education system. The University of

California, Santa Cruz, for example, has faced enormous pressures to standard-ize its unique curricular approaches and teaching philosophies as an institution of the University of California. The campus has gone from being a highly unorthodox interdisciplinary, teaching-centered institution, to a fairly tradi-tional research-oriented university. At the University of Wisconsin-Green Bay, the pressures imposed by a state-supported higher education system have also limited the campus' ability to maintain its free-spirited interdisciplinary and student-initiated educational activities. In the end, it seems that if a distinctive institution is to succeed in the public sector of higher education, it is essential that the campus retain some level of autonomy or self-governance, as in the case of Evergreen (which has its own independent board of trustees) and New College (which benefits from the New College Foundation). Other-wise, the campus is likely to be swallowed up by the traditional standards and goals of a state university system.

Shifts in Enrollments and Changes in the Student Generations

Second, long-lasting innovation may be jeopardized by enrollment downturns and changes in the attitudes and values of the student generations. Many distinctive colleges and universities faced budgetary cutbacks and enrollment pressures in the 1970s and were forced to sacrifice some of their innovative approaches to attract the more career-oriented students of the decade. The University of California, Santa Cruz, in the mid- to late 1970s, for example, was suffering from its reputation as a "hippie campus" that offered "weird" and unusual interdisciplinary degrees. When the institution began to lose students, the interdisciplinary courses in Santa Cruz's Colleges were abandoned and the university embraced traditional disciplinary departments and majors. At the University of Wisconsin-Green Bay, the early interdisciplinary mission was also jeopardized by severe enrollment problems in the 1970s. The campus moved to establish traditional disciplinary majors in the early 1980s to accom-modate the career ambitions and interests of local students. Even at New College, an institution that has been remarkably successful in preserving its distinctive heritage, some interviewees indicate that New College students have changed since the early days, and that over the years more students have been pursuing "standardized" (or course-based) learning contracts as opposed to the creative, field-based contracts of the start-up years.

Increasing Student-to-Faculty Ratios

Next, increasing student-to-faculty ratios may limit innovation. When an institution grows and if student-faculty ratios increase, there is often a sense of loss of the intimate, personalized feeling and engagement in the learner-centered ideals of the distinctive college or university. At the University of

Wisconsin-Green Bay, for example, the early individualized curriculum and the opportunities for close-knit interactions between faculty and students have largely disappeared as the proportion of students to faculty on campus has risen in recent decades. At UC Santa Cruz, the founding spirit of undergraduate teaching in a face-to-face learning community has also been sacrificed since the 1970s as enrollments have grown and the student-to-faculty ratios have increased. Those institutions that have been most successful in preserving their individualized curricular programs and distinctive educational approaches are those that have been able to maintain a relatively low student-to-faculty ratio (e.g., New College, Evergreen).

ISSUES AND CHALLENGES AT DISTINCTIVE COLLEGES AND UNIVERSITIES

What are some of the fundamental issues or challenges facing distinctive colleges and universities? According to the results of the case studies, there are six key issues or tensions that impact the lives of the students, faculty, and administrators at these institutions. These are retirements of founding faculty, campus stereotypes and image problems, student attrition, faculty overwork and burnout, faculty immobility, and the challenge to remain both innovative and innovating.

Founding Faculty Retirements

Perhaps the most serious and widespread concern among innovative colleges and universities today is the forthcoming retirements of charter faculty members. At all case study sites, long-time professors and administrators fear that the early dreams and innovative ideals of the institutions will be lost when the last of the academic pioneers retires over the next decade or two. Some interviewees express hope in the new generations of faculty who, they say, share a spark and passion for innovation and who will guide the institutions into the next century.

Campus Stereotypes and Image Problems

Distinctive institutions may also suffer from stereotypes and image problems, particularly in their early or start-up years. Misinformed outsiders and wary local citizens have labeled these campuses "hippie-dippie," flaky, anti-intellectual operations. Pitzer College, for example, has come up against distorted perceptions of the college as a "dope using," "sloppy," indulgent, nonacademic place, a "quirky" kid in The Claremont Colleges family. The University of California, Santa Cruz, has been accused of being a "haven for radicals," hippies, and "incompetents." Institutions that rebel against the standards and norms of conventional American education have always been the target of public skepticism and criticism.[1] Negative images and stereotypes have been particularly damaging in times of underenrollment, budgetary cutbacks, and public attitude shifts toward more conservative values or beliefs.

Student Attrition

> Don't expect experimental colleges to be happy campuses or little paradises tucked away in the woods. They're not. They are tough places in which to live and study. You need a great deal of reliance, knowledge of who you are and an idea of what you want to study.
>
> John Coyne and Tom Hebert, offering advice to prospective alternative college students in *This Way Out: A Guide to Alternatives to Traditional College Education in the United States, Europe and the Third World*, 1972, p. 144.

While many students thrive in an open or learner-directed environment, others may find themselves overwhelmed by the amount of freedom or responsibility that they are granted in designing their own educational programs. Some students flounder or eventually drop out of alternative institutions. Retention issues are a primary concern for a number of distinctive campuses in this study (including Pitzer College, New College, and Hampshire College).

This issue appears over and over again in the research and writings on experimental colleges and universities (e.g., Coyne and Hebert 1972; Gaff 1970; Grant and Riesman 1978; Meister 1982; Townsend et al. 1992). As early as 1967, Floyd Turner, an observer of the Experimental College at San Francisco State, noted: "It often takes [students here] a year to adjust to the shock of being responsible for their own learning" (Keyes 1967, 296). Grant and Riesman, Gaff, and Meister observed in their studies of experimental colleges that students at these campuses are sometimes unsure how to proceed with their educational programs. They hesitate. They question themselves and the world. Overwhelmed by the ambiguity of the "un-structured," they fill their faculty offices. Some "catch on." Others drift, "turn[ing] in their book bags for potters' wheels or join[ing] communes in the hills" (Grant and Riesman 1978, 254).

Faculty Overwork and Burnout

While the students flounder, the faculty may burn out. Intense seminar experiences, close-knit interactions with students and colleagues, participatory governance responsibilities, and the burden of having to write hundreds of narrative evaluations all take their toll on academics who devote their lives to teaching in innovative colleges and universities. Whether it is a Hampshire professor working seven days a week to complete various college projects or an

Evergreen teacher writing long, personalized narrative evaluations, the emotional and physical energy and intensity required of faculty at these campuses is often beyond belief. Similar concerns are, again, woven throughout the previous case studies and reports on innovative colleges and universities (e.g., Coyne and Hebert 1972; Grant and Riesman 1978; Holmquist, Nisonoff, and Rakoff 1984; Jones 1984).

Faculty Immobility

Next, there is the issue of faculty immobility. Academics at distinctive colleges and universities who devote themselves to innovative teaching and curriculum development may find themselves isolated from their disciplinary communities. Should these faculty members wish to transfer to other more traditional institutions, they may find that their mobility is limited. This issue emerged at all of the campuses in this study, particularly Evergreen and the University of Wisconsin-Green Bay (in the early years).

Innovative *and* Innovating

Last, at many of the institutions in this investigation, there was a sense of tension between remaining innovative (or true to the founding missions of the campus) while moving forward and "innovating," incorporating advances in technology, engaging in issues of cultural diversity, responding to shifting political and sociocultural trends and ideas. How does an innovative college or university preserve its distinctive founding ethos while flowing or moving with the times? Is there a necessary trade-off between being innovative and "innovating"?

Based on the findings of this investigation, the answer appears to be no. Those campuses that have successfully remained innovative (all for at least two and a half decades) have not only continued to embrace their innovative heritage in their educational missions and approaches, but have moved forward and incorporated new ideas and new concepts and issues. Pitzer College's emphasis on interdisciplinary and intercultural perspectives, the campus' outreach to the community, and student involvement in Third World nations; Hampshire's responsiveness to the exploration of new issues and areas in individualized learning; and Evergreen's ever-changing Coordinated Studies curriculum are all striking examples of the ways in which innovative institutions have remained true to their distinctive roots while confronting the challenges of the future.

IMPLICATIONS AND RECOMMENDATIONS

Each of the campuses in this study has at some point in its history dared to be different, to be a maverick, a rebel. Three decades since the dawn of the alternative higher education movement, some of these institutions are still rebelling, while others have settled into a more traditional or conventional pattern of being. Looking back over the lives and lessons of these six extraordinary colleges and universities, what are the overall lessons to be learned in the 1990s—the implications of the case studies for the larger higher education community? What are the implications for future innovators and leaders of distinctive colleges and universities? These questions are addressed in the two sections that follow.

Implications for the General Higher Education Community

- **Recognizing the need for alternatives in higher education.** First, this study turns our attention to the importance of providing alternatives, creative and nourishing educational places and spaces for students and scholars who are seeking unique, person-centered classrooms and programs in American higher education. The six campuses in this investigation are six islands of educational difference, each having evolved over the decades with at least some key elements of its original distinctive principles intact. One of the major lessons to be learned from this investigation is that traditional methods of higher education are not the sole means of educating students, and are not the most effective or appropriate strategies for all learners. Innovative colleges and universities fill a distinct niche in the higher education community, offering refuges for those who are dissatisfied with the mainstream practices and approaches of conventional higher education. They produce graduates who are successful entrepreneurs and leaders with imaginative hearts and spirits. Higher education would be wise to recognize and reward innovative campuses for their "genius." Philanthropical foundations and agencies should follow the lead of the John D. and Catherine T. MacArthur Foundation, which recently awarded grants of $750,000 apiece to six innovative liberal arts campuses (Alverno College, Antioch College, College of the Atlantic, Hampshire College, Johnson C. Smith University, and Marlboro College). These one-time grants were offered as part of a $5.9 million initiative to show support for distinctive institutions of higher education. In the words of Woodward A. Wickham, director of the MacArthur Foundation general grants program, "Parents are increasingly asking whether this kind of education is worth it. With these grants we wanted to say that it is absolutely worth it, and to help insure that liberal arts and these innovative colleges and others like them flourish" (Arenson 1996, B9).

- **Promotion.** In visiting distinctive campuses, you get the sense that you are uncovering hidden jewels or undiscovered treasures in American higher education. Nation-wide promotional strategies are needed to raise awareness of these unique teaching and learning communities. Educational organizations and professional associations should sponsor conferences and institutes on the topic of innovative higher education, where teams of participants from distinctive campuses across the country can gather to present their teaching and learning approaches. Joint research reports and local or regional workshops are also essential for building connections and providing networking opportunities across this family of creative institutions. National respect, recognition, and appreciation for the innovative sector of higher education are critical for combatting stereotypes and ensuring the survival of alternative colleges and universities.
- **Models and practices.** Many higher education institutions today are searching for creative strategies to improve or revitalize their teaching and learning environments. In these difficult budgetary times, when it may be impossible to develop new programs or campuses, mainstream colleges and universities should look to the practices of innovative colleges and universities and consider the merits of their unique approaches—for example, narrative evaluation systems, portfolio assessment for faculty. Evergreen's Washington Center for Improving the Quality of Undergraduate Education has made excellent strides in transmitting the Coordinated Studies model to colleges and universities throughout the state of Washington. Similar centers or offshoots could be founded across the nation to guide or assist traditional institutions in incorporating alternative, student-centered teaching and learning techniques.

Implications for Innovative Institutions of Higher Education

Now having considered the implications of this study for the broader higher education community, what are some of the lessons or teachings of this research for other innovative colleges and universities? Linking together the conclusions of each case study chapter, along with the cross-campus themes and analyses, I offer the following guidelines and strategies for ensuring long-lasting innovation in distinctive institutions of higher education.

- **Retain founding faculty.** First, to ensure that innovative ideals are passed down from one generation to the next, distinctive campuses should seek to retain a significant number of founding faculty members until the time of their retirements. Campuses should provide opportunities for interaction among charter professors and other academic cohorts (e.g., team teaching, educational workshops, or roundtable discussions).

- **Recruit new faculty and administrators who are committed to innovation.** Second, if innovative campuses are to maintain their imaginative principles or philosophies, it is critical that they recruit and retain faculty and administrators who value the distinctive ideals and missions of the institution. This will be especially important in the academic arena as these campuses seek to replace the majority of their founding faculty members in the coming decades.

- **Establish reward systems that value innovation.** Third, academic reappointment, promotion, and tenure systems that reward innovative approaches to teaching and curriculum development are critical to sustaining innovation. If creative, interdisciplinary teaching and learning approaches are to flourish at distinctive institutions, then faculty members must be actively supported and rewarded for innovative teaching and program development.

- **Provide open and flexible structures.** Fourth, open or flexible organizational structures are essential to the success of distinctive educational approaches and decision making. Institutions should strive to keep administrative hierarchies, academic committees, and disciplinary departments to a minimum. Governance structures should remain open and participatory. Faculty members should be given the freedom to experiment, to engage in creative approaches to teaching and scholarship. Students should be granted the space to design their own curricular pathways, to invent their own courses, majors, and/or independent study projects.

- **Affiliate with other institutions.** Finally, innovative campuses should seek out opportunities for affiliation with a consortium of institutions or neighboring colleges and universities. Opportunities will vary, of course, from one setting to another, but this kind of interinstitutional collaboration and exchange offers the small distinctive campus access to a wealth of information, resources, and shared facilities at other, more traditional or established institutions. The other campuses, in turn, benefit from the creative approaches, interdisciplinary teaching, and curricular activities of the innovative institution. It is a healthy partnership for all.

SUGGESTIONS FOR FUTURE RESEARCH

The study of innovative colleges and universities is an important and relatively undeveloped area of contemporary research. There are a number of ways in which future investigators could expand upon the findings of the present investigation by exploring additional issues or aspects of these very unusual and interesting institutions.

Studies of Other Innovative Campuses of the 1960s and 1970s

First, to broaden the findings of this investigation, qualitative research studies of the history and persistence of innovation should be conducted at other four-year distinctive institutions of the 1960s and 1970s. Investigators should examine the experiences of distinctive community colleges, nontraditional institutions for adults, and experimental subcolleges to understand how these campuses have evolved in a changing social, political, and economic climate. Further research could also be conducted at public innovative campuses to determine how issues of affiliation or control impact the life and longevity of other state-supported distinctive colleges and universities. The master inventory of innovative institutions in appendix B lists hundreds of innovative campuses of the 1960s and 1970s; it could serve as an excellent starting point and stimulus for future research.

Studies of Older Distinctive Campuses and Progressive Colleges

A scholarly comparison of the experiences of the six distinctive campuses in this study with those of the older experimental colleges of the late-nineteenth and early-twentieth centuries (e.g., Antioch College, Reed College, Deep Springs College) could yield important insights. What are the lessons to be learned about the history and transformation of innovation from the older and progressive-era innovative campuses, and how do these results compare and contrast with findings of the current investigation? These are important questions for future researchers.

Studies of Additional Issues or Topics at Innovative Institutions

There are a host of other important topics and concerns that deserve consideration in the writings about institutional reform in higher education. This study only touches the surface of some of the most pressing issues and tensions that are facing innovative colleges and universities in the 1990s. Future studies are needed to examine topics such as student and faculty life in the distinctive campus, alumnae/i outcomes and success, issues of student attrition and retention, faculty burnout, and faculty immobility. One important area for further investigation is the topic of institutional maturity. Future research is needed to determine how the aging or maturation of an innovative college or university (the life cycle of the campus from its newborn phase to its "adolescent" and "adult" years) impacts the endurance of distinctive missions.

Researchers should also turn their attention to the study of financial concerns and leadership issues, as well as multiculturalism and diversity in the innovative college or university. Future investigators should also conduct in-depth studies of the governance processes (e.g., open, participatory decision making), the nongraded or narrative evaluation systems, and the student-centered curricular models at these creative campuses to understand how these approaches could be applied or utilized in other college or university settings. There is much to be learned from the imaginative practices and programs of the innovative colleges and universities. The research pathways are open and this investigator invites others to join the journey.

Long-Term Follow-Up Studies

Looking ahead, investigators should revisit these six innovative campuses over the next two or three decades to follow up on the institutional stories, to examine how these institutions have (or have not) changed and developed over the ensuing decades. It will be especially important to observe how the distinctive colleges and universities have evolved in response to the retirements of the charter academics. As one founding faculty member said, "Come back and visit us in the next 20 years and see if we have changed."

FUTURE OUTLOOK

We are all the inheritors of the higher education revolution of the 1960s and 1970s. The future of the innovative college and university is in our hands and in the hands of tomorrow's campus visionaries. It will be up to the coming generations of reformers, kindred leaders, and educational rebels to preserve these distinctive institutions and to build new islands of educational difference.

Those whose lives have been touched by these campuses embark on the world with a new lens, a new way of seeing and being. These are transformative institutions and they produce transformative thinkers. Where there is room for empowering, learner-centered classrooms where students rise above conventional, competitive grading systems, there is room for the innovative campus. Where there is openness to egalitarian and participatory decision making, to communal togetherness, to a oneness among students and teachers, there is openness to the distinctive college or university. Where there is space for crossing over into new multidisciplinary fields of thought and inquiry, where rich frameworks and theories are imaginatively integrated, there is space for the alternative institution. And where there is hope for an education that will empower our children and our children's children to create and to follow their own academic pathways and dreams, there is hope, there is a future for the innovative college and university.

It will take all of our passion and commitment to sustain these kindred campuses and to energize new educational reform movements as we witness future revolutions in technology and social and cultural transformation. Respect, appreciation, consciousness raising, and continuing allocation of resources are vital to the future of alternative higher education. Let us pay tribute to the pioneers and visionaries who had the courage to experiment, to create unconventional institutions. Let us acknowledge their efforts. Let us share in their wonderment. Let us carry forward the nourishing spirit of the innovative campus, the legacy and dreams, into the twenty-first century.

NOTES

1. In the early years of Black Mountain College (an experimental college in North Carolina that survived from 1933 to 1956), Martin Duberman ([1972] 1993) writes, "the local people of Black Mountain village let it be known that they were upset by the 'goings on' at the college. To the suspicion that the community was a Godless place practicing free love was soon added the rumor that it was a nudist colony as well: students often wore shorts in warm weather, and several appeared in town, at a movie or at a square dance or while shopping, wearing sandals that revealed bare feet" (23).

REFERENCES

Arenson, K.W. 1996. Six colleges with 'genius' given $750,000 rewards. *The New York Times* (26 June): B9.

Clark, B.R. 1970. *The distinctive college: Antioch, Reed, and Swarthmore*. Chicago: Aldine.

Coyne, J., and T. Hebert. 1972. *This way out: A guide to alternatives to traditional college education in the United States, Europe and the Third World*. New York: E.P. Dutton.

Duberman, M. [1972] 1993. *Black Mountain: An exploration in community*. New York: W.W. Norton.

Gaff, J.G. 1970. Problems created and resolved. In *The cluster college*, J.G. Gaff and Associates, 216–38. San Francisco: Jossey-Bass.

Grant, G., and D. Riesman. 1978. *The perpetual dream: Reform and experiment in the American college*. Chicago: The University of Chicago Press.

Holmquist, F.W., L. Nisonoff, and R.M. Rakoff. 1984. The labor process at Hampshire College. In *Against the current: Reform and experiment in higher education*, edited by R.M. Jones and B.L. Smith, 183–214. Cambridge, Mass.: Schenkman.

Jones, R.M. 1984. Response to Youtz. In *Against the current: Reform and experiment in higher education*, edited by R.M. Jones and B.L. Smith, 119–25. Cambridge, Mass.: Schenkman.

Keyes, R. 1967. The free universities. *The Nation* (2 October): 294–99.

Meister, J.S. 1982. A sociologist looks at two schools - the Amherst and Hampshire experiences. *Change* (March): 26–34.

Townsend, B.K., L.J. Newell, and M.D. Wiese. 1992. *Creating distinctiveness: Lessons from uncommon colleges and universities*. ASHE-ERIC Higher Education Report No. 6. Washington, D.C.: The George Washington University, School of Education and Human Development.

Youtz, B.L. 1984. The Evergreen State College: An experiment maturing. In *Against the current: Reform and experiment in higher education*, edited by R.M. Jones and B.L. Smith, 93–118. Cambridge, Mass.: Schenkman.

APPENDIX A

Innovative College and University Consultant Panel

MEMBERS OF THE CONSULTANT PANEL

The following experts on American higher education and innovative colleges and universities participated in the process of nominating campuses for the case study sites.

1. **Dr. Alexander W. Astin**
   Allan Murray Cartter Professor, Division of Higher Education and Organizational Change, and Director, Higher Education Research Institute, University of California, Los Angeles

2. **Dr. Ernest L. Boyer**
   Former President, The Carnegie Foundation for the Advancement of Teaching; former U.S. Commissioner of Education; former Chancellor, State University of New York (now deceased)

3. **Dr. V. Ray Cardozier**
   Professor of Higher Education, University of Texas at Austin; second President and founding Vice President for Academic Affairs, University of Texas of the Permian Basin; editor, *Important Lessons from Innovative Colleges and Universities* (1993)

4. **Dr. Robert E. Engel**
   Emeritus Associate Professor, Department of Planning, Policy, and Leadership, University of Iowa; conducted field visits to a number of innovative colleges in the summer of 1970 as a part of the Committee to

Study Interdisciplinary Options for Undergraduate Education at the
University of Iowa

5. **Dr. Jerry G. Gaff**
   Vice President for Network and Academic Renewal, Association of
   American Colleges and Universities; coauthor, *The Cluster College*
   (Gaff and Associates 1970)

6. **Dr. Zelda F. Gamson**
   Director, New England Resource Center for Higher Education, University of Massachusetts at Boston; coauthor, *Academic Values and Mass
   Education* (Riesman, Gusfield, and Gamson 1970), a study of reform in
   higher education

7. **Dr. Russell Y. Garth**
   Executive Vice President, Council of Independent Colleges; former
   Deputy Director, Fund for the Improvement of Postsecondary Education

8. **Dr. Mildred M. Henry**
   Academic Vice President and Dean of the School of Humanities, New
   College of California

9. **Dr. Arthur E. Levine**
   President, Teachers College, Columbia University; author of several
   key works on innovation in higher education, including *Why Innovation
   Fails* (1980), *Handbook of Undergraduate Curriculum* (1978), and *Reform of Undergraduate Education* (with John Weingart, 1973)

10. **Dr. John D. Maguire**
    Former President, Claremont University Center and Graduate University; (1981–1998); former President, State University of New York,
    College at Old Westbury (1970–1981)

11. **Dr. Charles McCann**
    Founding President, The Evergreen State College

12. **Dr. Dean E. McHenry**
    Founding Chancellor, University of California, Santa Cruz; coauthor,
    Academic Departments: Problems, Variations, and Alternatives (McHenry
    and Associates, 1977), which includes chapters on UC Santa Cruz,
    University of Wisconsin-Green Bay, Hampshire College, and The Evergreen State College (now deceased)

13. **Dr. L. Jackson Newell**
    President, Deep Springs College; Professor of Higher Education, University of Utah; coauthor, *Creating Distinctiveness: Lessons from Uncommon Colleges and Universities* (Townsend, Newell, and Wiese 1992);
    coeditor, *Maverick Colleges: Ten Notable Experiments in American Undergraduate Education* (Newell and Reynolds 1993)

14. **Dr. Katherine C. Reynolds**
    Assistant Professor, College of Education, University of South Carolina; coeditor, *Maverick Colleges: Ten Notable Experiments in American Undergraduate Education* (Newell and Reynolds 1993)
15. **Dr. David Riesman**
    Professor Emeritus, Department of Sociology, Harvard University; coauthor, *The Perpetual Dream: Reform and Experiment in the American College* (Grant and Riesman 1978)
16. **Dr. Barbara Leigh Smith**
    Academic Vice President and Provost, The Evergreen State College; former Director, Washington Center for Improving the Quality of Undergraduate Education, The Evergreen State College; coeditor, *Against the Current: Reform and Experimentation in Higher Education* (Jones and Smith 1984)
17. **Dr. Page Smith**
    Founding Provost, Cowell College, University of California, Santa Cruz (now deceased)
18. **Dr. Peter Tommerup**
    Former Institutional Ethnographer, The Evergreen State College; author, *Adhocratic Traditions, Experience Narratives and Personal Transformation: An Ethnographic Study of the Organizational Culture and Folklore of The Evergreen State College, An Innovative Liberal Arts College* (1993)
19. **Dr. Edward W. Weidner**
    Founding Chancellor, University of Wisconsin-Green Bay

(1)   [Consultant Mailing]

Project for the Study of Innovative Colleges
Definition of Innovative Colleges and Institutional Selection Criteria

Definition of Innovative Colleges

In this study, "innovative" or "distinctive" colleges refer to those campuses that were founded amidst the social, political, economic, and demographic transformations of the 1960s and early 70s as alternatives to the mainstream American college or university. Specifically, innovative institutions are distinguished by the following characteristics (based on a review of the literature):

(1) Interdisciplinary teaching and learning: cross-disciplinary study and collaboration in curricular and co-curricular activity.

(2) Student-centered education: Students engineer or "take charge of" their academic programs (e.g., students invent their own majors, design courses, and assist in curricular planning and development).

(3) Egalitarianism (e.g., participatory governance structures -- town meetings, general assemblies, and/or community forums where administrators, faculty, and students share equal voice in decision making; an absence of status symbols, such as titles and ranks; narrative evaluations as opposed to letter grades; and cooperation and collaboration rather than competition in teaching and learning).

(4) Experiential education: Out-of-classroom projects, theses, and/or internships are integral to the academic program.

(5) An institutional focus on teaching rather than research and/or publication.

These criteria apply to the institution *at its inception.* While some colleges and universities today may refer to themselves as "distinctive" or "innovative," this study focuses specifically on those institutions that were founded as part of the educational reform movement of the 1960s and early 70s and that typically embody the five institutional characteristics described here.

Institutional Selection Criteria

As described in Attachment 2, several decision rules have guided the institutional selection process in this study. The innovative colleges under consideration are those that meet the following criteria: (1) The campus was founded in the United States in the 1960s or early 70s, (2) the campus is a free-standing innovative organization (rather than a subcollege or experimental unit of larger institution), and (3) the campus remains open in the 1990s. The research *excludes* nontraditional colleges for adults and/or distance-learning institutions, "free universities," and the small number of innovative community colleges and graduate-level institutions that that came into being during the 1960s and early 70s.

(2)   [Consultant Mailing]

Project for the Study of Innovative Colleges
Institution Nomination Form

In order to identify innovative colleges of the 1960s and early 70s and to determine which campuses have maintained their distinctive missions and which have abandoned their founding designs, I am seeking your expert assistance in the institutional "nomination" process. Please complete all applicable sections of this form. *Remember, responses will __not__ be reported or published. The purpose of this form is to guide the selection of institutions.*

Institutional Distinctiveness Rating

Please review the preliminary list of institutions below. In Column A (Rating at Founding), rate on a 1 to 5 scale, the extent to which you perceive this institution to have been innovative (in accordance with the definition provided on the preceding page) during the institution's early (say, first five to seven) years. In Column B (Current Rating), please rate on a 1 to 5 scale, the extent to which you perceive that this institution has remained innovative -- in keeping with its original conception.

Institution	Column A Rating at Founding	Column B Current Rating
1. Audrey Cohen College (formerly College for Human Services)	_____	_____
2. College of the Atlantic	_____	_____
3. The Evergreen State College	_____	_____
4. Hampshire College	_____	_____
5. Maharishi International University	_____	_____
6. The Naropa Institute	_____	_____
7. New College of California	_____	_____
8. New College of the University of South Florida	_____	_____
9. Pitzer College	_____	_____
10. Prescott College	_____	_____
11. Ramapo College of New Jersey	_____	_____
12. The Richard Stockton College of New Jersey (formerly Stockton State College)	_____	_____
13. State University of New York, College at Old Westbury	_____	_____
14. University of California, Santa Cruz	_____	_____
15. University of Wisconsin, Green Bay	_____	_____

Scale for Rating at Founding
1 = was not innovative
2 = was somewhat innovative
3 = was moderately innovative
4 = was quite innovative
5 = was highly innovative
DK = unsure/don't know

Scale for Current Rating
1 = does not remain innovative
2 = remains somewhat innovative
3 = remains moderately innovative
4 = remains quite innovative
5 = remains highly innovative
DK = unsure/don't know

Additional Institutions

Please list any additional innovative institutions that you believe should be included on this "nomination list" and that meet the project selection criteria outlined in the previous document. Please rate these campuses on a 1 to 5 scale following the instructions under Institutional Distinctiveness Rating (on the previous page).

Institution	Column A Rating at Founding	Column B Current Rating
1. _____	_____	_____
2. _____	_____	_____
3. _____	_____	_____
4. _____	_____	_____
5. _____	_____	_____

Additional Contacts

If there are other individuals who you feel might provide insight into the innovative college selection process, please list their names and contact information here:

name:	address:	phone #:	e-mail:

Comments/Suggestions

I would welcome any additional comments and/or suggestions that you might have regarding the institutional "nomination" process or the innovative college project. I am particularly interested in your feedback regarding the definition included in Attachment 3 (*please continue comments on the back of this page*).

Participant Information

Your name:_____

Your address:_____

phone number: _____   e-mail address:_____

Thank you for your participation! Please return this form within the next two weeks to Joy Rosenzweig, Center for Educational Studies, The Claremont Graduate School, 150 E. Tenth Street, Claremont, California 91711-6160   office phone: (909) 621-8075   fax: (909) 621-8734   e-mail: rosenzwj@cgs.edu

APPENDIX B

Master List of Innovative Institutions of the 1960s and 1970s

The master list is a comprehensive inventory of innovative colleges and universities that were founded in the 1960s and 1970s in the United States. The list was generated through an extensive review of the research literature, guidebooks, and reports on innovative colleges and universities, and in consultation with a panel of nationally recognized experts on reform in American higher education.

CRITERIA FOR INCLUSION ON THE MASTER LIST

The master list includes all institutions that were founded as innovative campuses in the United States in the 1960s and 1970s (i.e., those cited in the literature and/or in consultation with the expert panel).

The list *excludes* nontraditional campuses for adult learners, innovative colleges and universities that offer primarily external degree programs, and distance learning institutions that came into being during the 1960s and 1970s. The inventory also excludes the small number of innovative community colleges (distinctive two-year institutions that offer the *Associate of Arts degree*), upper division colleges, and graduate schools (and free-standing graduate institutions) that grew out of the 1960s and 1970s reform movement. Finally, the list includes only those innovative institutions that refer to themselves as "colleges," "universities," "schools," or "institutes." It excludes innovative "programs" and "divisions."

FORMAT AND ORGANIZATION OF THE MASTER LIST

The master list is organized alphabetically by institution name. Each entry includes the following information about the campus (where available): location, public or private affiliation, date of founding, references to the campus in studies or reports, and whether or not the institution has been identified as a free university and/or a subcollege.[1] Each entry includes *all available information* drawn from the hundreds of articles, reports, and studies reviewed in the institutional selection process.

In some cases, there may be duplicate entries (i.e., if the name of an institution has changed, but there is no record of the name change in the literature or guidebooks).

Abenaki Experimental College, the University of Maine (Orono, ME)
(public) (1970)
(Lichtman 1972, 1973) (free university)

Afro American Studies College of the State University of New York, College at Buffalo (Buffalo, NY) (public)
(Levine 1980*) (subcollege)

Allport College of Oakland University (Rochester, MI) (public) (1969)
(Gaff 1970; Grant and Riesman 1978; Jones and Smith 1984; Riesman, Gusfield, and Gamson 1970) (subcollege)

Alternative One College of Keene State College (Keene, NH) (public)
(1971)
(Coyne & Hebert 1972) (subcollege)

Alternate University of the University of Illinois, Chicago Circle Campus
(Chicago, IL) (public) (1969)
(Lichtman 1972, 1973) (free university)

Animas Free School (Hesperus, CO)
(Draves 1980) (free university)

Aquarian University (Baltimore, MD) (private)
(Coyne and Hebert 1972) (free university)

Arcata Free University (Arcata, CA) (1969)
(Lichtman 1972, 1973) (free university)

Artsworld Institute of Creative Arts (Ann Arbor, MI)
(Litkowski 1983) (free university)

---

* designates an article, chapter, book, or report devoted exclusively to this institution. References include materials reviewed prior to the field visits. Additional documents that were gathered during or following the campus visits are cited in the case study chapters (chapters 2–7). References for the master list are presented at the end of this appendix.

ASOSU Experimental College, Oregon State University (Corvallis, OR)
(public) (1970)
(Draves 1980; Lichtman 1972; Litkowski 1983) (free university)

Baltimore Free University, Johns Hopkins University (Baltimore, MD)
(private) (1960)
(Draves 1980; Lichtman 1972; Litkowski 1983) (free university)

Belleville Area Free University (BAFU) (Belleville, KS)
(Litkowski 1983) (free university)

Bensalem College of Fordham University (Bronx, NY) (private) (1967–
1971)
(Anzulovic 1976; Calabretta 1973;* Cardozier 1993; Coyne 1972;* Coyne
and Hebert 1972; Freeman 1972,* 1973;* Gaff 1970; Grant and Riesman
1978; Jerome 1970; Jones and Smith 1984; Levine 1978; MacDonald
1973a; MacDonald and Sewell 1973; Sewell 1973;* Wolfe 1970)
(subcollege)

Blake College (Eugene, OR) (private) (1966)
(Coyne and Hebert 1972)

Boulder Community Free School (Boulder, CO) (private) (1968)
(Draves 1980; Lichtman 1972, 1973; Litkowski 1983) (free university)

Boston Community School (Boston, MA)
(Draves 1980) (free university)

Boston University Free School (Boston, MA)
(Draves 1980; Litkowski 1983) (free university)

California Institute of the Arts (Valencia, CA) (private) (1964–present)
(Coyne and Hebert 1972; Greening 1981b)

Callison College of the University of the Pacific (Stockton, CA) (private)
(1967)
(Gaff 1970; Jones and Smith 1984; Heiss 1973; Litten 1971; Longsworth
1976; McHenry 1977a; Mason and Moore 1971;* Sullivan 1973)
(subcollege)

Centennial College of the University of Kansas (Lawrence, KS) (public)
(Heiss 1973) (subcollege)

Central University College of Eastern Kentucky University (Richmond, KY)
(public)
(Jones and Smith 1984) (subcollege)

Charter College of Oakland University (Rochester, MI) (public) (1965)
(Gaff 1970; Grant and Riesman 1978; Jones and Smith 1984; Riesman,
Gusfield, and Gamson 1970) (subcollege)

Cheap University of Southwest Missouri State University (Springfield, MO)
(public)
(Draves 1980) (free university)

College A of the State University of New York, College at Buffalo (Buffalo, NY) (public)
(Levine 1980*) (subcollege)

College of the Atlantic (Bar Harbor, ME) (private) (1969–present)
(Aranow 1983;* Coyne and Hebert 1972; Grant and Riesman 1978; Hall 1994;* Longsworth 1976; Townsend, Newell, and Wiese 1992; Wardle 1993*)

College B of the State University of New York, College at Buffalo (Buffalo, NY) (public)
(Levine 1980*) (subcollege)

College C of the State University of New York, College at Buffalo (Buffalo, NY) (public)
(Levine 1980*) (subcollege)

College D (Clifford Furnas College) of the State University of New York, College at Buffalo (Buffalo, NY) (public)
(Levine 1980*) (subcollege)

College Eight of the University of California, Santa Cruz (Santa Cruz, CA) (public) (1972–present)
(Grant and Riesman 1978; Levine 1978; McHenry 1977a; Von der Muhll 1984) (subcollege)

College of Ethnic Studies of Western Washington State College (now Western Washington University) (Bellingham, WA) (public) (1969)
(Fashing and Deutsch 1971) (subcollege)

College Five (now Porter College) of the University of California, Santa Cruz (Santa Cruz, CA) (public) (1969–present)
(Gaff 1970; Grant and Riesman 1978; Heiss 1973; Levine 1978; McHenry 1977a; Von der Muhll 1984) (subcollege)

College IV of Grand Valley State College (now University) (Allendale, MI) (public) (1973)
(Gamson 1979; Grant 1979; Grant and Riesman 1978) (subcollege)

College IV of the University of Massachusetts, Boston (Boston, MA) (public)
(Grant and Riesman 1978) (subcollege)

College H of the State University of New York, College at Buffalo (Buffalo, NY) (public)
(Levine 1980*) (subcollege)

College of Letters, Wesleyan University (Middletown, CT) (private) (1960)
(Gaff 1970; Jones and Smith 1984) (subcollege)

College of Mathematical Sciences of the State University of New York, College at Buffalo (Buffalo, NY) (public)
(Levine 1980*) (subcollege)

College of the Person (Washington, DC) (private)
  (Coyne and Hebert 1972; Grant and Riesman 1978)
College of the Potomac (Washington, DC) (1969)
  (Coyne and Hebert 1972; Heiss 1973; Jerome 1970)
College of Progressive Education (formerly New College of Modern Educa-
  tion) of the State University of New York, College at Buffalo (Buffalo,
  NY) (public)
  (Levine 1980*) (subcollege)
College of Public and Community Service (College III) of the University of
  Massachusetts, Boston (Boston, MA) (public)
  (Gamson 1979; Grant 1979; Grant and Riesman 1978) (subcollege)
College of Social Studies, Wesleyan University (Middletown, CT) (private)
  (1960)
  (Gaff 1970; Jones and Smith 1984) (subcollege)
Colleges-Within-The-College of the University of Kansas (Lawrence, KS)
  (public)
  (Coyne and Hebert 1972) (subcollege)
College of Urban Studies (a merger of College Z and C.P. Snow College) of
  the State University of New York, College at Buffalo (Buffalo, NY)
  (public)
College of the Virgin Islands (St. Thomas, Virgin Islands) (1963)
  (Coyne and Hebert 1972)
  (Levine 1980*) (subcollege)
College Within at Tufts University (Medford, MA) (private) (1972)
  (Grant and Riesman 1978; Heiss 1973) (subcollege)
College Z of the State University of New York, College at Buffalo (Buffalo,
  NY) (public)
  (Levine 1980*) (subcollege)
Colorado Springs Free U (Denver, CO)
  (Draves 1980) (free university)
Communications College of the State University of New York, College at
  Buffalo (Buffalo, NY) (public)
  (Levine 1980*) (subcollege)
Community Free School (also called Edwards County Free School) (Kinsley,
  KS)
  (Draves 1980; Litkowski 1983) (free university)
Community House Experimental School, the University of Maine, Presque
  Isle (Presque Isle, ME) (public) (1973)
  (Lichtman 1972) (free university)

Community School (Louisville, KY) (1968)
(Lichtman 1972) (free university)
Community University of Montana State University (Bozeman, MT)
(public)
(Draves 1980; Litkowski 1983) (free university)
Communiversity (Massachusetts)
(Lichtman 1973) (free university)
Communiversity (Rochester, NY) (private) (1971)
(Draves 1980; Lichtman 1972, 1973; Litkowski 1983) (free university)
Communiversity (San Francisco, CA)
(Draves 1980; Litkowski 1983) (free university)
Communiversity of Lake of the Ozarks Parish (Lake Ozark, MO)
(Litkowski 1983) (free university)
Communiversity of LaSalle College (now University) (Philadelphia, PA)
(private)
(Draves 1980) (free university)
Communiversity of the University of Illinois (Champaign, IL) (public)
(Draves 1980; Litkowski 1983) (free university)
Communiversity of the University of Missouri, Columbia (Columbia, MO)
(public)
(Draves 1980; Lichtman 1973; Litkowski 1983) (free university)
Communiversity of the University of Missouri, Kansas City (Kansas City,
MO) (public) (1970)
(Draves 1980; Lichtman 1972; Litkowski 1983) (free university)
Communiversity West of California State College (now University), Long
Beach (Long Beach, CA) (public) (1965)
(Lichtman 1972) (free university)
Communiverstiy of Western Illinois University (Macomb, IL) (public)
(Draves 1980) (free university)
Comparative Historical Studies College of the State University of New York,
College at Buffalo (Buffalo, NY) (public)
(Levine 1980*) (subcollege)
Cora P. Maloney College (formerly College E) of the State University of New
York, College at Buffalo (Buffalo, NY) (public)
(Levine 1980*) (subcollege)
Cowell College of the University of California, Santa Cruz (Santa Cruz, CA)
(public) (1965–present)
(Adams 1984; Gaff 1970; Grant and Riesman 1975, 1978; Hall 1991;
Heiss 1973; Levine 1978; Levine and Weingart 1973; McHenry 1964,

1977a; Ring 1971a; *Solomon's House* 1970;* Von der Muhll 1984)
(subcollege)

The Creative U of Texas Tech University (Lubbock, TX) (public)
(Litkowski 1983) (free university)

Crown College of the University of California, Santa Cruz (Santa Cruz, CA)
(public) (1967–present)
(Adams 1984; Gaff 1970; Grant and Riesman 1978; Heiss 1973; Levine
1978; Levine and Weingart 1973; McHenry 1977a; Ring 1971a; Von der
Muhll 1984) (subcollege)

Dartmouth Experimental College, Dartmouth College (Hanover, NH)
(private) (1967)
(Heiss 1973; Keyes 1967; Lichtman 1972) (free university)

The Defiance College (Defiance, OH)
(Draves 1980) (free university)

Delaware Free University of the University of Delaware (Newark, DE)
(public) (1971)
(Lichtman 1972, 1973) (free university)

Denver Free University (Denver, CO) (private) (1969)
(Draves 1980; Lichtman 1972, 1973; Litkowski 1983) (free university)

Disciplines College of the State University of New York, College at Old
Westbury (Old Westbury, NY) (public) (1969)
(Gaff 1970; Jones and Smith 1984) (subcollege)

Ecology College of the State University of New York, College at Buffalo
(Buffalo, NY) (public)
(Levine 1980*) (subcollege)

Eisenhower College (Seneca Falls, NY) (1968–1982)
(Berger 1984;* Dresser 1995;* Fleming 1986;* McGrath 1963;* Saunder
1975*)

Elbert Covell College of the University of the Pacific (Stockton, CA)
(private) (1963)
(Coyne and Hebert 1972; Gaff 1970; Grant and Riesman 1978; Heiss
1973; Jones and Smith 1984; Longsworth 1976; Mayhew 1965, 1977;
McHenry 1977a; Meyer 1964; Sullivan 1973) (subcollege)

The Evergreen State College (Olympia, WA) (public) (1967–present)
(Alpert 1980; Bergquist 1995; Boyer 1984; Cadwallader 1984; Cardozier
1993; Chance 1980;* Chance and Curry 1979;* Coyne and Hebert 1972;
Dodson 1991;* Elmendorf 1975; Fashing and Deutsch 1971; Gaff 1994;
Gehret 1972;* Grant 1984; Grant and Riesman 1975, 1978; Hahn 1984;
Hall 1991; Hall and Kevles 1982; Heiss 1973; Jones 1981,* 1984;* Jones
and Smith 1984; Kuh et al. 1991; Levine 1978; Levine and Weingart

1973; Longsworth 1976; Lyons 1991;* Marcus 1984; G.E. Martin 1982;*
W.B. Martin 1982; Mayhew 1977; McCann 1977;* McHenry 1977b;
Nkabinde 1993;* Perkins 1984; Schuster 1989a;* Tommerup 1993;*
Townsend, Newell, and Wiese 1992; Von Blum 1984; Wofford 1973;
Youtz 1984*)

Everybody's School (Westboro/West Lebanon, NH)
    (Lichtman 1972, 1973) (free university)

Everyone's U (Ashland, OR)
    (Draves 1980) (free university)

Experimental College at Berkeley, University of California, Berkeley (Berke
    ley, CA) (public) (1965–1969)
    (Bergquist 1995; Cadwallader 1984; Fashing and Deutsch 1971; Gaff
    1994; Grant and Riesman 1975, 1978; Hall 1991; Hefferlin 1969; Levine
    1978; Levine and Weingart 1973; Mayhew 1977; Meister 1982; Newell
    and Reynolds 1993; Riesman, Gusfield, and Gamson 1970; Schuster
    1989a; Suczek 1972;* Tussman 1969*) (subcollege)

Experimental College of California State College (now University), Fullerton
    (Fullerton, CA) (public) (1970)
    (Lichtman 1972, 1973) (free university)

Experimental College of California State College (now University), Los
    Angeles (Los Angeles, CA) (public) (1969)
    (Lichtman 1972, 1973) (free university)

Experimental College of California State University, Long Beach (Long
    Beach, CA) (public)
    (Lichtman 1973) (free university)

Experimental College of California State University, Northridge (Northridge,
    CA) (public)
    (Draves 1980; Lichtman 1973; Litkowski 1983) (free university)

Experimental College of California State University, Sacramento (Sacra
    mento, CA) (public)
    (Draves 1980) (free university)

Experimental College of City College of San Francisco (San Francisco, CA)
    (Lichtman 1972, 1973) (free university)

Experimental College of Cornell University (Ithaca, NY) (private)
    (Litkowski 1983) (free university)

Experimental College of Fresno State College (now California State Univer
    sity, Fresno) (Fresno, CA) (public)
    (Coyne and Hebert 1972; Grant and Riesman 1978) (subcollege)

Experimental College of Humboldt State University (Arcata, CA) (public)
    (Draves 1980) (free university)

Experimental College (Inner College) of the University of Connecticut
(Storrs, CT) (public) (1969)
(Coyne and Hebert 1972; Grant and Riesman 1978; Heiss 1973;
Lichtman 1972, 1973)
(free university) (subcollege)

Experimental College at Knox College (Galesburg, IL) (private)
(Draves 1980; Litkowski 1983) (free university)

Experimental College of Princeton University (Princeton, NJ) (private)
(Keyes 1967) (free university)

Experimental College of San Diego State College (now University) (San
Diego, CA) (public) (1967)
(Lichtman 1972, 1973) (free university)

Experimental College of San Fernando Valley State College (Northridge,
CA) (1967)
(Lichtman 1972) (free university)

Experimental College at San Francisco State College (now University) (San
Francisco, CA) (public) (1966–1969)
(Barlow and Shapiro 1971;* Bebout and Greening 1981; Draves 1980;
Fashing and Deutsch 1971; Grand and Bebout 1981;* Hefferlin 1969;
Heiss 1973; Keyes 1967; Lichtman 1973; Rogers 1983) (free university)

Experimental College of San Jose State College (now University) (San Jose,
CA) (public) (1965–1969)
(Cadwallader 1984;* Fashing and Deutsch 1971; Lichtman 1973;
McCann 1977) (subcollege)

Experimental College at the University of California, Davis (Davis, CA)
(public) (1966)
(Draves 1980; Levine 1978; Lichtman 1972, 1973; Litkowski 1983) (free
university)

Experimental College of the University of California, Irvine (Irvine, CA)
(public) (1970)
(Draves 1980; Lichtman 1972, 1973) (free university)

Experimental College of the University of Minnesota (MN) (public)
(Grant and Riesman 1978) (subcollege)

Experimental * College of the University of South Alabama (Mobile, AL)
(public) (1969)
(Lichtman 1972) (free university)

Experimental College of the University of Southern California (Los Angeles,
CA) (private) (1968)
(Lichtman 1972, 1973) (free university)

Experimental College of the University of Washington, Seattle (Seattle, WA) (public) (1968)
(Draves 1980) (free university)

Experimental University of the University of Virginia (Charlottesville, VA) (public) (1968)
(Lichtman 1972, 1973) (free university)

FACS (Free Apple Community School)
(Litkowski 1983) (free university)

Fairhaven College of Western Washington State College (now Western Washington University) (Bellingham, WA) (public) (1968–present)
(Cardozier 1993; Coyne and Hebert 1972; Fashing and Deutsch 1971; Gaff 1970; Harwood 1971;* Hefferlin 1969; Heiss 1973; Jones and Smith 1984; Litten 1971; MacDonald 1973a, 1973b;* MacDonald and Sewell 1973; Mayhew 1977) (subcollege)

Feminist Free University (San Diego, CA) (private)
(Draves 1980; Litkowski 1983) (free university)

Flint Freedom School (also called Learning Exchange) (Burton, MI)
(Draves 1980) (free university)

Franklin Pierce College (Rindge, NH) (private) (1962–present)
(Coyne and Hebert 1972; Elmendorf 1975)

Free College of Emory University (Atlanta, GA) (private) (1970)
(Lichtman 1972, 1973) (free university)

Free Community School of Detroit (Detroit, MI) (private) (1971)
(Lichtman 1972, 1973) (free university)

Free Community School (Port Jefferson, NY) (private) (1971)
(Lichtman 1972) (free university)

Free School of Clinton, Kirkland-Hamilton College (Clinton, NY) (1972)
(Draves 1980; Lichtman 1972) (free university)

Free School of New Haven, Yale University (New Haven, CT) (private) (1967)
(Lichtman 1972, 1973) (free university)

Free School of Southern Illinois University, Carbondale (Carbondale, IL) (public)
(Draves 1980) (free university)

Free University (Albuquerque, NM)
(Litkowski 1983) (free university)

Free University (Salina, KS)
(Draves 1980) (free university)

Free University (Syracuse, NY)
(Draves 1980) (free university)

Free University of Ann Arbor, the University of Michigan, Ann Arbor (Ann
   Arbor, MI) (public) (1971)
   (Draves 1980; Lichtman 1972, 1973) (free university)
Free University of Baylor University (Waco, TX) (private) (1971)
   (Draves 1980; Lichtman 1972) (free university)
Free University of Bethlehem Lutheran Church (Indianapolis, IN) (private)
   (1970)
   (Lichtman 1972) (free university)
Free University of Berkeley (Berkeley, CA) (public) (1964–1972)
   (Draves 1980; Levine 1978; Lichtman 1972, 1973) (free university)
Free University of Boston College (Chestnut Hill, MA) (private)
   (Draves 1980; Litkowski 1983) (free university)
Free University of The Catholic University (now the Catholic University of
   America) (Washington, DC) (private)
   (Draves 1980) (free university)
Free University of DeKalb (Illinois)
   (Keyes 1967) (free university)
Free University of Denton (Denton, TX)
   (Draves 1980) (free university)
Free University of Depauw University (Greencastle, IN) (private)
   (Keyes 1967) (free university)
Free University of Duke University (Durham, NC) (private) (1971)
   (Lichtman 1972, 1973) (free university)
Free University of Eastern Kentucky University (Richmond, KY) (public)
   (Draves 1980) (free university)
Free University of Edinboro State College (Edinboro University of Pennsyl-
   vania) (Edinboro, PA) (public) (1967)
   (Lichtman 1972, 1973) (free university)
Free University of the Fenway (Boston, MA) (1971)
   (Draves 1980; Lichtman 1972) (free university)
Free University of Georgia Institute of Technology (Atlanta, GA) (public)
   (1969)
   (Lichtman 1972, 1973) (free university)
Free University of Indiana Memorial Union (Bloomington, IN) (1969)
   (Lichtman 1972) (free university)
Free University of John Carroll University (Cleveland, OH) (private) (1970)
   (Draves 1980; Lichtman 1972, 1973) (free university)
Free University of Lewis and Clark College (Portland, OR) (private)
   (Draves 1980) (free university)

Free University of Louisiana State University (Louisiana State University is
now called Louisiana State University and Agricultural and Mechanical
College) (Baton Rouge, LA) (public)
(Lichtman 1972) (free university)

Free University of Mary Washington College (Fredericksburg, VA) (public)
(1970)
(Lichtman 1972) (free university)

Free University of Maryland, the University of Maryland (Beltsville, MD)
(Draves 1980; Litkowski 1983) (free university)

Free University of Michigan State University (East Lansing, MI) (public)
(Lichtman 1973) (free university)

Free University of Mississippi (State College, MS) (private) (1968)
(Lichtman 1972) (free university)

Free University of Montgomery Junior College (now called Montgomery
College, Takoma Park Campus) (Takoma Park, MD) (public) (1968)
(Lichtman 1972) (free university)

Free University of Muncie, Ball State University (Muncie, IN) (public)
(1969)
(Lichtman 1972, 1973) (free university)

Free University of Muskingum College (New Concord, OH) (private)
(Litkowski 1983) (free university)

Free University of Nashville, Vanderbilt University (Nashville, TN) (private)
(1969)
(Lichtman 1972, 1973) (free university)

Free University of Northern Michigan University (Marquette, MI) (public)
(Draves 1980; Litkowski 1983) (free university)

Free University of Ohio State University (public)
(Keyes 1967) (free university)

Free University of Pittsburgh State University (Pittsburgh, KS) (public)
(Draves 1980) (free university)

Free University of New Orleans (New Orleans, LA) (1970)
(Draves 1980; Lichtman 1972, 1973; Litkowski 1983) (free university)

Free University of New York (FUNY)
(Draves 1980) (free university)

Free University of Newark State College (Union, NJ) (1971)
(Lichtman 1972) (free university)

Free University of Oklahoma
(Lichtman 1973) (free university)

Free University of Pennsylvania State University (University Park, PA)
(public) (1970)
(Draves 1980; Lichtman 1972, 1973; Litkowski 1983) (free university)

Free University of Pennsylvania, University of Pennsylvania (Philadelphia, PA) (private) (1966)
(Keyes 1967; Lichtman 1972, 1973) (free university)
Free University of Rochester Institute of Technology (Rochester, NY) (private) (1970)
(Draves 1980; Lichtman 1972) (free university)
Free University of San Diego (Solana Beach, CA) (private) (1970)
(Lichtman 1972, 1973) (free university)
Free University of Seattle (Seattle, WA)
(Keyes 1967) (free university)
Free University of Seton Hall University (South Orange, NJ) (private) (1971)
(Draves 1980; Lichtman 1972, 1973) (free university)
Free University of Southern Methodist University (Dallas, TX) (private)
(Draves 1980; Lichtman 1972) (free university)
Free University of St. Joseph College (now University) (Philadelphia, PA) (private) (1969)
(Lichtman 1972) (free university)
Free University—Saint Louis (Saint Louis, MO)
(Draves 1980) (free university)
Free University of Student's College (Duluth, MN)
(Litkowski 1983) (free university)
Free University of Temple University (Philadelphia, PA) (public) (1968)
(Lichtman 1972) (free university)
Free University of Texas A&M University (College Station, TX) (public)
(Draves 1980) (free university)
Free University of Tucson (also called Tucson Free University), the University of Arizona (Tucson, AZ) (public) (1969)
(Draves 1980; Lichtman 1972; Litkowski 1983) (free university)
Free University of the United Ministry (Tulsa, OK) (private) (1969)
(Lichtman 1972) (free university)
Free University of the University of Alabama, Huntsville (Huntsville, AL) (public)
(Draves 1980; Litkowski 1983) (free university)
The Free University of the University of Arkansas (Fayetteville, AR) (public) (1969)
(Lichtman 1972) (free university)
Free University of the University of Kansas (Lawrence, KS) (public)
(Draves 1980; Lichtman 1972) (free university)

Free University of the University of Kentucky (Lexington, KY) (public)
(1969)
(Draves 1980; Lichtman 1972) (free university)

Free University of the University of Minnesota, Duluth (Duluth, MN)
(public)
(Draves 1980) (free university)

Free University of the University of North Carolina at Charlotte (Charlotte,
NC) (public)
(Litkowski 1983) (free university)

Free University of the University of South Carolina, Columbia (Columbia,
SC) (public)
(Draves 1980; Litkowski 1983) (free university)

Free University of University Station (Murray, KY)
(Draves 1980) (free university)

Free University of the University of Tennessee, Knoxville (Knoxville, TN)
(public) (1972)
(Draves 1980; Lichtman 1972) (free university)

Free University of the University of Texas, El Paso (El Paso, TX) (public)
(1970)
(Lichtman 1972) (free university)

Free University of the University of Wisconsin, LaCrosse (LaCrosse, WI)
(public)
(Draves 1980) (free university)

Free University of the University of Wisconsin, River Falls (River Falls, WI)
(public)
(Draves 1980) (free university)

Free University of Utah, University of Utah (Salt Lake City, UT) (public)
(1967)
(Lichtman 1972, 1973) (free university)

Free University of Wayne State University (Detroit, MI) (public) (1968)
(Lichtman 1972, 1973) (free university)

Free University of Wisconsin (Madison, WI) (private) (1966)
(Lichtman 1972, 1973) (free university)

Freedom University (Albuquerque, NM)
(Draves 1980) (free university)

Freespace Alternate U (New York, NY)
(Draves 1980) (free university)

Friends World College (Westbury, NY) (private) (1965–present); now
Friends World Program at Southampton College, Long Island Univer-

sity—Friends World affiliated with Long Island University in 1991 and moved to Southampton, NY.
(Coyne and Hebert 1972; Fashing and Deutsch 1971; Heiss 1973; Jerome 1970)

The General College at Michigan State University (East Lansing, MI) (public) (closed)
(Newell and Reynolds 1993) (subcollege)

Georgetown Free University, Georgetown University (Washington, DC) (private) (1967)
(Lichtman 1972; Litkowski 1983) (free university)

Grand Valley State University (formerly Grand Valley State College) (Allendale, MI) (public) (1960–present)
(Gamson 1979;* Grant and Riesman 1978; Mayhew 1965, 1977) (an amalgamation — has several subcolleges)

Gumbo University, the University of Southwestern Louisiana (Lafayette, LA) (public)
(Draves 1980; Litkowski 1983) (free university)

Hackensack Open University (Hackensack, MN)
(Draves 1980) (free university)

Hampshire College (Amherst, MA) (private) (1965–present)
(Alderman 1971;* Alpert 1980;* Astin et al. 1991;* Birney 1972,* 1993;* Bloch and Nylen 1974;* Calabro 1975;* Cardozier 1993; Coyne and Hebert 1972; Elmendorf 1975; Frazier 1977;* Gamson and Catlin 1984; Grant 1984; Grant and Riesman 1975, 1978; Hahn 1984; Hall 1991; Hefferlin 1969; Heiss 1973; Holmquist, Nisonoff, and Rakoff 1984;* Jones and Smith 1984; Levine 1978; Levine and Weingart 1973; Longsworth 1976, 1977;* Magner 1989; Marcus 1984; Mayhew 1977; McHenry 1977a, 1977b; Meister 1982; Patterson and Longsworth 1966;* Riesman, Gusfield, and Gamson 1970; Townsend, Newell, and Wiese 1992; Von Blum 1984; Wofford 1973; Wolfe 1970)

Health and Life University (Walla Walla, WA)
(Draves 1980) (free university)

Health and Society College of the State University of New York, College at Buffalo (Buffalo, NY) (public)
(Levine 1980*) (subcollege)

Heliotrope Free University (Palo Alto, CA) (1968)
(Lichtman 1972, 1973) (free university)

The Hillel School (Boston, MA)
(Draves 1980; Litkowski 1983) (free university)

Holy Cross College of St. Edwards University (Austin, TX) (private) (1967)
(Gaff 1970; Jones and Smith 1984) (subcollege)

Hutchins School of Liberal Studies (also called Hutchins College), Sonoma
State College (now University) (Rohnert Park, CA) (public) (1969–
present)
(Coyne and Hebert 1972; Gaff 1970; Heiss 1973; Jones and Smith 1984)
(subcollege)

Huxley College of Western Washington State College (now Western
Washington University) (Bellingham, WA) (public) (1969)
(Fashing and Deutsch 1971; Heiss 1973) (subcollege)

Immaculate Heart College (Los Angeles, CA) (private) (closed, 1980)
(Bebout and Greening 1981; Glass and Glass 1981; Grant and Riesman
1975, 1978; Rogers 1974,* 1983)

Indianapolis Free University (Indianapolis, IN)
(Draves 1980; Lichtman 1973; Litkowski 1983) (free university)

International College of the State University of New York, College at Buffalo
(Buffalo, NY) (public)
(Levine 1980*) (subcollege)

Invisible University (Chapel Hill, NC) (private) (1970)
(Lichtman 1972) (free university)

Iola Communiversity (Iola, KS)
(Draves 1980; Litkowski 1983) (free university)

James Madison College of Michigan State University (East Lansing, MI)
(public) (1967)
(Gaff 1970; Garfinkel 1971;* Grant and Riesman 1978; Hahn 1984; Heiss
1973; Jones and Smith 1984; Litten 1971; Sullivan 1973) (subcollege)

Johnston College (now Johnston Center) of the University of Redlands
(Redlands, CA) (private) (1969–present)
(Anderson 1981; Bebout and Greening 1981; Blume 1981;* Childs
1981;* Coyne and Hebert 1972; Dodson 1991; Elmendorf 1975; Gaff
1970; Grant 1984; Grant and Riesman 1975, 1978; Greening 1981a;*
Greening 1981b;* Hahn 1984; Hall 1991; Heiss 1973; Jones and Smith
1984; Litten 1971; McCoy 1971;* McDonald and O'Neill 1988;* Owada
1981;* Rogers 1983; Thompson 1981; Watt 1981;* Williams 1981*)
(subcollege)

The Judson Life School (Minnesota)
(Lichtman 1973) (free university)

Justin Morrill College of Michigan State University (East Lansing, MI)
(public) (1965)
(Coyne and Hebert 1972; Elmendorf 1975; Gaff 1970; Grant 1979; Grant
and Riesman 1978; Hefferlin 1969; Heiss 1973; Jones and Smith 1984;

Levine 1978; Levine and Weingart 1973; Litten 1971; Martin 1968;
Rohman 1971; Sullivan 1973; Wolfe 1970) (subcollege)

Kaw Valley Free University (Wamego, KS)
(Draves 1980; Litkowski 1983) (free university)

Kresge College of the University of California, Santa Cruz (Santa Cruz, CA)
(public) (1970–present)
(Bebout and Greening 1981; Grant 1984; Grant and Riesman 1975, 1978;
Hall 1991; Heiss 1973; Jones and Smith 1984; Kahn 1981a,* 1981b;*
Levine 1978; Levine and Weingart 1973; McHenry 1977a; Potter 1980;
Rogers 1983; Von der Muhll 1984; Wolgemuth 1993*) (subcollege)

Lavender U (San Francisco, CA)
(Draves 1980) (free university)

Law and Society College of the State University of New York, College at
Buffalo (Buffalo, NY) (public)
(Levine 1980*) (subcollege)

Leisure Learning (Mini School), Southern Connecticut State College (now
University) (New Haven, CT) (public)
(Litkowski 1983) (free university)

Leisure Learning School of the State University College of Arts and Sciences
(the State University College of Arts and Sciences is now called the State
University of New York, College at Geneseo) (Geneseo, NY) (public)
(Litkowski 1983) (free university)

Little House Free University (Overland Park, KS)
(Draves 1980) (free university)

Living College of Oregon Institute of Technology (Klamath Falls, OR)
(public)
(Litkowski 1983) (free university)

Livingston College of Rutgers University, the State University of New Jersey
(New Brunswick, NJ) (public) (1969)
(Coyne and Hebert 1972; Gaff 1970; Heiss 1973; Horowitz and
Feigenbaum 1980;* Jones and Smith 1984; Lynton 1972;* Wolfe 1970)
(subcollege)

Louisville Free University, University of Louisville (Louisville, KY) (public)
(Draves 1980; Litkowski 1983) (free university)

Ludlow 4H Free University (Ludlow, KY)
(Litkowski 1983) (free university)

Lyman Briggs College of Michigan State University (East Lansing, MI)
(public) (1967) (There is now a "Lyman Briggs School" at Michigan State
University.)

(Coyne and Hebert 1972; Gaff 1970; Grant and Riesman 1978; Hahn 1984; Jones and Smith 1984; Sullivan 1973) (subcollege)

Maharishi International University (now the Maharishi University of Management) (Fairfield, IA) (private) (1971–present)
(Brown 1977;* Jones and Smith 1984; Levine 1978; Moss 1980;* Newell and Reynolds 1993; Rowe 1981;* Townsend, Newell, and Wiese 1992)

Mark Hopkins College (Brattleboro, VT) (private) (1964)
(Coyne and Hebert 1972)

Marquette Free University, Marquette University (Milwaukee, WI) (private) (1971)
(Lichtman 1972) (free university)

Maryhill College of St. Edwards University (Austin, TX) (private) (1967)
(Gaff 1970; Jones and Smith 1984) (subcollege)

Maryland Free University, the University of Maryland, College Park (College Park, MD) (public) (1971)
(Lichtman 1972) (free university)

Marysville Free University (Marysville, KS)
(Draves 1980; Litkowski 1983) (free university)

Merrill College of the University of California, Santa Cruz (Santa Cruz, CA) (public) (1968–present)
(Gaff 1970; Grant and Riesman 1978; Heiss 1973; Levine 1978; McHenry 1977a; Ring 1971a; Von der Muhll 1984) (subcollege)

Michigan State Perversity, Michigan State University (East Lansing, MI) (public) (1966)
(Lichtman 1972) (free university)

Midpeninsula Free University (formerly Free University of Palo Alto) (Palo Alto, CA) (1966–1970)
(Draves 1980; Fashing and Deutsch 1971; Lichtman 1973) (free university)

Mini-U (Chicago, IL)
(Draves 1980) (free university)

Miniversity, Roger Williams College (Worcester, MA) (1970)
(Lichtman 1972) (free university)

Minnesota Free University (Minneapolis, MN) (private) (1967)
(Lichtman 1972, 1973) (free university)

Modern College of the State University of New York, College at Buffalo (Buffalo, NY) (public)
(Levine 1980*) (subcollege)

Mount Sunflower University for Higher Education (Wallace, KS)
(Litkowski 1983) (free university)

Muir College of the University of California, San Diego (La Jolla, CA)
(public) (1967–present)
(Gaff 1970; Heiss 1973; Jones and Smith 1984) (subcollege)

Multiversity (Laramie, WY)
(Draves 1980) (free university)

The Naropa Institute (Boulder, CO) (private) (1974–present)
(Halterman 1983)

Nebraska Free University, the University of Nebraska, Lincoln (Lincoln, NE)
(public)
(Lichtman 1972) (free university)

Neosho River Free School (Emporia, KS)
(Draves 1980; Litkowski 1983) (free university)

New College of California (San Francisco, CA) (private) (1971–present)
(Halterman 1983; Mayhew 1977)

New College of Drake University (Des Moines, IA) (private)
(Draves 1980) (free university)

New College at Hofstra University (Hempstead, NY) (private) (1965)
(Chickering 1984; Coyne and Hebert 1972; Boyer 1984; Elmendorf 1975;
Gaff 1970; Grant and Riesman 1978; Jones and Smith 1984; Levine and
Weingart 1973; Mayhew 1965, 1977; Newell and Reynolds 1993)
(subcollege)

New College of Nasson College (Springvale, ME)
(Heiss 1973) (subcollege)

New College of Oakland University (Rochester, MI) (public) (1967)
(Coyne and Hebert 1972; Gaff 1970; Riesman, Gusfield, and Gamson
1970) (subcollege)

New College of San Jose State University (San Jose, CA) (public)
(Heiss 1973; Jones and Smith 1984) (subcollege)

New College of the University of Alabama (Tuscaloosa, AL) (public) (1970–
present)
(Berte 1972;* Cardozier 1993; Coyne and Hebert 1972; Elmendorf 1975;
Grant and Riesman 1978; Heiss 1973; Jones and Smith 1984; Levine
1978, 1980b) (subcollege)

New College of the University of Hawaii (Honolulu, HI) (public) (1970)
(Coyne and Hebert 1972; Heiss 1973) (subcollege)

New College of the University of South Florida (Sarasota, FL) (public)
(1960–present)
(Alpert 1980; Bergquist 1995; Cardozier 1993; Chickering 1984; Coyne
and Hebert 1972; Elmendorf 1971,* 1975;* Gaff 1994; Grant and
Riesman 1975, 1978;* Gustad 1964;* Heiss 1973; Johnson 1964; Jones

and Smith 1984; Levine 1978; Levine and Weingart 1973; Litten 1971; Longsworth 1976; W.B. Martin 1982; Mayhew 1965, 1977; McHenry 1977a; Riesman 1975;* Riesman, Gusfield, and Gamson 1970; Scheuerle 1979;* Sullivan 1973; Wolfe 1970)

New Lane University (Lecompton, KS)
(Draves 1980) (free university)

New School (San Francisco, CA)
(Draves 1980) (free university)

New University (Washington, DC) (private) (1970)
(Lichtman 1972) (free university)

The New University of Santa Fe (Santa Fe, NM) (private) (1972)
(Lichtman 1972) (free university)

Northwest Free University of Western Washington State College (now Western Washington University) (Bellingham, WA) (public) (1968)
(Draves 1980; Fashing and Deutsch 1971) (free university) (subcollege)

Oakes College of the University of California, Santa Cruz (Santa Cruz, CA) (public) (1971–present)
(Grant and Riesman 1978; Levine 1978; McHenry 1977a; Von der Muhll 1984) (subcollege)

Oberlin Experimental College (Oberlin, OH)
(Litkowski 1983) (free university)

Off-Campus College of the State University of New York, Binghamton (Binghamton, NY) (public) (1970)
(Coyne and Hebert 1972) (subcollege)

Ohio Wesleyan Free University, Ohio Wesleyan University (Delaware, OH) (private) (1965)
(Lichtman 1972) (free university)

Open University (also called Open University of Washington DC) (Washington, DC) (1975)
(Draves 1980; Litkowski 1983) (free university)

Open University of the University of Arkansas, Little Rock (Little Rock, AR) (public)
(Draves 1980; Litkowski 1983) (free university)

Oshkosh Free University, the University of Wisconsin, Oshkosh (Oshkosh, WI) (public) (1970)
(Lichtman 1972) (free university)

The Paracollege at St. Olaf College (Northfield, MN) (private) (1969–present)
(Cardozier 1993; Coyne and Hebert 1972; Jones and Smith 1984; Newell 1984) (subcollege)

Pawnee Rock Free University (Pawnee Rock, KS)
(Draves 1980; Litkowski 1983) (free university)

Peoples' School '71 (Missouri)
(Lichtman 1973) (free university)

Pitzer College (Claremont, CA) (private) (1963–present)
(Elmendorf 1975; Glass and Glass 1981)

Post Rock University (Beloit, KS)
(Litkowski 1983) (free university)

Pre-University of the University of Wisconsin, Milwaukee (Milwaukee, WI)
(public)
(Keyes 1967) (free university)

Prescott College (Prescott, AZ) (private) (1966–present)
(Adams 1993;* Anzulovic 1976;* Coyne and Hebert 1972; Elmendorf
1975; Hahn 1984; Heiss 1973; Levine 1978; Levine and Weingart 1973;
Newell 1993)

Providence Free University (Providence, RI)
(Draves 1980) (free university)

Purchase College, State University of New York (formerly State University of
New York, College at Purchase) (Purchase, NY) (public) (1967–present)
(Coyne and Hebert 1972; Grant and Riesman 1978; Heiss 1973; Riesman,
Gusfield, and Gamson 1970)

Rachel Carson College of the State University of New York, College at
Buffalo (Buffalo, NY) (public)
(Levine 1980*) (subcollege)

Ramapo College of New Jersey (Mahwah, NJ) (public) (1969–present)
(Alpert 1980; Bergquist 1995; Cardozier 1993; Coyne and Hebert 1972;
Grant and Riesman 1978; Hahn 1984; Hall 1991; Jones and Smith 1984;
Potter 1980)

Raymond College of the University of the Pacific (Stockton, CA) (private)
(1962)
(Coyne and Hebert 1972; Gaff 1967,* 1969,* 1970a, 1994; Heiss 1973;
Jones and Smith 1984; Kolker 1972;* Levine 1978; Longsworth 1976;
Martin 1968; Mayhew 1965, 1977; McHenry 1977a; Meyer 1964;
Riesman, Gusfield, and Gamson 1970; Sullivan 1973) (subcollege)

The Residential College at the University of Michigan (Ann Arbor, MI)
(public) (1967)
(Cardozier 1993; Gaff 1970; Gamson, Boyk, and Gipson 1977;* Grant
and Riesman 1978; Hefferlin 1969; Jones and Smith 1984; Levine and
Weingart 1973; Litten 1971; Newcomb et al. 1971;* Riesman, Gusfield,
and Gamson 1970) (subcollege)

The Richard Stockton State College of New Jersey (formerly Stockton State
    College) (Pomona, NJ) (public) (1969–present)
    (Cardozier 1993; Coyne and Hebert 1972; Grant and Riesman 1978;
    Hahn 1984; Hodgkinson 1974; Jones and Smith 1984; Schuster 1989b*)
Royalton College (South Royalton, VT) (private) (1966)
    (Coyne and Hebert 1972)
San Jose Free University (San Jose, CA) (private) (1968)
    (Lichtman 1972, 1973) (free university)
Sherwood Oaks Experimental College (California)
    (Lichtman 1973) (free university)
Sierra Nevada College (Incline Village, NV) (private) (1969)
    (Coyne and Hebert 1972)
Simon's Rock College of Bard (Great Barrington, MA) (private) (1964–
    present)
    (Cardozier 1993; Coyne and Hebert 1972; Grant and Riesman 1978;
    Heiss 1973; Levine 1978; Longsworth 1976)
Smith Experimental College, Smith College (Northampton, MA) (private)
    (1971)
    (Lichtman 1972, 1973) (free university)
Social Science College of the State University of New York, College at
    Buffalo (Buffalo, NY) (public)
    (Levine 1980*) (subcollege)
Sociotechnical Systems College of the State University of New York, College
    at Buffalo (Buffalo, NY) (public)
    (Levine 1980*) (subcollege)
Southeast Denver Free University (Denver, CO)
    (Draves 1980; Litkowski 1983) (free university)
Southwest Minnesota State College (public) (1967) (Marshall, MN) (public)
    (1963)
    (Grubb 1984;* Jones and Smith 1984)
Southwest State University (Marshall, MN) (public) (1963–present)
    (Bergquist 1995)
State University of New York, College at Old Westbury (Old Westbury, NY)
    (public) (1965–present)
    (Bergquist 1995; Cadwallader 1984; Cardozier 1993; Chickering 1984;
    Coyne and Hebert 1972; Dunn 1973;* Elmendorf 1975; Gehret 1972;
    Grant and Riesman 1975, 1978; Greening 1981b; Hall 1991; Hall and
    Kevles 1982; Heiss 1973; Jerome 1970; Jones and Smith 1984; Lichtman
    1973; MacDonald 1973a; MacDonald and Sewell 1973; Maguire 1971,*

1972,* 1982;* Mayhew 1977; McCann 1977; Riesman, Gusfield, and Gamson 1970; Wofford 1970,* 1973;* Wolfe 1970)

Stevenson College of the University of California, Santa Cruz (Santa Cruz, CA) (public) (1966–present)
(Adams 1984; Gaff 1970; Grant and Riesman 1978; Levine 1978; Levine and Weingart 1973; McHenry 1977a; Ring 1971a; Von der Muhll 1984) (subcollege)

Strawberry College of the University of California, Berkeley (also called Strawberry Creek College) (Berkeley, CA) (public)
(Hahn 1984; Jones and Smith 1984; McHenry 1977b) (subcollege)

Student Center College (Mendocino, CA) (private)
(Coyne and Hebert 1972)

Sundry School of the University of Houston (Houston, TX) (public)
(Draves 1980; Litkowski 1983) (free university)

The Third College of the University of California, San Diego (La Jolla, CA) (public)
(Heiss 1973) (subcollege)

Thomas Jefferson College of Grand Valley State College (now University) (Allendale, MI) (public) (1968)
(Coyne and Hebert 1972; Gaff 1970; Gamson 1979; Grant and Riesman 1978; Hahn 1984; Heiss 1973; Jones and Smith 1984) (subcollege)

Tolstoy College (formerly College F) of the State University of New York, College at Buffalo (Buffalo, NY) (public)
(Levine 1980*) (subcollege)

Tufts Experimental College (Medford, MA) (private) (1964)
(Anzulovic 1976; Coyne and Hebert 1972; Levine 1978; Levine and Weingart 1973) (subcollege)

UCLA Experimental College, University of California, Los Angeles (Los Angeles, CA) (public) (1966)
(Draves 1980; Fashing and Deutsch 1971; Lichtman 1972, 1973) (free university)

Universidad de los Barrios (San Antonio, TX)
(Lichtman 1972) (free university)

University of California, Irvine (Irvine, CA) (public) (1965–present)
(Grant and Riesman 1978)

University of California, Santa Cruz (Santa Cruz, CA) (public) (1962–present)
(Adams 1984;* Alpert 1980; Bergquist 1995; Cardozier 1993; Carter 1971;* Coyne and Hebert 1972; Dodson 1991; Elmendorf 1975; Euben 1984; Fashing and Deutsch 1971; Gaff 1994; Grant 1984; Grant and

Riesman 1978; Hall 1991; Hall and Kevles 1982; Heiss 1973; Johnson
1964; Jones and Smith 1984; Kahn 1981a; Levine 1978, 1980b; Levine
and Weingart 1973; Litten 1971; Longsworth 1976; Magner 1989;
Maguire 1971; Martin 1968; Mayhew 1965, 1977; McCoy 1971;
McHenry 1964,* 1977a,* 1977b, 1993;* Newell and Reynolds 1993;
"Rethinking the Dream" 1980;* Ring 1971a,* 1971b*, 1972a,* 1972b;*
Solomon's House 1970; Townsend, Newell, and Wiese 1992; Von der
Muhll 1984;* Wolfe 1970)

University for Man, Kansas State University (Manhattan, KS) (public)
(1968)
(Draves 1980; Lichtman 1972, 1973; Litkowski 1983) (free university)

University for Man, Monterey Peninsula College (Monterey, CA) (public)
(1969)
(Draves 1980; Lichtman 1972, 1973; Litkowski 1983) (free university)

University of Man, Lamar University (Beaumont, TX) (public)
(Litkowski 1983) (free university)

University for Many, Vanderbilt University (Nashville, TN) (private)
(Draves 1980; Lichtman 1973; Litkowski 1983) (free university)

University of Northern Colorado Open University (Greeley, CO) (public)
(Draves 1980; Litkowski 1983) (free university)

University of Thought, the University of Houston (Houston, TX) (public)
(1969)
(Lichtman 1972, 1973) (free university)

University II of Villanova University (Villanova, PA) (private)
(Litkowski 1983) (free university)

University of Wisconsin-Green Bay (Green Bay, WI) (public) (1965–
present)
(Bergquist 1995; Cardozier 1993; Coyne and Hebert 1972; Elmendorf
1975; Grant 1984; Grant and Riesman 1978; Hahn 1984; Heiss 1973;
Jones and Smith 1984; Kolka 1972;* Levine and Weingart 1973;
Longsworth 1976; Maier 1972;* Marcus 1984; Mayhew 1977; McHenry
1977a, 1977b; Weidner 1977;* Weidner and Kuepper 1993*)

Urban Studies College at the State University of New York, College at Old
Westbury (Old Westbury, NY) (public) (1969)
(Gaff 1970) (subcollege)

Vico College of the State University of New York, College at Buffalo (Buf
falo, NY) (public)
(Levine 1980*) (subcollege)

Villanova Free University of Villanova University (Villanova, PA) (private)

(Draves 1980; Lichtman 1973) (free university)

Washington Area Free University (Washington, DC) (private) (1969)
(Draves 1980; Lichtman 1972, 1973) (free university)

Washington International College (Washington, DC) (private) (1971)
(Coyne and Hebert 1972)

Waterfield Free School (Marblehead, MA) (private) (1971)
(Lichtman 1972, 1973) (free university)

Wichita Free University, Wichita State University (Wichita, KS) (public)
(1968)
(Draves 1980; Litkowski 1983) (free university)

William James College of Grand Valley State College (now University)
(Allendale, MI) (public) (1971)
(Coyne and Hebert 1972; Gamson 1979; Grant and Riesman 1978; Jones
and Smith 1984; Perkins 1984) (subcollege)

Wingspan Free University (Paonia, CO)
(Draves 1980) (free university)

Women's Studies College of the State University of New York, College at
Buffalo (Buffalo, NY) (public)
(Levine 1980*) (subcollege)

World Campus Afloat, Chapman College (now University) (Orange, CA)
(private) (1965) [a floating university]
(Coyne and Hebert 1972) (subcollege)

Wyoming Free University (Casper, WY)
(Draves 1980) (free university)

YMCA Free University (Blacksburg, VA)
(Draves 1980) (free university)

NOTE

1. "Subcolleges" are innovative or experimental colleges that are affiliated with a larger
   institution. "Free universities" are community-centered or student-run alternative
   campuses that grew out of the free speech movement and that have been identified in
   the guidebooks and literature on free universities. (A free university may or may not be
   a subcollege of a larger institution.)

REFERENCES

Adams, E.A. 1993. Prescott: From parson to parsimony. In *Maverick colleges: Ten notable experiments in American undergraduate education*, edited by L.J. Newell and K.C. Reynolds 89–103. Salt Lake City: Utah Education Policy Center, Graduate School of Education, The University of Utah.

Adams, W. 1984. Getting real: Santa Cruz and the crisis of liberal education. *Change* (May-June):19–27.

Alderman, J.D. 1971. Financial approach at Hampshire is innovative, too. *College Management* 24–26.

Alpert, R.M. 1980. Professionalism and educational reform: The case of Hampshire College. *Journal of Higher Education* 51 (5): 497–518.

Anderson, W. 1981. Comment. *Journal of Humanistic Psychology* 21 (2); 141–42.

Anzulovic, B. 1976. The rise and fall of Prescott College. *The University Bookman*, XVI (3): 51–57.

Aranow, B. 1983. *Such a frail bark: An oral history of College of the Atlantic's early years*. Bar Harbor, Maine: College of the Atlantic.

Astin, H.S., J.F. Milem, A.W. Astin, P. Ries, and T. Heath. 1991. *The courage and vision to experiment: Hampshire College, 1970–1990*. Los Angeles: Higher Education Research Institute, Graduate School of Education, University of California, Los Angeles.

Barlow, W., and P. Shapiro. 1971. *An end to silence: The San Francisco State College student movement in the '60s*. New York: Pegasus.

Bebout, J., and T. Greening. 1981. Commentary by the editors. *Journal of Humanistic Psychology* 21 (2): 1.

Berger, I.M. 1984. The death of a college: A faculty reminiscence of Eisenhower College. *Liberal Education* 70 (4): 401–8.

Bergquist, W.H. 1995. *Quality through access, access with quality: The new imperative for higher education*. San Francisco: Jossey-Bass.

Berte, N.R. 1972. New College. In *Innovations in undergraduate education: Selected institutional profiles and thoughts about experimentalism*, edited by N.R. Berte, 12–33. Tuscaloosa: The University of Alabama.

Birney, R. 1972. Hampshire College. In *Innovations in undergraduate education: Selected institutional profiles and thoughts about experimentalism*, edited by N.R. Berte, 41–44. Tuscaloosa: The University of Alabama.

Birney, R.C. 1993. Hampshire College. In *Important lessons from innovative colleges and universities*, edited by V.R. Cardozier,9–22. *New Directions for Higher Education* 82 (summer).

Bloch, P., and N. Nylen. 1974. Hampshire College: New intents and old realities. *Change* (October): 38–42.

Blume, F. 1981. The role of personal growth groups at Johnston College. *Journal of Humanistic Psychology* 21 (2): 47–61.

Boyer, E. 1984. Introduction. In *Against the current: Reform and experimentation in higher education*, edited by R.M. Jones and B.L. Smith, xiii–xxi. Cambridge, Mass.: Schenkman.

Brown, M. 1977. Higher education for higher consciousness: A study of students at Maharishi International University. *Dissertation Abstracts International* 38 (02): 649. (University Microfilms No. AAC 77-15619)

Cadwallader, M.L. 1984. Experiment at San Jose. In *Against the current: Reform and experiment in higher education*, edited by R.M. Jones and B.L. Smith, 343–66. Cambridge, Mass.: Schenkman.

Calabretta, R. 1973. Beyond the old and the new. In *Five experimental colleges: Bensalem, Antioch-Putney, Franconia, Old Westbury, Fairhaven*, edited by G.B. MacDonald, 38–48. New York: Harper and Row.

Calabro, H. 1975. Curricular relevance for today's youth. *Improving College teaching and learning* 23 (1): 49–50.

Cardozier, V.R. 1993. Editor's notes. In *Important lessons from innovative colleges and universities*, edited by V.R. Cardozier, 1–7. *New Directions for Higher Education* 82: (summer).

Carter, L.J. 1971. U. of California at Santa Cruz: New deal for undergraduates? *Science* 171 (15 January): 153–57.

Chance, W. 1980. *Institutional reviews by state-level agencies: The Evergreen study*. Paper presented at the Annual Advanced Leadership Seminar for State Academic Officers Association, San Antonio, Tex., July. (ERIC Document Reproduction Service No. ED 202 313)

Chance, W., and D.J. Curry. 1979. *The Evergreen study: Report and recommendations on The Evergreen State College: A report in response to Substitute Senate Bill 3109* (Report No. 79-7). Olympia, Wash.: Washington State Council for Postsecondary Education. (ERIC Document Reproduction Service No. ED 168 412)

Chickering, A.W. 1984. Alternatives for the 80's: The Goddard-Pitkin legacy. In *Against the current: Reform and experiment in higher education*, edited by R.M. Jones and B.L. Smith, 303–19. Cambridge, Mass.: Schenkman.

Childs, B. 1981. The obligatory inspirational commencement address (Johnston College graduation, May 1980). *Journal of Humanistic Psychology* 21 (2): 143–46.

Coyne, J. 1972. Bensalem: When the dream died. *Change* (October): 39–44.

Coyne, J., and T. Hebert. 1972. *This way out: A guide to alternatives to traditional college education in the United States, Europe and the Third World*. New York: E.P. Dutton.

Dodson, D. 1991. Evergreen: Prototype or dinosaur? In *The role and contribution of student affairs in involving colleges*, edited by G.D. Kuh and J.H. Schuh, 199–206. Washington, D.C.: The National Association of Student Personnel Administrators.

Draves, B. 1980. *The free university: A model for lifelong learning*. Chicago: AssociationPress.

Dresser, D.L. 1995. *Eisenhower College: The life and death of a living memorial.* Interlaken, N.Y.: Heart of the Lakes Publishing.

Dunn, J.A., Jr. 1973. Old Westbury I and Old Westbury II. In *Academic transformation: Seventeen institutions under pressure,* edited by D. Riesman and V.A. Stadtman, 199–224. New York: McGraw-Hill.

Elmendorf, J. 1971. New College: Sarasota, Florida. In *The new colleges: Toward an appraisal,* edited by P.L. Dressel, 177–83. Iowa City: The American College Testing Program and the American Association for Higher Education.

———. 1975. *Transmitting information about experiments in higher education: New College as a case study.* New York: Academy for Educational Development.

Euben, J.P. 1984. Disciplinary professionalism — response: To Weaver and Hahn. In *Against the current: Reform and experiment in higher education,* edited by R.M. Jones and B.L. Smith, 35–40. Cambridge, Mass.: Schenkman.

Fashing, J., and S.E. Deutsch. 1971. *Academics in retreat: The politics of educational innovation.* Albuquerque: University of New Mexico Press.

Fleming, J.S. 1986. The Eisenhower College silver dollar legislation: A case of politics and higher education. *Journal of Higher Education* 57, no. 6 (November-December): 569–605.

Frazier, N. 1977. Freedom and identity at Hampshire College. *Change* (November): 14–17.

Freeman, K.D. 1972. Bensalem: An analysis. In *Innovations in undergraduate education: Selected institutional profiles and thoughts about experimentalism,* edited by N.R. Berte, 80–96. Tuscaloosa: The University of Alabama.

———. 1973. Realities: Bensalem: An Analysis. In *Five experimental colleges: Bensalem, Antioch-Putney, Franconia, Old Westbury, Fairhaven,* edited by G.B. MacDonald, 13–37. New York: Harper and Row.

Gaff, J.G. 1967. *Innovations and consequences: A study of Raymond College, University of the Pacific.* (Research Project No. 6-1257) Berkeley: Department of Health, Education, and Welfare, U.S. Office of Education.

———. 1969. Innovation and evaluation: A case study. *Educational Record* 50 (3): 290–99.

———. 1970. The cluster college concept. In *The cluster college,* J.G. Gaff and Associates, 3–32. San Francisco: Jossey-Bass.

———. 1994. *The Meiklejohn Experimental College at Wisconsin, 1927–32: Relevance to the current reform movements in liberal education.* The Alexander Meiklejohn Lecture for 1994, University of Wisconsin, Madison, Wis., April.

Gamson, Z.F. 1979. Assuring survival by transforming a troubled program: Grand Valley State Colleges. In *On competence: A critical analysis of competence-based reforms in higher education,* edited by G. Grant, P. Elbow, T. Ewens, Z. Gamson, W. Kohli, W. Neumann, V. Olesen, and D. Riesman, 410–38. San Francisco: Jossey-Bass.

Gamson, Z.F., and J.B. Catlin. 1984. Preparing students to use what they learn. In *Liberating education*, Z.F. Gamson and Associates, 51–65. San Francisco: Jossey-Bass.

Gamson, Z.F., B. Boyk, and G. Gipson. 1977. Experimental college grads: Getting theirs. *Change* (September): 48–49.

Garfinkel, H. 1971. James Madison College: Michigan State University. In *The new colleges: Toward an appraisal*, edited by P.L. Dressel, 229–55. Iowa City: The American College Testing Program and the American Association for Higher Education.

Gehret, K.G. 1972. Reports: Washington's Evergreen College. *Change* (May): 17–19.

Glass, J., and J. Glass. 1981. Humanistic education: A tale of two professors. *Journal of Humanistic Psychology* 21 (2): 71–77.

Grand, I.J., and J. Bebout. 1981. Passionate discourse: The experimental college at San Francisco State. *Journal of Humanistic Psychology* 21 (2): 79–95.

Grant, G. 1979. New methods for the study of a reform movement. In *On competence: A critical analysis of competence-based reforms in higher education*, edited by G. Grant, P. Elbow, T. Ewens, Z. Gamson, W. Kohli, W. Neumann, V. Olesen, and D. Riesman, 439–90. San Francisco: Jossey-Bass.

——. 1984. Whither the progressive college? *Liberal Education* 70 (4): 315–21.

Grant, G., and D. Riesman. 1975. An ecology of academic reform. *Daedalus, Journal of the American Academy of Arts and Sciences* 2 (winter): 166–91.

——. 1978. *The perpetual dream: Reform and experiment in the American college*. Chicago: The University of Chicago Press.

Greening, T. 1981a. The first days of Johnston College. *Journal of Humanistic Psychology* 21 (2): 3–15.

——. 1981b. Power, decision making, and coercion in experimental colleges. *Journal of Humanistic Psychology* 21 (2): 97–109.

Grubb, C. 1984. Innovative politics in defense of innovative education: A case study of a faculty's struggle for survival. In *Against the current: Reform and experiment in higher education*, edited by R.M. Jones and B.L. Smith, 153–81. Cambridge, Mass.: Schenkman.

Gustad, J.W. 1964. New College: D minus five months. In *Experimental colleges: Their role in higher education*, edited by W.H. Stickler, 49–56. Tallahassee: Florida State University.

Hahn, J. 1984. Disciplinary professionalism: Second view. In *Against the current: Reform and experiment in higher education*, edited by R.M. Jones and B.L. Smith, 19–33. Cambridge, Mass.: Schenkman.

Hall, J.W. 1991. *Access through innovation: New colleges for new students*. New York: The National University Continuing Education Association, American Council on Education, and MacMillan.

Hall, J.W., and B.L. Kevles. 1982. A model college education: From an atraditional viewpoint. In *In opposition to core curriculum: Alternative models for undergraduate education*, edited by J.W. Hall and B.L. Kevles, 197–220. Westport, Conn.: Greenwood.

Hall, M. 1994. A distaste for walls. *Harvard Magazine* (November-December): 52–57.

Halterman, W.J. 1983. *The complete guide to nontraditional education*. New York: Facts on File.

Harwood, C. 1971. Fairhaven College. In *The new colleges: Toward an appraisal*, edited by P.L. Dressel, 89–98. Iowa City: The American College Testing Program and the American Association for Higher Education.

Hefferlin, JB L. 1969. *Dynamics of academic reform*. San Francisco: Jossey-Bass.

Heiss, A. 1973. *An inventory of academic innovation and reform*. Berkeley: The Carnegie Commission on Higher Education.

Hodgkinson, H.L. 1974. *The campus senate: Experiment in democracy*. Berkeley: Center for Research and Development in Higher Education, University of California Press.

Holmquist, F.W., L. Nisonoff, and R.M. Rakoff. 1984. The labor process at Hampshire College. In *Against the current: Reform and experiment in higher education*, edited by R.M. Jones and B.L. Smith, 183–214. Cambridge, Mass.: Schenkman.

Horowitz, I.L., and J. Feigenbaum. 1980. Experiment perilous: The first year of Livingston College of Rutgers University. *Urban Education* 15 (2): 131–68.

Jerome, J. 1970. Friends World College, Bensalem, the College of the Potomac: Portrait of three experiments. *Change* (July-August): 40–54.

Johnson, B.L. 1964. Behold, you have created a new thing: Summary and critique. In *Experimental colleges: Their role in higher education*, edited by W.H. Stickler, 173–85. Tallahassee: Florida State University.

Jones, R.M. 1981. *Experiment at Evergreen*. Rochester, Vt.: Schenkman.

———. 1984. Response to Youtz. In *Against the current: Reform and experiment in higher education*, edited by R.M. Jones and B.L. Smith, 119–25. Cambridge, Mass.: Schenkman.

Jones, R.M., and B.L. Smith, eds. 1984. *Against the current: Reform and experiment in higher education*. Cambridge, Mass.: Schenkman.

Kahn, M. 1981a. The Kresge experiment. *Journal of Humanistic Psychology* 21 (2): 63–69.

———. 1981b. The seminar: An experiment in humanistic education. *Journal of Humanistic Psychology* 21 (2): 119–27.

Keyes, R. 1967. The free universities. *The Nation* (2 October): 294–99.

Kolka, J.W. 1972. *Una experiencia de universidad interdisciplinaria*. Paper presented at the Seminario de Interdisciplinaridad de la Eseñanza e Investigación, Vigo, Spain, July.

Kolker, B.L. 1972. The transformation of Raymond College. Redesigning the halls of ivy: Innovations in higher education. *Compact* 6, no. 5 (October): 6–8.

Kuh, G.D., J.H. Schuh, E.J. Whitt, R.E. Andreas, J.W. Lyons, C.C. Strange, L.E. Krehbiel, and K.A. MacKay. 1991. *Involving colleges: Successful approaches to fostering student learning and development outside the classroom.* San Francisco: Jossey-Bass.

Levine, A. 1978. *Handbook on undergraduate curriculum.* San Francisco: Jossey-Bass.

——. 1980. *Why innovation fails.* Albany: State University of New York Press.

Levine, A., and J. Weingart. 1973. *Reform of undergraduate education.* San Francisco: Jossey-Bass.

Lichtman, J. 1972. *Free university directory.* Washington, D.C.: American Association for Higher Education.

——. 1973. *Bring your own bag: A report on free universities.* Washington, D.C.: American Association for Higher Education.

Litkowski, T. 1983. Free universities and learning referral centers 1981. Washington, D.C.: National Center for Education Statistics.

Litten, L.H. 1971. We know that you're out there, but what are you doing? In *The new colleges: Toward an appraisal*, edited by P.L. Dressel, 257–83. Iowa City: The American College Testing Program and the American Association for Higher Education.

Longsworth, C.R. 1976. Experimental colleges: Agents of change. *Today's Education, NEA Journal* (January-February): 73–76.

——. 1977. Academic organization by schools at Hampshire College. In *Academic departments: Problems, variations, and alternatives*, D.E. McHenry and Associates, 117–46. San Francisco: Jossey-Bass.

Lynton, E. 1972. Livingston College, Rutgers University. In *Innovations in undergraduate education: Selected institutional profiles and thoughts about experimentalism*, edited by N.R. Berte, 38–40. Tuscaloosa: The University of Alabama.

Lyons, J.W. 1991. An eclipse of the usual: The Evergreen State College. In *The role and contribution of student affairs in involving colleges*, edited by G.D. Kuh and J.H. Schuh, 173–98. Washington, D.C.: The National Association of Student Personnel Administrators.

MacDonald, G.B. 1973a. Meditation. In *Five experimental colleges: Bensalem, Antioch-Putney, Franconia, Old Westbury, Fairhaven*, edited by G.B. MacDonald, 229–32). New York: Harper and Row.

——. 1973b. Realities: Growth by fire. In *Five experimental colleges: Bensalem, Antioch-Putney, Franconia, Old Westbury, Fairhaven*, edited by G.B. MacDonald, 196–227. New York: Harper and Row.

MacDonald, G.B., and E. Sewell. 1973. Introduction. In *Five experimental colleges: Bensalem, Antioch-Putney, Franconia, Old Westbury, Fairhaven*, edited by G.B. MacDonald, ix–xii. New York: Harper and Row.

Magner, D.K. 1989. Innovative colleges find their unorthodox ways can bring headaches. *The Chronicle of Higher Education* (31 May): A9, A12.

Maguire, J. 1972. State University of New York, College at Old Westbury. In *Innovations in undergraduate education: Selected institutional profiles and thoughts about experimentalism*, edited by N.R. Berte, 73–79. Tuscaloosa: The University of Alabama.

Maguire, J.D. 1971. Less than a year into a presidency: Or, what's a sober guy like me doing in a place like this. *Soundings* 44 (4): 12–22.

———. 1982. The disadvantaged student and the undergraduate curriculum. In *In opposition to core curriculum: Alternative models for undergraduate education*, edited by J.W. Hall and B.L. Kevles, 147–56. Westport, Conn.: Greenwood.

Maier, R.H. 1972. Ecology U. is alive and healthy. In *Innovations in undergraduate education: Selected institutional profiles and thoughts about experimentalism*, edited by N.R. Berte, 1–11. Tuscaloosa: The University of Alabama.

Marcus, R. 1984. The Rollins College conferences on progressive education, 1931 and 1983: Introduction. *Liberal Education* 70 (4): 293–95.

Martin, G.E. 1982. Encounter with education: Impact of an alternative college on student development. *Dissertation Abstracts International* 43-10A: 3234. (University Microfilms No. AAG83-04032)

Martin, W.B. 1968. *Alternative to irrelevance: A strategy for reform in higher education*. New York: Abingdon.

———. 1982. The legacy of the sixties: Innovation - bloodied but unbowed. *Change* (March): 35–38.

Mason, B.B., and D.R. Moore. 1971. Toward a strategy of evaluation for a new college. In *The new colleges: Toward an appraisal*, edited by P.L. Dressel, 155–76. Iowa City: The American College Testing Program and the American Association for Higher Education.

Mayhew, L.B. 1965. The new colleges. In *Higher education: Some newer developments*, edited by S. Baskin, 1–26. New York: McGraw-Hill.

———. 1977. *Legacy of the seventies: Experiment, economy, equality, and expediency in American higher education*. San Francisco: Jossey-Bass.

McCann, C.J. 1977. Academic administration without departments at The Evergreen State College. In *Academic departments: Problems, variations, and alternatives*, D.E. McHenry and Associates, 147–69. San Francisco: Jossey-Bass.

McCoy, P.C. 1971. Johnston College: An experimenting model. In *The new colleges: Toward an appraisal*, edited by P.L. Dressel, 53–87. Iowa City: The American College Testing Program and the American Association for Higher Education.

McDonald, W., and K. O'Neill. 1988. *"As long as you're havin' a good time." A history of Johnston College 1969–1979*. San Francisco and Redlands, Calif.: Forum Books.

McGrath, E.J. 1963. *Eisenhower College: An adventure in college education*. Seneca Falls, N.Y.: Committee for the Promotion of a New Liberal Arts College.

McHenry, D.E. 1964. The University of California, Santa Cruz. In *Experimental colleges: Their role in American higher education*, edited by W.H. Stickler, 133–44. Tallahassee: Florida State University.

———. 1977a. Academic organizational matrix at the University of California, Santa Cruz. In *Academic departments: Problems, variations, and alternatives*, D.E. McHenry and Associates, 86–116. San Francisco: Jossey-Bass.

———. 1977b. Toward departmental reform. In *Academic departments: Problems, variations, and alternatives*, D.E. McHenry and Associates, 210–24. San Francisco: Jossey-Bass.

———. 1993. University of California, Santa Cruz. In *Important lessons from innovative colleges and universities*, edited by V.R. Cardozier, 37–53. *New Directions for Higher Education* 82 (summer).

Meister, J.S. 1982. A sociologist looks at two schools - the Amherst and Hampshire experiences. *Change* (March): 26–34.

Meyer, S.L. 1964. The University of the Pacific and its "cluster colleges." In *Experimental colleges: Their role in higher education*, edited by W.H. Stickler, 73–89. Tallahassee: Florida State University.

Moss, J.E. 1980. Education and the growth of consciousness. *Dissertation abstracts international* 41 (04): 1469. (University Microfilms No. AAC80-21485)

Newcomb, T.M., D.R. Brown, J.A. Kulik, D.J. Reimer, and W.R. Revelle. 1971. The University of Michigan's Residential College. In *The new colleges: Toward an appraisal*, edited by P.L. Dressel, 99–141. Iowa City: The American College Testing Program and the American Association for Higher Education.

Newell, L.J. 1993. Deep Springs: Loyalty to a fault? In *Maverick colleges: Ten notable experiments in American undergraduate education*, edited by L.J. Newell and K.C. Reynolds, 32–46. Salt Lake City: Utah Education Policy Center, Graduate School of Education, The University of Utah.

Newell, L.J., and K.C. Reynolds, eds. 1993. *Maverick colleges: Ten notable experiments in American undergraduate education*. Salt Lake City: Utah Education Policy Center, Graduate School of Education, The University of Utah.

Newell, W.H. 1984. Interdisciplinary curriculum development in the 1970's: The Paracollege at St. Olaf and the Western College Program at Miami University. In *Against the current: Reform and experiment in higher education*, edited by R.M. Jones and B.L. Smith, 127–47. Cambridge, Mass.: Schenkman.

Nkabinde, Z. 1993. Evergreen: Ever green? In *Maverick colleges: Ten notable experiments in American undergraduate education*, edited by L.J. Newell and K.C. Reynolds, 104–17. Salt Lake City: Utah Education Policy Center, Graduate School of Education, The University of Utah.

Owada, Y. 1981. Prefigurative education: A discovery at Johnston College. *Journal of Humanistic Psychology* 21 (2): 129–40.

Patterson, F., and C. Longsworth. 1966. The making of a college. Cambridge, Mass.: MIT Press.

Perkins, J.H. 1984. Comments on Newell. In *Against the current: Reform and experiment in higher education*, edited by R.M. Jones and B.L. Smith, 149–51. Cambridge, Mass.: Schenkman.

Potter, G.T. 1980. Innovation, experimentation, and higher education: Is the perpetual dream a nightmare? *Liberal Education* 66 (3): 307–14.

Rethinking the dream at Santa Cruz. 1980. *Science* 207, no. 4427 (January): 157–60.

Riesman, D. 1975. The noble experiment that . . . ? New College. *Change* (May): 34–43.

Riesman, D., J. Gusfield, and Z. Gamson. 1970. *Academic values and mass education: The early years of Oakland and Monteith*. New York: Doubleday.

Ring, L.J. 1971a. Evaluation for Santa Cruz. In *The new colleges: Toward an appraisal*, edited by P.L. Dressel, 185–227. Iowa City: The American College Testing Program and the American Association for Higher Education.

———. 1971b. *Innovation at Santa Cruz — more than tinkering*. Paper presented at the 1971 Conference of the American Association for Higher Education, Chicago, March. (ERIC Document Reproduction Service No. ED 056 667)

———. 1972a. Cluster colleges: Viable steps into the future. Redesigning the halls of Ivy: Innovations in higher education. *Compact* 6 (5): 16–20.

———. 1972b. University of California, Santa Cruz. In *Innovations in undergraduate education: Selected institutional profiles and thoughts about experimentalism*, edited by N.R. Berte, 45–63. Tuscaloosa: The University of Alabama.

Rogers, C.R. 1974. The project at Immaculate Heart: An experiment in self-directed change. *Education* 95 (2): 172–96.

———. 1983. *Freedom to learn for the 80's*. Columbus, Ohio: Charles E. Merrill.

Rohman, D.G. 1971. Evaluating change in new colleges. In *The new colleges: Toward an appraisal*, edited by P.L. Dressel, 143–53. Iowa City: The American College Testing Program and the American Association for Higher Education.

Rowe, R.L. 1981. A case study of Maharishi International University: An innovative institution of higher education. *Dissertation Abstracts International* 41 (11): 4622. (University Microfilms No. AAC81-08369)

Saunder, G.F. 1975. Eisenhower College: From riches to rages — and back? *Change* (November): 13–16.

Scheuerle, W.H. 1979. New College of the University of South Florida. *Alternative Higher Education* 3 (3): 154–60.

Schuster, J.H. 1989a. The Evergreen State College. Site visit report for the Carnegie Foundation for the Advancement of Teaching's Campus Community Project, Claremont, Calif., 27 June. Draft.

———. 1989b. *Stockton State College*. Report of the consultant to the Faculty Assembly, Claremont, Calif.

Sewell, E. 1973. Dreams: Start with people. In *Five experimental colleges: Bensalem, Antioch-Putney, Franconia, Old Westbury, Fairhaven*, edited by G.B. MacDonald, 2–9. New York: Harper and Row.

Solomon's house: A self-conscious history of Cowell College. 1970. Felton, Calif.: Big Trees Press.

Suczek, R.F. 1972. *The best laid plans*. San Francisco: Jossey-Bass.

Sullivan, H. 1973. The experimental college: A cool medium. *Improving College and University Teaching and Learning* 21 (August): 265–68.

Thompson, L. 1981. A view from the trenches. *Journal of Humanistic Psychology* 21 (2): 23–40.

Tommerup, P.D. 1993. Adhocratic traditions, experience narratives and personal transformation: An ethnographic study of the organizational culture and folklore of The Evergreen State College, an innovative liberal arts college. *Dissertation Abstracts International* 54 (03): 1051. (University Microfilms No. AAC93-20067)

Townsend, B.K., L.J. Newell, and M.D. Wiese. 1992. *Creating distinctiveness: Lessons from uncommon colleges and universities*. ASHE-ERIC Higher Education Report No. 6. Washington, D.C.: The George Washington University, School of Education and Human Development.

Tussman, J. 1969. *Experiment at Berkeley*. New York: Oxford University Press.

Von Blum, P. 1984. Marginality, survival or prosperity: Interdisciplinary education in large research universities — Berkeley and U.C.L.A. In *Against the current: Reform and experiment in higher education*, edited by R.M. Jones and B.L. Smith, 227–48. Cambridge, Mass.: Schenkman.

Von der Muhll, G. 1984. The University of California at Santa Cruz: Institutionalizing Eden in a changing world. In *Against the current: Reform and experiment in higher education*, edited by R.M. Jones and B.L. Smith, 51–92. Cambridge, Mass.: Schenkman.

Wardle, B. 1993. College of the Atlantic: Spirit of time and place. In *Maverick colleges: Ten notable experiments in American undergraduate education*, edited by L.J. Newell and K.C. Reynolds, 118–28. Salt Lake City: Utah Education Policy Center, Graduate School of Education, The University of Utah.

Watt, J. 1981. Johnston College: A retrospective view. *Journal of Humanistic Psychology* 21 (2): 41–45.

Weidner, E.W. 1977. Problem-based departments at the University of Wisconsin-Green Bay. In *Academic departments: Problems, variations, and alternatives*, D.E. McHenry and Associates, 63–85. San Francisco: Jossey-Bass.

Weidner, E.W., and W.G. Kuepper. 1993. University of Wisconsin-Green Bay. In *Important lessons from innovative colleges and universities*, edited by V.R. Cardozier, 23–35. *New Directions for Higher Education* no. 82 (summer).

Williams, E. 1981. A confirmation and critique. *Journal of Humanistic Psychology* 21 (2): 17–21.

Wofford, H. 1973. Dreams and realities: How big the wave? In *Five experimental colleges: Bensalem, Antioch-Putney, Franconia, Old Westbury, Fairhaven*, edited by G.B. MacDonald, 158–91. New York: Harper and Row.

Wofford, H., Jr. 1970. New College at Old Westbury. In *The cluster college*, J.G. Gaff and Associates, 179–98. San Francisco: Jossey-Bass.

Wolfe, A. 1970. The experimental college — noble contradiction. *Change* (March-April): 26–32.

Wolgemuth, H.W. 1993. Kresge College (U.C. Santa Cruz) in the late 1980's: An ethnographic portrait. *Dissertation Abstracts International* 55-04A: 0833. (University Microfilms No. AAG94-22816)

Youtz, B.L. 1984. The Evergreen State College: An experiment maturing. In *Against the current: Reform and experiment in higher education*, edited by R.M. Jones and B.L. Smith, 93–118. Cambridge, Mass.: Schenkman.

APPENDIX C

Candidate List of Innovative Institutions

Appendix C
Candidate List of Innovative Institutions

Institution	Founding Year	Carnegie Classification[a]	Control	Location (State)	Enroll- ment	Writings/ Reports[b]	Presumed Status[c]
1. California Institute of the Arts	1964	Art	Private	CA	1,061		M
2. College of the Atlantic	1969	BA I	Private	ME	217		M
3. The Evergreen State College	1967	BA II	Public	WA	3,477	X	M
4. Franklin Pierce College	1962	BA II	Private	NH	3,012		?
5. Grand Valley State University (former Grand Valley State College)	1960	MA I	Public	MI	13,384		?
6. Hampshire College	1965	BA I	Private	MA	1,050	X	M
7. Maharishi International University	1971	MA I	Private	IA	628		M
8. The Naropa Institute	1974	Other	Private	CO	550		M
9. New College of California	1971	BA II	Private	CA	7,500		?
10. New College of the University of South Florida	1960	not listed*	Public	FL	526	X	M
11. Pitzer College	1963	BA I	Private	CA	890		NM

Table continues

Appendix C: Candidate List of Innovative Institutions (continued)

Institution	Founding Year	Carnegie Classification[a]	Control	Location (State)	Enroll-ment	Writings/ Reports[b]	Presumed Status[c]
12. Prescott College	1966	BA II	Private	AZ	829		M
13. Purchase College, State University of New York (formerly, State University of New York, College at Purchase)	1967	BA II	Public	NY	3,978		?
14. Ramapo College of New Jersey	1969	BA II	Public	NJ	4,683		NM
15. The Richard Stockton College of New Jersey (formerly Stockton State College)	1969	BA I	Public	NJ	5,619		NM
16. Sierra Nevada College	1969	BA II	Private	NV	437		?
17. Simon's Rock College of Bard	1964	BA I	Private	MA	314		M
18. Southwest State University	1963	BA II	Public	MN	2,637		?
19. State University of New York, College at Old Westbury	1965	BA II	Public	NY	3,947		NM
20. University of California, Irvine	1965	Res I	Public	CA	16,773		?
21. University of California, Santa Cruz	1962	Res II	Public	CA	10,173	X	NM
22. University of Wisconsin–Green Bay	1965	MA II	Public	WI	5,205		NM

Table notes follow on the next page

Notes to Appendix C: Candidate List of Innovative Institutions

Note. The data in column 3 are from *A Classification of Institutions of Higher Education 1994 Edition*, 1994, Princeton, NJ: The Carnegie Foundation for the Advancement of Teaching. The data in columns 2, 4, 5, and 6 are from the *1995 Higher Education Directory* by M.P. Rodenhouse (Ed.), 1995, Falls Church, VA: Higher Education Publications.

[a] Art = Schools of art, music, and design; BA I = Baccalaureate I institutions; BA II = Baccalaureate II institutions; MA I = Master's institutions; MA II = Master's II institutions; Res I = Research I institutions; Res II = Research II institutions; Other = Other specialized institutions (*A Classification of Institutions of Higher Education*, 1994).

[b] X = The institution has been the subject of six or more journal articles, books, chapters in edited volumes, and/or scholarly reports.

[c] M = Presumption that the institution *maintained* its founding principles, NM = Presumption that the institution *did not maintain* its founding principles, ? = *Don't know* whether the institution maintained or did not maintain its founding principles. (Based on a review of the literature and current campus catalogs, and consultation with a panel of experts on innovation in American higher education.)

*The Carnegie classification for the University of South Florida is Res II.

APPENDIX D

Research Methodology

T o understand how and why innovative colleges and universities sustained their founding principles or transformed their visionary start-up missions, field visits were conducted to six distinctive campuses across the United States in the fall and winter of the 1995-96 academic year. The case study sites, in the order in which the visits occurred, were Pitzer College in Claremont, California; New College of the University of South Florida in Sarasota; Hampshire College in Amherst, Massachusetts; the University of Wisconsin (UW)-Green Bay; the University of California (UC), Santa Cruz; and The Evergreen State College in Olympia, Washington.

This appendix expands upon the methodological discussion in the introduction by presenting additional details about the research design, campus selection, and data analysis procedures in this study. The first section examines the rationale for a qualitative research approach and explains the qualitative method. The next section describes the institutional selection process. This is followed by a discussion of the procedures for gaining access to the six campus sites. The next two sections describe the data gathering techniques (interviews, observations, document analysis) and the methods used to ensure the trustworthiness of the research findings. The final section reviews the data analysis procedures.

THE QUALITATIVE RESEARCH METHOD

Qualitative research methods (case studies, interviews, observations, document analysis) formed the methodological basis for this investigation. According to Masland (1991), qualitative or field research techniques provide researchers with the tools for uncovering institutional histories, sagas, cultural life, and activity. They enable the investigator to enter the worlds of college and university campuses, to talk with participants, to observe events and scenes. When it comes to studying reform periods or movements in American higher education, Grant (1979) writes, qualitative methodologies are the best means of "produc[ing] the greatest yield of useful knowledge to policy makers and potential participants in such a movement or reform" (440). In their classic and current investigations of innovative colleges and universities, Grant and Riesman (1978), Kuh et al. (1991), Newell and Reynolds (1993), and Levine (1980) all draw upon the qualitative (or sometimes called "ethnographic") technique. This study follows their lead.

What is the qualitative technique? Qualitative research is about talking and watching and listening (Whitt 1991). Its paramount goal is to understand social settings, to gain insight into the ways in which participants make meaning of their experiences, their social worlds. The qualitatively oriented researcher, Grant (1979) explains, seeks to discover and to describe a system "in such a way that the participants recognize it as a portrait of their world" (452). The observer strives to look at, appreciate, and uncover the "insider" perspective, the "native" point of view. How is this accomplished? Crowson (1993) offers: The researcher "assume[s] a mantle of almost childlike curiosity, trying to understand—or . . . trying to 'find out how a situation ticks'" (171). Seymour Sarason suggests that researchers "indulge in a bit of fantasy— examining our educational institutions as if we were beings from outer space poised on invisible platforms above these institutions and trying to figure out 'what's going on'" (cited in Crowson 1993, 170). A bit of this sci-fi, outer-space posturing and child-like curiosity allows the qualitative investigator to "make the familiar strange," to see the ordinary, the known, as the new and exotic (Spindler and Spindler 1988).

The qualitative research approach also emphasizes holistic perspectives or the search for interconnections or patterns of meaning among pieces or slices of data (stories, sagas, legends, etc.) gathered in the field. Findings are analyzed inductively, from the ground up—ideas and inspirations emerge out of the experiences in the social setting (Crowson 1993; Lincoln and Guba 1985).

Masland (1991) imagines the researcher stepping inside an organization and peering through "windows" on an institution's culture, taking in the rich landscape of day-to-day moments, experiences. The qualitative observer immerses himself or herself in a natural setting to learn the life and language of the people living in it, to capture emergent forms, features, and themes (Levine 1980). This was the goal—and the driving spirit—of this investigation: to immerse myself as much as possible in the cultures of the innovative colleges and universities (and taking some of that magical, child-like curiosity with me), to paint a finely detailed portrait of the campus worlds that I observed and experienced. This research strategy called for a multi-site, case study technique.

Why multi-site? As discussed in the literature review in the introduction, few authors in the innovative college and university arena have conducted investigations that compare findings across institutions. There seemed to be room for research and research methodologies that stepped beyond individual campus boundaries, that looked both within and across kindred campuses, that wove together findings into a tapestry of common themes and threads of life and experience. The beauty of cross-institutional analysis is that it allows for a broader understanding of the processes of innovation among a family of unorthodox institutions, while preserving in-depth institutional data and insight—the rich stories and storytelling that grow out of the single case study inquiry (Crowson 1993; Herriott and Firestone 1983; Whitt and Kuh 1993).

INSTITUTIONAL SELECTION

Jane Lichtman (1973) in her spirited study of alternative campuses or "free universities," makes mention of the "hidden" or buried treasure quality of these inventive institutions:[1] "In 1970, I knew that free universities existed, but where?" (iv). This proved to be one of the dilemmas and delights of the current investigation. While there had been guidebooks and directories published on innovative colleges and universities and nontraditional and interdisciplinary programs in higher education (e.g., Bear 1980; Coyne and Hebert 1972; Halterman 1983; Heiss 1973; Lichtman 1972; Newell 1986), there were no comprehensive, up-to-date inventories that cataloged the family of institutions—the scores of distinctive campuses (including the subcolleges and free universities)—that came to life in the 1960s and 1970s. Part of the task of this investigation was to construct such a directory or list—a "master guide" of innovative colleges and universities in the United States that would serve as a "population" of potential reform sites in this investigation. (Using the "master list," I would be able to select a sample of six geographically and academically diverse campuses for the case studies. It was also envisioned that the master list might serve as a tool or a stimulus for further research or referral in the area of reform in higher education.)

The Master List

The master list of institutions was generated from an extensive review of the research literature and the guidebooks on alternatives in higher education. "Nominations" of campuses were also sought through consultation (correspondence and telephone conversations) with a panel of experts on reform in higher education (see "Innovative College and University Consultant Panel," later in this appendix).

To limit the size of the master inventory, nontraditional campuses for adults, innovative colleges and universities that offered primarily external degree programs, and distance learning institutions that came into being during the 1960s and 1970s were excluded from the list (e.g., Empire State College, Metropolitan State University). The inventory also excluded the older and progressive experimental colleges that were founded in the late nineteenth century and in the first three decades of the twentieth century (e.g., Antioch, Berea, Deep Springs, Bennington). The institutions under investigation were those that grew out of the revolutionary reforms of the 1960s.[2]

The end result was a master inventory of 314 innovative colleges and universities and subcolleges in the United States that were founded in the 1960s and 1970s. (The master list is presented in appendix B.)

Next, a "candidate list" of possible research sites was compiled from the master inventory of institutions. To narrow down the number of potential research sites, subcolleges and free universities were excluded from this list. For ease of research and accessibility to participants in the campus communities, the list was confined to those innovative (and once-innovative) colleges and universities that remained open in the 1990s (e.g., The Evergreen State College, UC Santa Cruz, Ramapo College). (Many of the alternative campuses that were listed on the master list had closed in the 1960s or 1970s.) To determine which of the campuses on the master list remained open, I consulted the *Higher Education Directory*, an annual catalog of accredited, degree-granting postsecondary institutions in the United States (Rodenhouse 1995), along with the research literature. The result was a list of 22 freestanding innovative institutions from which the final sample of campus sites would be drawn (see appendix C).

Four decision rules guided the process of campus selection from the candidate list. First, I attempted to choose institutions from different regions of the country. Geographical diversity was an important factor in this investigation because of the reported influence of locale and neighboring institutional collaboration on the life and longevity of innovative campuses. (Previous research had shown that proximity to or affiliation with nearby "traditional" higher education institutions tended to enhance the longevity of distinctive campuses.) (Frazier 1977; Meister 1982) More generally, Kuh and Whitt

(1988) relate, "the mores of the host community or region of the country where a college is located influence the attitudes of students who attend the college. Whether an institution is in a major metropolitan area on the East Coast or on the outskirts of a small town in Iowa influences faculty and student behaviors that are tolerated and the degree of social cohesion developed" (43–44). Thus, it was necessary to include a range of regional contexts to encompass a broad spectrum of national life and institutional experiences.

Second, every effort was made to select at least some institutions that had not been thoroughly investigated in the research. One of the underlying goals of this work was to tell the stories of distinctive colleges and universities that had yet to be told, to push past the boundaries of the previous research and to raise awareness about some of the undiscovered settings of reform and innovation in American higher education.

Third, I tried to achieve a balance between public and private institutions. Past writings had formed a connection between private status and distinctive campus longevity (e.g., Hahn 1984). Ensuring a mix of public and private institutions would take into account this finding and build on the previous research.

Fourth, in keeping with the research mission of understanding how and why innovative campuses preserve or transform their original distinctive ideals or visions, I tried to select both those campuses that seemed to have preserved their founding ideals and those that appeared to have transformed themselves or moved away from their original missions. To determine which institutions on the candidate list had kept hold of their alternative visions and which had not, I reviewed campus catalogs and documents (present and founding year), comparing each campus today with the campus of the past. I also sought the advice of a panel of experts on reform in higher education.

Innovative College and University Consultant Panel

Twenty-eight experts on higher education reform were identified, and 19 participated as consultants in the campus nomination process (appendix A). Each consultant was contacted (via mail) in the summer of 1995 and was asked to complete a confidential "Institution Nomination Form" with a preliminary list of innovative colleges and universities (drawn from the master list of institutions).[3] The experts were asked to provide two ratings of "institutional distinctiveness" for each campus on the list: (1) "Rating at Founding" ("the extent to which you perceive this institution to have been innovative . . . during the institution's early [say, first five to seven] years") and (2) "Current Rating" ("the extent to which you perceive that this institution has remained innovative—in keeping with its original conception"). Consultants were also invited to list any additional innovative colleges or universities "that you believe should be included on this 'nomination list'" (along with institutional distinctiveness ratings), and to suggest names of other individuals who might serve as contact persons in the campus selection process. (The Institution Nomination Form is included in appendix A.)

The expert panel of consultants offered valuable guidance in the selection of the final sample of institutions. While most of the consultants provided feedback by completing the nomination form, three consultants (Russell Y. Garth, vice president of the Council of Independent Colleges; Arthur E. Levine, president of Teachers College, Columbia University; and Page Smith, the late founding provost of Cowell College at UC Santa Cruz) shared their comments in an interview over the telephone. John Maguire, then president of The Claremont University Center and Graduate University (and former president of the State University of New York, College at Old Westbury), invited me to his office to offer in person his impressions and insights about the research project and the nomination form.

Responses to the nomination form were compiled and analyzed by computing the means of the institutional distinctiveness ratings (at founding and today) for each college or university on the list. In general, the feedback provided by the expert panel's impressions (on the nomination forms and in the interviews) supported the findings of initial catalog and literature reviews regarding the extent to which institutions had preserved their innovative founding missions. The advice and input of the consultants figured prominently in the final selection of the six case study sites.

GAINING ENTRY TO THE SIX CAMPUSES

Once the final sample of case study sites was selected, the next stage of the research involved negotiating entry into the six institutions. In the fall of 1995, letters were sent to the president or chancellor at each campus,[4] explaining the purposes of the study, describing the plans for field research (including the proposed dates of the visit), specifying efforts to maintain confidentiality (i.e., protecting the identity of interview participants), and inviting the institution to participate. Approximately one week after the letters were sent, the president or chancellor at each campus was called to confirm the institution's involvement, to review the dates of the research visit, and to request assistance in scheduling the interviews, perhaps with the assistance of a campus contact or liaison. (All six presidents or chancellors agreed to the campus visit.) The phone conversation was followed by a letter confirming the site visit and requesting campus materials and information (e.g., a college or university catalog; student, faculty, and staff handbooks; an institutional mission statement; campus histories; annual reports).

DATA-GATHERING TECHNIQUES: CAPTURING THE DREAMS

Four- to five-day site visits were conducted at each of the six innovative campuses between the months of September 1995 and February 1996. Data collection was based on three qualitative research techniques: interviews, observations, and document analysis.

Interviews

Interviews formed the heart of the data gathering. At each campus, approximately 25 50-minute, semi-structured interviews were conducted with the present and past players in the life of the college or university: the president or chancellor (current and founding, if available), faculty and administrators, key trustees, and selected students and active alumnae/i. Altogether, 151 interviews were conducted during the six field visits with 164 faculty, administrators, students, trustees, and alumnae/i. (Table D1 provides a demographic profile of the interview participants.)

Interviewees were identified in two ways: with the assistance of a campus liaison who had been designated by the president or chancellor to facilitate the campus visit; and through "snowball sampling" (i.e., identifying one interviewee and then asking that individual to recommend the names of others who would be able to provide additional insight into the history and endurance of campus innovation) (Dobbert 1984). Snowball sampling served as the primary means of identifying interviewees for the field visits at Pitzer College and UC Santa Cruz. At New College, Hampshire College, UW-Green Bay, and Evergreen, a campus contact person assisted in the scheduling of the interviews.

Interview Questions

The interview questions were designed to "explore" or "probe" the histories, legends, and "sagas" of the institutions as well as the present life and culture of the campuses. Participants were encouraged to reflect upon the unique nature of the college or university today and, where possible, to look back to the early days or start-up years, to think about how the institution had transformed (and/or recreated) itself. The goal of the interviews was to capture the voices, the stories of where and how the distinctive founding dreams of the campuses had persisted or flourished and where and how the early visions had changed or faded. A protocol of the interview questions is presented below:

1. What are some of the innovative educational principles or missions upon which this institution was founded?
2. To what extent has this institution maintained the innovative principles upon which it was founded?

TABLE D1

DEMOGRAPHIC PROFILE OF INTERVIEW PARTICIPANTS ACROSS CAMPUS SITES

Characteristics of Interview Participants	Pitzer College	New College of USF	Hampshire College	U. of Wisconsin-Green Bay	U. of California, Santa Cruz	The Evergreen State College	Totals
Overall Statistics							
Total # Interviews Conducted	27	23	26	26	27	22	**151**
Total # Persons Interviewed	25	23	33	34	27	22	**164**
Average # Years at Institution	19.2	16.8	19.2	21.4	22.9	21.3	**120.8**
Breakdown by Gender							
# male	13	17	17	25	23	13	**108**
# female	12	6	16	9	4	9	**56**
Role or Affiliation [a]							
# faculty	14	11	15	21	20	15	**96**
# administrators	9	15	12	15	16	10	**77**
# alumnae/i	5	5	3	3	2	4	**22**
# students	0	1	9	4	0	1	**15**
# trustees	2	0	1	0	0	0	**3**

[a] Some interviewees occupied more than one role at the institution.

3. How important has it been for this institution to maintain the innovative principles upon which it was founded?

4. Is the campus today a better place for education than it was in the early years?

5. Many of the campuses that were founded as innovative institutions in the 1960s and 1970s were closed in the late 1960s or in the 1970s. Why do you think this institution has managed to "survive" (or to remain open)?

6. What are some of the "lessons" or "teachings" of this institution and its history of innovation for other colleges and universities in the United States?

Prior to each interview, participants were presented with a written overview of the research project and a biographical sketch of the principal investigator. Individuals were also asked to complete an "Interview Participant Profile Form" requesting demographic information about the interviewee.[5] All interviews were tape recorded on a microcassette recorder, with the permission of the interviewees. In nearly all 151 cases, the tapes were transcribed verbatim to ensure accuracy of information for data analysis. All interviewees were assured of confidentiality—the names of the individual interviewees would be kept confidential in the write-up of the case studies.

Observations

Wherever possible, interview data were supplemented by observations of campus programs and events (i.e., regularly scheduled activities such as administrative meetings, convocations, programs, etc., and spontaneous happenings—"frisbee matches on the green") (Kuh et al. 1991). Visiting these campuses, and watching and listening and participating in innovative college or university goings-on (both scheduled and spur-of-the-moment activities) enabled me to pull together impressions and insights about campus history, culture, and tradition. Campus observations also served as a means of developing topics for future interviews and cross-checking the accuracy of the data ("triangulating" the results) gathered during the interview sessions.

Document Analysis

Document analyses were conducted prior to, during, and following the field visits. In letters and communication with the presidents or chancellors (and/or contact persons) at each institution, I requested a copy of the current campus catalog, viewbook, faculty/staff handbook, annual reports, and institutional histories to review prior to the field visits. These documents served as an orienting point and a source of information about the innovative history and current educational mission of the campus. According to Tuckman (1988),

"The first step in conducting a qualitative study is to obtain copies of all available documents. . . . This is the best and most objective way to orient yourself to the situation that you are about to study" (398).

During the campus visits, I tried to gather as many documents as possible that would provide insight into the history and current life and direction of the institution. At each campus, I spent time reviewing the institutional archives—current and founding year catalogs, organizational charts, viewbooks, policy handbooks, mission statements, accreditation reports, minutes of meetings, early campus newspapers, yearbooks, planning statements, and institutional histories. Archival document review was essential for the historical analysis— that is, for understanding the founding ideals or opening missions of the institution as well as the present-day institutional culture and mission, and for verifying and supplementing the statements and recollections that were offered by the veteran faculty and staff and early alumnae/i in the interviews.

ESTABLISHING TRUSTWORTHINESS

How can a researcher "persuade his or her audiences (including self) that the findings of an inquiry are worth paying attention to"? (Lincoln and Guba 1985, 290). How can the investigator ensure the "trustworthiness" of his or her findings? According to Lincoln and Guba, there are four standards or criteria used for establishing the trustworthiness of qualitative research data: credibility, transferability, dependability, and confirmability. The following paragraphs describe how these criteria were integrated into the research design to ensure the trustworthiness of the data in this study.

First, to establish the credibility of the findings (i.e., that the results "ring true" to the participants in the field), institutional data were collected and captured through multiple lenses or triangulation (interviews, observations, document analysis, interactions with members of six different innovative college or university communities). Immediately following the interviews, participants were invited to offer additional comments or clarification to verify the accuracy of the information gathered in the interview session.

For further verification, a preliminary draft of the case study report was circulated to the president or chancellor at all six sites for comment and clarification. Each president or chancellor was asked to read the draft and to offer input or clarification on the write-up, especially with regard to matters of fact and interpretation. They were also invited to circulate the draft to others on campus, including veteran faculty and administrators for additional input and feedback. The President's or Chancellor's Office at four of the campuses— New College, UW-Green Bay, UC Santa Cruz, and Evergreen—provided responses to the drafts and shared the report with others at the institution.

(Drafts of the Pitzer College and Hampshire College chapters were circulated to interviewees and other individuals on campus for comment and review.) The New College draft was read by the dean and warden, the director of special project development, the director of admissions, the chair of humanities, and a former director of student affairs. The University of Wisconsin-Green Bay chapter benefited from the review of the current chancellor; a former chancellor; the assistant vice chancellor for enrollment services; the dean of humanities, social sciences, and general education; an alumnus and director of assessment and testing services; the associate dean of general education; and the assistant chancellor for planning and budget. The UC Santa Cruz chapter was read by the executive vice chancellor, who had been employed at the university since 1971. The Evergreen State College draft was reviewed by the president; academic vice president and provost; and the founding president of the institution. The Pitzer College chapter was read by the director of communications; the director of the Pitzer History and Archives Project, who is a founding faculty member; and another charter member of the Pitzer faculty. The Hampshire College case study was reviewed by the associate dean of faculty and a former dean of students.

This valuable feedback was incorporated into the final writing of the campus case study reports. According to Lincoln and Guba (1985), the "member check" is the most crucial technique for establishing the credibility of results. Every attempt was made to ensure that I got the campus stories "right."

Second, to establish the transferability of the data (the usefulness of the findings in another context), the case studies and stories incorporated "thick descriptions." Fetterman (1993) describes this narrative technique in his wonderfully titled "Recording the Miracle: Writing." "Ethnographers," he says, "take great pains to describe a cultural scene or event in tremendous detail. The aim is to convey the feel as well as the facts of an observed event" (499). A detailed portrait of the institutions in this study, their founding and history (along with the use of quotations and background or contextual descriptions) would provide the reader with a means of contextual comparison: The reader, it was hoped, would be able to assess the similarities between the innovative college or university environment that was captured in the case study (the "sending context") and his or her own ("receiving") context—campus setting or community (Lincoln and Guba 1985; Whitt 1991).

Third, the dependability of the findings (the results take into account changes over time) and the confirmability of the evidence (the information can be verified by someone besides the investigator) were demonstrated through the use of an "audit trail" (Lincoln and Guba 1985), a carefully collected and documented record of the study, its data, and resources. What goes into the audit trail? Lincoln and Guba suggest that the researcher have on hand the following: (1) raw data (interview notes, tapes, documents); (2) products of data analysis and reduction (write-ups of field notes, theoretical notes); (3) products of data synthesis and reconstruction (descriptions of categories or themes, interim case reports, records of ongoing findings or conclusions); (4) process notes (notes on research design and trustworthiness criteria); (5) materials relating to the disposition and intentions of the researcher (the research proposal, personal notes, notes on expectations); and (6) information on instrument development (pilot test questions, observation formats). All of the above ingredients, including research materials, data, recordings, interview transcripts, notes, and proposals relating to the investigation, were carefully collected and compiled to enable an outsider to track the research processes in this study.

DATA ANALYSIS

"Imagine a large gymnasium in which thousands of toys are spread out on the floor. You are given the task of sorting them into piles according to a scheme that you are going to develop. You walk around the gym looking at the toys, picking them up, and examining them" (Bogdan and Biklen 1992, 165). In many ways, the data analysis process in this study was like looking around such a gym and picking up and examining and sorting the thousands of toys—the rich stories and insights gleaned in the interviews and documents about the six innovative colleges and universities.

Data were analyzed inductively (from the ground up) both within and across sites. For each campus case study, I carefully reviewed the interview transcripts, document summaries, and observation notes, identifying key categories and then coding the information into clusters of emergent themes (e.g., "Hampshire College's Distinctive Early Ideals:" "Individualism," "Egalitarianism," "Undergraduate Teaching and Faculty Freedom," and "Interdisciplinary Education"). A coding guide was developed in the process of transcribing the interviews and reviewing the documents and observation notes. Nearly all 151 interviews were transcribed verbatim, generating rich insights, institutional themes, and quotations that captured the essence or spirit of innovation at the six colleges and universities.

When the individual analyses of the six campus sites were completed, the case study results were compiled to present a cross-campus portrait of the general findings about innovation in higher education (chapter 8). The cross-institutional analyses yielded comparative data about the commonalities and differences in the history and endurance of educational innovation among the six distinctive colleges and universities.

NOTES

1. Free universities ("free u's") are those student-run experimental educational centers and alternative community institutions that grew out of the free school and free speech movement of the 1960s. Many of the innovative subcolleges are referred to or are identified as "free universities" by Lichtman (1972, 1973) and other researchers (e.g., Draves 1980; Litkowski 1983).
2. The master list also excluded the small number of innovative community colleges (distinctive two-year institutions that offer the associate of arts degree such as Miami-Dade Community College), upper division colleges (e.g., Sangamon State University), and graduate schools (and free-standing graduate institutions) (e.g., The California Institute of Integral Studies) that grew out of the 1960s and 1970s reform movement (Coyne and Hebert 1972; Heiss 1973).
3. Along with the Institution Nomination Form, each consultant received an abstract of the research project; a preliminary list of institutions; a definition of "innovative colleges" and the institutional selection criteria used to identify the campuses in this investigation; and a self-addressed, stamped return envelope in which to enclose the nomination form. Follow-up letters (including a second copy of the institution nomination form; project abstract; institution list; definition and selection criteria; and self-addressed, stamped return envelope) were sent to all individuals who had not responded within three weeks of the initial mailing. Thank you letters were mailed to all consultants who participated in the campus nomination process.
4. The highest ranking official at New College is the provost or "dean and warden."
5. In some cases, the project overview and interview questions were made available to individuals prior to the interview date. All interview participants at UW-Green Bay received a copy of the project abstract and the interview questions, accompanied by a letter from the researcher and a cover letter from the chancellor of UW-Green Bay.

REFERENCES

Bear, J. 1980. *The alternative guide to college degrees & non-traditional higher education*. New York: Stonesong.

Bogdan, R.C., and S.K. Biklen. 1992. *Qualitative research for education: An introduction to theory and methods*. Boston: Allyn and Bacon.

Coyne, J., and T. Hebert. 1972. *This way out: A guide to alternatives to traditional college education in the United States, Europe and the Third World*. New York: E.P. Dutton.

Crowson, R.L. 1993. Qualitative research methods in higher education. In *Qualitative research in higher education: Experiencing alternative perspectives and approaches*, edited by C. Conrad, A. Neumann, J.G. Haworth and P. Scott, 167–208. ASHE Reader. Needham Heights, Mass.: Ginn Press.

Dobbert, M.L. 1984. *Ethnographic research: Theory and application for modern schools and societies*. New York: Praeger.

Draves, B. 1980. *The free university: A model for lifelong learning*. Chicago: Association Press.

Fetterman, D.M. 1993. Recording the Miracle: Writing. In *Qualitative research in higher education: Experiencing alternative perspectives and approaches*, edited by C. Conrad, A. Neumann, J.G. Haworth, and P. Scott, 493–502. ASHE Reader. Needham Heights, Mass.: Ginn Press.

Frazier, N. 1977. Freedom and identity at Hampshire College. *Change* November 14–17.

Grant, G. 1979. New methods for the study of a reform movement. In *On competence: A critical analysis of competence-based reforms in higher education*, edited by G. Grant, P. Elbow, T. Ewens, Z. Gamson, W. Kohli, W. Neumann, V. Olesen and D. Riesman, 439–90. San Francisco: Jossey-Bass.

Grant, G., and D. Riesman. 1978. *The perpetual dream: Reform and experiment in the American college*. Chicago: The University of Chicago Press.

Hahn, J. 1984. Disciplinary professionalism: Second view. In *Against the current: Reform and experiment in higher education*, edited by R.M. Jones and B.L. Smith, 19–33. Cambridge, Mass.: Schenkman.

Halterman, W.J. 1983. *The complete guide to nontraditional education*. New York: Facts on File.

Heiss, A. 1973. *An inventory of academic innovation and reform*. Berkeley: The Carnegie Commission on Higher Education.

Herriott, R.E., and W.A. Firestone. 1983. Multisite qualitative policy research: Optimizing description and generalizability. *Educational Researcher* 12, 14–19.

Kuh, G.D., and E.J. Whitt. 1988. *The invisible tapestry: Culture in American colleges and universities*. ASHE-ERIC Higher Education Report No. 1. Washington, D.C.: Association for the Study of Higher Education.

Kuh, G.D., J.H. Schuh, E.J. Whitt, R.E. Andreas, J.W. Lyons, C.C. Strange, L.E. Krehbiel, and K.A. MacKay. 1991. *Involving colleges: Successful approaches to fostering student learning and development outside the classroom*. San Francisco: Jossey-Bass.

Levine, A. 1980. *Why innovation fails*. Albany, N.Y.: State University of New York Press.

Lichtman, J. 1972. *Free university directory*. Washington, D.C.: American Association for Higher Education.

———. 1973. *Bring your own bag: A report on free universities*. Washington, D.C.: American Association for Higher Education.

Lincoln, Y.S., and E.G. Guba. 1985. *Naturalistic inquiry*. Newbury Park, Calif.: Sage.

Litkowski, T. 1983. *Free universities and learning referral centers 1981*. Washington, D.C.: National Center for Education Statistics.

Masland, A.T. 1991. Organizational culture in the study of higher education. In *Organization and governance in higher education* (4th ed.), edited by M.W. Peterson, E.E. Chaffee, and T.H. White, 118–25. ASHE Reader. Needham Heights, Mass.: Ginn Press.

Meister, J.S. 1982. A sociologist looks at two schools - the Amherst and Hampshire experiences. *Change* (March) 26–34.

Newell, L.J., and K.C. Reynolds, eds. 1993. *Maverick colleges: Ten notable experiments in American undergraduate education.* Salt Lake City: Utah Education Policy Center, Graduate School of Education, The University of Utah.

Newell, W.H. 1986. *Interdisciplinary undergraduate programs: A directory.* Oxford, Ohio: Association for Integrative Studies.

Rodenhouse, M.P., ed. 1995. *1995 higher education directory.* Falls Church, Va.: Higher Education Publications.

Spindler, G., and L. Spindler. 1988. Roger Harker and Schonhausen: From familiar to strange and back again. In *Doing the ethnography of schooling: Educational anthropology in action*, edited by G. Spindler, 20–43. Prospect Heights, Ill.: Waveland Press.

Tuckman, B.W. 1988. *Conducting educational research*, 3rd ed. New York: Harcourt Brace Jovanovich.

Whitt, E.J. 1991. Artful science: A primer on qualitative research methods. *Journal of College Student Development* 32: 406–15.

Whitt, E.J., and G.D. Kuh. 1993. Qualitative methods in a team approach to multiple-institution studies. In *Qualitative research in higher education: Experiencing alternative perspectives and approaches*, edited by C. Conrad, A. Neumann, J.G. Haworth, and P. Scott, 253–66. ASHE Reader. Needham Heights, Mass.: Ginn Press.

INDEX

by Linda Webster